Political Quietism in Islam

Political Quietism in Islam

Sunnī and Shīʿī Practice and Thought

Edited by Saud al-Sarhan

I.B.TAURIS

LONDON • NEW YORK • OXFORD • NEW DELHI • SYDNEY

I.B. TAURIS
Bloomsbury Publishing Plc
50 Bedford Square, London, WC1B 3DP, UK
1385 Broadway, New York, NY 10018, USA
29 Earlsfort Terrace, Dublin 2, Ireland

BLOOMSBURY, I.B. TAURIS and the I.B. TAURIS logo are trademarks of
Bloomsbury Publishing Plc

First published in Great Britain 2020
Paperback edition published 2021

Cover image: Drawing of the holy mosque in Mecca, from Dala'il al-Khayrat,
by Muhammad b. Sulayman al-Jazuli (d. 870 AH/1465 AD). Courtesy of the King Faisal
Center for Research and Islamic Studies, Saudi Arabia.

A catalogue record for this book is available from the British Library.

A catalog record for this book is available from the Library of Congress

ISBN HB: 978-1-8386-0219-2
PB: 978-0-7556-4504-6
ePDF: 978-1-8386-0765-4
ePub: 978-1-8386-0766-1

Series: King Faisal Center for Research and Islamic Studies

KFCRIS
KING FAISAL CENTER FOR
RESEARCH AND ISLAMIC STUDIES

Typeset by Integra Software Services Pvt. Ltd.

To find out more about our authors and books visit www.bloomsbury.com
and sign up for our newsletters.

Contents

List of Illustrations vii
Contributors viii
Acknowledgments xi
Introduction 1

Part I The Concept of Political Quietism: Its Problematics and the Islamic Context

1 Making Sense of "Political Quietism": An Analytical Intervention *Jan-Peter Hartung* 15
2 Expressions of Political Quietism in Islamic History *Ebrahim Moosa and Nicholas Roberts* 33

Part II Political Quietism in Classical Islam

3 The Rightly Guided Caliphs: The Range of Views Preserved in *Ḥadīth* *Christopher Melchert* 63
4 "Patience in Our Situation is Better than Sedition": The Shift to Political Quietism in the Sunnī Tradition *Saud al-Sarhan* 81
5 Quietism and Political Legitimacy in Imāmī Shīʿī Jurisprudence: al-Sharīf al-Murtaḍā's *Treatise on the Legality of Working for the Government* Reconsidered *Robert Gleave* 99

Part III Political Quietism in Modern and Contemporary Islamic Thought

6 "I'm Only a Village Farmer and a Dervish": Between Political Quietism and Spiritual Leadership: Early Modern Shīʿī Sufism and the Challenge of Modernity *Alessandro Cancian* 131
7 Legal Discourses on *Hijra* in the Caucasus after the Fall of the Caucasus Imamate: *al-Risāla al-Sharīfa* by the Dagestani Scholar ʿAbd al-Raḥmān al-Thughūrī *Magomed Gizbulaev* 145
8 Constitutionalism as Quietist Strategy: The Case of Tunisia *Jeremy Kleidosty* 171

9 "Dropping a Thick Curtain of Forgetting and Disregard": Modern Shīʿī Quietism beyond Politics *Rainer Brunner* 185
10 Public Piety and the Politics of Preaching among Female Preachers in Riyadh *Laila Makboul* 209
11 The Gülen Movement in Azerbaijan: Political Quietism or *Taqiyya*? *Fuad Aliyev* 225
12 The Neo-Traditionalist Critique of Modernity and the Production of Political Quietism *Walaa Quisay* 241

Index 259

List of Illustrations

7.1	Sogratl after it was burned to the ground in November 1877	146
7.2	The first picture of Imam Shāmil was made by I. G. Nostitz in September 1859 in Chiryurt	150
7.3	*al-Risāla al-sharīfa*	154
7.4	Officers and non commissioned officers of the Dagestan irregular cavalry division in 1871 (see Kozubskii, "History of the Dagestan Cavalry Division")	156
11.1	The Gülen network scheme in Azerbaijan before 2014	229

Contributors

Saud al-Sarhan (PhD, University of Exeter) is Secretary General at the King Faisal Center for Research and Islamic Studies (KFCRIS) in Riyadh, Saudi Arabia. He was previously the Director of Research at KFCRIS. He is also an Honorary Senior Research Fellow in the College of Social Sciences and International Studies at Exeter University, UK, an Associate Fellow at the International Centre for the Study of Radicalisation (ICSR) at King's College London, and a Distinguished International Affairs Fellow of the National Council on US-Arab Relations, USA.

Fuad Aliyev (PhD, Azerbaijan State University of Economics) is an expert on Islam in post-Soviet countries and Islamic political economy. He was the Fulbright Scholar in 2011–12 at the John Hopkins University School of Advanced International Studies, Central Asia–Caucasus Institute. He was a Hubert Humphrey fellow in 2005–06, affiliated with the University of North Carolina in Chapel Hill and with the Brookings Institution. Dr. Aliyev teaches at ADA University and Khazar University in Azerbaijan. He has written several publications on Islamic economics and finance, the political economy of transition, and economic reforms.

Rainer Brunner (PhD, University of Freiburg) has been Director of Research at the CNRS and PSL Research University Paris (Laboratoire d'Études sur les monothéismes) since 2005. Prior to that, he was a fellow at the Institute for Advanced Studies at the Hebrew University of Jerusalem; a member at the Institute for Advanced Study in Princeton, New Jersey; and more recently, visiting professor for Islamic Studies at the University of Heidelberg. He also serves as editor of the journal *Die Welt des Islams* (Leiden). His main research areas are Shīʿī Islam, Sunnī–Shīʿa relations, Islamic modernism, and the history of Islamic studies.

Alessandro Cancian (PhD, University of Siena) is Senior Research Associate in the Qur'anic Studies unit at the Institute of Ismaili Studies, London. He is a review editor for the *Journal of Shiʿa Islamic Studies*, and has edited and published articles and papers, contributed book chapters and encyclopedia entries, and delivered numerous lectures. His areas of interest and expertise are the intellectual history of Shīʿism, Shīʿī Sufism in early modern times, the anthropology of Islam, and

Shīʿism and modern Iran. He is currently working on a Shīʿī mystical exegesis of the Qurʾān, its influences, and reception in modern times and on a monograph on Sulṭān ʿAlī Shāh's *Tafsīr Bayān al-saʿāda*.

Magomed Gizbulaev (PhD, Dagestan Scientific Center of the Russian Academy of Sciences) is Research Fellow in the Department of Ancient and Medieval History of Dagestan, Institute of History, Archaeology and Ethnography, Dagestan Scientific Center of the Russian Academy of Sciences. His research interests include the history of the medieval Caucasus, Islamic intellectual culture in Dagestan, Russian-Dagestan relations after the Great Caucasian War, and early Arabic historical and geographical sources of Caucasian history.

Robert Gleave (PhD, University of Manchester) is Professor of Arabic Studies and Director of the Centre for the Study of Islam, Institute of Arab and Islamic Studies, University of Exeter. His areas of research are Islamic law and legal theory, with a particular emphasis on the history of Shīʿī jurisprudence. He is currently the director of two projects: Understanding Shariʿa; and Law, Authority and Learning in Imami Shiʿite Islam. He is the author of *Inevitable Doubt: Two Shii Theories of Jurisprudence* (2000), *Scripturalist Islam* (Brill 2007), and *Islam and Literalism* (2012).

Jan-Peter Hartung (PhD, University of Erfurt, and Senior PhD, University of Bonn) is currently an ERC senior research fellow at the Institute of Social Anthropology at the University of Goettingen, Germany. Prior to that, he taught the study of Islam at the universities of Erfurt, Bonn, and Bochum, all in Germany, and for a decade at SOAS, University of London. His most recent monograph is *A System of Life: Mawdūdī and the Ideologisation of Islam* (London and New York 2013); he is currently preparing a book manuscript on the religious trajectories that led to the emergence of the Taliban and a special issue on Salafi Islam outside the Near and Middle East for *Die Welt des Islams*.

Jeremy Kleidosty (PhD, University of St. Andrews) is Researcher at the University of Helsinki's Centre of Excellence on Reason and Religious Recognition. He specializes in constitutionalism and the comparison of political norms, institutions, and texts across wide swaths of time and space with a focus on how philosophy and political theory influence their development, legitimacy, and effectiveness. His research highlights the cross-fertilization of these political ideas and norms from the Middle Ages onward, and demonstrates that comparative political theory offers tools that go beyond dialogue to create new hybrid ideas to better serve today's increasingly interconnected and global communities while still respecting local narratives and traditions.

Laila Makboul (PhD candidate, University of Oslo) holds an MA in Middle Eastern and North African Studies from the University of Oslo. Her main field of research and the subject of her PhD thesis are the discourse and practice of intellectual female preachers in Saudi Arabia.

Christopher Melchert (PhD, University of Pennsylvania) is Professor of Arabic and Islamic Studies at the University of Oxford. He has written over sixty articles in journals and edited collections. His first book, *The Formation of the Sunni Schools of Law, Ninth-Tenth Centuries C.E.*, was published in 1997; his second, *Ahmad ibn Hanbal*, came out in 2006. He is presently at work on *Before Sufism: Early Islamic Renunciant Piety.*

Ebrahim Moosa (PhD, University of Cape Town) is Professor of Islamic Studies in the Keough School of Global Affairs at the University of Notre Dame. Moosa is the author of *What Is a Madrasa*? (2015), as well as the prize-winning book *Ghazali and the Poetics of Imagination* (2005). He coedited *Islam in the Modern World* (2014) and *Muslim Family Law in Sub-Saharan Africa: Colonial Legacies and Post-Colonial Challenges* (2010). He also edited the last manuscript of the late Fazlur Rahman, *Revival and Reform in Islam: A Study of Islamic Fundamentalism* (2000).

Nicholas Roberts' (PhD candidate, University of Notre Dame) dissertation focuses on modern Omani history and Ibadi political theology. His publications include *Political Islam and the Invention of Tradition* (2015).

Walaa Quisay (PhD candidate, University of Oxford) is researching neo-traditionalist religious scholars in the West. She is a visiting research fellow at Istanbul Sehir University's Sociology Department.

Acknowledgments

I would like to acknowledge here, briefly, the work of others who have helped bring this collection to life. Any book is the work of many more than just its author, a collected edition even more so. I would like to acknowledge and thank first and foremost the King Faisal Center for Research and Islamic Studies in Riyadh for supporting the publication of the book, as well as for their support of the Annual Islamic Political Thought Conference. Faisal Abualhassan has been helpful every step of the way. In addition, the encouragement of Iradj Bagerzade until his retirement last year was an unparalleled source of support. Finally, I would like to thank Natana Delong-Baz for her comments on an early draft of the book.

Introduction

Much has been written on Islamic conceptions of political ideology, philosophy, and ideas of governance. Since the term "political quietism" was introduced into the field of Islamic studies in 1981 by Michael Cook, Western academics have used it in various ways to describe specific beliefs or actions in both classical and modern Islam. According to Cook, Islam is a political religion, in which the *umma* and *imāma* (imamate, or leadership) are political and religious concepts with pertinent significance to the broader Islamic society. As Cook notes, (political) "activism" is a given in Islam, and it is the advocates of "quietism" who must endeavor to dissuade activists from engaging in political action.[1] Cook used the concept of "quietism" in reference to action; since then, however, the concept of quietism has been introduced in Islamic studies and used by scholars to describe many different beliefs and actions. The only common factor among the various uses and typologies of quietism is the way in which quietism is contrasted to what is described as activism. Arabic-language concepts deriving from early Islamic theology and jurisprudence such as *khurūj* (rebellion) and *quʿūd* (sitting [i.e., action-neutral]) or *muwādaʿa* (quietism) have often been associated with other concepts such as *sharʿiyya* (legitimacy), *ṭāʿa* (obedience), and *bayʿa* (allegiance). On a closer examination of the theologies of various schools and traditions in the Sunnī and Shīʿī traditions, two types of quietist and activist relations emerge; these focus on belief, or deeds.

Does Islamic political theory draw a distinction between heartfelt beliefs and the practice of those beliefs? This important differentiation raises questions as to the sincerity of belief without practice. The dynamics of individual versus community obligations and responsibilities also come into play. Does a believer have a greater obligation to God to live his or her life in the right way as an individual than he or she does to serve the needs of the community as an expression of his or her belief in God? These are questions to keep in mind while reading this volume. Generally, the concept of quietism (that is to say, political nonaction that results from theological beliefs and religious commitments) in relation to the deeds of an individual does not *ipso facto* correlate to a belief in the legitimacy of rulers, neither does it carry an inherent assumption of loyalty (to the said ruler). As a concept, quietism can be understood as an approach to comparing and contrasting religious scholasticism and theological orthodoxy with the exercise of political authority and power. In the third-/ninth-century creeds of traditionalists, some state, for example, "No sword shall be raised upon the nation of Muḥammad" (*wa-lā narā l-sayf ʿalā aḥadin min ummat Muḥammad*). This is a quietist position against revolutionaries such as the Khārijīs and the Muʿtazilīs. By contrast, the same creeds insist on performing *jihād* declared by the ruler, regardless of the piety (or lack) of the ruler, and attending the Friday prayers behind the same ruler. In this instance, the action (and not the *quʿūd*) is quietist in nature.[2] In such cases, quietism in action was understood as a sign of those revolutionary in heart; in this example, theological orthodoxy is maintained inwardly, while stability and the common good (*maṣlaḥa*) provided by an imperfect ruler are maintained outwardly.[3] Another interesting example is that of the *qaʿadat al-Khawārij* (the quietist Khārijīs) who believed in Khārijī doctrines but did not act on them.[4] Therefore, like its eponym derived from Pyrrhonic skepticism in the Euro-Christian context, "political quietism" has no clear and established translation in Arabic in the study of Islamic thought.

Several of the chapters in this volume allude to the concept's direct and/or indirect Christian origins that date to the seventeenth-century Spanish mystic and priest Miguel de Molinos, the standard-bearer of Christian quietism (itself an elaboration on Eastern Orthodox and Byzantine prayer techniques and theological teachings inspired by Pyrrhonism). These mystical trends emerged in Iberian monasteries over the course of the sixteenth century with such figures as the Franciscan friar Saint Peter of Alcántara (1499–1562), who wrote *De oratione et meditatione* ("On oration and meditation"), widely considered the first treatise in what became the "quietist" revivalist movement; the Carmelite nun Saint Teresa of Ávila (1515–82); and the mystic Miguel de Molinos (1628–96), who pursued a life of mysticism based on contemplation and meditation. De Molinos later codified this approach in his teachings and writings, in which he emphasized two paths toward religiosity: one an outward life of action and (visible) piety and another an inward life of contemplation and meditation, focused on strengthening the heart and soul (which de Molinos considered the "fortress of God"). Little to no concrete evidence exists linking the conceptions of quietism in Roman Catholic monastic society to what Western orientalists in the twentieth century termed "quietism" in Islamic scriptural interpretation. It is interesting to note, however, that similarities and claims of intellectual genealogy between Islamic and Catholic mystics have been noted before, including by a contemporary of de Molinos himself: the French orientalist Barthélemy d'Herbelot (1625–95) saw de Molinos as a renewer of illuminist spirituality, which had "passed with the Arabs into Spain." Two centuries later, the Spanish priest and orientalist scholar Miguel Asín Palacios (1871–1944) devoted much of his career to studying Islamic influences on Christianity in general and on Spanish mysticism in particular.[5]

In the histories of Islamic societies, there exists some observable form of an intentional and theologically sound silence, or quietness, on part of the *ʿulamāʾ* (religious scholars) in the face of rulings and actions by sultanic dynasties that unquestionably run counter to the preserved knowledge of the *ʿulamāʾ*. Sometimes, this has led to a deference on part of the *ʿulamāʾ*, at other times on part of the rulers. No clear theological pattern emerges. Is this in fact just pragmatism? And if so, how "quiet" could political quietism really be? Such a broad approach to religion and politics in Islamic thought is rather ambitious and obviously cannot be addressed entirely in a single book. In this collection, we neither endorse nor reject the concept (or invocation of the concept) of "political quietism." Rather, we seek to create a space to explore the concept itself as it is used or understood by scholars who interpret it according to their own disciplinary and scholarly background.

Overview

This book explores various perspectives on political quietism throughout the histories of Islamic societies, from the era of the immediate successors to the Prophet Muḥammad in first-/seventh-century Arabia, to contemporary Muslim scholars in the West. The approaches, disciplines, and subject matter of the authors include Islamic studies, history, philosophy, anthropology, and political science (among others). These scholars question the concept of political quietism itself and explore the applications of various interpretations of political quietism in both historic and contemporary cases.

In the first chapter, "Making Sense of 'Political Quietism'—An Analytical Intervention," Jan-Peter Hartung describes the timeline and conceptualization of the term and puts forward the conceptual pair "governance-orientation" and "guidance-orientation," first used in 1992 by Ahmed Mukarram in his doctoral dissertation at Oxford. Hartung argues that those to whom the label "political quietism" is usually applied fall under the category of "governance-orientation," as they are concerned with overall societal affairs and thus cannot be labeled "quietists." In his exploration of "guidance-orientation," Hartung considers the challenges of differentiating stances toward rulers who commit *kufr*, and in such cases he proposes conceptual tripartite categories of "state-sustaining," "action-neutral," and "confrontational" and further discusses and challenges scholars to reformulate the semantics of the field.

Ebrahim Moosa and Nicholas Roberts's chapter on expressions of political quietism in Islamic history presents a genealogical overview of interpretations on Muslim expressions of political obligations based on commitment to religion over three historical periods, each with a set of factors that determines different outcomes for political expressions. For Moosa and Roberts, "Muslim expressions of quietist political theologies are tied to the changes in Muslim political institutions, societies, political philosophies, ethics, and doctrines that have unfolded over time."

In the third chapter, titled "The Rightly Guided Caliphs: The Range of Views Preserved in *Ḥadīth*," Christopher Melchert examines the range of views in early Sunnī *ḥadīth*s on the conceptualization of "the rightly guided caliphs" (*al-khulafāʾ al-rāshidūn*), who were generally understood in Islamic theological history as the successors to Muḥammad as head of state, and whose words and deeds were especially reliable as guides to belief and conduct. He examines the context of various definitions of those considered "rightly guided" and discusses the interpretation of such historic diversity. By more generally discussing the versatility of orthodox Islamic scriptures, Melchert reinforces what he describes as a well-known feature of Islamic law: that is, the "answers" to questions possess a range of possible responses, as opposed to a sole answer or ruling. Melchert concludes, "Discouragement of indignation over such points also seems to suggest encouragement of political quietism." Quietism appears here as a way of interrupting the past by accepting and accommodating a variety of answers.

Saud al-Sarhan examines the shift to political quietism among Sunnī Muslims, primarily through a case study comparing and contrasting the "quietist" doctrine of the founder of the Ḥanbalī school of jurisprudence, Aḥmad b. Ḥanbal, and the context and practice of his relationship to authority in his time (on the eve of the ʿAbbāsid Empire). Al-Sarhan argues that until the second half of the third/ninth century, two trends coexisted among early Islamic traditionalists; these argued for political activism and quietism, respectively. He credits Aḥmad b. Ḥanbal (d. 241/855) with the quietism that eventually became the formal doctrine of the Sunnīs for the better part of premodern Islamic history. In examining the methods that Aḥmad b. Ḥanbal used to support quietism and to undermine Islamic traditions that seemed to endorse activism, al-Sarhan explores and discusses various understandings about Ibn Ḥanbal's relationship with the authorities in his time and demonstrates how Aḥmad b. Ḥanbal's "passive approach had far-reaching consequences for the Ḥanbalīs, but rarely obstructed the agendas of their rulers, just or otherwise."

Robert Gleave's chapter (5) reconsiders al-Sharīf al-Murtaḍā's *Mas'ala fī ʿamal maʿa l-sulṭān* ["The issue of working for the government"] in light of contemporary research that reexamines the "quietist" nature assumed of Twelver Shīʿī orthodoxy vis-à-vis working with, or for, governments (traditionally understood as somewhat illegitimate during or due to the occultation of the twelfth Imam). Using Muslim juristic discussions to interpret and define a political theory, Gleave explores the question of "working for the Imam" and finds vague links between legitimacy and practices and theories that could be understood as quietist in early Twelver Shīʿī jurisprudence. This pattern not only is found in Islamic law generally but, Gleave argues, also is evident in the interpretations of the Sunnī counterparts of early Twelver Shīʿī clerics.

Alessandro Cancian's aptly titled chapter (6), "'I'm Only a Village Farmer and a Dervish': Between Political Quietism and Spiritual Leadership: Early Modern Shīʿī Sufism and the Challenge of Modernity," addresses alternative views on religious government as formulated by various voices in modern Shiʿism and focuses on the approach of modern Shīʿī-Sufi masters to activism. He attempts to demonstrate how traditional Shīʿī quietist positions were negotiated by Sufis to better claim spiritual authority and religious legitimacy and were also adapted to the modern challenges of the state. Cancian insists that the views and actions taking by these Shīʿī mystics-turned-republican leaders must be considered in the traditional Shīʿī jurisprudential pluralism that evolved apart from modernist theories and contemporary political activism.

Magomed Gizbulaev's chapter (7), entitled "Legal Discourses on *Hijra* in the Caucasus after the Fall of the Caucasus Imamate: *al-Risāla al-sharīfa*," attempts to more profoundly understand the development of legal discourse on *hijra* (Muslim expatriation from lands ruled by non-Muslims to those under Muslim rule) after the Russian conquest of the Caucasus. He does so through a case study of the understudied treatise *al-Risāla al-sharīfa* by the Dagestani scholar ʿAbd al-Raḥmān al-Thughūrī. Gizbulaev's chapter traces the development of the concept of *hijra* as the basis for a Muslim's obligation to leave the territory of *dār al-ḥarb*. Despite the centrality of the concept in Islamic thinking, Gizbulaev finds that, in the Caucasian experience, Muslim jurists felt relatively free to decide when it should be applied and when it should be disregarded. His chapter presents an interesting conundrum with regard to quietism: How might one understand the debate of whether to emigrate or remain under non-Muslim rule in the spectrum of "activist" or "quietist?"

Moving to another historical context and exploration of strategies conceived as quietist, in Chapter 8 Jeremy Kleidosty explores "Constitutionalism as a Quietist Strategy: The Case of Tunisia" by outlining the thought of the mid-to-late nineteenth-century Tunisian reformer and constitutional author Khayr al-Dīn al-Tūnisī from his treatise *Aqwam al-masālik fī maʿrifat aḥwāl al-mamālik* (translated as *The Surest Path to Knowledge Concerning the Conditions of Countries*). The case of Tunisia in the 1860s is interesting, as it was involved in dual imperial entanglements with the Ottoman and French empires. Kleidosty thus understands al-Tūnisī's approach as pragmatic: "if you can't beat them, join them"; al-Tūnisī asserted that Tunisian independence from colonialism could only be salvaged by developing its own form of national modernity compatible with both European norms and Islamic law. In exploring the revolutionary ideas of traditional notions of religious and political authority in the Islamic context with the pressure to adopt a Europeanized modernity, Kleidosty presents al-Tūnisī as someone who engaged in what was, perhaps, one of the earliest prototypes of contemporary conceptions and debates on Islam and politics, quietism and activism, and the role of religious scholars in contemporary Muslim-governed states.

In Chapter 9, Rainer Brunner returns to the Shīʿī tradition in his discussion of Shīʿī quietism beyond politics. He initially challenges the notion that, over time, Twelver Shīʿism (*al-shīʿa al-ithnā ʿashariyya*) has been considered the dominant school of thought in the Shīʿī tradition and that other branches of Shīʿism, such as the Zaydiyya, Ismāʿīliyya, and ʿAlawiyya, were merely splinter groups of an establishment Twelver orthodoxy. Brunner examines various conceptions of political authority, obedience, the relations of Shīʿīs to powers (both Sunnī and Shīʿī), and the various ecumenical movements (as well as their lack of success and reasons for such) with Sunnīs prior to the Islamic revolution in Iran. He understands these events prior to 1979—particularly the ecumenicalism—as evidence that a "defensive, careful, i.e., quietist approach to history can and did exist in modern Shīʿism, and that the offensive, political, i.e., activist approach is not necessarily the only logical outcome of history."

In Chapter 10, Laila Makboul uses her ongoing research of female Saudi preachers in Riyadh to further explore the deconstruction of semantics. Thus, she opens the debate on semantics in the study of political quietism in Islam not only to include what is political, and what is quietism, but also to ask:

What is public? What is activism? And what is the difference between politics and religion, especially among self-declared nonpolitical female preachers in twenty-first-century Riyadh? In attempting to answer some of these questions that revolve around the semantics of the study of political quietism in Islam, she proposes several solutions. An overarching theme of these proposed semantic and epistemological solutions does not attempt to define activist or quietist, but instead classifies them as governance-orientation or guidance-orientation, and secondarily at confrontational, or what Hartung terms "action-neutral."

Fuad Aliyev (Chapter 11) highlights a similar phenomenon in relation to the Gülenist movement in post-Soviet Azerbaijan, where followers of the exiled Turkish scholar focus on nonpolitical social change through secular institutions as an investment in its potential political future. Aliyev also invokes the use of a discourse on "moderate Islam" by Gülenists in Azerbaijan and elsewhere; he is not alone in examining the somewhat ambiguous concept of "moderate Islam" as a form of political quietism.

Finally, in Chapter 12, Walaa Quisay describes the development of "political Islam" through epistemic structures of modernity—a sort of "Protestantization" of Islam, not unlike allusions to modernist influences over the past two centuries described elsewhere in this collection. Quisay finds the neo-traditionalist critique of modernity and activist political Islam/Islamism deeply intertwined.

Coming together

Throughout these chapters, we can identify three individual and collective themes: (i) the discussion of semantics and temporal context, (ii) the challenge of ideological and theological purity versus a diverse selection of pragmatic approaches, and (iii) conclusions regarding the political nature of political quietism.

Semantics and context

Contemporary narratives in the political and academic worlds all too often operate on a timeline of pre- and post-1979: the year the Islamic revolution in Iran overthrew the Western-aligned and increasingly secular Iranian monarchy, eventually culminating in a government as envisioned by Ayatollah Ruhollah Khomeini's understanding of *wilāyat al-faqīh*. Yet this artificial date ignores the historical coexistence of what could be considered activist and quietist trends among Iranian Shīʿī clergy, as Rainer Brunner describes in his chapter on modern Shīʿī quietism beyond politics. Many other authors in this collection would readily agree with such an assessment in relation to other societies and political systems.

Similarly, many if not most of the contributors to this volume, either directly or indirectly, question the activist–quietist binary in the study of Islam. Jan-Peter Hartung's analysis of the concept, and indeed the words "political quietism," investigates the terminology surrounding "quietism," "political quietism," and "politics" in the Arab and Islamic traditions. Alessandro Cancian's chapter on early modern Sufi Shīʿism and the challenges of modernity likewise presents a similar investigative and skeptical approach. Both Hartung's analysis and the chapter of Ebrahim Moosa and Nicholas Roberts on expressions of political quietism throughout Islamic history explore the Jesuit and Euro-Christian origins of the concept of "quietism," while many others in this collection at least touch on the Western academic and philosophical origins of applying these concepts to Islam, particularly in relation to the Orientalist historiography of the activist–quietist binary presented by Cook (1981) and Lewis (1988). Cancian's chapter, as well as those of Robert Gleave on quietism and political legitimacy in Twelver Shīʿism and Walaa Quisay on neo-traditionalists' critiques of modernity and the production of political quietism, sheds light on the role of reformist ʿ*ulamā*ʾ in the late nineteenth century who traveled and observed imperial Europe, and brought back new concepts, as well as dogmatic translations of concepts such as "state" (*dawla*) and "politics" (*siyāsa*), among others (to which Hartung dedicates a significant portion of his analysis). An important distinction is made between political quietism and being apolitical. This comparison is most clear in Moosa and Roberts's chapter, as well as in Saud al-Sarhan's chapter on the shift to political quietism in the Sunnī tradition via the founder of the Ḥanbalī school of thought, Aḥmad b. Ḥanbal.

Purity versus pragmatism

Another theme that emerges is the historical evolution of Islamic scholarly approaches to governance and the guidance of rulers. This evolution is evident from the slow progress of the egalitarian tradition of Arabian tribal society to the adoption of an Islamic form of caesaropapism (as is evident in the absorption of Byzantine and Persian Sasanian imperial socio-administrative cultures), up through the collapse of the Ottoman Empire in the early twentieth century. Contemporary debates and indeed conflicts have emerged as the result of a lack of clarity on this subject.

Whether or not clarity exists or even ought to exist is a core premise of Christopher Melchert's chapter on the range of ideas preserved in *ḥadīth*, particularly in the concept of the "rightly guided caliphs" and who, if any, deserve this distinction. Melchert claims that in jurisprudence, Sunnī orthodoxy allows for disagreements, yet these differences should not bring about fighting and violent chaos (*fitna*).

Many essays in this collection analyze the very challenge of pragmatism versus (theological) purity. Moosa and Roberts explore the challenge of obeying the ruler while maintaining political obligations of faith. In his chapter on constitutionalism as a form of political quietism in Tunisia since the nineteenth century, Jeremy Kleidosty examines the challenge of balancing the absolute autocracy of the Ottoman sultan and local bey (and later secular presidents) with the constitutionalism outlined in Khayr al-Dīn al-Tūnisī's (*c.* 1820–90) work, *The Surest Path to Knowledge Concerning the Condition of Countries*. Al-Tūnisī proposed legitimatizing the role of the *ʿulamāʾ* as a constitutional check and balance against the ruler, limiting their actions to the *sharīʿa*, and paving the way for more contemporary understandings of rulers and *ʿulamāʾ* in political Islam. Looking to the Shīʿī tradition, particularly that of early modern Iran, Cancian examines how Sufi Shīʿīs continuously negotiated a form of political quietism in order to claim spiritual authority and religious legitimacy, all the while attempting to adapt to challenges posed by newly ascendant and Western-educated secularists, as well as other political revolutionaries with religiously inspired modernist ideologies.

This is not a recent challenge, as Melchert's chapter demonstrates, citing early Islamic jurists' proposals of a variety of orders of preference, numberings, etc., as a way to please those in power while still justifying their own theological beliefs. al-Sarhan's chapter presents us with a case of ascetic jurisprudential "purism" with little room for pragmatism in the first two generations of Ḥanbalī scholars. Thus, various forms of pragmatism appear to have emerged. Moosa and Roberts describe early jurisprudential rulings in the Sunnī tradition on obeying a ruler despite his flaws, as well as *taqiyya*, or religious dissimulation in (largely) Shīʿī traditions, as one example.

Other authors in this collection allude, in varying ways, to the development, over the generations, of a general trend preferring stability and security over jurisprudential purity, as noted. Makboul mentions the Albanian-Syrian scholar Muḥammad Nāṣir al-Dīn al-Albānī (1914–99) and his preference to focus on purification and education before political reform projects, according to the citations of several female preachers in Saudi Arabia. Quisay also brings up a similar trend as an approach and attempt by mainstream scholars to maintain hierarchy and authority in Islam, an authority that has been gradually eroded by modernism. What is described as political quietism, then, is not necessarily apolitical. As al-Albānī famously reminded his followers, "from politics is to leave politics", abstaining from politics is essentially a political play.

Elsewhere, the deliberate abstention from certain politics among female Saudi preachers described by Makboul relates to the question Aliyev asks of the Gülenist movement in Azerbaijan: Is their political quietism an ideology or a chameleon-like pragmatism? As Quisay notes, the moderate discourse is dismissed by neo-traditionalists, yet even the neo-traditionalists can be considered pragmatic tools in the discourses of Western governments; their discourses are essentially politicized to fit the requirements of the "rulers" of Western Europe and North America. This is hardly traditionalist, at least not in the sense that al-Sarhan describes Aḥmad b. Ḥanbal and traditional precolonial Sunnī dogma.

Conclusion

The idea that political quietism is an apolitical response to a supposed binary political activism, or Islamism in the Islamic context, is a gross simplification, as all of the essays in this collection reveal to varying degrees in varying contexts. The binary taxonomy can be better understood as a continuum, one that has always existed and continues to evolve with time, context, and experience.

In seeking to create a space to explore the concept of political quietism, this collection successfully achieves its mandate—and nothing more. Just as we argue here that the concept itself is open to the interpretation of any individual scholar, so too the arguments are presented to the informed reader for his or her own acceptance, rejection, or interpretation.

Finally, it is worth noting that this collection was based on the papers (apart from Chapter 2) presented in the second annual conference on political Islamic thought entitled "Political Quietism in Sunni, Shia, and Sufi Jurisprudence: The Classics and the Contemporary," which was held in 2016 in Riyadh.

Saud al-Sarhan
Faisal Abullhassan

Notes

1 Michael Cook, "Activism and Quietism in Islam: The Case of the Early *Murjiʾa*," in *Islam and Power*, ed. Alexander Cudsi and Ali Dessouki (London: Croom Helm, 1981), 21.

2 Saud al-Sarhan, "The Creeds of Aḥmad Ibn Ḥanbal," in *Books and Bibliophiles: Studies in Honour of Paul Auchterlonie on the Bio-Bibliography of the Muslim World*, ed. Robert Gleave (Cambridge: Gibb Memorial Trust, 2014), 29–44.

3 Saud Saleh al-Sarhan, "Early Muslim Traditionalism: A Critical Study of the Works and Political Theology of Aḥmad Ibn Ḥanbal" (PhD dissertation, University of Exeter, 2011), 181–193.

4 ʿAlī b. Ismāʿīl al-Ashʿarī, *Maqālāt al-islāmiyyīn wa-ikhtilāf al-muṣallīn*, ed. Hellmut Ritter (Wiesbaden: Franz Steiner, 1963), 86–87; Muḥammad b. Aḥmad al-Azharī, *Tahdhīb al-lugha*, ed. ʿAbd al-Salām Hārūn (Cairo: Dār al-Miṣriyya li-l-Taʾlīf wa-l-Tarjama, 1964), 1:205.

5 See Chapter 1 in this collection.

Part One

The Concept of Political Quietism: Its Problematics and the Islamic Context

1

Making Sense of "Political Quietism": An Analytical Intervention

Jan-Peter Hartung

These days, many conceptual terms flutter around the academic landscape that are, in fact, heavily presuppositional, including even the study of Islam and its manifold auxiliaries. Unfortunately, more often than not, theoretically, these concepts do not appear to be sufficiently grounded; this fact creates the impression that these terms correspond with actual empirical entities. All-time favorites in this regard include "discourse" and "network," and not least, also "quietism." With Katrin Jomaa's entry "Quietism and Activism" in *The Princeton Encyclopedia of Islamic Political Thought*, the concept has become almost canonized and thus suggests that there is an overall consensus that allows for the meaning of a term to be enshrined in such a reference work.[1] However, I think that this conceptual pair merits further reflection, as do the other overblown concepts listed above.

Most of these concepts, it seems, have sprung from the various social sciences; yet, we must be careful not to adopt them simply because they sound sophisticated and make an academic argument appear even more academic. In fact, we may want to consider the careful and well-considered use of language as one, if not *the*, core criterion of any kind of academic pursuit. Therefore, it is reasonable to thoroughly investigate the conceptual term "quietism"—be it alone or in combination with various attributes, such as "political"—and see to what extent we can employ the term sustainably. In this context, we must also consider whether "quietism" is indeed an antonym of "activism"; a cursory glance shows that this may not be the case, as the antonym of "active" is usually "passive," not "quiet." Therefore, if "quietism" and "activism" are to form a conceptual pair, then we should be able to make an argument for such a pair. This chapter is meant to stimulate a deeper terminological reflection.

First, we need to remember that almost all conceptual terms were derived from objective ones, that is, they are words that have emerged not from a scientific context but rather life-world experiences. To raise objective terms from their empirical embeddedness to abstract analytical terms requires a lot of substantiation; otherwise, one is tempted to read abstract notions against one's own empirically grounded experience—many of Max Weber's ideal types have thus been equally misread as Hegel's earlier imaginaries in his *Lectures on the Philosophy of History*.[2]

Therefore, my first step is to introduce the historical origins of "quietism," then I illustrate how the term was embraced by scholars in the study of Islam in the 1980s and then perpetuated, and further expanded upon, from the early 2000s. Third, I relate the historical term and its semantic implications to the term that is used in the study of Islam and indicate the odd semantic pitfall that makes the application of this term in our context problematic, at least without serious efforts to conceptualize it as logically consistent in itself.

I conclude that, in our context, the usefulness of "quietism" indeed depends on what we understand as "political"—in fact, "political" is the attribute upon which the term "quietism" reacts.

The starting point: The historical semantics of "quietism"

In 1675, the Spaniard Miguel de Molinos (d. 1696), initially educated by the Jesuits, released his *Guida spirituale che disinuolge l'anima e la conduce per l'interior camino all' acquisito della perfetta contemplazione e del ricco tesoro della pace interiore*, "The spiritual guide which releases the soul and conducts it through the interior path to acquire the perfect contemplation and rich treasure of interior peace." In this work, de Molinos pleads for the supremacy of the "prayer of quiet" (*orazione di quiete*), which—by annihilating one's own will in favor of God's—he believed would lead inevitably to the highest level of mystical contemplation and nearness to God.[3]

The idea of obliterating one's own will through contemplative prayer provoked almost instant rebuke by the representatives of established spirituality. Thus, three years after the publication of de Molinos's work, the Jesuit Gottardo Bell'uomo (d. 1690) responded with his own *Pregio e l'ordine dell' orazioni ordinarie e mistiche* [The merit and order of ordinary and mystical prayers]. In this work, the term "quietism" appears for the first time[4] and obviously with polemical intent.

Despite the fact that Bell'uomo nowhere mentioned his name explicitly, de Molinos responded with a defense of his own views, this time in Spanish, although he ultimately refrained from having it published. A reason for this may be that while he praised the *Spiritual Exercises* of Ignacius of Loyola (d. 1556), founder of the Jesuit order, as "most holy, most useful, and worthy of infinite praise," he nonetheless claims that "they are not an immediate means to raise the soul to union and perfection,"[5] that is, he implicitly criticized the founder of the order.

Indeed, the following and often quite polemical critiques of de Molinos's *Spiritual Guide* came from within the Jesuit order.[6] It may be useful to briefly examine its self-image, indicated already by the fact that the order was founded by the Roman Catholic Church in an effort to counteract the popular pull of the Reformation movements throughout Europe that began in the early 1500s. The figureheads of those movements, in turn, emphasized what culminated in, approximately 300 years later, the Pietistic movements; they also inspired Max Weber's theory of the interdependence of the Calvinist work ethic and the rise of capitalism in what is now called the "Global North"—just to employ yet another *en vogue* conceptual term.[7] Indeed, the Jesuit reaction was an inner-worldly one, emphasizing the work in and for the community, *caritas* and *humanitas*: this turned out to be a rather successful strategy to bring stray sheep back into the flock of the Catholic Church and win over all of humanity. They worked on a global scale, setting up missions, translating works, and blending in with local populations.

Thus, when Jesuits polemicized against other Jesuits who advocated quietism from among their own, then we are confronted with a matter that touches on the very identity of the order and the post-Reformation Catholic Church as a whole. This conflict within the Jesuit order was ultimately decided in 1704 by the papal decision to list the works of de Molinos and those who followed him in the index of prohibited books,[8] very much in line with the view of Ignacius of Loyola that "to be right in everything, we ought always to hold that the white which I see, is black, if the Hierarchical Church so decides it."[9] That is, the matter was closed, at least as far as the Catholic Church was concerned.

Decontextualized application: The current use of the term in the study of Islam and conceptual problems

How is it possible, we must ask, that a term with a rather clear-cut and culturally specific historical meaning became entrenched in the study of Islam and, moreover, was coupled with the attribute "political"? Taking into consideration its dissociation from its historically concrete meaning and its eventual lexicographical determination in English—"what is called by the poets apathy or dispassion, by the scepticks [*sic*] indisturbance, by the Moulinists *Quietism*, by common men peace of conscience seems all to mean but great tranquility of mind"[10]—the question becomes even more compelling when we look for a direct correspondent of the term in Arabic, Persian, Turkish, or other written Muslim languages. Almost all the dictionaries I consulted refer to core elements of Sufi practice (*taṣawwuf*): tranquility, calmness, silence, and deference (Ar. *ṭumaʾnīna*; *sukūt*; Tk. *digincilik/taslīm*; P. and Urdu *riżā*; *tavakkul*; *be-khabarī*)[11]; none of these terms seems suitable to refer, in a straightforward way, to something "political."

Alternatively, the term *muwādaʿa* has been used to capture the idea of "quietism," not least in the Arabic title of the conference from which this volume emerged. While *muwādaʿa* seems to be much more closely related to the wider field of politics, we must ask ourselves whether "(political) quietism" is the best possible English rendering of a term that—at least in its classical usage—refers more to conducting a truce between two or more conflicting parties or to the cessation of hostilities.[12]

The at times controversial Orientalist Bernard Lewis seems to be responsible for bringing together these terms with reference to Islamic contexts. In an article in the *New York Review of Books* from 1988, he stated the following:

> There are in particular two political traditions, one of which might be called quietist, the other activist. The arguments in favor of both are based, as are most early Islamic arguments, on the Holy Book and on the actions and sayings of the Prophet. The quietist tradition obviously rests on the Prophet as sovereign, as judge and statesman. But before the Prophet became a head of state, he was a rebel. Before he traveled from Mecca to Medina, where he became sovereign, he was an opponent of the existing order. He led an opposition against the pagan oligarchy of Mecca and at a certain point went into exile and formed what in modern language might be called a "government in exile," with which finally he was able to return in triumph to his birthplace and establish the Islamic state in Mecca. … The Prophet as rebel has provided a sort of paradigm of revolution—opposition and rejection, withdrawal and departure, exile and return. Time and time again movements of opposition in Islamic history tried to repeat this pattern.[13]

Let us summarize the salient points. For Lewis, "quietism" was clearly no longer a mystical inner disposition, but rather a conscious individual position toward a prevailing political, social, economic, etc., order: opposing such an order is "activism," accepting it is "quietism."[14] Now, one could argue that renouncing the world also translates to opposition to the prevailing order: the original Christian mystical concept of "quietism" would then become "activism." Such an obvious logical contradiction hardly serves our quest for a clearly defined and analytically distinct terminology. Such an analytically useful lexicon, however, is necessary if one wishes to avoid the confusion that arises from the application of terms that were used, initially, in historically specific contexts and then applied to temporally and spatially different ones: an explicit definition is therefore an absolute requirement.

The second and perhaps most crucial problem of Lewis's notion is his rather unspecified use of the "existing order." It may be easiest to confine oneself to the foundational period of Islam, which, for lack of sufficient contemporaneous Arabic sources, we know predominantly from the established Muslim narrative. I would contest, on the basis of a wealth of literature by historians who aim to conceptualize the state in a historical and comparative perspective, whether or not we may indeed speak of a "state" with regard to the polity of Medina under the leadership of the Prophet Muḥammad, as Lewis suggests.[15] After all, none of the Arabic terms usually employed for "state" captures the specific semantics of the early modern European concept: *dawla* refers to (dynastic) cycles of rule, while *ḥukūma* indicates the praxis of exerting power, and *salṭana* relates to the disposition of power.[16] None of these terms indicates, first and foremost, the fiscal administration of a community that is perhaps best captured by the French word *état*.[17] However, assuming that the Prophet Muḥammad did not aim to establish dynastic rule over Medina and the territories in the Arabian Peninsula that were later attached to it,[18] the term *dawla* could be more loosely rendered as "civilizational cycle," while the semantic shift to "dynastic cycle" may be attributed to the dynastic aspirations of the early *ahl al-bayt*, mainly the ʿAlids and ʿAbbāsids.[19] There might be some virtue in this consideration, as we see below.

For the moment, we return to Lewis, who was not the first to employ the binary "activism *vs.* quietism" for Islamic contexts. Seven years prior to his article, we find the conceptual pair in reflections on the early Murjiʾa by the medievalist historian Michael Cook.[20] In a way that is rather unusual for him, Cook seems to regard "quietism" in this context as "compliant support of the existing regime" and "Umayyad-phily"[21]; thus, he understands "quietism" as a nonconfrontational attitude toward the prevailing political authorities.

Cook's colleague at Princeton, Muhammad Qasim Zaman, took what Cook regarded as the "political quietism" of the medieval Murjiʾa and used it in a contemporary context. This label was used to characterize those against whom Saḥwīs like Safar b. ʿAbd al-Raḥmān al-Ḥawālī (b. 1950) polemicized; first and foremost among them was Muḥammad Naṣīr al-Dīn al-Albānī (d. 1999).[22] While Zaman appears careful not to put too much stress on the notion of "*political* quietism," it is nonetheless remarkable that he tacitly establishes it as an antonym to "*religious* activism."[23] If we take this further, then the notions of "political" and "religious" become seriously blurred; this is problematic in terms of logic, but makes some sense for those who advocate that "Islam" in reality is both, *dīn wa-dawla*. Translating this phrase—as is often done—as "religion and state" falls rather short and distorts the culturally specific origins of both terms. It is here, therefore, that the rendering of *dawla* as a "civilizational cycle" might help to preserve the culturally distinct semantics of a broad Arabic term, while *dīn* urgently requires a similar reconsideration.[24]

With regard to the overuse of the term "quietism" in the study of Islam, we note that, recently, the term has even been used in the titles of important and path-breaking works on contemporary Salafī scholars: Joas Wagemakers' work on Abū Muḥammad ʿĀṣim al-Maqdisī (b. 1959), who is labeled "a quietist Jihādī-Salafist," is the most prominent to date.[25] Here, I see two possible readings, both of which depend on how *jihād* is understood. If al-Maqdisī promoted *jihād* as the one against one's weaker self (*jihād al-nafs*), then he was embracing a "quietism" much in the sense of de Molinos and his followers. In fact, this is not the case; what Wagemakers considers "quietist" in al-Maqdisī's thought is the theological basis for his legal declaration that a ruler is an infidel (*takfīr al-ḥākim*), a declaration that allows al-Maqdisī to oppose rebelling against an oppressive ruler.[26] In this context, *jihād* refers not to the struggle against one's weaker self but to the militant fight against the enemies of Islam. If I am correct here, then the label "quietist *jihādī*" is equivalent to a "quietist activist," and this surely amounts to a clear logical fallacy. Moreover, in his otherwise excellent work on the theological references of militant Salafists, Daniel Lav even calls such a position "ultra-quietist."[27]

While neither Wagemakers nor Lav explicitly states their reasons for choosing the term "quietism" in their works over other possible concepts, they may have a point. After all, it is scholars like al-Maqdisī, in particular, who make our conceptual work so difficult. I return to this matter below. First, however, we need to make sense of the attribute "political" and inquire whether or not we can rightfully assign this to a historically rather distinct religious concept.

Defining the "political"

Indeed, I think that the usefulness of the term "quietism" in conjunction with the attribute "political" stands and falls with our definition of the latter. When employing such terms, we must explicitly define what we wish our readers and auditors to understand.

Our investigation must go deeper than merely acknowledging the term *siyāsa* as equivalent to "politics." Here, the approach of Conceptual History is useful because it requires us to delve deeper into the semantics of the term itself and tie it to a semantic field or to related concepts.[28] Thus, we discover that the Semitic verbal root *s-w-s* in the pre-Islamic era refers to either an entity of livestock (see the Hebrew *sûs*: "horse") or its management, as the early Arabic *sāʾis* (animal trainer) suggests.[29] From here, it is a short step to relate the management of livestock to the dichotomy *rāʿī* and *raʿiyya*[30]; this dichotomy assumed a prominent role in medieval and early modern Islamic political theory: here the title of Taqī l-Dīn Aḥmad b. Taymiyya's (d. 1328) work on the "management in line with the *sharīʿa*" (*al-siyāsa al-sharʿiyya*) serves as a prominent indicator.[31]

Here I conclude that "politics" is understood to be a fairly hierarchical structure in which an inspired, and thus capable, individual administers, in a top-down style, the rest of the population, who are perceived to be incapable of managing their own affairs. This understanding is perpetuated by thinkers as diverse as Abū Naṣr al-Fārābī (d. 950), Abū l-Ḥasan al-Māwardī (d. 1058), Abū Ḥāmid al-Ghazālī (d. 1111), and, once more, Ibn Taymiyya.[32] The latter is of special significance because he constitutes a link between premodern debates and those in today's Salafist circles, for which the label "political quietism" is most frequently employed.

Next, however, hierarchical relationships must be investigated, because we are confronted with the idea of cascading hierarchies, each one confined to distinct social and even physical spaces. So, what is the extent of the family in which the male householder assumes the role of the *rāʿī*; and subsequently, what are the confines of the *raʿiyya*, over which a ruler assumes management responsibilities? In other words, is there any space that remains unmolested by the encroachment of top-down administration or, in the parlance of contemporary social sciences, a "public–private" divide?

On this point, we may apply what we have learned about the historical origins of "quietism." I would argue that the ultimate private space is within one's own conscience, a realm that is by definition beyond the discretionary powers of legal thought. This in turn—and I am well aware of my potential presumptuousness—begs the question of whether it makes sense to speak of "political quietism in jurisprudence."

This seems a good moment to return to Abū Muḥammad al-Maqdisī, because I think that his alleged "political quietism"—characterized by his call to not carry out a sentence against a political officeholder accused of apostasy (*takfīr*)—was informed by his theologically grounded distinction between *kufr akbar* and *kufr aṣghar*. Legally, however, he still argues for the pronouncement of *takfīr* of a ruler (and all that this entails in terms of his expulsion from the *umma* and loss of protection) and the unconditional need for rule in accordance with the *sharīʿa*; this, in my eyes, still makes him a political activist with regard to both his theological and legal thought.

A conciliatory proposal

Of course, to criticize and leave it at that is always easy. It is much harder to provide an alternative, and thus to render my concerns about the analytical usefulness of applying the term "quietism" to the matters at hand. Just to settle one thing right away: I do not have a secret solution up my sleeve; all I can offer is a brief reflection on conceptual binaries that we may want to consider in place of "political quietism" and "political activism."

The first conceptual pair that I offer is that of "governance-orientation" and "guidance-orientation." I have employed this pair, established in 1992 by Ahmed Mukarram in his doctoral dissertation at Oxford,[33] in an earlier monograph on the Indian scholar Abū l-Ḥasan ʿAlī l-Nadwī (d. 1999).[34] Ultimately, however, the pair was derived from Max Weber's systematic considerations on the sociology of religion[35]—I, too, am prey to the pull of the social sciences. What Mukarram and I call "guidance-orientation" and "governance-orientation" correspond well to Weber's ideal-typical dichotomy of basic ethical attitudes in "ultimate ends" and "politics"—the latter in the sense of "political rule." As such, the horizon of values that underlies eventual orientations in practice is considered in both concepts.

"Guidance-orientation" is a double-edged sword, as it allows for egocentric world renunciation in the sense of the historical "quietism," but also entails a more activist possibility that encompasses social activities at the grassroots level, ranging from communal kitchens to public study circles, and these are activities that must be kept analytically separate from "quietism." As social activism, it is the evil twin of the "governance-orientation": they differ only in their respective appraisal of the relationship between political rule and the religious constitution of the society. While advocates of "governance-orientation" hold fast to the conviction that a sound political superstructure is inevitably necessary to enable members of a society to lead a life in compliance with the *sharīʿa*, the adherents of "guidance-orientation" do not require a particular political superstructure but refer the responsibility for one's fidelity back to the basis of society. First and foremost, it is important that this falls equally under the category "activism"; this, in turn, allows us to confine "quietism" to the more mystical and individualistic approach that it has had historically and, moreover, it allows us to abandon the problematic notion of "political quietism."

I argue that the Salafī authors to whom the label "political quietism" is usually applied all fall well under the category of "governance-orientation." After all, they are still very much concerned with overall societal affairs—as such, they cannot be labeled, with any accuracy, "quietists."

The category "governance-orientation," however, still requires further subdividing, because—and here I certainly agree with authors like Wagemakers—we need to account for the great variety of theologically sustained legal positions in the variety of people who can be considered Salafīs. To me, it appears as if the main difference lies in how the stance toward a ruler who has been declared as having committed any kind of *kufr*—be it greater or lesser—translates into legally grounded actions. Here, perhaps a tripartite subdivision into "state-sustaining," "action-neutral," and "confrontational" may be helpful.

"State-sustaining" would include those who do not extend the practice of *takfīr* to the political ruler and confine themselves to admonitions and counsel—examples include scholars of the Hayʾat Kibār al-ʿUlamāʾ (lit., "council of senior scholars")[36] of Saudi Arabia, such as key Salafist figures like ʿAbd al-ʿAzīz b. Bāz (d. 1999) and Muḥammad b. Ṣāliḥ al-ʿUthaymīn (d. 2001). People in this category appear in the focus of polemics by those subsumed under the other two categories[37] and therefore are easily discernible. At the other end of the spectrum are those who proclaim the ruler an infidel and are not overly concerned with the finer theological and legal points of *kufr*; therefore, they legitimize violent confrontation against the ruler as a religious duty. From here, the spectrum extends from the militant activists of al-Qāʿida and its various affiliates to the *Dawla Islāmiyya fī l-ʿIrāq wa-l-Shām* (ISIS). Finally, "action-neutral" would include people like al-Qāʿida sympathizer Abū Muḥammad al-Maqdisī, who deem it necessary to practice *takfīr al-ḥākim* but, because they rate a ruler's *kufr* as a lesser (*aṣghar*) *kufr*, they argue for abstinence from violently punishing the offending ruler. According to my proposed taxonomy, al-Maqdisī would no longer be considered a "quietist *jihādī*," but rather a "governance-oriented, yet action-neutral, Salafist."

Yet, the reality appears more complex. If the classification of al-Maqdisī has currency, then the Jordanian scholar must maintain one and the same position throughout; this, in turn, assumes that a person is absolutely consistent and fixed in his positions.[38] Such an anthropology, however, is entirely unwarranted by empirical observation: humankind, in its overwhelming majority, is predominantly contingent, to the extent even of arbitrariness. Every person classed above holds a myriad of positions, usually dependent on ever-changing circumstances. Thus, al-Maqdisī's early writings, prominently among them *Millat Ibrāhīm* (1984), present a rather confrontational position that was informed by his years in Saudi Arabia in the late 1970s and by his participation with the *mujāhidīn* in the borderland between Pakistan and Afghanistan in the early 1980s.[39] Changed contexts, informed not least by al-Maqdisī's experience of imprisonment since the mid-1990s, have led to a less "confrontational"—thus, "action-neutral"—position: in his *Waqfāt maʿa thamarāt al-jihād* (2004), al-Maqdisī was outspoken in his criticism of the militant option, as advocated by those he had earlier associated with, prominently among them Abū Muṣʿab al-Zarqāwī (killed 2006).[40]

What can be gathered from this is that we need to duly recognize the fact that a person may be classed in one category at a point in time (t_1) and fall into another at a different moment in time (t_2). In light of this, my above classification of al-Maqdisī as "governance-oriented, yet action-neutral, Salafist" requires a necessary expansion that credits the time factor. Thus, while in 1985, for example, he would have been a "governance-oriented confrontational Salafist," two decades later, he had become a "governance-oriented, yet action-neutral, Salafist," which is where he was initially classed. The advantage of this categorization is that it allows for the contingency of human beings, who elude definite and persistent categorization.

***

Do the above considerations help us explain things better? Ultimately, I suggest, this is what conceptual, or analytical, terms are supposed to do.

Along with an acknowledgment of the historical semantics of "quietism," we have become sensitive to the fact that we must be careful whenever we ascribe new meaning to a term. To avoid potential confusion over the use of a concept with a rather distinct historical meaning, at the least, we should make explicit what we wish our readers and auditors to understand when we use the term "quietism." Still, our definitions need to take into consideration the historical roots of the term; otherwise, "quietism" would be equivalent to a mathematical variable that can stand for anything.

Apparently, the semantic reformulation that is taking place, especially in the study of Islam, has so far almost ignored the historical semantics of the term. Unfortunately, it was tacitly lumped together with the attribute "political"; thus, the term already gains a new meaning, even without comprehensive conceptual reflection and the subsequent justification of this semantic twist. We have seen that even in its appearance in the authoritative *Princeton Encyclopedia of Islamic Political Thought*, the term is loosely defined and little clarity is achieved. Moreover, I argue that the phenomena that we aim to capture with the term "(political) quietism" could be equally, and perhaps with an even higher degree of differentiation, well framed with alternative conceptual terms. As such, I have introduced the skeleton of a heuristic model that we may want to apply to our material, to see if it provides us with greater conceptual clarity. For now, however, there is little more left for me than to invite my learned peers to test it, critique it, and by doing so, refine it, or eventually abandon it for a conceptual framework that has even stronger explanatory force.

Notes

1 See Katrin Jomaa, "Quietism and Activism," in *The Princeton Encyclopedia of Islamic Political Thought*, ed. Gerhard Böwering et al. (Princeton, NJ: Princeton University Press, 2013), 446–447.

2 See Jan-Peter Hartung, "(Re-)Presenting the Other?—Erkenntniskritische Überlegungen zum Orientalismus," in *Räume der Hybridität: Postkoloniale Konzepte in Theorie und Literatur*, ed. Christof Hamann and Cornelia Sieber (Hildesheim: Olms, 2002), 138n3.

3 See Dottor Michele di Molinos Sacerdote, *Guida spirituale che disinuolge l'anima e la conduce per l'interior camino all' acquisito della perfetta contemplazione e del ricco tesoro della pace interiore* (Rome: Michel 'Ercole, 1681 [reprint]), esp. 27, 31, and 86–96.

4 See Gottardo Bell'huomo [*sic*], *Il pregio e l'ordine dell' orazioni ordinarie e mistiche* (Modona: Soliani, 1678), 101.

5 Miguel de Molinos, *Defensa de la contemplación*, ed. Francisco Trinidad Solano (Madrid: Editora nacional, 1983), 132.

6 The next polemic was Paolo Segneri's *Concordia tra la fatica e la quiete nell' orazione* from 1680, which again triggered a response, this time from Cardinal Pier Matteo Petrucci (d. 1701), in *Della contemplazione mistica acquistata* (1682).

7 See Caroline Levander and Walter Mignolo, "Introduction: The Global South and World Dis/Order," *Global South* 5, no. 1 (2011), 1–11.

8 See *Index Librorum prohibitorum Innoc. XI.P.M. jusse editus usque ad annum 1681. Eidem accedit in fine Appendix usque ad mensem Junij 1704* (Rome: Typis. Rev. Cam. Apost., 1704), 9f, 376, and 550.

9 Ignatius [de Loyola], *Exercitia Spiritualia* (Rome: Antonio Blado, 1548), 211 (trans. Elder Mullan, SJ).

10 See "Quietism," in *A Dictionary of the English Language*, ed. Samuel Johnson (London: W. Strahan, 1755), 2:442. The semantics of "quietism" in the eighteenth century did not change significantly until the early twentieth century, as proven by the first edition of the *Oxford English Dictionary*, ed. the Philological Society (Oxford: Clarendon Press, 1884–1928), 8:60.

11 For Turkish, see, for example, J. W. Redhouse, *Redhouse's Turkish Dictionary, Part I: English and Turkish* (London: Bernhard Quaritch, 1880), 252; Bedia Akarsu, *Felsefe Terimleri Sözlüğü* (Ankara: Türk Dil Kurumu Yayınları, 1975), 50; for Persian, see ʿAbbās Āryānpūr and Manūchihr Āryānpūr, *Farhang-i dānishgāhī: inglīsī-fārsī* (Tehran: Sipihr, 1369Sh/1987), 2:1,787; for Urdu, see Jamīl Jālibī (ed.), *Qawmī angrezī-urdū lughat* (Islamabad: Idāra-yi Muqtadira-yi Qawmī Zabān, 1992), 1,607. Both the Persian and Urdu dictionaries make explicit reference to de Molinos.

12 See Abū l-Faḍl b. Manẓūr, *Lisān al-ʿarab* (Cairo: al-Maṭbaʿa al-Kubrā l-Mīriyya, 1300–07 AH), 10:266 (s.v. *w-d-ʿ*).

13 Bernard Lewis, "Islamic Revolution," *New York Review of Books* 34, nos. 21–22 (January 21, 1988), 4.

14 It appears that Lewis's rather feeble definition is still widely embraced today, as illustrated by Jomaa's entry in *The Princeton Encyclopedia of Islamic Political Thought* more than two decades later; she states that "quietism" "can generally be defined as passivism in politics" (446). Thus, she suggests, what is, in my view, a rather problematic synonymity of "quiet" and "passive."

15 See the entries "Reich" (Stephan Wendehorst), "Staat" (Roland G. Asch), and "Staatenbildung, außereuropäische: Islam" (Stephan Conermann), in *Enzyklopädie der Neuzeit*, ed. Friedrich Jaeger (Stuttgart: Metzler, 2005–12), 10:874–888, 12:494–509, and 522–532.

16 See Ibn Manẓūr, *Lisān*, 13:267–270 (s.v. *d-w-l*), with the initial meaning of *dawla* as "victory (over those who dominate the former cycle of rule)"; 15:30–34 (s.v. ḥ-*k-m*), esp. 31f; 9:192–194 (s.v. *s-l-ṭ*).

17 See Louis de Jaucourt, s.v. "État," in *Encyclopédie ou Dictionnaire raisonné des sciences, des arts et des métiers*, ed. Denis Diderot and M. D'Alembert (Paris: Briasson, 1751–72), 6:16–30, esp. 19–28.

18 See Michael Cook, "Did the Prophet Muḥammad Keep Court?" in *Court Cultures in the Muslim World: Seventh to Nineteenth Centuries*, ed. Albrecht Fuess and Jan-Peter Hartung (London and New York: Routledge, 2011), 23–29.

19 Compare the notion of *dawla* in *Ṣaḥīḥ al-Bukhārī*, K. al-jihād wa-l-sayr, bāb qawl Allāh taʿālā "hal tarabbusūna binā illā iḥday al-ḥusnayayn" wa-l-ḥarb sijāl 1, no. 2: 841; and Nuʿaym b. Ḥammād al-Marwāzī, *Kitāb al-fitan*, ed. Suhayl Zakkār (Beirut: Dār al-Fikr, 1414/1993), 120; during the campaign that eventually brought the ʿAbbāsids to power, the ʿAlids were labeled *aṣḥāb al-dawla*. The ʿAbbāsid historiographer Aḥmad b. Yaḥyā l-Baladhūrī put this meaning into the mouth of an Umayyad commander who reprimanded his ruler with the words "We are fighting for your dynasty [*dawlatikum*] while you betray it" (*Kitāb jumal min ansāb al-ashrāf*, ed. Suhayl Zakkār and Riyāḍ Ziriklī [Beirut: Dār al-Fikr, 1417/1996], 4:112). Slightly earlier, Abū Jaʿfar Muḥammad al-Ṭabarī clearly associated this meaning with the ʿAbbāsids when he used the expression "our cycle/dynasty" (*dawlatunā*); see *Taʾrīkh al-Ṭabarī*, ed. Nawāf al-Jarrāḥ (Beirut: Dār Ṣādir, 1424/2003), 4:1,525, 1,543, and 1,549.

20 See Michael Cook, "Activism and Quietism in Islam: The Case of the Early *Murjiʾa*," in *Islam and Power*, ed. Alexander S. Cudsi and Ali E. Hillal Dessouki (London: Croom Helm, 1981), 15–23.

21 See ibid., 18.

22 See Muhammad Qasim Zaman, *The Ulama in Contemporary Islam: Custodians of Change* (Princeton, NJ, and Oxford: Princeton University Press, 2002), 157. More recent scholars on al-Albānī perpetuate the label "political quietist" with regard to him, yet still without substantiating the term. See Jacob Olidort, "The Politics of 'Quietist' Salafism," *Analysis Paper of the Brookings Project on U.S. Relations with the Islamic World* 18 (February 2015).

23 See Zaman, *Ulama*, 157.

24 On the problematic character of translating *dīn* as "religion," see Reinhold Glei and Stefan Reichmuth: "Religion between Last Judgement, Law and Faith: Koranic *dīn* and Its Rendering in Latin Translations of the Koran," *Religion* 42, no. 2 (2012), 247–271.

25 See Joas Wagemakers, *A Quietist Jihadi: The Ideology and Influence of Abu Muhammad al-Maqdisi* (Cambridge: Cambridge University Press, 2012).

26 See ibid., 67–75.

27 Daniel Lav, *Radical Islam and the Revival of Medieval Theology* (Cambridge: Cambridge University Press, 2012), 148.

28 For the entire discussion about the attempt to establish a semantic field of "the political" in the Muslim context, see Jan-Peter Hartung, "Appropriations and Contestations of the Islamic Nomenclature in Muslim North India: Elitism, Lexicography, and the Meaning of *The Political*," in *Contributions to the History of Concepts* 12, no. 2 (2017): 76–110.

29 See Bernard Lewis, "Siyāsa," in *In Quest of an Islamic Humanism: Arabic and Islamic Studies in Memory of Mohamed al-Nowaihi*, ed. Arnold H. Green (Cairo: American University in Cairo Press, 1984), 3–14, here 3; *Biblia Hebraica Stuttgartensia*, ed. K. Ellinger and W. Rudolph (Stuttgart: Deutsche Bibelgesellschaft, 1997), 109 (Ex 14.9), 408 (Judg 5.22), 530 (2 Sam 15.1), 586 (1 Kings 10.28), 678, 683, and 720 (Isa 2.7, 5.28, 30.16), 1,049 (Hab 1.8), 1,270 (Job 39.18f).

30 The binary *rāʿin–raʿiyya* in Islamic political theory dates back to the prophetic *ḥadīth* "kullukum rāʿin wa-kullukum masʾūlun ʿan raʿiyyatih" (see *Ṣaḥīḥ Muslim*, Kitāb al-imāra, bāb faḍīlat al-imām al-ʿādil wa-ʿuqūbat al-jāʾir wa-l-ḥathth ʿalā l-rifq bi-l-raʿiyya wa-l-nahy ʿan idkhāl al-mashaqqa ʿalayhim 4, no. 4,617; *Sunan Abī Dāwūd*, Kitāb al-kharāj wa-l-imāra wa-l-fayʾ, bāb mā yalzamu l-imām min ḥaqq al-raʿiyya 1, no. 2,928; *al-Jāmiʿ al-ṣaḥīḥ*, Kitāb al-jihād, bāb mā jāʾ fī l-imām 1, no. 1,705; *Musnad Aḥmad b. Ḥanbal*, no. 6,020).

31 See Taqī l-Dīn Abū ʿAbbās Aḥmad b. Taymiyya, *Kitāb al-siyāsa al-sharʿiyya fī iṣlāḥ al-rāʿī wa-l-raʿiyya*, ed. Lajnat Iḥyāʾ al-Turāth al-ʿArabī fī Dār al-Āfāq al-Jadīda (Beirut: Dār al-Jīl, 1408/1988). For an explicit reference to the *ḥadīth* "kullukum rāʿin," see ibid., 13.

32 See Abū Naṣr al-Fārābī, *Kitāb ārāʾ ahl al-madīna al-fāḍila*, ed. Albīr Naṣrī Nādir (Beirut: Dār al-Mashriq, 1991); Abū l-Ḥasan ʿAlī b. Muḥammad al-Māwardī, *Kitāb al-aḥkām al-sulṭāniyya* (Beirut: Dār al-Fikr, 1422/2002); Abū Ḥāmid Muḥammad al-Ghazālī, *al-Mustaṣfā min ʿilm al-uṣūl*, ed. Muḥammad al-Bilbaysī l-Ḥusaynī (Baghdad: Maktabat al-Muthannā, 1970; reprint of the 1322–24 AH Bulaq edition); Ibn Taymiyya, *Siyāsa sharʿiyya*.

33 See Ahmed Mukarram, "Some Aspects of Contemporary Islamic Thought: Guidance and Governance in the Work of Mawlana Abul Hasan Ali Nadwi and Mawlana Abul Aala Mawdudi" (PhD dissertation, University of Oxford, 1992).

34 See Jan-Peter Hartung, *Viele Wege und ein Ziel: Leben und Wirken von Sayyid Abū l-Ḥasan Ḥasanī Nadwī (1914–1999)* (Würzburg: Ergon, 2004), 123–125.

35 See Max Weber, *Wirtschaft und Gesellschaft. Grundriß der verstehenden Soziologie* (Tübingen: Mohr, 1972), 267–268 and 355–359.

36 The Hayʾat Kibār al-ʿUlamāʾ is a council of scholars chosen by the royal family; numerous especially younger Salafīs are deeply suspicious of it, largely because of the criteria on which the regime chooses these scholars.

37 See, for example, Abū Muḥammad ʿĀṣim al-Maqdisī, *Millat Ibrāhīm wa-daʿwat al-anbiyāʾ wa-l-mursalīn* [*wa-asālīb al-ṭughāt fī tamyīʿihā wa-ṣarf al-duʿāt ʿanhā*] (N.p.: Minbar al-Tawḥīd wa-l-Jihād, 1431 AH [originally 1984]), 65–72, esp. 68f, where the Mecca-based Muslim World League (Rābiṭat al-ʿĀlam al-Islāmī) is mentioned explicitly as an example of a tool employed by the Saudi government to co-opt *ʿulamāʾ* for its own—for al-Maqdisī sinister—ends. It is perfectly clear that for al-Maqdisī, the Hayʾat Kibār al-ʿUlamāʾ falls into the same context.

38 I am much indebted to Saʿūd al-Sarḥān for raising this issue in the discussion following the presentation of my argument at the conference in Riyadh and thus substantially helping me sharpen my analytical tools. The problem of biography-related contingencies of literary output, however, already determined my approach in the above-mentioned work on Abū l-Ḥasan ʿAlī l-Nadwī. See Hartung, *Viele Wege*, 18–34.

39 See al-Maqdisī, *Millat Ibrāhīm*, 21–24 and 66–69; also, al-Maqdisī, *Kitāb iʿdād al-qāda al-fawāris bi-hajr fasād al-madāris* (N.p.: Minbar al-Tawḥīd wa-l-Jihād, 1422 AH [originally 1986–87]); al-Maqdisī, *al-Kawāshif al-jaliyya fī kufr al-dawla al-Suʿūdiyya* (N.p.: Minbar al-Tawḥīd wa-l-Jihād, 1421 [originally 1989]), 72–74 and 165–167.

40 See al-Maqdisī, *Waqfāt maʿa thamarāt al-jihād bayn al-jahl fī l-sharʿ wa-l-jahl bi-l-wāqiʿ* (N.p.: Minbar al-Tawḥīd wa-l-Jihād, 1425 AH [originally 2004]), 124f and 127.

Bibliography

Abū Dāwūd. *Sunan Abī Dāwūd*. K. al-kharāj wa-l-imāra wa-l-fayʾ, bāb mā yalzamu l-imām min ḥaqq al-raʿiyya.

Akarsu, Bedia. *Felsefe Terimleri Sözlüğü*. Ankara: Türk Dil Kurumu Yayınları, 1975.

Āryānpūr, "ʿAbbās and Manūchihr Āryānpūr." In *Farhang-i dānishgāhī: inglīsī-fārsī*. 2 vols. Tehran: Sipihr, 1369 Sh/1987.

Asch, Roland G. "Staat." In *Enzyklopädie der Neuzeit*, edited by Friedrich Jaeger, 12:494–509. 16 vols. Stuttgart: Metzler, 2005–12.

al-Baladhūrī, Aḥmad b. Yaḥyā. *Kitāb jumal min ansāb al-ashrāf*. Edited by Suhayl Zakkār and Riyāḍ Ziriklī. 13 vols. Beirut: Dār al-Fikr, 1417/1996.

Bell'huomo, Gottardo. *Il pregio e l'ordine dell' orazioni ordinarie e mistiche*. Modona: Soliani, 1678.

Biblia Hebraica Stuttgartensia. Edited by K. Ellinger and W. Rudolph. Stuttgart: Deutsche Bibelgesellschaft, 1997.

al-Bukhārī. *Ṣaḥīḥ al-Bukhārī*. K. al-jihād wa-l-sayr, bāb qawl Allāh taʿālā "hal tarabbusūna binā illā iḥday al-ḥusnayayn" wa-l-ḥarb sijāl.

Conermann, Stephan. "Staatenbildung, außereuropäische: Islam." In *Enzyklopädie der Neuzeit*, edited by Friedrich Jaeger, 12:522–532. 16 vols. Stuttgart: Metzler, 2005–12.

Cook, Michael. "Activism and Quietism in Islam: The Case of the Early *Murjiʾa*." In *Islam and Power*, edited by Alexander S. Cudsi and Ali E. Hillal Dessouki, 15–23. London: Croom Helm, 1981.

Cook, Michael. "Did the Prophet Muḥammad Keep Court?" In *Court Cultures in the Muslim World: Seventh to Nineteenth Centuries*, edited by Albrecht Fuess and Jan-Peter Hartung, 23–29. London and New York: Routledge, 2011.

al-Fārābī, Abū Naṣr. *Kitāb ārāʾ ahl al-madīna al-fāḍila*. Edited by Albīr Naṣrī Nādir. Beirut: Dār al-Mashriq, 1991.

al-Ghazālī, Abū Ḥāmid Muḥammad. *al-Mustaṣfā min ʿilm al-uṣūl*. Edited by Muḥammad al-Bilbaysī l-Ḥusaynī. 2 vols. Baghdad: Maktabat al-Muthannā, 1970; reprint of Bulaq, 1322–24.

Glei, Reinhold, and Stefan Reichmuth. "Religion between Last Judgement, Law and Faith: Koranic *dīn* and Its Rendering in Latin Translations of the Koran." *Religion* 42, no. 2 (2012): 247–271.

Hartung, Jan-Peter. "Appropriations and Contestations of the Islamic Nomenclature in Muslim North India: Elitism, Lexicography, and the Meaning of *The Political*." *Contributions to the History of Concepts* 12, no. 2 (2017): 76–110.

Hartung, Jan-Peter. "(Re-)Presenting the Other?—Erkenntniskritische Überlegungen zum Orientalismus." In *Räume der Hybridität: Postkoloniale Konzepte in Theorie und Literatur*, edited by Christof Hamann and Cornelia Sieber, 135–150. Hildesheim: Olms, 2002.

Hartung, Jan-Peter. *Viele Wege und ein Ziel: Leben und Wirken von Sayyid Abū l-Ḥasan Ḥasanī Nadwī (1914–1999)*. Würzburg: Ergon, 2004.

Ibn Ḥanbal. *Musnad Aḥmad b. Hanbal*. Edited by Shuʿayb al-Arnawūṭ, ʿĀdil Murshid et al., 50 vols. (Beirut: Muʾassasat al-Risāla 1421/2001), VIII: 83 (no. 4,795), IX: 156 (no. 5,176), X: 139 (no. 5,901) and X: 220 (no. 6,026).

Ibn Manẓūr, Abū l-Faḍl. *Lisān al-ʿarab*. 20 vols. Cairo: al-Maṭbaʿa al-Kubrā l-Amīriyya, 1300–07.

Ibn Taymiyya, Taqī l-Dīn Abū ʿAbbās Aḥmad. *Kitāb al-siyāsa al-sharʿiyya fī iṣlāḥ al-rāʿī wa-l-raʿiyya*. Edited by Lajnat Iḥyāʾ al-Turāth al-ʿArabī fī Dār al-Āfāq al-Jadīda. Beirut: Dār al-Jīl, 1408/1988.

Ignatius [de Loyola]. *Exercitia spiritualia*. Translated by Elder Mullan. Rome: Antonio Blado, 1548.

Index Librorum prohibitorum Innoc. XI.P.M. jusse editus usque ad annum 1681. Eidem accedit in fine Appendix usque ad mensem Junij 1704. Rome: Typis. Rev. Cam. Apost., 1704.

Jālibī, Jamīl (ed.). *Qawmī angrezī-urdū lughat*. Islamabad: Idāra-yi Muqtadira-yi Qawmī Zabān, 1992.

de Jaucourt, Louis. "État." In *Encyclopédie ou Dictionnaire raisonné des sciences, des arts et des métiers*. Edited by Denis Diderot and M. D'Alembert. 17+11 vols, 6:16–30. Paris: Briasson and others, 1751–72.

Jomaa, Katrin. "Quietism and Activism." In *The Princeton Encyclopedia of Islamic Political Thought*, edited by Gerhard Böwering et al. Princeton, NJ: Princeton University Press, 2013: 446–447.

Lav, Daniel. *Radical Islam and the Revival of Medieval Theology*. Cambridge: Cambridge University Press, 2012.

Levander, Caroline, and Walter Mignolo. "Introduction: The Global South and World Dis/Order." *The Global South* 5, no. 1 (2011): 1–11.

Lewis, Bernard. "Islamic Revolution." *New York Review of Books* 34, nos. 21–22 (January, 1988). Online: http://www.nybooks.com/issues/1988/01/21/. Accessed March 6, 2018.

Lewis, Bernard. "Siyāsa." In *In Quest of an Islamic Humanism: Arabic and Islamic Studies in Memory of Mohamed al-Nowaihi*, edited by Arnold H. Green, 3–14. Cairo: American University of Cairo Press, 1984.

al-Maqdisī, Abū Muḥammad ʿĀṣim. *al-Kawāshif al-jaliyya fī kufr al-dawla al-Suʿūdiyya*. N.p.: Minbar al-Tawḥīd wa-l-Jihād, 1421 [1989].

al-Maqdisī, Abū Muḥammad ʿĀṣim. *Kitāb iʿdād al-qāda al-fawāris bi-hajr fasād al-madāris*. N.p.: Minbar al-Tawḥīd wa-l-Jihād, 1422 [1986–87].

al-Maqdisī, Abū Muḥammad ʿĀṣim. *Millat Ibrāhīm wa-daʿwat al-anbiyāʾ wa-l-mursalīn* [*wa-asālīb al-ṭughāt fī tamyīʿihā wa-ṣarf al-duʿāt ʿanhā*] N.p.: Minbar al-Tawḥīd wa-l-Jihād, 1431 [1984].

al-Maqdisī, Abū Muḥammad ʿĀṣim. *Waqfāt maʿa thamarāt al-jihād bayn al-jahl fī l-sharʿ wa-l-jahl bi-l-wāqiʿ*. N.p.: Minbar al-Tawḥīd wa-l-Jihād, 1425 [2004].

al-Māwardī, Abū l-Ḥasan ʿAlī b. Muḥammad. *Kitāb al-aḥkām al-sulṭāniyya*. Beirut: Dār al-Fikr, 1422/2002.

al-Marwāzī, Nuʿaym b. Ḥammād. *Kitāb al-fitan*. Edited by Suhayl Zakkār. Beirut: Dār al-Fikr, 1414/1993.

de Molinos, Miguel [Michele]. *Defensa de la contemplación*. Edited by Francisco Trinidad Solano. Madrid: Editora nacional, 1983.

de Molinos, Miguel [Michele]. *Guida spirituale che disinuolge l'anima e la conduce per l'interior camino all' acquisito della perfetta contemplazione e del ricco tesoro della pace interiore*. Rome: Michel 'Ercole, 1681.

Mukarram, Ahmed. "Some Aspects of Contemporary Islamic Thought: Guidance and Governance in the Work of Mawlana Abul Hasan Ali Nadwi and Mawlana Abul Aala Mawdudi." PhD dissertation, University of Oxford, 1992.

Muslim. *Ṣaḥīḥ Muslim*. K. al-imāra, bāb faḍīlat al-imām al-ʿādil wa-ʿuqūbat al-jāʾir wa-l-ḥathth ʿalā l-rifq bi-l-raʿiyya wa-l-nahy ʿan idkhāl al-mashaqqa ʿalayhim.

Olidort, Jacob. "The Politics of 'Quietist' Salafism." *Analysis Paper of the Brookings Project on U.S. Relations with the Islamic World* 18 (February 2015). Online: www.brookings.edu/wp-content/uploads/2016/07/Brookings-Analysis-Paper_Jacob-Olidort-Inside_Final_Web.pdf. Accessed March 6, 2018.

Oxford English Dictionary. Edited by the Philological Society. 10 vols. Oxford: Clarendon Press, 1884–1928.

"Quietism." In *A Dictionary of the English Language*, edited by Samuel Johnson, 2:442. 2 vols. London: W. Strahan, 1755.

Redhouse, J. W. *Redhouse's Turkish Dictionary, Part I: English and Turkish*. London: Bernhard Quaritch, 1880.

al-Ṭabarī, Abū Jaʿfar Muḥammad. *Taʾrīkh al-Ṭabarī*. Edited by Nawāf al-Jarrāḥ. 6 vols. Beirut: Dār Ṣādir, 1424/2003.

al-Tirmidhī. *al-Jāmiʿ al-ṣaḥīḥ*, K. al-jihād, bāb mā jāʾ fī l-imām.

Wagemakers, Joas. *A Quietist Jihadi: The Ideology and Influence of Abu Muhammad al-Maqdisi*. Cambridge: Cambridge University Press, 2012.

Weber, Max. *Wirtschaft und Gesellschaft. Grundriß der verstehenden Soziologie*. Tübingen: Mohr, 1972.

Wendehorst, Stephan. "Reich." In *Enzyklopädie der Neuzeit*, edited by Friedrich Jaeger, 10:874–888. 16 vols. Stuttgart: Metzler, 2005–12.

Zaman, Muhammad Qasim. *The Ulama in Contemporary Islam: Custodians of Change*. Princeton, NJ, and Oxford: Princeton University Press, 2002.

2

Expressions of Political Quietism in Islamic History

Ebrahim Moosa and Nicholas Roberts

> Babaji was known for his piety and scholarship, and his followers included men and women of every faith—Hindus, Muslims, Sikhs and untouchables. Although on the face of it Babaji had nothing to do with politics, it was an open secret that no political movement in the Punjab could begin or end without his clearance. To the government machinery, he was an unsolved puzzle. There was always a smile on his face, which could be interpreted in a thousand ways.
>
> Saadat Hasan Manto, "The Price of Freedom," in *Mottled Dawn*

Introduction

Political quietism is one expression of political theology in Islamic history. Political theology is a discourse capturing the nexus of how the elements of God, humans, and the world intersect in an ever-changing relationship of political community and religious order.[1] It articulates the relationship between "power [or authority, *Herrschaft*] and salvation [*Heil*]."[2] Modern students of Islam have drawn on European, Christian categories of "quietism," a tradition in Christian political theology, to explain certain religiopolitical phenomena in Islam. "Quietism" originally referred to a devotional movement in Catholicism led by the Spanish priest Miguel de Molinos.[3] In other modern European and Christian contexts, political quietism generally refers to styles of thought that combine pietism with conservative politics. For example, Johann Albrecht Bengel (d. 1752), a Lutheran reformist invested in biblical piety, tended to a "pessimistic outlook and political quietism."[4] The authoritative *Encyclopedia of Religion* differentiates between quietism and the generic use of the word *quietistic*, "which implies withdrawal or passivity with regard to politics or ethics."[5]

Strands of political quietism in Islam have been expressed along a spectrum of Muslim political theologies stretching from the early formation of the faith to the modern period. In early Islamic history, tensions between the motivations of piety and the politics of responsibility laid the groundwork for myriad expressions of quietism that continue, in different iterations, in the modern period. Historically, an important element in strands of mainstream Sunnī and Shīʿī theology involves the notion of obedience to those in power. Many theologians have refrained from making political judgments on errant or unjust rulers, usually in the interest of personal and communal preservation and stability. Modern scholars of Islam, when referencing these events, have used the label "political quietism." These Muslim expressions of quietism resemble similar expressions in Christian history. In the Bible, in Romans (13:1-2), St. Paul commands Christians to obey those in authority and warns that whoever rebels against them is rebelling against God. In Christendom and Europe, this was used by rulers to legitimate the divine right of kings.[6] Similarly, the Qurʾān enjoins Muslims to obey God, the Prophet, and those in authority (4:59). In Muslim history, this verse formed the basis for obedience (*ṭāʿa*) to political leaders. Very early, the public manifestation of the authority of an Islamic ruler meant that he or his representative exercised the office of leading the public liturgy and prayers, regardless of how unfit he was for such a role.[7] A practice of toleration for such leaders was captured in the aphorism that one may "perform the *ṣalāt* behind a pious man or a malefactor."[8]

In this chapter, we take a genealogical approach to the interpretation of Muslim expressions of political obligation based on the commitment to *dīn*, a set of salvation practices inspired by faith. Such an approach precludes neat divisions of history into binaries of "quietist" versus "activist" tendencies or tying origins to subsequent developments. Historians must uncover a tangled history of how Muslims have interpreted political obligations, power, and knowledge, and how these mutated over time. Grasping the motives, contexts, and environments in which Muslim expressions of quietism occurred is more important than trying to find a neat and coherent meaning of quietism that remained consistent and transcendent. Political quietism means very different things in different contexts and eras. The details surrounding political quietism evolved in tandem with the transformation of Muslim politics and political institutions over time. This historical study is divided into three broadly defined periods, each with a set of crucial factors that determine different outcomes of political expressions. These periods are the early caliphate, the era of empire, and the modern era.[9]

Political contestation, expressed as quietist or activist, is a major element in Muslim political theology. For our purpose, the central question in early Muslim political theology was this: Is the commandment to adhere to a political-moral obligation to command what is right and forbid what is wrong (*al-amr bi-l-maʿrūf wa-l-nahy ʿan al-munkar*) an absolute and unfettered command, or can it be subject to the dictates of human reason, political expediency, and strategy? The most extreme answer came from the Khawārij in the first/seventh century. The Khawārij believed this political-moral obligation was an absolute command that Muslims must adhere to, even if it meant using violence to overthrow a ruler deemed unjust. From their political theology, a spectrum of different iterations of "quietism" emerged under a variety of names and orientations.

Quietist political theology in Islam should not be understood as apolitical or a way to avoid political debates. One form of political quietism (*taqiyya*) was a term used by Muslims in distinctive ways throughout history as a pragmatic or strategic mode of political contestation and self-preservation. Contrary to the literal meaning of the nomenclature "political quietism," another form of political activism was exercised; this form depended on context. Hence, for some early Muslims the idea of quietism more closely approximated the prevention of strife or the pursuit of social and political stability (*ittiqāʾ al-fitna*). However, this did not presuppose that these Muslims were apolitical. Even self-described "quietists" in the modern era, such as certain Shīʿī clerics or Salafis, use the idea of quietism, or nonengagement, as a form of political protest or political preservation. And both protest and strategies of preservation are expressions of power. Power influences relations between people, and it can determine the conduct of others. As Michel Foucault reminds us: "There is no power without potential refusal or revolt."[10] If politics is the expression of power, then quietism is a form of power demonstrated by refusal, restraint, or the absence of overt political action in the service of an inarticulate motive.

The early caliphate

The historian Marshall Hodgson (d. 1968) made a valuable observation when he explained that the early Muslim community understood political responsibilities "as an essential consequence of their faith."[11] Hodgson illustrated that the idea of "political responsibility" was an intrinsic aspect of the sociopolitical milieu of early Arabia, where Islam began. The egalitarian ethos of Arabia gave this political responsibility a "strikingly egalitarian" hue, among a people who "disliked structures of authority."[12] For Hodgson, political responsibility was imprinted into the fabric of Islam. This politics of responsibility or founding political theology was tested as Islam reached into domains outside Arabia and meshed with neighboring Byzantine and Persian political traditions. In these encounters, new political vocabularies mingled with inherited norms of political responsibility, based on the Arabian experience of Islam. These confrontations peaked in the early years of the Umayyad caliphate. As Hodgson astutely observed, "It was almost a corollary of the political responsibility called for by Islam that the tradition of faith proved to be developed most actively in an atmosphere of political opposition to the ruling forms."[13]

As the Muslim polity grew and percolated with norms and customs from foreign lands, Muslims imagined new vocabularies for expressing their faith and acted upon their perceived political obligations. These expressions of faith and political responsibility triggered intense political-theological debates, resulting in the schism of the Muslim community into sects. Debates between these sects revolved around political responsibility and at their core was the Qurʾānic mandate to command what is right and forbid what is wrong (*al-amr bi-l-maʿrūf wa-l-nahy ʿan al-munkar*), also known as *ḥisba*.[14]

Historian Michael Cook tells us that early Muslims interpreted this Qurʾānic injunction to mean that "executive power of the law of God is vested in each and every Muslim."[15] "Under this conception," he adds, "the individual believer as such has not only the right, but also the duty, to issue orders pursuant to God's law, and to do what he can to see that they are obeyed."[16] Cook also points out that this moral and political obligation defied social hierarchy, and even laymen remained the equal of political superiors in terms of fulfilling God's order to command the right and forbid the wrong. But, in the early centuries, the egalitarian, socially homogenous tradition that the Arabs from the Arabian Peninsula brought to their faith was gradually challenged as the caliphate, now located in newly conquered territories in Syria and Iraq, took on hues of absolutism. The transformation of the caliphate into something resembling a royal court was new political territory for Muslims, and the litmus test of their faith was how they imagined their political responsibilities in this changing milieu. Threads of political activism or quietism must be understood in the multiple ways in which Muslims disputed commanding the right and forbidding the wrong.

The first civil war (36–41/656–61) fragmented any sense of community and raised questions about political legitimacy and religious duties for Muslims. Opposing the political theologies of the proto-Shīʿa and the Khawārij were the Murjiʾa, who proposed that the community should withhold passing a verdict on the moral status of political leaders. In making this argument, they drew upon the Qur'ānic use of the expression *irjā'* in *Sūrat al-Tawba*; this term meant postponing or deferring judgment. This verse encourages believers to defer the judgment of others to God, for only God can judge whether someone shall be punished or forgiven (Q 9:106).[17] This position, "itself the mark of a political attitude," to borrow the phrase of Montgomery Watt, had consequential outcomes for Muslim politics.[18]

The Murji'a argued that the best way to fulfill the duty of *ḥisba* was to defer judgment to God. Indeed, as with other sects, the early Murji'a considered this duty to be "an ideal of higher priority over any other interest."[19] Political and moral accountability was an especially critical topic for Muslims living in Kufa, the fulcrum of Murji'ī thought. One especially important Kufan figure was Abū Ḥanīfa (d. 150/767); many claim that he espoused a form of political theology of postponement (*irjā'*) in a text attributed to him, *al-Fiqh al-akbar* [The major discernment].[20]

This text falls squarely within the realm of Hodgson's binary of faith and political responsibility. His answer to the defining question of his time—what Muslims should do about a ruler who is deemed unjust—was a clear exposition on the legitimacy of political protest and activism. Abū Ḥanīfa began by objecting to the basis of Khārijī political theology: "We do not consider anyone to be an infidel on account of sin; nor do we deny his faith."[21] Abū Ḥanīfa also defied the position of the proto-Shī'a: "We disavow none of the Companions of the Apostle of Allah; nor do we adhere to any of them exclusively."[22] Both these political positions are within the realm of moral and political accountability. "We enjoin what is just," declared Abū Ḥanīfa, "and prohibit what is evil."[23]

For Abū Ḥanīfa, maintaining the unity of the Muslim community was paramount. As Watt puts it: "The earliest Murji'ites were essentially men who wanted to preserve the unity of the Islamic community." The Murji'īs attempted to preserve unity with minimal expressions of political responsibility, without appearing to endorse tyranny or abet anarchy. So, we also see Abū Ḥanīfa wrestling with the idea of how to practice *ḥisba.* If *ḥisba* is moral responsibility and political accountability, and as Hodgson reminds us, faith requires political responsibility, the question for Abū Ḥanīfa was this: Should one practice moral accountability to such an extent that it destabilizes and jeopardizes the Muslim polity? In answering this question, Abū Ḥanīfa developed the idea that a Muslim who failed to be politically accountable and morally responsible could be deemed a sinner, but remain a believer. "We do not proclaim any Muslim an unbeliever on the account of any sin, however great," he announced. "Nor does he forfeit the name of belief; we continue to call him a believer in essence. It is possible to be a sinful believer without being an unbeliever."[24]

The category of a sinful believer allowed the Murjiʾa to develop a political position in opposition to the hardline Shīʿa and Khawārij. This position was not necessarily one of neutrality. In the early period, expressions of "quietism" did not mean the removal of oneself from political questions. Rather, quietism was expressed politically in unconventional ways or as politics of another kind. Perhaps someone like Abū Ḥanīfa was caught between his obligation to be loyal to the caliph, and his obligation to provide sage political counsel, and quell or mediate in rebellions. Those we would label today as political quietists are persons who were entangled in multiple agendas. Another example of this is Aḥmad b. Hanbal, the eponym of the Ḥanbalī *madhhab* and an important voice in early debates over political power and authority. Some modern scholars claim that political quietism is central to Ḥanbalī political doctrine.[25] As the Saudi scholar Saud al-Sarhan noted, political expressions that have subsequently been labeled "quietist"—especially by those Muslims who later became part of the Ḥanābila—were generally rooted in the idea of conforming to the Muslim community (*luzūm jamāʿat al-muslimīn*). Commenting on the first civil war, Ibn Ḥanbal averred that preserving community was a "mercy" while division was a "torment," drawing on a teaching of the Prophet Muḥammad.[26]

One of the questions Ibn Ḥanbal debated was *tafḍīl,* or preference among the first four caliphs. Debates over this issue took the form of superlatives, and Muslims argued about who among the first four caliphs "was the best." There is some disagreement over precisely what Ibn Ḥanbal's position was on this issue,[27] but the fact that he was engaged in such a debate demonstrates the complexity of the Ḥanbalī expression of quietism.[28] Ibn Ḥanbal might, in theory, have advocated obedience to the ruler, but we also know from history that he and his students and followers were, nonetheless, actively engaged in political protest and the debates of their time.

Years of political contestation following the civil war led the Umayyad caliphs, based in Damascus, to demand unconditional obedience. This was referred to as "Syrian obedience," or *ṭāʿa shāmiyya.* The mufti of Damascus, Sulaymān b. Mūsā (d. 119/737), for example, argued that the perfect Muslim was one who combined Ḥijāzī knowledge, Iraqi behavior, and Shāmī obedience.[29] Expressions of the political, however, must be understood in both a top-down fashion and a bottom-up fashion. As al-Sarhan cogently describes, despite the caliph's insistence on total obedience, many Muslims in this time did not accept it. Opponents insisted that obedience to the rulers should be conditional, based on their performance of "good" (*ma'rūf*), not their immersion in sin.[30] Thus, the issue of quietism, or obedience to the rulers, was dependent on how Muslims interpreted the political obligations of their faith. The development of certain traditions from this time suggests that many Muslims placed obligations to their faith before obligations of quietism to the ruler.[31]

This dichotomy between obedience to the ruler and political obligations of the faith is evident in Ibn Ḥanbal's complex positions. In his writings, we see expressions of political quietism or activism that seem to depend on varying contexts. While Ibn Ḥanbal and his contemporaries might have argued that obedience to the ruler was, in fact, necessary, they also argued that Islam demanded that Muslims place obedience to God and His laws above all other forms of obedience. Although modern scholars such as Cook and Crone depict the traditionalist Ibn Ḥanbal as a political quietist, al-Sarhan demurs, reminding us, "Other traditionalists were not against commanding and forbidding the rulers against certain actions … "[32] Quietism for Ibn Ḥanbal and his followers was an expression of political protest that understood the limits of activism. Given the expanding power of the caliphal state, expressions of quietism were also demonstrative of many Muslims' pragmatic acceptance of their inability to influence the caliph or other rulers.[33]

For the early Muslim community, questions of religious allegiance were entwined with duties that stemmed from political commitments. The Shīʿa sect emerged from this milieu and can be interpreted as an early iteration of political quietism in Islam. Early Shīʿī writers such as Muḥammad al-Bāqir (d. 117/735) and Jaʿfar al-Ṣādiq (d. 148/765) explicitly rejected the idea of using armed rebellion to achieve their community's particular political-theological goals and urged their followers to "differentiate" their religious identity from the early state. The early Shīʿī community represents perhaps a two-pronged version of political quietism. Intellectual leaders such as Jaʿfar al-Ṣādiq urged his followers not to engage in rebellion against the broader, Sunnī polity in which they were a minority. But, as Said Arjomand points out, Jaʿfar al-Ṣādiq also "developed the notion of authority stemming from the divine guidance of mankind into a principle of absolute and infallible authority."[34] Thus, the early development of "the fundamentally quietistic feature" of the Shīʿa sect can be interpreted as strategic dissimulation before the more powerful Sunnī majority.[35]

A quintessential statement describing the early Shīʿī concept of dissimulation and quietism (*taqiyya*) comes from Shaykh al-Mufīd (d. 413/1032). Urging his community to reject armed rebellion and affirming the lawfulness of *taqiyya*, al-Mufīd argued that the Shīʿa community must bide their time and wait for the reappearance of the "hidden imam," or Mahdī. "Far from holding it a religious duty to rise in armed revolt against their enemies," al-Mufīd wrote, the Mahdī's ancestors "disapproved of any incitement to such action, and ... the religion by which they approach God consisted of dissimulation [*taqiyya*], restraining the hand and guarding the tongue, carrying out the prescribed worship, and serving God exclusively by good works."[36]

The era of empire

It has become something of a cliché in modern scholarship on Islam that, by the medieval period, Muslim politics was characterized by absolutism and thus required a political theology of quietism. Bernard Lewis articulated this standard line of thinking: "Except for the early caliphate, when the anarchic individualism of tribal Arabia was still effective, the political history of Islam is one of almost unrelieved autocracy." He continues, "For the last thousand years ... the political thinking of Islam has been dominated by such maxims as 'tyranny is better than anarchy' and 'whose power is established, obedience to him is incumbent.'" Lewis then cites a passage from the Syrian jurist Ibn Jamāʿa (d. 733/1333), who wrote about "forced homage," to a system of politics in which "it was of no consequence" whether the ruler was "illiterate, unjust or vicious, that he be even a slave or a woman." Further, Ibn Jamāʿa argued, "Whoever has effective power has the right to obedience ... for a government, even the worst one, is better than anarchy, and of two evils one should choose the lesser."[37]

History certainly vindicates the claim that the absolutism of the medieval caliphs existed alongside the political quietism of the populace. Maxims like "tyranny is better than anarchy" nourished political theologies that contended with rapidly changing geopolitical circumstances, from the beginning of the crusades in 488/1095 to the Mongol invasions, which climaxed with the sack of Baghdad in 656/1258 that incapacitated the ʿAbbāsid caliphate. The political strife of the first centuries of Islam led the political theorist Hamid Enayat to conclude that, by the medieval period, Muslims had reached "a point at which the supreme value in politics appeared to be not justice but security." Muslim political thinking, in his view, did not revolve so much around the demands of justice from rulers as it required "the ability to rule and maintain 'law and order.'"[38]

Ibn Taymiyya (d. 728/1328) was a classic exponent of a political theology that valorized security. In the wake of Mongol destruction, Ibn Taymiyya argued that the worst political situation for Muslims would be not having a ruler at all—this was a fate worse than an unjust ruler. "Sixty years with an unjust ruler," he said, repeating a well-known maxim, "is better than one night without a ruler."[39] Yet Ibn Taymiyya's political postures are ambiguous. He advocated quietism when it was strategic to do so, and at other times he advocated activism, even going so far as to specify that it was a religious duty for Muslims to overthrow an unjust ruler.[40] As Yahya Michot notes, Ibn Taymiyya's "outspoken personality" and "noncompliance" landed him in prison six times between 706/1306 and 729/1328. In fact, Ibn Taymiyya argued that the notion of absolute obedience imposed by Mongol rulers was "of a pre-Islamic, ignorant (*jāhilī*) nature."[41]

By the medieval period, the Muslim polity fell in line with a top-down, political theology of empire characteristic of most human societies at the time; it favored the sovereignty of the caliphs or emperors and the subservience and obedience of their subjects. It is not surprising that major intellectuals such as Ibn Jamāʿa characterized the caliph as "the shadow of God on earth."[42] Although rule became absolute and the Muslim community grew into an empire that saw quietism as a feature of the virtuous subject, it was in this period that a thriving genre of scholarship known as *naṣīḥa*, or advice, literature emerged. The goal of these works was to "preserve principles of communal consensus and election when it came to political authority."[43] The proliferation of these works can be interpreted as a pragmatic, or quietist, form of activism. Works such as *Siyāsat nāma* by Niẓām al-Mulk (d. 485/1092), *Naṣīḥat al-mulūk* by al-Ghazālī (d. 505/1111), and *al-Siyāsa al-sharʿiyya* by Ibn Taymiyya tacitly accepted the divinely sanctioned absolutism of the caliph but also exemplified a spirit of political activism.

In the Sunnī and Shīʿī traditions, these works were known as "mirrors for princes." Many of them were written by theologians contracted by political leaders to work for the state, positions that many Shīʿī scholars accepted only begrudgingly, fearing that involvement with politics would distract them from their scholarly, theological pursuits. For example, when Mullā Muḥsin Fayḍ Kāshānī (d. 1090/1679) was invited by Shah ʿAbbās II (d. 1078/1667) of the Ṣafavid Empire, he wrote, "I wavered between accepting that command and rejecting it because of the afflictions it entailed through the sons of this world and their affairs." Kāshānī then added that he only accepted the court position "because of the possibility of propagating the religion."[44] Although many of these tracts emphasized the duty of Muslims to remain obedient to their rulers, many of them can also be interpreted as pragmatic, subtle expressions of political activism calling for equitable, sound governance. As Said Arjomand notes, the *Qavāʿid al-salāṭīn*, written in 1081/1670 by an *ʿālim* who was a descendant of

Shaykh ʿAlī l-Karakī (d. 940/1534), "mentions twelve principles of rulership, illustrating each with edifying stories of the exemplary behavior of past kings ... First and foremost among these principles is justice (*ʿadālat*)."[45]

In the Sunnī tradition, one of the most famous works from this genre is the *Aḥkām al-sulṭāniyya wa-l-dīniyya* [The ordinances of government and religious positions] by the jurist and political theorist al-Māwardī (d. 450/1058). In the introduction to his work, he makes clear that his audience is "those in authority." And although he acknowledges that he owes obedience to them, he writes to ensure that the ruler "honours the dictates of justice ... and aspires to equity in establishing his claims and in the fulfilment of others' claims."[46] Al-Māwardī's first chapter describes the imamate in terms of a contract (*ʿaqd*) between the community of Muslims and the ruler. To link expressions of quietism with political activism, al-Māwardī draws on a verse from the sixth-century pre-Islamic poet al-Afwah al-Awdī. "There is no benefit to a leaderless people when disorder reigns, and they will never have a leader if the ignorant amongst them leads."[47] The first half confirms what modern scholars have labeled quietism, while the second half endorses what many Muslims view as a duty to counsel the ruler to secure just and equitable rule, according to the teachings of the *sharīʿa*.

For Shīʿa Muslims, expressions of political quietism were rooted in a historical experience different from that of their Sunnī counterparts. As a minority group, Shīʿī history is largely characterized by persecution, especially in territories ruled by Sunnī majorities. Shīʿī expressions of political activism fell on a spectrum but generally reflected a strong Muʿtazilī influence. This is particularly evident in the Zaydī emphasis on principles of divine justice and commanding the right and forbidding the wrong. The Zaydī applied their duty to command right and forbid wrong to notions of political authority and legitimacy, and they developed an activist political theology that "justified (and even necessitated) the overthrow of an unjust ruler via armed insurrection."[48] As Racha el Omari and Najam Haider write, "Rhetoric highlighting free will, the desire to establish justice, and the duty to enjoin good/forbid wrong became staples of the oaths of allegiance administered by most Zaydī *imams*."[49] On the other side of the Shīʿī spectrum of political expression were the Imāmī or Twelver Shīʿa. Prominent intellectuals associated with this sect were al-Shaykh al-Mufīd (d. 413/1032) and al-Sharīf al-Murtaḍā (d. 436/1044). Unlike their Zaydī counterparts, the Twelvers advocated what is described, today, as political quietism. They argued that Muslims should have as little to do with politics as possible until the return of the imam.[50]

As previously stated, the concept of *taqiyya* (strategic dissimulation in pursuit of self-preservation) is an important element in Shīʿī expressions of political quietism.[51] Throughout their history, in times of oppression, not only in the formative years, the Shīʿa drew upon this concept to dissimulate their convictions on political questions. Dissimulation of the faith, or what contemporary scholars might call quietism, is a theme throughout the Shīʿī political-theological canon and is included in the foundational works of Nāṣir al-Dīn al-Ṭūsī (d. 672/1274). The traditionist (Akhbārī) Shīʿīs embraced this concept as early as the third/ninth century and "could live with patrimonial monarchy and even its leadership in religious matters."[52] The other school of Shīʿīs, the principled discursive school (Uṣūlīs), could not reconcile with that position.

Sufism (*taṣawwuf*) formed yet another expression of the Muslim understanding of political obligations of the faith. The Chishtiyya can be interpreted as adhering closely to ideas of quietism.[53] The order spread throughout the Indian subcontinent under the spiritual guidance of Shaykh Niẓām al-Dīn Awliyāʾ (d. 725/1325). The Chishtiyya "scrupulously avoid" identification with those who held political office and, by principle, refuse to involve themselves in government service.[54] Despite their initial unwillingness to engage in politics, the Chishtiyya understood "'social service' as the supreme object of all their spiritual exercises."[55] Although the Chishtiyya attempted to avoid any involvement with the rulers of the Delhi sultanate, they became entwined with state politics as early as Sultan Muḥammad b. Tughluq's reign in India (724–52/1324–51). The arrival of young Chishtī saints in provincial towns under the reign of Tughluq coincided with the rise of provincial kingdoms throughout India, in which young saints were actively involved.[56] Despite the urging of Shaykh Niẓām al-Dīn and other Chishtī elders to refrain from political involvement, "traditions of the saints of the first cycle were consequently discarded," Nizami writes, "and the comfortable theory was expounded that mystics should consort with kings and high officers in order to influence them for the good."[57]

The case of the Chishtiyya illustrates that life cannot be neatly divided between the social and the political, in which quietist notions of faith or spirituality are kept separate from worldly notions of politics. Chishtī elders sought to create a social system in which individuals could pursue moral purity and oneness with God. But social values such as these have important implications for the politics of the state in which they exist. We can understand politics to be subsumed under the realm of worldly "facts," as opposed to "values" or matters of faith. But as social theorist Philip Gorski notes, "The fact/value divide is leaky. Values have a way of seeping into facts; and facts have a way of seeping into values."[58] The

Chishtiyya trajectory resembles some of the quietist stance of some Sufis, but over time their political and social roles varied enormously.[59]

The modern era

By 1800, the balance of global power had drifted from Muslim empires and dynasties to emerging European powers. The turnover of Muslim dynasties and the emergence of massive reform programs aimed at Westernization reflected a new world in which European power was hegemonic. As historian Immanuel Wallerstein states, the Europeans "were able to establish the rules of the game in the interstate system, to dominate the world economy (in production, commerce, and finance), to get their way politically … and to formulate the cultural language with which one discussed the world."[60] Some Muslims argued that European hegemony was, as with everything on Earth, the will of God, and Muslims should therefore quietly accept their lot. For example, the Muslim poet Mirza Ghalib (d. 1869) argued that the 1857 Indian Muslim rebellion against the British was wrong because revolt brought nothing but disaster.[61] "When the Lord confers sovereignty he confers dignity also and the talent for victory," reasoned Ghalib in support of the new political status quo, adding, "It is fitting for the people of the world to obey those whom the Lord has blessed with good fortune and, in obeying them, they should consider it obedience to the Lord himself."[62]

In supporting his argument for a quietist response to British hegemony in India, Ghalib cited a verse from the Persian poet Saʿdī of Shiraz (d. 691/1292): "The slave must bow his head before the master. The ball has no choice but to follow the swing of the mallet."[63] Saʿdī's creative verse is symbolic of another expression of quietism as articulated by Ottoman Tanzimat-era reformers like Rifāʿa Rāfiʿ al-Ṭahṭāwī (d. 1873). Rather than rebel against the European powers, Tanzimat-era intellectuals viewed Europe as a sort of ally or guide and studied its history, culture, and political philosophy to glean certain insights into how to improve the Muslim community.[64] In this context, political quietism meant benefiting from the products of European knowledge, and not resisting it politically, as some more orthodox elements were inclined to do. This expression of political quietism involved acquiescence to European epistemology and its consequences in private and public life, ranging from the family to political economy. Political activism meant resisting European epistemology and knowledge as a matter of principle, and strategically adopting only what was needed, such as technological expertise, but not cultural and political modernity.

Al-Ṭahṭāwī championed this new form of political quietism. Upon his return to Egypt from living in France, he argued, "There is a moral obligation on those who share the same *waṭan* (homeland) to work together to improve it and perfect its organization."[65] Yet al-Ṭahṭāwī's exhortation for Muslims to "improve" and "perfect" their homelands was limited. It did not mean rebelling against colonialism or protesting rulers; rather, it meant following the rule of law by accepting the new modernizing political order of Muḥammad ʿAlī. Al-Ṭahṭāwī urged his compatriots not to rebel and argued that citizens should live in a state of freedom, but added, "patriots are not characterized by freedom except when they follow the law of the land and assist in its implementation."[66]

The political and reformist labor of the revolutionary Jamāl al-Dīn al-Afghānī (d. 1315/1897) and his disciple Muḥammad ʿAbduh (d. 1323/1905) represents another political expression. In his diagnosis of the relative weakness of the global Muslim community (*umma*) on the world stage, al-Afghānī was a realist. But ideologically, he was a revolutionary and stated that Muslims must change their personal relationship with God and Islam before they could improve the political position of their states. This could be interpreted as another modern expression of quietism, namely, one that calls for work on the interior self and the creation of a new pedagogy for the modern Muslim self. In one essay, al-Afghānī sought to explain that turning inward was necessary to correct the "sad situation" of the *umma*. He wrote that Muslims had lost true faith, for when they were "true Muslims," "the world bears witness to their excellence." He continued, "As for the present, I will content myself with this holy text: 'Verily, God does not change the state of a people until they change themselves inwardly' [Q 13:11]."[67]

Granted, al-Afghānī called for political reform in Muslim societies, especially an end to authoritarian rule. In this sense, he was an activist. But his frequent calls for Muslims to quietly turn inward and reevaluate the nature of their faith were an important dimension of Muslim political theology in the late modern era. In many ways, al-Afghānī's quietist strand of thought was a response to his contemporary, Sir Sayyid Ahmed Khan of India (d. 1898), whom he accused of calling "openly for the abandonment of all religions."[68] In the exchange between al-Afghānī and Khan, the idea of political activism and quietism became much more complex. Al-Afghānī's version of quietism was not to resist but to remain open to a limited amount of Western knowledge, but he was opposed to the political bondage of colonialism. Khan was quietist in both politics and knowledge and was viewed, by many, as an Anglophile. He was content to let new knowledge of modernity rewrite the narrative of Islam. In the late modern period, activism and quietism were not so much about the nature of politics but the politics of the body and the body-politic: What kind of knowledge governs the body as well as body-politic of the modern colonial and postcolonial subject? Who acquiesces to the politics and power of Western political and scientific technology and who resists it is difficult to define. It is here that, in the modern era, the category of political quietism and activism became superfluous, because in an age of globalization and fluid boundaries, activism and quietism are one of individual choice. One expression of political quietism called for the acceptance of the new of order of knowledge and politics, which is based on the experience of Christian Europe in the form of the nation-state, in the belief that this acceptance would give rise to a new Islamic political theology.[69] And that new political theology regulating the nation-state required a separation of religion from politics.

The controversial writing of ʿAlī ʿAbd al-Rāziq (d. 1386/1966) is perhaps the most explicit example of the advocacy of Islamic secularism (a new political theology). In *Islam and the Foundations of Political Power*, ʿAbd al-Rāziq argues that neither the Qurʾān nor the sunna provides compelling reasons to view the caliphate as a religious duty. Throughout history, he argued, there was no legitimate consensus (*ijmāʿ*) on the obligation to establish a caliphate. The history of the caliphate proved that it was a negative and despotic experience for the Muslim community that led to Islam's decline on the world stage. ʿAbd al-Rāziq never overtly drew on the concept of *irjāʾ* or the Murjiʾa; nonetheless, his concern was to preserve the solidarity of the Muslim community as a religious, not a political, community.

"The control that the Prophet exercised over the believers was strictly an extension of his Prophetic function," ʿAbd al-Rāziq declared. "It had none of the characteristics of temporal power. In all certainty, it was not a government; it was not a state; nor a political movement; neither was it the sovereignty of kings and princes."[70] We can interpret his line of analysis here as a quietist move to accept the emerging status quo. But unlike earlier forms of quietism, when favoring the status quo was necessary for self-preservation in an asymmetrical power relationship with a potentate, here quietism meant benefiting from the new political and epistemological European order. ʿAbd al-Rāziq attempted to remove the dualism of secular politics versus religion. For most of ʿAbd al-Rāziq's critics, this epistemological move in the direction of quietism, which involved reinterpreting the political history of Islam to legitimate a separation of religion and politics, was a betrayal of Islam itself. Muḥammad Sayyid Kīlānī, documenting the trial of ʿAbd al-Rāziq, described his "evil views" (*al-ārāʾ al-khabītha*) as insulting and a reproach (*ṭaʿn*) of the Prophet and the Companions.[71] ʿAbd al-Rāziq was charged with portraying Islam "exclusively as a spiritual norm" (*sharīʿa rūḥiyya maḥḍa*). His critics argued that his new order of politics was reassuring to Christian missionaries, who congratulated him on his writings, and confirmed that politically, he did not oppose European colonialism nor did he support a political struggle (*jihād*) in support of independence and freedom.[72]

In the modern era, certain Shīʿī clerics, such as the Grand Ayatollah Sayyid Ḥusayn Burūjirdī (d. 1961), represent a less explosive form of quietism. Burūjirdī was involved in many charitable works, such as establishing schools, but on pressing political issues, he remained virtually silent throughout his life. Despite his position as a leader of Iran's Shīʿī Muslims, Burūjirdī never commented on events such as the overthrow of Mohammad Mosaddegh, the Israel–Palestine conflict, or even British and American interference in Iranian national interests.[73] Yet, Burūjirdī was not completely apolitical. Rather, his political positions should perhaps be characterized as silent protest rather than public activism. This protest was framed using religious concepts and symbols. In the 1950s, when the Fidāʾiyyān-i Islām ("devotees of Islam") embarked on a series of political assassinations, Burūjirdī denounced their actions as un-Islamic. He was involved in protesting the anti-Baha'i campaigns of another prominent Shīʿī cleric, Abū l-Qāsim Falsafī, and also protested the Shah's land reform programs that began in 1951. In fact, according to Neguin Yavari, Burūjirdī's public denouncement of the Shah's program was the first instance of open confrontation between the clergy and the Shah's government.[74]

What we see in Burūjirdī's thinking is an implicit separation between religious and political spheres of knowledge and engagement with public life. Burūjirdī protested the Shah's land reform program because he deemed it to be contrary to Islamic law and tradition. Some theorists might consider his protest to be of a more religious than political nature, which would confirm Burūjirdī's own thinking. The difference between Burūjirdī and ʿAbd al-Rāziq is that the latter might have considered the land reform acts, which were related to property, to be a secular and not a religious issue, and for that reason he might not have protested them. By contrast, Burūjirdī fully believed that *sharīʿa* norms applied to people's lives and therefore he protested the government's actions. In fact, after Burūjirdī's death, more radical and politically active clergymen rose to prominence in Qum. These clergymen frequently criticized Burūjirdī's quietist, apolitical policies and sought to assert Islamic doctrines as a major factor in shaping politics.

Burūjirdī's quietist strand of political protest was maintained by Grand Ayatollah Sayyid Abū l-Qāsim al-Khūʾī (d. 1413/1992) of Najaf, Iraq. At the time of his death, al-Khūʾī was the spiritual leader of much of the Shīʿī world. Despite his prominence, most of al-Khūʾī's activism was centered on social welfare and charity. He established the Imam al-Khoei Foundation in London and New York and founded numerous cultural centers in Pakistan and other Muslim countries. Al-Khūʾī represented a strand in Shīʿī thought that disapproved of the involvement of the clergy in politics. He accepted that religion and politics occupied separate spheres of public life and thus he was opposed to Khomeini's doctrine of the governance of the jurist (*wilāyat-i faqīh*). He was even critical of the activism of Muḥammad Bāqir al-Ṣadr, a leading cleric executed by Saddam Hussein in 1401/1980.[75]

Al-Khūʾī's expression of quietism, with some exceptions, amounted to the complete avoidance of the political realm. During the decade-long Iran–Iraq war, al-Khūʾī maintained a strict position of "absolute silence."[76] Al-Khūʾī even refused to allow himself to be photographed with Iraqi government officials who visited shrines in Najaf. In 1991, during the post-Gulf war Shīʿī uprising, al-Khūʾī appeared on television to denounce the rebellions among Shīʿī communities throughout Iraq—but only under tremendous pressure from Saddam Hussein. Al-Khūʾī argued that such rebellions were prohibited by Islam and that Muslims should not revolt against their leader.[77]

Ayatollah al-Khūʾī's mode of political quietism has its counterpart in Sunnī Islam, among the Salafīs. Various iterations of Salafism have been described as either "purist" or "quietist," but what underlies this form of contention is political protest.[78] As one *jihādī* Salafist told Quintan Wiktorowicz: "The split is not in thought; it is in strategy."[79] "Purist" or "quietist" Salafīs do not generally advocate violence in any form, rather they express themselves politically through *daʿwa,* the Islamic concept of community outreach that involves spreading the faith, and education. Quietist Salafīs disagree with overt, full-throttle participation in a political system deemed to be inherently Western in nature or un-Islamic. As Wiktorowicz puts it, "They view politics as a diversion that encourages deviancy."[80]

One of the most prominent Salafī intellectuals who is often labeled a quietist is the Jordanian-Palestinian Abū Muḥammad al-Maqdisī.[81] Al-Maqdisī represents a distinct mode of political expression. Nearly all of al-Maqdisī's writings are political, but his quietism stems from his views that Muslims should not participate in a system of politics that is not authentically Islamic. Interestingly, he believes that certain traditional Islamic concepts and symbols would become tarnished if used in the contemporary, Western-dominated world of politics. For example, al-Maqdisī admits to supporting various forms of *jihād* in principle—both offensive and defensive. But in 2004, al-Maqdisī published a book in which he berated many *mujāhidūn* "for their lack of knowledge about Islam and their surroundings, their extreme paranoia or dangerous negligence and their reckless use of violence."[82] He followed this work with another tract aimed squarely at critiquing his former student, al-Zarqāwī, in which he urged al-Zarqāwī to refrain from the indiscriminate use of violence and anathematizing (*takfīr*) entire groups of people "because it is wrong to do so and hurts the image of Islam."[83]

Quietist Salafism is characterized by a hesitation to participate in strategies or systems deemed un-Islamic and damaging to the image of Islam. The Western-imposed system of nation-states throughout the world, and the strong alliances between many Muslim states and Western powers, has brought about a new phase in expressions of quietism and activism in Muslim politics. At the core of quietists' political contentions is the question of what Muslims should do about a ruler who is deemed unjust or unworthy of obedience. This contention is rooted in the concept of *kufr*, or unbelief. On this issue, the Murjiʾa position of quietism, in the sense of deferring conclusions regarding belief and sin to God, has undergone two major changes in modern Islam.

One group of "quietist" Salafis included Muḥammad Nāṣir al-Dīn al-Albānī (d. 1420/1999) and the former Grand Mufti of Saudi Arabia, ʿAbd al-ʿAzīz b. Bāz (d. 1420/1999). They argued that Muslim rulers who applied "man-made laws" were in a state of "lesser unbelief" (*kufr aṣghar*). These Salafis argue that the application of some "man-made laws" does not necessarily constitute wholesale unbelief, and therefore they do not anathematize (*takfīr*) secular Muslims. Another group of "quietists," including al-Maqdisī, Muḥammad b. al-ʿUthaymīn (d. 1422/2001), and the former Saudi Grand Mufti Muḥammad b. Ibrāhīm Āl al-Shaykh (d. 1389/1969), sees the systematic application of man-made laws as full-scale unbelief (*kufr akbar*).[84] Here, al-Maqdisī's position reveals how difficult it is for scholars to apply categories of "quietism" or "activism." Al-Maqdisī's defiance of the legitimacy of Muslim rulers is overtly political, but his choice *not* to use the political system itself to protest these rulers is quietist. Rather, al-Maqdisī resorts to private writings and *daʿwa* to spread his concerns.

In discussions of quietism in Salafi political theology, experts often mention many clerics from Saudi Arabia. In defining their role as guardians of the faith, Saudi clerics draw upon a *ḥadīth* in which the Prophet Muḥammad states that the *ʿulamāʾ* are heirs of the prophets.[85] Members of the *ʿulamāʾ* thus view themselves as protectors of Muslim tradition rooted in the model of the Prophet Muḥammad. They generally do not comment or get involved in the overtly political matters of the kingdom. But the quietism of the Saudi clerics, as defenders of "tradition," can be interpreted as expressions of the political, for tradition has the power to conserve as well as conquer.[86] The Saudi *ʿulamāʾ* might be quietist in the sense that they do not instigate rebellion or political reforms such as democratization, but as upholders of tradition, they are, nonetheless, inherently political and engaged in a project of shaping the future of their society through the narratives of faith.

Conclusion

Muslim expressions of quietist political theologies are tied to the changes in Muslim political institutions, societies, political philosophies, ethics, and doctrines that have unfolded over time. Shifting interpretations of how Muslims could best respond to the moral obligation of *ḥisba* were central to these divisions and internal variations. In the early period, the Muslim polity was relatively small and socially homogenous, and politics was deeply imbued in the Arab tribal ethos of consultation (*shūrā*), consensus (*ijmāʿ*), and the oath of allegiance (*bayʿa*). As Muslim society became more heterogeneous and diverse, the political culture also underwent changes. This political culture required a delicate balance and a continuous reconciliation between the normative imprint of Islam's original impulse, which remained in tension with new cultures that arose within the emerging and growing Islamic imperium.

Politics was the bedrock of the unfolding of Islam. Political quietism was a product of that milieu and an expression of a political theology. Multiple religious traditions underwent similar challenges as they tried to balance political, pietistic, and ethical impulses within a coherent narrative. Political quietism is a balancing act that tries to retain some of the old theology and accommodate new conditions without creating instability and anarchy. Modernists either weighed in favor of the status quo politics of colonialism and post-colonialism or proposed alternative interpretations of Islam, to make Islam adapt to the status quo. Some call it Islamic reform, while critics would consider it political quietism and acquiescence, since it is not sufficiently revolutionary. While political quietism might not reflect all forms of Islamic reform, it is the impulse that drives nonrevolutionary Islamic reform.

The Italian philologist Giorgio Levi Della Vida (d. 1967) once said, "Islam is so complex that it cannot be made to coincide with anything other than itself."[87]

Della Vida's attempt to articulate an Islamic exceptionalism ought not be heeded. Indeed, historians of Islam repeatedly untangle the ways in which a multiplicity of ideas from different origins become entwined with the lifeworlds of Muslim societies, cultures, and politics. Quietism is one form of political theology. As with the Indian guru Babaji's smile, these multiple expressions of political quietism can be interpreted in a number of ways.

Notes

1 Mark Lilla, *The Stillborn God: Religion, Politics, and the Modern West* (New York: Knopf, 2007), 19–21.

2 Jan Assman, *Herrschaft und Heil: Politische Theologie in Altägypten, Israel und Europa* (Munich: Hanser, 2000), 24; as quoted in Hent de Vries and Lawrence E. Sullivan (eds.), *Political Theologies: Public Religion in a Post-Secular World* (New York: Fordham University Press, 2006), 25.

3 S.v. "Quietism," in *Britannica Academic*, online: http://academic.eb.com; T. K. Connolly, s.v. "Quietism," in *New Catholic Encyclopedia* (Detroit: Gale, 2003).

4 Werner Raupp, Heiner F. Klemme, and Manfred Kuehn, "Johann Albrecht Bengel," in *The Dictionary of Eighteenth-Century German Philosophers* (New York: Continuum, 2010), online: www.oxfordreference.com/view/10.1093/acref/9780199797097.001.0001/acref-9780199797097-e-0042.

5 Leszek Kolakowski, "Quietism," in *Encyclopedia of Religion*, ed. Lindsay Jones (Detroit: Macmillan Reference, 2005).

6 "Divine Right of Kings—Oxford Reference," (accessed May 11, 2017), online: http://www.oxfordreference.com/view/10.1093/oi/authority.20110810104754564 (accessed January 4, 2018).

7 Ignaz Goldziher, *Introduction to Islamic Theology and Law* (Princeton: Princeton University Press, 1981), 73.

8 Ibid.

9 All divisions of historical time are, inevitably, somewhat arbitrary. For clarity of narrative, however, we divide these periods as the early caliphate (revelation–750 CE), era of empire (750–1800 CE), and modern (1800–present).

10 Michel Foucault, *Power*, ed. James D. Faubion, trans. Robert Hurley, *Essential Works of Foucault, 1954–1984* (New York: New Press, 2000), 324.

11 Marshall G. S. Hodgson, *The Venture of Islam: Conscience and History in a World Civilization* (Chicago: University of Chicago Press, 1974), 1:241.

12 Louise Marlow, *Hierarchy and Egalitarianism in Islamic Thought* (New York: Cambridge University Press, 1997), 1–6; Robert G. Hoyland, *Arabia and the Arabs:*

From the Bronze Age to the Coming of Islam (New York: Routledge, 2001), 117; Nicholas P. Roberts, *Political Islam and the Invention of Tradition* (Washington, DC: New Academia Publishing, 2015), 136.

13 Hodgson, *Venture*, 1:241.

14 This order is given throughout the Qurʾān. See 3:104, 110, 114; 9:112; 22:41. As Mohammad Hashim Kamali states, the duty of *ḥisba* is a collective obligation on the community of Muslims, or *wājib/farḍ kifāʾī*. See Muhammad Hashim Kamali, *Principles of Islamic Jurisprudence* (Cambridge: Islamic Texts Society, 2003), 415.

15 Michael A. Cook, *Commanding Right and Forbidding Wrong in Islamic Thought* (New York: Cambridge University Press, 2001), 9.

16 Ibid.

17 W. Madelung, "Murdjiʾa," *Encyclopaedia of Islam*, 2nd ed. (Leiden: Brill, 1993), 7:605–607.

18 W. Montgomery Watt, *The Formative Period of Islamic Thought* (Edinburgh: Edinburgh University Press, 1973), 125.

19 Khalil Athamina, "The Early Murjiʾa: Some Notes," *Journal of Semitic Studies* 35, no. 1 (1990), 122. The early biographer and historian Ibn Saʿd (d. 230/845), in his *Kitāb al-ṭabaqāt al-kubrā,* surveys eighteen prominent Murjiʾīs, eleven of whom were from Kufa. See Watt, *Formative Period*, 122.

20 The Muslim scholar Mulla ʿAlī Qārī assumes this text was that of Abū Ḥanīfa; however, some modern scholars challenge this. Joseph Schacht claims that the opinions in *al-Fiqh al-akbar* are authentic and those of Abū Ḥanīfa, but he doubts that Abū Ḥanīfa composed the text itself. See Abū Ḥanīfa Nuʿmān b. Thābit, *Kitāb al-fiqh al-akbar*, ed. Mulla ʿAlī Qārī ʿAlī b. Sulṭān Muḥammad al-Harawī (Cairo: Dār al-Kutub al-ʿArabiyya al-Kubrā, 1909); Joseph Schacht, "Abū Ḥanīfa al-Nuʿmān," in *Encyclopaedia of Islam*, 2nd ed. (Leiden: Brill, 1960), 1:123–124.

21 Abū Ḥanīfa, *al-Fiqh al-akbar*, online: http://shamela.ws/browse.php/book-6388/page-21 (accessed September 18, 2017).

22 A. J. Wensinck, *The Muslim Creed: Its Genesis and Historical Development* (London: Cambridge University Press, 1932), 103–104.

23 Ibid.

24 Abū Ḥanīfa, "al-Fiqh al-akbar," trans. Hamid Algar, 3, online: https://archive.org/details/Al-fiqhAl-akbareng.-AbuHanifah.pdf (accessed January 4, 2018).

25 Michael A. Cook, "Activism and Quietism in Islam," in *Islam and Power*, ed. Alexander S. Cudsi and Ali E. Hillal (London: Croom Helm, 1981), 22; Patricia Crone, *God's Rule: Government and Islam* (New York: Columbia University Press, 2004), 135–139; Muhammad Qasim Zaman, *Religion and Politics Under the Early ʿAbbāsids: The Emergence of the Proto-Sunnī Elite* (Leiden: Brill, 1997), 73; as cited in Saud Saleh al-Sarhan, "Early Muslim Traditionalism: A Critical Study of the Works and Political Theology of Aḥmad Ibn Ḥanbal" (PhD dissertation University of Exeter, 2011), 171.

26 Al-Sarhan, "Early Muslim Traditionalism," 171–172.

27 For example, according to Ibn al-Jawzī, Ibn Ḥanbal once stated that because ʿAlī was "a member of the Prophet's household," no one, caliph or otherwise, could compare with him. See Ibn al-Jawzī, *The Life of Ibn Ḥanbal*, trans. Michael Cooperson (New York: New York University Press, 2016), 80.

28 Al-Sarhan, "Early Muslim Traditionalism," 121.

29 Ibn ʿAbd al-Barr, *Jāmiʿ bayān al-ʿilm wa-faḍlih*, ed. Abū l-Ashbāl al-Zuhayrī (Saudi Arabia: Dār Ibn al-Jawzī, 1994), 2:824–825; as cited in al-Sarhan, "Early Muslim Traditionalism," 176.

30 Al-Sarhan, "Early Muslim Traditionalism," 177.

31 One saying from al-Bukhārī's collection of traditions states, "[There is] no obedience in disobedience to God; obedience is required only in what is good." Another similarly states, "A Muslim has to listen to and obey [the orders of his ruler] whether he likes it or not, as long as these orders do not involve one in disobedience [to God]; but if an act of disobedience [to God] is imposed, one should not listen to it or obey it." Ibid.

32 Ibid., 193.

33 Ibid., 198–199.

34 Said Amir Arjomand, *The Shadow of God and the Hidden Imam* (Chicago: University of Chicago Press, 1984), 35.

35 "'Imam'—the mere word—is an invitation to obedience. More: It is a command to believe," writes Hamid Dabashi in *Theology of Discontent: The Ideological Foundations of the Islamic Revolution in Iran* (New York: New York University Press, 1993), 482.

36 Arjomand, *Shadow of God*, 61.

37 Bernard Lewis, "Communism and Islam," in *The Middle East in Transition*, ed. Walter Z. Laqueur (New York: Frederick A. Praeger, 1958), 318–319; Roberts, *Political Islam*, xviii.

38 Hamid Enayat, *Modern Islamic Political Thought* (Austin: University of Texas Press, 1982), 12.

39 Aḥmad b. ʿAbd al-Ḥalīm Ibn Taymiyya, *Minhāj al-sunna al-nabawiyya fī naqḍ kalām al-Shīʿa wa-l-Qadariyya*, edited by Muḥammad Rashād Sālim, 4 vols. (Cairo: Maktabat Dār al-ʿUrūba, 1962), 1:371; Ibn Taymiyya, *al-Siyāsa al-sharʿiyya* (Cairo: Dār al-Shaʿb, 1971), 185; Enayat, *Modern Islamic Political Thought*, 12.

40 For an excellent overview of contested interpretations of Ibn Taymiyya, see Yossef Rapoport and Shahab Ahmed, *Ibn Taymiyya and His Times* (New York: Oxford University Press, 2010).

41 Yahya Michot, "Ibn Taymiyya," in *The Princeton Encyclopedia of Islamic Political Thought*, ed. Gerhard Böwering et al. (Princeton: Princeton University Press, 2013).

42 Albert Hourani, *Arabic Thought in the Liberal Age, 1798–1939* (Cambridge and New York: Cambridge University Press, 1983), 15.

43 Paul Heck, "Advice," in *The Princeton Encyclopedia of Islamic Political Thought*, ed. Gerhard Böwering et al. (Princeton: Princeton University Press, 2013).

44 Said Amir Arjomand (ed.), *Authority and Political Culture in Shiʿism* (Albany: State University of New York Press, 1988), 267–268.

45 Ibid., 13.

46 Al-Mawardi, *al-Ahkam as-Sultaniyyah*, trans. Asadullah Yate (London: Ta-Ha Publishers Ltd., 1996), 7–8.

47 Ibid., 10.

48 Racha el Omari, Najam Haider, and Emad El-Din Shahin, "Muʿtazilah," in *The Oxford Encyclopedia of Islam and Politics* (New York: Oxford University Press, 2014). For more on this, see Hussein Ali Abdulsater, *Shiʿi Doctrine, Muʿtazili Theology: Al-Sharif al-Murtaḍā and Imami Discourse* (Edinburgh: Edinburgh University Press, 2017).

49 Ibid.

50 Ibid.

51 This should not be construed, however, as a categorical description of Shīʿism as a quietist political theology. Many important Shīʿī intellectuals, such as Ali Shariʿati, argued strongly against the traditional Shīʿī understanding of *taqiyya*. See Dabashi, *Theology of Discontent*, 114. Dabashi's work *Shiʿism: A Religion of Protest* demonstrates, by its mere title, the complex interplay between expressions of quietism and activism in Shīʿī history. See Hamid Dabashi, *Shiʿism: A Religion of Protest* (Cambridge, MA: Belknap Press, 2011).

52 Antony Black, *The History of Islamic Political Thought: From the Prophet to the Present* (Edinburgh: Edinburgh University Press, 2011), 228. R. Strothmann et al., s.v. "Taḳiyya," in *Encyclopaedia of Islam*, 2nd ed. (Leiden: Brill, 2000), 10:134–136.

53 For this insight, we thank Mohammad Ali, PhD candidate at Jamia Millia Islamia in New Delhi, India.

54 K. A. Nizami, "Čishtiyya," in *Encyclopaedia of Islam*, 2nd ed. (Leiden: Brill, 1965), 2:50–56.

55 K. A. Nizami, *Some Aspects of Religion and Politics in India during the Thirteenth Century* (New Delhi: Caxton Press P. Ltd., 1961), 236. Other Sufi orders, such as the Suhrawardiyya, understood that the faith-based obligation of social service required active participation with the state, as Nizami points out (248). Nizami adds, "If a man became ego-centric, limited his sympathies and cut himself off completely from the energizing currents of social life, he failed to fulfill the mystic mission."

56 Jürgen Paul argues that, as with the Chishtiyya, "the Khwājagān's attitude towards the powers that be was at first quietist and even apolitical and [then] they became more involved with politics … their attitude towards the way Transoxiana was

being ruled became more outspoken, when their influence grew," in Paul L. Heck (ed.), *Sufism and Politics: The Power of Spirituality* (Princeton: Markus Wiener Publishers, 2007), 141. See also the introduction to K. A. Nizami, *Some Aspects of Religion*, x–xi.

57 Nizami, "Čishtiyya."

58 Philip Gorski, "Beyond the Fact/Value Distinction: Ethical Naturalism and the Social Sciences," *Society* 50, no. 6 (2013): 548, doi: 10.1007/s12115-013-9709-2.

59 Black, *History of Islamic Political Thought*, 133.

60 Immanuel Wallerstein, *World-Systems Analysis: An Introduction* (Durham and London: Duke University Press, 2004), 57–58.

61 We wish to again thank Mohammad Ali of Jamia Millia Islamia in New Delhi for this insight and source.

62 Mirza Asadullah Khan Ghalib, *Dastanbūy: A Diary of the Indian Revolt of 1857*, trans. Khwaja Ahmed Faruqi (New York: Asia Publishing House, 1970), 275.

63 Ibid.

64 Roberts, *Political Islam*, 37.

65 As cited in Hourani, *Arabic Thought in the Liberal Age*, 79.

66 Rifāʿa Rāfiʿ al-Ṭahṭāwī, "The Extraction of Gold, or an Overview of Paris and the Honest Guide for Girls and Boys," in *Modernist Islam: A Sourcebook, 1840–1940*, ed. Charles Kurzman (New York: Oxford University Press, 2002), 34–35.

67 Jamāl al-Dīn al-Afghānī, "Refutation of the Materialists," in *An Islamic Response to Imperialism: Political and Religious Writings of Sayyid Jamāl ad-Dīn "al-Afghānī,"* ed. Nikki R. Keddie (Berkeley: University of California Press, 1983), 173.

68 Jamāl al-Dīn al-Afghānī, "The Materialists in India," in *Islamic Response*, ed. Keddie, 177.

69 Ebrahim Moosa, "Political Theology in the Aftermath of the Arab Spring," in *The African Renaissance and the Afro-Arab Spring*, ed. C. Villa-Vicencio, E. Doxtader, and E. Moosa (Washington, DC: Georgetown University Press, 2015), 101–119.

70 Ali Abdel Razek, *Islam and the Foundations of Political Power*, trans. Maryam Loutfi, ed. Abdou Filali-Ansary (Edinburgh: Edinburgh University Press, 2012), 95–96.

71 Muḥammad Sayyid Kīlānī, "Dhayl al-milal wa-l-niḥal," in *al-Milal wa-l-niḥal* (Beirut: Dār al-Maʿrifa, 1402), 74–75.

72 Ibid.

73 Roy P. Mottahedeh, *The Mantle of the Prophet: Religion and Politics in Iran* (New York: Simon and Schuster, 1985), 237–238.

74 Neguin Yavari, "Hosayn Borujerdi," in *Encyclopedia of the Modern Middle East and North Africa* (New York: Macmillan Reference, 2004).

75 Edmund A. Ghareeb (ed.), "Ayat-Allah al-Khui," in *Historical Dictionary of Iraq* (Lanham, MD: Scarecrow Press, 2004).

76 Majid Mohammadi, "Abo al-Qasem Khoʾi," *Encyclopedia of Islam and the Muslim World*, ed. Richard C. Martin (Farmington Hills, MI: Gale, 2016).

77 Ghareeb, "Ayat-Allah al-Khui."

78 See, for example, Joas Wagemakers, *A Quietist Jihadi: The Ideology and Influence of Abu Muhammad al-Maqdisi* (New York: Cambridge University Press, 2012); Quintan Wiktorowicz, "Anatomy of the Salafi Movement," *Studies in Conflict and Terrorism* 29, no. 3 (2006): 207–240, doi: 10.1080/10576100500497004. Jacob Olidort argues that "quietist" is an inadequate label for certain Salafis, such as Muḥammad Nāṣir al-Dīn al-Albānī (d. 1999) and his followers because they are, in fact, politically active. See "The Politics of 'Quietist' Salafism," Analysis Paper, *Brookings Project on U.S. Relations with the Islamic World* (Washington, DC: Brookings, February 2015).

79 Wiktorowicz, "Anatomy of the Salafi Movement," 208.

80 Ibid.

81 See, for example, Wagemakers, *A Quietist Jihadi*.

82 Ibid., 46–47.

83 Ibid. As Wagemaker notes, for important analyses of the debate between al-Maqdisī and al-Zarqawī, see Steven Brooke, "The Preacher and the Jihadi," *Current Trends in Islamist Ideology* 3 (2006), 119; Nibras Kazimi, "A Virulent Ideology in Mutation: Zarqawi Upstages Maqdisi," *Current Trends in Islamist Ideology* 2 (2005), 109.

84 Wagemakers, *A Quietist Jihadi*, 64–66.

85 Nabil Mouline, *The Clerics of Islam: Religious Authority and Political Power in Saudi Arabia* (New Haven: Yale University Press, 2014), 1.

86 This insight is derived from Maurice Blondel, *The Letter on Apologetics and History and Dogma*, trans. Alexander Dru and Illtyd Trethowan (London: Harvill Press, 1964), 267; Mouline, *The Clerics of Islam*, 10.

87 As cited in Shahab Ahmed, *What Is Islam?: The Importance of Being Islamic* (Princeton, NJ: Princeton University Press, 2016), 301.

Bibliography

Abdel Razek, Ali. *Islam and the Foundations of Political Power*. Translated by Maryam Loutfi. Edited by Abdou Filali-Ansary. Edinburgh: Edinburgh University Press, 2012.

Abū Ḥanīfa, Nuʿmān b. Thābit. "al-Fiqh al-akbar." Translated by Hamid Algar. Online: https://archive.org/details/Al-fiqhAl-akbareng.-AbuHanifah.pdf. Accessed January 4, 2018.

Abū Ḥanīfa, Nuʿmān b. Thābit. *Kitāb al-fiqh al-akbar*. Edited by Mulla ʿAlī Qārī ʿAlī b. Sulṭān Muḥammad al-Harawī. Cairo: Dār al-Kutub al-ʿArabiyya al-Kubrā, 1909.

al-Afghānī, Jamāl al-Dīn. "The Materialists in India." In *An Islamic Response to Imperialism: Political and Religious Writings of Sayyid Jamāl ad-Dīn "al-Afghānī."* Edited by Nikki R. Keddie, 175–180. Berkeley: University of California Press, 1983.

al-Afghānī, Jamāl al-Dīn. "Refutation of the Materialists." In *An Islamic Response to Imperialism: Political and Religious Writings of Sayyid Jamāl ad-Dīn "al-Afghānī."* Edited by Nikki R. Keddie, 73–83. Berkeley: University of California Press, 1983.

Ahmed, Shahab. *What Is Islam?: The Importance of Being Islamic*. Princeton, NJ: Princeton University Press, 2016.

Arjomand, Said Amir (ed.). *Authority and Political Culture in Shiʿism*. Albany: State University of New York Press, 1988.

Arjomand, Said Amir. *The Shadow of God and the Hidden Imam*. Chicago: University of Chicago Press, 1984.

Assman, Jan. *Herrschaft und Heil: Politische Theologie in Altägypten, Israel und Europa*. Munich: Hanser, 2000.

Athamina, Khalil. "The Early Murjiʾa: Some Notes." *Journal of Semitic Studies* 35, no. 1 (1990): 109–130.

Black, Antony. *The History of Islamic Political Thought: From the Prophet to the Present*. Edinburgh: Edinburgh University Press, 2011.

Blondel, Maurice. *The Letter on Apologetics and History and Dogma*. Translated by Alexander Dru and Illtyd Trethowan. London: Harvill Press, 1964.

Brooke, Steven. "The Preacher and the Jihadi." *Current Trends in Islamist Ideology* 3 (2006): 52–66.

Connolly, T. K. "Quietism." *New Catholic Encyclopedia*. Detroit: Gale, 2003.

Cook, Michael A. "Activism and Quietism in Islam." In *Islam and Power*, edited by Alexander S. Cudsi and Ali E. Hillal, 15–22. London: Croom Helm, 1981.

Cook, Michael A. *Commanding Right and Forbidding Wrong in Islamic Thought*. New York: Cambridge University Press, 2001.

Crone, Patricia. *God's Rule: Government and Islam*. New York: Columbia University Press, 2004.

Dabashi, Hamid. *Shiʿism: A Religion of Protest*. Cambridge, MA: Belknap Press, 2011.

Dabashi, Hamid. *Theology of Discontent: The Ideological Foundations of the Islamic Revolution in Iran*. New York: New York University Press, 1993.

"Divine Right of Kings—Oxford Reference." Online: http://www.oxfordreference.com/view/10.1093/oi/authority.20110810104754564. Accessed January 4, 2018.

El Omari, Racha, Najam Haider, and Emad El-Din Shahin. "Muʿtazilah." *The Oxford Encyclopedia of Islam and Politics*. New York: Oxford University Press, 2014. Online: http://www.oxfordreference.com/view/10.1093/acref:oiso/9780199739356.001.0001/acref-9780199739356-e-0057. Accessed March 6, 2018.

Enayat, Hamid. *Modern Islamic Political Thought*. Austin: University of Texas Press, 1982.

Foucault, Michel. *Power*. Edited by James D. Faubion. Translated by Robert Hurley. New York: New Press, 2000.

Ghalib, Mirza Asadullah Khan. *Dastanbūy: A Diary of the Indian Revolt of 1857*. Translated by Khwaja Ahmed Faruqi. New York: Asia Publishing House, 1970.

Ghareeb, Edmund A. (ed.). "Ayat-Allah al-Khui." *Historical Dictionary of Iraq*. Historical Dictionaries of Asia, Oceania, and the Middle East 44. Lanham, MD: Scarecrow Press, 2004.

Goldziher, Ignaz. *Introduction to Islamic Theology and Law*. Princeton, NJ: Princeton University Press, 1981.

Gorski, Philip. "Beyond the Fact/Value Distinction: Ethical Naturalism and the Social Sciences." *Society* 50, no. 6 (2013): 543–553. Online: https://link.springer.com/article/10.1007/s12115-013-9709-2.

Heck, Paul. "Advice." *The Princeton Encyclopedia of Islamic Political Thought*, edited by Gerhard Böwering et al. Princeton, NJ: Princeton University Press, 2013.

Heck, Paul (ed.). *Sufism and Politics: The Power of Spirituality*. Princeton, NJ: Markus Wiener Publishers, 2007.

Hodgson, Marshall G. S. *The Venture of Islam: Conscience and History in a World Civilization*. 3 vols. Chicago: University of Chicago Press, 1974.

Hourani, Albert. *Arabic Thought in the Liberal Age, 1798–1939*. Cambridge and New York: Cambridge University Press, 1983.

Hoyland, Robert G. *Arabia and the Arabs: From the Bronze Age to the Coming of Islam*. New York: Routledge, 2001.

Ibn ʿAbd al-Barr, Yusūf b. ʿAbdallāh. *Jāmiʿ bayān al-ʿilm wa-faḍlih wa-mā yanbaghī min riwāyatih wa-ḥamlih*. Edited by Abū l-Ashbāl al-Zuhayrī. 2 vols. Saudi Arabia: Dār Ibn al-Jawzī, 1994.

Ibn al-Jawzī. *The Life of Ibn Ḥanbal*. Translated by Michael Cooperson. New York: New York University Press, 2016.

Ibn Taymiyya, Taqī l-Dīn Aḥmad. *Minhāj al-sunna al-nabawiyya fī naqd kalām al-shīʿa al-Qadariyya*. Vol. 1. Cairo, 1962.

Ibn Taymiyya, Taqī l-Dīn Aḥmad. *al-Siyāsa al-sharʿiyya*. Cairo, 1951.

Kamali, Muhammad Hashim. *Principles of Islamic Jurisprudence*. Cambridge: Islamic Texts Society, 2003.

Kazimi, Nibras. "A Virulent Ideology in Mutation: Zarqawi Upstages Maqdisi." *Current Trends in Islamist Ideology* 2 (2005): 59–73.

Kīlānī, Muḥammad Sayyid. "Dhayl al-milal wa-l-niḥal." In *al-Milal wa-l-niḥal*. Beirut: Dār al-Maʿrifa, 1402.

Kolakowski, Leszek. "Quietism." Edited by Lindsay Jones. *Encyclopedia of Religion*. Detroit: Macmillan Reference, 2005.

Lewis, Bernard. "Communism and Islam." In *The Middle East in Transition*, edited by Walter Z. Laqueur, 311–324. New York: Frederick A. Praeger, 1958.

Lilla, Mark. *The Stillborn God: Religion, Politics, and the Modern West*. New York: Knopf, 2007.

Madelung, W. "Murdjiʾa." In *Encyclopaedia of Islam*, 2nd ed., edited by P. Bearman, Th. Bianquis, C. E. Bosworth, E. van Donzel, and W. P. Heinrichs. 7:605–607. Leiden: Brill, 1993.

Marlow, Louise. *Hierarchy and Egalitarianism in Islamic Thought*. New York: Cambridge University Press, 1997.

al-Mawardi, Abu'l-Hasan. *al-Ahkam as-sultaniyyah*. Translated by Asadullah Yate. London: Ta-Ha Publishers Ltd., 1996.

Michot, Yahya. "Ibn Taymiyya." In *The Princeton Encyclopedia of Islamic Political Thought*, edited by Gerhard Böwering et al, 238–241. Princeton, NJ: Princeton University Press, 2013.

Mohammadi, Majid. "Abo al-Qasem Khoʾi." In *Encyclopedia of Islam and the Muslim World*, edited by Richard C. Martin, 393. Farmington HIlls, MI: Gale, 2016.

Moosa, Ebrahim. "Political Theology in the Aftermath of the Arab Spring." In *The African Renaissance and the Afro-Arab Spring*, edited by C. Villa-Vicencio, E. Doxtader, and E. Moosa, 101–119. Washington, DC: Georgetown University Press, 2015.

Mottahedeh, Roy P. *The Mantle of the Prophet: Religion and Politics in Iran*. New York: Simon and Schuster, 1985.

Mouline, Nabil. *The Clerics of Islam: Religious Authority and Political Power in Saudi Arabia*. New Haven: Yale University Press, 2014.

Nizami, K. A. *Some Aspects of Religion and Politics in India during the Thirteenth Century*. New Delhi: Caxton Press, 1961.

Nizami, K. A. "Čishtiyya." In *Encyclopaedia of Islam*, 2nd ed., edited by P. Bearman, Th. Bianquis, C. E. Bosworth, E. van Donzel, and W. P. Heinrichs. 2:50–56. Leiden: Brill, 1965.

Olidort, Jacob. "The Politics of 'Quietist' Salafism." Analysis Paper. *The Brookings Project on U.S. Relations with the Islamic World*. Washington, DC: Brookings, February 2015.

"Quietism." *Britannica Academic*. Online: academic.eb.com.

Rapoport, Yossef, and Shahab Ahmed. *Ibn Taymiyya and His Times*. New York: Oxford University Press, 2010.

Raupp, Werner, Heiner F. Klemme, and Manfred Kuehn. "Johann Albrecht Bengel." In *The Dictionary of Eighteenth-Century German Philosophers*. New York: Continuum, 2010: 92–95.

Roberts, Nicholas P. *Political Islam and the Invention of Tradition*. Washington, DC: New Academia Publishing, 2015.

al-Sarhan, Saud Saleh. "Early Muslim Traditionalism: A Critical Study of the Works and Political Theology of Aḥmad Ibn Ḥanbal." PhD thesis, University of Exeter, 2011.

Schacht, Joseph. "Abū Ḥanīfa al-Nuʿmān." In *Encyclopaedia of Islam*, 2nd ed., edited by P. Bearman, Th. Bianquis, C. E. Bosworth, E. van Donzel, and W. P. Heinrichs, 1:123–124. Leiden: Brill, 1960.

Strothmann, R., and Moktar Djebli. "Taḳiyya." In *Encyclopaedia of Islam*, 2nd ed., edited by P. Bearman, Th. Bianquis, C. E. Bosworth, E. van Donzel, and W. P. Heinrichs, 10:134–136. Leiden: Brill, 2000.

al-Ṭahṭāwī, Rifāʿa Rāfiʿ. "The Extraction of Gold, or an Overview of Paris and the Honest Guide for Girls and Boys." In *Modernist Islam: A Sourcebook, 1840–1940*, edited by Charles Kurzman, 31–39. New York: Oxford University Press, 2002.

Vries, Hent de, and Lawrence E. Sullivan (eds.). *Political Theologies: Public Religion in a Post-Secular World*. New York: Fordham University Press, 2006.

Wagemakers, Joas. *A Quietist Jihadi: The Ideology and Influence of Abu Muhammad al-Maqdisi*. New York: Cambridge University Press, 2012.

Wallerstein, Immanuel. *World-Systems Analysis: An Introduction*. Durham and London: Duke University Press, 2004.

Watt, W. Montgomery. *The Formative Period of Islamic Thought*. Edinburgh: Edinburgh University Press, 1973.

Wensinck, A.J. *The Muslim Creed: Its Genesis and Historical Development*. London: Cambridge University Press, 1932.

Wiktorowicz, Quintan. "Anatomy of the Salafi Movement." *Studies in Conflict and Terrorism* 29, no. 3 (2006): 207–240. doi: 10.1080/10576100500497004.

Yavari, Neguin. "Hosayn Borujerdi." *Encyclopedia of the Modern Middle East and North Africa*. New York: Macmillan Reference, 2004.

Zaman, Muhammad Qasim. *Religion and Politics Under the Early ʿAbbāsids: The Emergence of the Proto-Sunnī Elite*. Leiden: Brill, 1997.

Part Two

Political Quietism in Classical Islam

3

The Rightly Guided Caliphs: The Range of Views Preserved in *Ḥadīth*

Christopher Melchert

Sunnī *ḥadīth* literature of the third/ninth century preserves numerous different opinions as to which caliphs were righteously guiding and guided. There is support for a theory of just two, Abū Bakr and ʿUmar, for these two plus ʿUthmān, for these three plus ʿAlī, with variants that give only half-honors to ʿUthmān or ʿAlī. It is hard to find *ḥadīth* only preferring ʿAlī to ʿUthmān in these collections, although some prominent Sunnī traditionists were quoted as upholding such a preference. The suggestion seems to be that some disagreement was legitimate and should not occasion fighting.

The problem here concerns the range of views preserved in early Sunnī *ḥadīth* collections on the "rightly guided caliphs" (*al-khulafāʾ al-rāshidūn*), meaning most broadly the successors to Muḥammad (as head of state) whose words and deeds were considered reliable as guides to belief and conduct.[1] These collections were assembled in the mid-third/ninth century. There are two aspects to the problem. First, we ought to go back a hundred years or so to see what led up to the situation in the mid-third/ninth century. Second, how can we interpret such diversity as remained in the mid-third/ninth century? A major theoretical desideratum involves disentangling the two problems of the caliphate and preference. The caliphate (*al-khilāfa*) concerns the problem of who was a caliph and who was not. The major question was whether ʿAlī or Muʿāwiya was the fourth after the Prophet. Preference (*tafḍīl*) concerns the problem of who was the best after the Prophet. Was ʿAlī better than ʿUthmān? than Ṭalḥa and al-Zubayr?[2]

With regard to views in the century before the mid-200s/800s, the following review from Aḥmad b. Saʿīd al-Dārimī (d. 253/867–8) is useful:

> The jurisprudents disagreed. Among them were those who said Abū Bakr and ʿUmar, then stopped. Among them were al-Shaʿbī [Kufan, d. after 100/718–19]; Ibrāhīm [Kufan, d. 96/714?]; and the Kufans, Saʿīd b. Jubayr [Kufan, d. 95/714?], Abū l-Bakhtarī [Kufan client, d. 83/702–703], and others; also ʿUbayd b. ʿUmayr [Meccan *qāṣṣ*, d. before 73/692–693] and a number of the people of Basra who stopped. A number said Abū Bakr, ʿUmar, ʿUthmān, and ʿAlī. There was a group called the Shīʿa who were not rebels or associated with innovation who said Abū Bakr, ʿUmar, and ʿAlī. There was a group called the ʿUthmāniyya who said Abū Bakr, ʿUmar, ʿUthmān, then fell silent. Among them were Saʿīd b. Abī ʿArūba [Basran client, d. 156/772–773?], Ḥammād b. Zayd [Basran, d. 179/795–796], Hishām b. Abī ʿAbdallāh [al-Dastuwāʾī, Basran Qadarī, d. 154/770–771], and others. There was a group of the people of Basra who would not choose between ʿAlī and ʿUthmān. Among them were Yaḥyā b. Saʿīd [al-Qaṭṭān, d. 198/813], Sulaymān al-Taymī [b. Ṭarkhān, d. 143/760–761], Muʿtamir b. Sulaymān [d. 187/802–803], and Khālid b. al-Ḥārith [d. 186/802].[3]

"Those who said Abū Bakr and ʿUmar, then stopped" effectively held that there were just two rightly guided caliphs. To judge by *isnād*s, this position was most popular in Kufa. By means of a Kufan *isnād*, ʿAbdallāh b. Aḥmad quotes ʿAlī himself in support of such a theory: "The Messenger of God preceded (everyone else). He put Abū Bakr in charge of the prayer. He made ʿUmar the third. After that, we were a group struck by the tribulation (*fitna*) of what God willed."[4] (It is surprising to see ʿUmar described as the third, not the second. He did come third as head of the Islamic state. Perhaps the formula is archaic, reflecting a time when propagandists for the Umayyads extolled the caliphate as virtually equal to prophethood.[5]) ʿAlī is quoted as saying that Abū Bakr and ʿUmar had a covenant with the Messenger of God, he and ʿUthmān only with the people.[6] And the Kufan *mukhaḍram,* Ṣaʿṣaʿa b. Ṣūḥān (d. after 40/661), is quoted as saying in a sermon that God chose Abū Bakr and ʿUmar, whereas the people chose ʿUthmān.[7] Likewise through Kufan *isnād*s, the Prophet is widely quoted as saying, "Follow the lead of (*iqtadū bi-*) those two after me, Abū Bakr and ʿUmar."[8] ʿĀʾisha is quoted as saying, mainly by Kufan *isnād*s, "The Messenger of God … was taken away without having appointed a successor. The Messenger of God said, 'If I were to appoint a successor, I would appoint Abū Bakr and ʿUmar.'"[9]

According to Aḥmad b. Ḥanbal, "The people of Kufa prefer ʿAlī to ʿUthmān save for two men: Ṭalḥa b. Muṣarrif [d. 112/730–731?] and ʿAbdallāh b. Idrīs [d. 192/807–808]." Asked whether Zubayd al-Yāmī (d. 122/739–40?) was not another, he said, "No, he used to love ʿAlī," meaning (presumably ʿAbdallāh's gloss) he preferred ʿAlī to ʿUthmān.[10] It may seem odd, then, for Kufa to be the center of a two-caliph hypothesis. My guess would be that ʿAlī having such strong support in Kufa, a two-caliph hypothesis was the safest option for Kufan supporters of the Umayyads or at least quietists who resisted active opposition to the Umayyads. Al-Shaʿbī was characterized as taking a strong position against the Shīʿa, meaning those who preferred ʿAlī to ʿUthmān and probably also those who thought the rightful caliphs after ʿAlī had to be among his descendants. "If the Shīʿa were among the birds," he is quoted as saying, "they would be vultures. If they were among the beasts, they would be asses."[11] Ibn Idrīs's preference for ʿUthmān may have been an assertion of his independence of the ʿAbbāsids, also perhaps disdain for Kufa. He was known for being close to the scholars of Medina, normally allied with the Basrans.

Al-Dārimī's first proponents of a three-caliph hypothesis are "the ʿUthmāniyya who said Abū Bakr, ʿUmar, ʿUthmān, then fell silent." A *ḥadīth* report with a Basran *isnād* states "that the Messenger of God … ascended Uḥud with Abū Bakr, ʿUmar, and ʿUthmān. It shook them, whereupon the Prophet of God … said, 'Be firm, Uḥud, for on you are only a prophet, a saint, and two martyrs.'"[12] A yet more prominent *ḥadīth* report quotes Ibn ʿUmar with a Medinan/Baghdadi *isnād*: "We used to, in the time of the Prophet … , consider no one equal to Abū Bakr, then ʿUmar, then ʿUthmān. Then we would leave the Companions of the Prophet … , not preferring any to another."[13] In Ibn Abī ʿĀṣim (by Kufan and Basran *isnād*s), ʿAlī himself implies that Abū Bakr, ʿUmar, and ʿUthmān were the best Muslims after the Prophet, in descending order.[14]

To the same effect is a longer story from Ibn ʿUmar (Medinan *isnād*):

> The Messenger of God … took a ring of gold or silver and put its jewel (*faṣṣ*) next to his palm. Its inscription was "Muḥammad is the Messenger of God." The people took up the like of that. When he saw that they had taken them up, he threw his away, saying, "I will never wear it." Then he took up a ring of silver, so the people took up rings of silver. There wore the ring after the Prophet … Abū Bakr, then ʿUmar, then ʿUthmān, till it fell from ʿUthmān into the well of Arīs.[15]

One version from Ibn Saʿd recounts that it was on the hand of ʿUthmān for precisely six years before being lost in the well. The *isnād* suggests that this was a Basran interpretation, connecting the loss of the ring with the theory that ʿUthmān's caliphate comprised six good years and six bad years.[16] Another version, likewise Basran, states that the ring remained on ʿUthmān's hand so long as he did the work of his two predecessors.[17]

Another, apparently opposing, version with a Kufan *isnād* goes back to a Shīʿī imam, ʿAlī b. al-Ḥusayn (Zayn al-ʿĀbidīn, d. Medina, 95/714): "The ring of the

Messenger of God … was with Abū Bakr and ʿUmar. When ʿUthmān took it, it fell and was lost. ʿAlī … inscribed his own inscription."[18] Thus, ʿAlī b. al-Ḥusayn recognizes the legitimacy of Abū Bakr and ʿUmar, in the Zaydī style, while rejecting ʿUthmān. Yet another opposing report with a Medinan *isnād* goes back to Saʿīd b. al-Musayyab (d. 94/712–3?): "The Messenger of God … did not wear a ring (*mā takhattama*) until he met God. Neither did Abū Bakr until he met God, nor ʿUmar until he met God, nor ʿUthmān until he met God."[19]

There is also a three-caliph tradition that finds Abū Bakr, ʿUmar, and ʿUthmān all legitimate caliphs, but decreasing in virtue. Here is one example recounted by Abū Dāwūd, al-Tirmidhī, and al-Nasāʾī with a Basran *isnād*:

> Prophet: "Who of you has had a dream?" A man: "I dreamt as if a scale came down from heaven. You and Abū Bakr were weighed on it. You outweighed him. Abū Bakr and ʿUmar were weighed, Abū Bakr outweighing (ʿUmar). ʿUmar and ʿUthmān were weighed, ʿUmar outweighing (ʿUthmān)." Abū Bakra: "We saw dislike on the face of the Messenger of God …."[20]

This report endorses the classical order of preference (*tafḍīl*) among the first three. Perhaps the Prophet disliked what he heard because he knew things would only get worse from there. Another example, recounted in Aḥmad's *Musnad* also with a Basran *isnād*, includes an interpretation by the Prophet:

> The Messenger of God liked a good dream. He would ask about it. One day, the Messenger of God said, "Which of you has dreamt a dream?" A man said, "I, O Messenger of God. dreamt as if a scale came down from heaven. You were weighed on it against Abū Bakr, whom you outweighed. Then Abū Bakr was weighed against ʿUmar, whom he outweighed. Then ʿUmar was weighed against ʿUthmān, whom he outweighed. Then the scale was drawn up." The Messenger of God … was displeased by this. He said, "[There will be proper] succession to prophethood (*khilāfat nubuwwa*), then God will give power (*mulk*) to whomever he pleases."[21]

Again, we have the classical order of preference among the first three, also a limitation of righteous succession to the first three, making ʿAlī no better than Muʿāwiya and the Umayyads after him—indeed, making it a matter of indifference whether one recognized ʿAlī as a caliph at all or dismissed him as merely an unsuccessful pretender.

This account of a dream from the Prophet himself (Basran *isnād*) gives an even more negative view of ʿUthmān:

> I saw as if a bucket descended from the sky. Abū Bakr came and took it by its handles, drinking from it a weak draught … Then ʿUmar came and took it by its

handles and drank till he was full. Then ʿUthmān came and took it by its handles and drank till he was full. But it shook, so some of it spilt onto him.[22]

Here are three righteous caliphs, but ʿUthmān is besmirched, perhaps for being overly eager to take power. I infer in the end that the three-caliph hypothesis of Abū Bakr, ʿUmar, and ʿUthmān had its strongest support in Basra, with opposition from different directions in Kufa and Medina. (This slightly qualifies van Ess's assertion that the three-caliph hypothesis, recognizing Abū Bakr, ʿUmar, and ʿUthmān, prevailed in Basra and Medina.[23] Of course, there were characteristically majority and minority views in each center.)

As indicated by al-Dārimī and Aḥmad b. Ḥanbal, others, especially Kufan, held an alternative three-caliph hypothesis, mainly that Abū Bakr, ʿUmar, and ʿAlī were three rightly guided caliphs.[24] ʿAbd al-Razzāq includes a *ḥadīth* report from ʿAbdallāh b. Masʿūd apparently endorsing this list:

> I was with the Prophet … the night when the delegation of *jinn* came to him. He sighed, so I said, "What is with you, O Messenger of God?" He said, "I have been told of my own death, O Ibn Masʿūd." I said, "So appoint a successor." He said, "Whom?" I said, "Abū Bakr." He was silent. Some time passed, then he sighed. I said, "What is with you, O Messenger of God?" He said, "I have been told of my own death, O Ibn Masʿūd." I said, "So appoint a successor." He said, "Whom?" I said, "ʿUmar." He was silent. Some time passed, then he sighed. I said, "What is with you, O Messenger of God?" He said, "I have been told of my own death, O Ibn Masʿūd." I said, "So appoint a successor." He said, "Whom?" I said, "ʿAlī b. Abī Ṭālib." He said, "By him in whose hand is my soul, if they obey him, they will all enter paradise, every one."[25]

On the whole, though, it is difficult to find express Kufan endorsements of a three-caliph hypothesis, Abū Bakr, ʿUmar, then ʿAlī, in Sunnī *ḥadīth* collections.

ʿAbd al-Razzāq fits into "a group called the Shīʿa who were not rebels or associated with innovation."[26] This is commonly identified as the Zaydī position, and is probably what Ibn al-Nadīm (d. 380/990?) had in mind when he said of the Zaydiyya, "most of the traditionists, such as Sufyān b. ʿUyayna, Sufyān al-Thawrī, and Ṣāliḥ b. Ḥayy and his sons, upheld this position."[27] As late as Ibn Ḥajar, Sunnī authors distinguished between *tashayyuʿ*, a forgivable preference for ʿAlī over ʿUthmān, and *rafḍ*, a preference for ʿAlī over Abū Bakr and ʿUmar, which may put one outside the community. Moreover, the seriousness of preferring ʿAlī might depend on whether one actively promoted such a preference. According to the Ḥanbalī *qāḍī* Abū Yaʿlā b. al-Farrāʾ (d. 458/1065), for example, a witness was not disqualified for preferring ʿAlī to the three unless he was an active propagandist.[28]

Surprisingly, al-Dārimī concludes with Basrans who would not choose between ʿAlī and ʿUthmān, with examples from the mid- to late second/eighth century. On the face of it, this is the position of the early Murjiʾa (*al-murjiʾa al-ūlā*), who refrained from saying whether either ʿUthmān or ʿAlī was a believer.[29] Ibn Saʿd mentions, about the Kufan *qāḍī* Muḥārib b. Dithār (d. 116/734–5?), "He was among the first Murjiʾa who put off (*yurjūna*) a decision concerning ʿAlī and ʿUthmān, not testifying to either faith or infidelity."[30] To refrain from deciding is the express position of *Fiqh akbar* I, the short creed usually attributed to Abū Muṭīʿ al-Balkhī (al-Ḥakam b. ʿAbdallāh b. Maslama, d. 199/814?), a *qāḍī* who claimed to relate it from Abū Ḥanīfa himself.[31] Early on, Abū Muṭīʿ was denounced as a Murjiʾ.[32] The *Waṣiyya*, which is attributed to Abū Ḥanīfa, endorses the position of the later Murjiʾa concerning faith, that it neither increases nor decreases, but takes what became the orthodox Sunnī position concerning the caliphs, namely that Abū Bakr, ʿUmar, ʿUthmān, and ʿAlī were the best of the Muslims after the Prophet, in descending order.[33]

To my surprise, I have not found independent confirmation that Yaḥyā b. Saʿīd al-Qaṭṭān, Sulaymān al-Taymī, Muʿtamir b. Sulaymān, and Khālid b. al-Ḥārith (all highly reputable traditionists) actually took the position ascribed to them by al-Dārimī, namely that they refused to decide between ʿUthmān and ʿAlī. To the contrary, Ibn Saʿd states that Sulaymān al-Taymī inclined toward ʿAlī.[34] Aḥmad ascribes neutrality as between ʿUthmān and ʿAlī to his teacher Yazīd b. Hārūn (a client from Wasit, d. 206/821–2), or at least that he said *ahl al-sunna* were not to be blamed if they preferred one or the other, either ʿUthmān or ʿAlī.[35]

There seem to have been four stages to the development of the ʿUthmāniyya, the group named by al-Dārimī: (1) loyalists opposed to ʿAlī; (2) supporters of the three-caliph hypothesis; (3) supporters of the four-caliph hypothesis with ʿUthmān the third best, ʿAlī the fourth; and finally (4) a shadowy, evanescent pro-Umayyad party.[36] Al-Dārimī's description fits stage two. His examples of shaykhs who endorsed this ranking are all Basrans of the later second/eighth century. Similarly, Ibn Saʿd applies the term *ʿUthmānī* mainly to Basrans of the later second/eighth century: ʿAbdallāh b. ʿAwn (d. 151/768?), Ḥammād b. Zayd (d. 179/795), Yazīd b. Zurayʿ (d. Basra, 182/798), and Bishr b. al-Mufaḍḍal (d. 186/802).[37] Ibn Saʿd applies the term more sparingly outside Basra: to the Egyptian Muʿāwiya b. Ḥudayj (fl. first/seventh century) and the Kufan Abū Ḥaṣīn (d. 128/745–6?).[38]

In the middle, but without any named examples, al-Dārimī puts those who upheld the four-caliph hypothesis: the first four, righteous caliphs were, in order,

Abū Bakr, ʿUmar, ʿUthmān, and ʿAlī. Al-Dārimī does not distinguish between the caliphate and preference, but the classical Sunnī doctrine of preference ranked them in chronological order as to virtue as well as legitimate leadership of the community. This is famously expressed in the *ḥadīth* report of Abū ʿAbd al-Raḥmān Safīna, the Prophet's freedman (Basran *isnād*):

> Prophet: "Succession to prophecy (*khilāfat nubuwwa*) will be for thirty years, then God will give power (*al-mulk*) or His power (*mulkahu*) to whomever he wills." Saʿīd (b. Jumhān, d. Basra, 136/753–754) < Safīna: "Consider (*amsik ʿalayk*, literally 'hold onto') Abū Bakr at two years, ʿUmar ten, ʿUthmān twelve, and ʿAlī so-and-so." Saʿīd: "I said to Safīna, 'Those assert that ʿAlī was not a caliph.' She said, 'The anuses of Banī l-Zarqāʾ have lied,' meaning Banī Marwān."[39]

This is the *ḥadīth* report to which Aḥmad b. Ḥanbal appeals:

> The *sunna* with regard to *tafḍīl*, which we endorse, is what is related of Ibn ʿUmar, saying Abū Bakr, then ʿUmar, then ʿUthmān. As for the caliphate, we go by the *ḥadīth* report of Safīna, saying Abū Bakr, ʿUmar, ʿUthmān, and ʿAlī among the caliphs. We harmonize (*nastaʿmil*) the two *ḥadīth* reports. We do not rebuke anyone who makes ʿAlī the fourth on account of his blood and marriage relationships, his early conversion, and his probity.[40]

The following is a story of the Prophet and his most important Companions on a mountain that shakes:

> The Messenger of God … was on Mount Ḥirāʾ along with Abū Bakr, ʿUmar, ʿUthmān, ʿAlī, Ṭalḥa, and al-Zubayr. The rock moved. The Messenger of God … said, "Be still, for there is no one on you but a prophet, a saint, and a martyr."[41]

This incident is placed outside Mecca rather than Medina. It represents most closely the mature Sunnī position that not only are Abū Bakr, ʿUmar, ʿUthmān, and ʿAlī all righteous, but the Companions, such as Ṭalḥa and al-Zubayr, who opposed ʿAlī are likewise righteous. They could be equally righteous because their opposition was entirely political, not religious, politics and religion being entirely separate concerns. (Sunnī dogma on this point is of course opposed by Shīʿī dogma, which holds that opposition to ʿAlī was intensely religious.) A variant mentions Saʿd b. Abī Waqqāṣ as well. Another variant, mentioning the first four caliphs of the Sunnīs, Ṭalḥa, al-Zubayr, ʿAbd al-Raḥmān b. ʿAwf, and Saʿīd b. Zayd, was blamed on the Kufan Muḥammad b. Ṭalḥa (d. 167/783–4).[42] If its fabricator is indeed the man indicated, this provides a fairly early *terminus post quem* for the four-caliph hypothesis in Kufan ʿUthmānī circles; however, it is very uncertain whether it was transmitted from him in just these words. Considering how common the term became later, it seems odd that Aḥmad b. Ḥanbal is not quoted as upholding the four-caliph hypothesis in terms of who was rightly guided. Most obviously, he would not quote it because the report (through the Companion al-ʿIrbāḍ b. Sāriya) that the Prophet enjoined obedience to the rightly guided caliphs does not mention who they were.[43]

It was Sunnī dogma, of course, that the Prophet never appointed a successor, and hence, among other things, a quotation such as, "If I were to appoint a successor …." The Rāfiḍī position was that prophets and imams do, on the contrary, appoint their successors. They hold that the Prophet clearly designated ʿAlī as his successor at Ghadīr Khumm, where the Prophet said, "Of whomever I am the patron (*mawlā*), ʿAlī also is his patron." The story of Ghadīr Khumm appears in some Sunnī collections as well as Shīʿī, but it is interpreted as related to the division of spoils, not the caliphate.[44] Ibn Abī Shayba apparently quotes a Meccan tradition by which ʿUthmān used language similar to that of ʿAbdallāh b. al-Zubayr: refusing to go out to fight the rebellious Egyptians, ʿUthmān declared, "Whoever owes hearkening and obedience to me, let him obey ʿAbdallāh b. al-Zubayr."[45] Ibn al-Zubayr would go on to fight against ʿAlī at the Battle of the Camel and was widely recognized as caliph in succession to Yazīd, before he was overthrown by the Marwānids. The quotation suggests how the ʿUthmāniyya might be anti-Umayyad.

There is also a five-caliph hypothesis, quoted by Abū Dāwūd of Sufyān al-Thawrī: "The caliphs are five: Abū Bakr, ʿUmar, ʿUthmān, ʿAlī, and ʿUmar b. ʿAbd al-ʿAzīz."[46] In Abū Dāwūd's collection of Aḥmad b. Ḥanbal's opinions, it seems to be specifically rejected:

> I more than once heard [someone] ask Aḥmad, "It is said that whatever Abū Bakr, ʿUmar, ʿUthmān, and ʿAlī did was *sunna*." He said, "Yes." Once, he said of the *ḥadīth* report of the Messenger of God …, 'Incumbent on you is my *sunna* and that of the rightly-guided caliphs (*al-khulafāʾ al-rāshidīn*),' "He called it *sunna*." He was asked about ʿUmar b. ʿAbd al-ʿAzīz but he said, "No." He was asked, "Was he not an *imām*?" He said, "Yes (he was)."[47]

ʿUmar b. ʿAbd al-ʿAzīz (r. 99–101/717–720) was sometimes even named as one of three rightly guided caliphs. Saʿīd b. al-Musayyab, the prominent Medinan who reputedly denied that Abū Bakr and the others wore a ring, is also quoted as telling an obscure man named Ḥabīb as they stood on ʿArafa, "The caliphs are just three." Ḥabīb asked him, "Who are the caliphs?" Saʿīd said, "Abū Bakr, ʿUmar, and ʿUmar." Ḥabīb said, "These are Abū Bakr and ʿUmar, whom we know, but who is this third ʿUmar?" Saʿīd said, "If you live, you will meet him. If you die, he will come after you."[48] In an alternative story, ʿUmar b. ʿAbd al-ʿAzīz stayed in the cell of a Mesopotamian monk, who recognized him as the just imam corresponding to Rajab. Someone explained that the sacred months were three in a row, corresponding to Abū Bakr, ʿUmar, and ʿUthmān, then Rajab by itself, hence an unconventional four-caliph hypothesis.[49] ʿUmar b. ʿAbd al-ʿAzīz himself is quoted as endorsing the two-caliph hypothesis: "Is it not that whatever the Messenger of God … and his two comrades (*ṣāḥibāh*) laid down as the pattern to follow (*sunna*), it is religion (*dīn*), which we take up and do not go beyond (*nantahī ilayh*)? Whatever anyone else laid down as a *sunna*, we put it off (*nurjiʾuh*)."[50]

There is also some ambiguity over the caliphate of al-Ḥasan b. ʿAlī. Safīna's *ḥadīth* report of thirty years sometimes mentions that ʿAlī's caliphate was six years, sometimes refrains. ʿAlī was acclaimed caliph in 35/656, assassinated in 40/661, so it may have been felt that counting out a full six (to make a full thirty from Abū Bakr's accession in 11/632) implied the caliphate of al-Ḥasan as well, which ended in 41/661. (Abū Dāwūd al-Ṭayālisī's version anticipates the problem by expressly counting the caliphate of Abū Bakr and ʿUmar as twelve years and six months, so that al-Ḥasan's six months are not needed to make up the thirty.[51])

When I am asked about the position of Islam on something, my answer is usually that it is a disputed question. This is a well-known feature of Islamic law: what is offered concerning most questions is not a single rule but a range of possibilities. The four-caliph hypothesis definitely won, defining Sunnism from the third/ninth century until today. From the point of view of a believer, it is possible to harmonize most of these reports: the *ḥadīth*s about two and three caliphs describe a subset of the four, while preference for ʿAlī over ʿUthmān was a forgivable error. From a historian's point of view, these different reports have to represent contending versions of orthodoxy, most of which were ultimately unsuccessful. (I think the evidence is strong that a two-caliph hypothesis was prevalent in second-/eighth-century Kufa, a three-caliph hypothesis in Basra; the evidence is perhaps weaker, although to my mind still preponderant, that the Murjiʾa position evolved out of the two-caliph hypothesis, and the Rāfiḍa were one later reaction to it.) What impresses me is the way the tradition preserves them side by side, one after another. Abū Dāwūd al-Sijistānī is particularly clear, presenting a section on preference, which begins with the first three in chronological order, then apparently a five-caliph hypothesis, followed by a section on the caliphs that has *ḥadīth* about three caliphs, then about four. Implicitly, then, it is possible to uphold any of these positions and be an orthodox adherent of the *sunna*.

Indeed, this is just the approach of the earliest commentator on Abū Dāwūd's *Sunan*, al-Khaṭṭābī (d. 388/988?). He states by turns that Ibn ʿUmar's stopping at ʿUthmān does not necessarily derogate ʿAlī, that Sufyān al-Thawrī once said that the Sunnīs of Kufa thought the order of precedence was Abū Bakr, ʿUmar, ʿAlī, and ʿUthmān; the Sunnīs of Basra [thought it was] Abū Bakr, ʿUmar, ʿUthmān, and ʿAlī (also that he himself was with the Kufans); [and] that there were recent authorities who put Abū Bakr first from the point of view of Companionship, ʿAlī from the point of view of blood relationship, and so on.[52] Centuries later, Ibn Ḥajar (d. 852/1449) would quote him with approval, although observing that Sunnī opinion had by then settled (*taqarrara*) on preference for ʿUthmān over ʿAlī.[53] Discouragement of indignation over such points also seems to suggest encouragement of political quietism.

Notes

1 The full expression in the relevant *ḥadīth* report, implicitly assumed here, is *al-khulafāʾ al-rāshidūn al-mahdiyyūn*, meaning "the rightly guiding and guided caliphs," on which more below. In context, confirmed by Aḥmad b. Ḥanbal's comments, their status as guiding, not just guided, was crucial.

2 The regional dynamics of different positions on the caliphate were opened up, above all, by Wilferd Madelung, *Der Imam al-Qāsim ibn Ibrāhīm und die Glaubenslehre der Zaiditen* (Berlin: Walter de Gruyter, 1965). The theological parties of the second/eighth and early third/ninth centuries have also been masterfully surveyed by Josef van Ess, *Theologie und Gesellschaft im 2. und 3. Jahrhundert Hidschra* (Berlin: Walter de Gruyter, 1991–95). I make comparisons here with a convenient précis, Josef van Ess, "Political Ideas in Early Islamic Religious Thought," *British Journal of Middle Eastern Studies* 28 (2001): 151–164.

3 Ḥarb al-Kirmānī, *Masāʾil al-imām Aḥmad b. Muḥammad b. Ḥanbal wa-Isḥāq b. Rāhūyah*, ed. Nāṣir b. Saʿūd b. ʿAbdallāh al-Salāma (Riyadh: Maktabat al-Rushd, 1425), 441.

4 ʿAbdallāh b. Aḥmad b. Ḥanbal, *al-Sunna*, ed. ʿAbdallāh b. Ḥasan b. Ḥusayn (Mecca: al-Maṭbaʿa al-Salafiyya, 1349), 199, five other versions 201–203, 211 (all references are to this edition unless noted as ed. Zaghlūl) = ed. Abū Hājir Muḥammad Saʿīd b. Basyūnī Zaghlūl (Beirut: Dār al-Kutub al-ʿIlmiyya, 1405/1985), 229, five other versions 230, 232, 240. Ibn Saʿd quotes ʿAlī to similar effect, *Kitāb al-ṭabaqāt al-kabīr*, ed. Eduard Sachau et al. (Leiden: E. J. Brill, 1904–40), 6:89 (all references are to this edition unless noted as Dār Ṣādir edition) = *al-Ṭabaqāt al-kubrā* (Beirut: Dār Ṣādir, 1957–68), 6:130.

5 Patricia Crone and Martin Hinds, *God's Caliph: Religious Authority in the First Centuries of Islam* (Cambridge: University Press, 1986), 26–32. But compare also a report from the Prophet blamed on an unreliable transmitter of the early third/ninth century: "I am the first, Abū Bakr the second, and ʿUmar the third, while the people after us will be one after another": Ibn ʿAdī l-Qaṭṭān, *al-Kāmil fī ḍuʿafāʾ al-rijāl*, ed. ʿĀdil Aḥmad ʿAbd al-Mawjūd and ʿAlī Muḥammad Muʿawwaḍ (Beirut: Dār al-Kutub al-ʿIlmiyya, 1418/1997), 2:96.

6 ʿAbdallāh b. Aḥmad b. Ḥanbal, *al-Sunna*, 191–192; ed. Zaghlūl, 220–221.

7 ʿAbdallāh b. Aḥmad b. Ḥanbal, *al-Sunna*, 193–194; ed. Zaghlūl, 223.

8 ʿAbdallāh b. Aḥmad b. Ḥanbal, *al-Sunna*, 208–209; ed. Zaghlūl, 238; Aḥmad b. Ḥanbal, *al-Musnad* (Cairo: al-Maṭbaʿa al-Maymaniyya, 1313/1895), 5:382, 385, 402 (all references are to this edition unless noted as ed. Arnaʾūṭ) = ed. Shuʿayb al-Arnaʾūṭ et al. (Beirut: Muʾassasat al-Risāla, 1413–21/1993–2001), 38:280–282, 309–311, 418–419; al-Tirmidhī, *al-Jāmiʿ, al-manāqib* 37, no. 3805; Ibn Māja, *al-Sunan, al-sunna* 11, *fī faḍāʾil aṣḥāb rasūl Allāh*, no. 97; Ibn Saʿd, *Ṭabaqāt* 2/2:98; Dār Ṣādir edition, 2:334; Ibn Abī Shayba, *al-Muṣannaf*, ed. Ḥamad ʿAbdallāh al-Jumʿa and Muḥammad Ibrāhīm al-Luḥaydān (Riyadh: Maktabat al-Rushd, 1425/2004), 11:104 (all references are to this edition, unless noted as ed. ʿAwwāma) = ed. Muḥammad ʿAwwāma (Jedda: Dār al-Qibla and Damascus: Muʾassasat ʿUlūm al-Qurʾān, 1427/2006), 17:35-36.

9 Al-Nasāʾī, *al-Sunan al-kubrā, al-manāqib* 2, *faḍl Abī Bakr wa-ʿUmar*, no. 8118.

10 Aḥmad b. Ḥanbal, *Kitāb al-ʿilal wa-maʿrifat al-rijāl*, ed. Waṣī Allāh b. Muḥammad ʿAbbās (Beirut: al-Maktab al-Islāmī, 1988), 2:535 (all references are to this edition, unless noted as ed. Bayḍūn) = ed. Muḥammad Ḥusām Bayḍūn (Beirut: Muʾassasat al-Kutub al-Thaqāfiyya, 1410/1990), 2:47; also Ṣāliḥ b. Aḥmad, *Masāʾil al-imām Aḥmad b. Ḥanbal*, ed. Ṭāriq b. ʿAwaḍ Allāh b. Muḥammad (Riyadh: Dār al-Waṭan, 1420/1999), 210, with a similar gloss.

11 Ibn Saʿd, *Ṭabaqāt* 6:173; Dār Ṣādir edition, 6:248; ʿAbdallāh b. Aḥmad b. Ḥanbal, *al-Sunna*, 193; ed. Zaghlūl, 222, with more instances, 193; ed. Zaghlūl, 222–223. On al-Shaʿbī's loyalty to the Umayyads, see Steven C. Judd, *Religious Scholars and the Umayyads* (London: Routledge, 2014), 41–51.

12 Al-Tirmidhī, *al-Jāmiʿ, manāqib* 18, *manāqib ʿUthmān b. ʿAffān*, no. 3697; similarly, Ibn Abī ʿĀṣim, *al-Sunna*, ed. Muḥammad Nāṣir al-Dīn al-Albānī (Beirut: al-Maktab al-Islāmī, 1400/1980), 2:594 (all references are to this edition, unless noted as Dār Ibn Ḥazm edition) = (Beirut: Dār Ibn Ḥazm, 1424/2004), 300, with the scene shifted from Uḥud near Medina to Thubayr near Mecca. Cf. van Ess, "Political Ideas," 155.

13 Al-Bukhārī, *al-Ṣaḥīḥ, faḍāʾil aṣḥāb al-nabī* 7, *bāb manāqib ʿUthmān b. ʿAffān*, no. 3698; similarly, no. 3655. Also Abū Dāwūd, *al-Sunan, al-sunna* 7, *bāb fī l-tafḍīl*, nos. 4627–4628; Ibn Hānī, *Masāʾil al-imām Aḥmad b. Ḥanbal*, ed. Zuhayr al-Shāwīsh

(Beirut: al-Maktab al-Islāmī, 1400), 2:170; ʿAbdallāh b. Aḥmad b. Ḥanbal, *al-Sunna*, 206–208; ed. Zaghlūl, 236–237 (11 versions, in one of which, however, with a Kufan *isnād*, Ibn ʿUmar mentions only Abū Bakr and ʿUmar; the same in Ibn Abī Shayba, 11:102; ed. ʿAwwāma, 17:31–32); Ibn Abī ʿĀṣim, *Sunna* 2:539, Dār Ibn Ḥazm edition, 264 (in which, uniquely, Ibn ʿUmar specifies that this is with regard to the caliphate; Medinese *isnād*). Cf. Ibn Abī ʿĀṣim, *al-Sunna* 2:569–571; Dār Ibn Ḥazm edition, 276–278 (Syrian/Medinan *isnād*, Abū Hurayra instead of Ibn ʿUmar).

14 Ibn Abī ʿĀṣim, *al-Sunna* 2:569–570; Dār Ibn Ḥazm edition, 277.

15 Al-Bukhārī, *al-Jāmiʿ*, *al-libās* 6, *bāb khātam al-fiḍḍa*, no. 5866. Similarly, Muslim, *al-Ṣaḥīḥ*, Kitāb al-libās wa-l-zīna 12, *lubs al-nabī … khātaman min wariq*, no. 2091; Abū Dāwūd, *al-Sunan*, Kitāb al-khātam 1, no. 4218; al-Nasāʾī, *al-Mujtabā*, Kitāb al-zīna 53, *nazʿ al-khātam ʿinda dukhūl al-khalāʾ*, no. 5220; al-Nasāʾī, *al-Sunan al-kubrā*, al-zīna 73, *dhikr ikhtilāf alfāẓ al-nāqilīn li-khabar Nāfiʿ ʿan Ibn ʿUmar fī khātam al-dhahab*, nos. 9048, 9550; Ibn Saʿd, *Ṭabaqāt* 1/2:162–163, 165; Dār Ṣādir edition, 1:472–473, 476–477; Ibn Abī Shayba, 8:340; ed. ʿAwwāma, 12:583–584.

16 Ibn Saʿd, *Ṭabaqāt* 1/2:165; Dār Ṣādir edition, 1:476–477.

17 Ibn Abī ʿĀṣim, *al-Sunna* 2:542; Dār Ibn Ḥazm edition, 265.

18 Ibn Saʿd, *Ṭabaqāt* 1/2:165; Dār Ṣādir edition, 1:477.

19 Ibn Saʿd, *Ṭabaqāt* 1/2:166; Dār Ṣādir edition, 1:477–478.

20 Abū Dāwūd, *al-Sunna*, 8, *bāb fī l-khulafāʾ*, nos. 4634–4635 (also a third version, no 4636, in which it is the Prophet's own dream); al-Tirmidhī, *al-Jāmiʿ*, *abwāb al-ruʾya* 10, *bāb mā jāʾa fī ruʾyā l-nabī … fī l-mīzān wa-l-dalw*, no. 2287; al-Nasāʾī, *al-Sunan al-kubrā*, *al-manāqib* 3, *faḍāʾil Abī Bakr wa-ʿUmar wa-ʿUthmān*, no. 8136. Other versions of the story of three caliphs weighed against each other, sometimes with Kufan *isnād*s, at Ibn Abī Shayba, 10:327–328, 11:108–109; ed. ʿAwwāma, 16:40–43, 17:46–47; and Aḥmad b. Ḥanbal, *al-Musnad* 2:76, ed. Arnaʾūṭ, 9:338–339.

21 Aḥmad b. Ḥanbal, *al-Musnad* 5:44; ed. Arnaʾūṭ. 34:94–97; similarly, 5:50; ed. Arnaʾūṭ, 34:140–142.

22 Aḥmad b. Ḥanbal, *al-Musnad* 5:21; ed. Arnaʾūṭ, 33:384–386. Cf. Ibn Abī Shayba, 10:329; ed. ʿAwwāma, 16:43–44 (Medinan *isnād*, Abū Bakr and ʿUmar only); Abū Dāwūd, *al-Sunna* 8, *bāb fī l-khulafāʾ*, no. 4637 (Basran *isnād*, Abū Bakr, ʿUmar, ʿUthmān, and ʿAlī, the last of whom is the one besmirched); similarly, Ibn Abī ʿĀṣim, *al-Sunna*, 2:540; Dār Ibn Ḥazm edition, 264.

23 Van Ess, "Political Ideas," 155.

24 As observed by ibid.

25 ʿAbd al-Razzāq, *al-Muṣannaf*, ed. Ḥabīb al-Raḥmān al-Aʿẓamī (Johannesburg: Majlis Ilmi, 1390–2/1970–21), 1:317–318.

26 A detailed study plausibly concludes that ʿAbd al-Razzāq's Shīʿism was fairly mild, extending to the occasional denigration of ʿUthmān and possibly those who fought against ʿAlī, but not to the wholesale rejection of the Companions: Asmāʾ

Ibrāhīm Saʿūd ʿAjīn, *Manhaj al-ḥāfiẓ ʿAbd al-Razzāq al-Ṣanʿānī* (Amman: al-Dār al-ʿUthmāniyya and Cairo: al-Maktaba al-Islāmiyya, 1429/2008), 79–91.

27 Ibn al-Nadīm, *Kitāb al-fihrist, maqāla* 5, *fann* 6, ed. Gustav Flügel with Johannes Roediger and August Müller (Leipzig: F. C. W. Vogel, 1872), 178. The sources tend to agree as to Ṣāliḥ b. Ṣāliḥ b. Ḥayy (d. 153/770), little is said of the theological position of Ibn ʿUyayna (d. 198/814), while a wide variety of positions are ascribed to Sufyān al-Thawrī (d. 161/777?), which I will not detail here. All three started out in Kufa, although Ibn ʿUyayna died in Mecca and al-Thawrī in Basra.

28 Al-Mardāwī, *al-Inṣāf fī maʿrifat al-rājiḥ min al-khilāf*, ed. Muḥammad Ḥāmid al-Fiqī (Cairo: Maṭbaʿat al-Sunna al-Muḥammadiyya, 1955–58; repr. n.p.: Dār Iḥyāʾ al-Turāth al-ʿArabī, 1419/1998), 12:36.

29 Michael Cook argues that this tendency originated in Kufa in opposition to Kufan Shīʿism: "Activism and Quietism in Islam: The Case of the Early *Murjiʾa*," in *Islam and Power*, ed. Alexander S. Cudsi and Ali E. Hillal Dessouki (London: Croom Helm, 1981), 15–23. This agrees with my supposition concerning the two-caliph hypothesis.

30 Ibn Saʿd, *Ṭabaqāt* 6:214; Dār Ṣādir edition, 6:307.

31 A. J. Wensinck, *The Muslim Creed* (Cambridge: Cambridge University Press, 1932; repr. New Delhi: Oriental Books Reprint Corp., 1979), 104. On Abū Muṭīʿ, see Ibn Abī l-Wafāʾ, *al-Jawāhir al-muḍiyya fī ṭabaqāt al-ḥanafiyya*, ed. ʿAbd al-Fattāḥ Muḥammad al-Ḥulw (Cairo: Dār Iḥyāʾ al-Kutub al-ʿArabiyya, 1398–1408/1978–88, repr. Giza: Hajr, 1413/1993), 4:87–88; also al-Dhahabī, *Tārīkh al-islām*, ed. ʿUmar ʿAbd al-Salām Tadmurī (Beirut: Dār al-Kitāb al-ʿArabī, 1407–21/1987–2000), 14:158–160, with further references; and van Ess, *Theologie* 2:536–539.

32 Ibn Saʿd, *Ṭabaqāt* 7/2:106; Dār Ṣādir edition, 7:374. See also Ibn Abī Ḥātim, *Kitāb al-jarḥ wa-l-taʿdīl* (Hyderabad: Jamʿiyyat Dāʾirat al-Maʿārif al-ʿUthmāniyya, 1360–71, repr. Beirut: Dār Iḥyāʾ al-Turāth al-ʿArabī, n.d.), 3:122.

33 Wensinck, *Muslim Creed*, 125, 127. As to who actually came up with *al-Waṣiyya*, Wensinck will say no more than that it originated some time before the mid-ninth century (*Muslim Creed*, 187).

34 Ibn Saʿd, *Ṭabaqāt* 7/2:18; Dār Ṣādir edition, 7:253.

35 Aḥmad b. Ḥanbal, *ʿIlal* 3:473; ed. Bayḍūn, 2:272.

36 P. Crone, s.v. "ʿUthmāniyya," in *Encyclopaedia of Islam*, 2nd ed. (Leiden: Brill, 2000), 10:952–954.

37 Ibn Saʿd, *Ṭabaqāt*, 7/2:24–25, 42, 44–45; Dār Ṣādir edition, 7:261–262, 286, 289–290.

38 Ibn Saʿd, *Ṭabaqāt*, 6:224, 7/2:195; Dār Ṣādir edition, 6:321, 7:503.

39 Abū Dāwūd, *al-Sunna*, 8, *bāb fī l-khulafāʾ*, no. 4646; similarly, al-Tirmidhī, *al-Jāmiʿ*, *al-fitan* 48, *bāb mā jāʾa fī l-khilāfa*, no. 2226, also al-Nasāʾī, *al-Sunan al-kubrā*, *manāqib* 5, *Abū Bakr wa-ʿUmar wa-ʿUthmān wa-ʿAlī*, no. 8155; Aḥmad b. Ḥanbal,

al-Musnad 5:220–221; ed. Arnaʾūṭ, 36:248–250, 252–253, 256–257. Cf. ʿAbdallāh b. Aḥmad b. Ḥanbal, *al-Sunna*, 215; ed. Zaghlūl, 244, where Safīna expressly counts six years for ʿAlī and denies that the Marwānids are caliphs, and Abū Dāwūd al-Ṭayālisī, *Musnad Abī Dāwūd al-Ṭayālisī* (Hyderabad: Maṭbaʿat Majlis Dāʾirat al-Maʿārif al-Niẓāmiyya, 1321, repr. Beirut: Dār al-Maʿrifa, n.d.), 151, no. 1107, where Safīna expressly names Muʿāwiya as first of the kings.

40 ʿAbdallāh b. Aḥmad b. Ḥanbal, *al-Sunna*, 214; ed. Zaghlūl, 243. But Aḥmad is also quoted as making Ibn ʿUmar identify the caliphs as Abū Bakr, ʿUmar, ʿUthmān, and ʿAlī: ʿAbdallāh b. Aḥmad b. Ḥanbal, *al-Sunna*, 206; ed. Zaghlūl, 235. There is some disagreement over exactly where Aḥmad put ʿAlī. See Christopher Melchert, "A Response to Saud al-Sarhan's 'The Creeds of Aḥmad ibn Ḥanbal,'" in *Books and Bibliophiles: Studies in Honour of Paul Auchterlonie*, ed. Robert Gleave (N.p.: Gibb Memorial Trust, 2014), 46–47.

41 Muslim, *Ṣaḥīḥ Muslim, faḍāʾil al-ṣaḥāba* 6, *min faḍāʾil Ṭalḥa wa-l-Zubayr*, no. 2417; al-Tirmidhī, *al-Jāmiʿ*, *manāqib* 18, *manāqib ʿUthmān b. ʿAffān*, no. 3696; al-Nasāʾī, *al-Sunan al-kubrā, manāqib* 5, *Abū Bakr wa-ʿUmar wa-ʿUthmān wa-ʿAlī*, no. 8156.

42 Ibn ʿAdī l-Qaṭṭān, *Kāmil*, 7:475.

43 Abū Dāwūd, *al-Sunna*, 5, *bāb fī luzūm al-sunna*, no. 4607; al-Tirmidhī, *al-Jāmiʿ*, *abwāb al-ʿilm* 16, *bāb mā jāʾa fī l-akhdh bi-l-sunna wa-ijtināb al-bidaʿ*, no. 2676; Ibn Māja, *al-Sunan*, 6, *bāb ittibāʿ sunnat al-khulafāʾ al-rāshidīn al-mahdiyyīn*, nos. 42–44; al-Dārimī, *Sunan, muqaddima* 16, *bāb ittibāʿ al-sunna*; Aḥmad b. Ḥanbal, *al-Musnad* 4:126–127; ed. Arnaʾūṭ, 28:367–368, 373–379.

44 See Henri Laoust, "Le role de ʿAli dans la *sira* chiite," *Revue des études islamiques* 30 (1963), 25–26.

45 Ibn Abī Shayba, 14:187–188; ed. ʿAwwāma, 21:299.

46 Abū Dāwūd, *al-Sunna* 7, *bāb fī l-tafḍīl*, no. 4631. For further examples, see Murād, "Umar II's view," 53 n. 41.

47 Abū Dāwūd, *Kitāb masāʾil al-imām Aḥmad*, ed. Muḥammad Bahja al-Bayṭār (Cairo: Dār al-Manār, 1353/1934, repr. Beirut: Muḥammad Amīn Damj, n.d.), 277.

48 Aḥmad b. Ḥanbal, *al-Zuhd*, ed. ʿAbd al-Raḥmān b. Qāsim (Mecca: Maṭbaʿat Umm al-Qurā, 1357), 292; reprinted with new pagination (Beirut: Dār al-Kutub al-ʿIlmiyya, 1403/1983), 356; Abū Nuʿaym, *Ḥilya*, 5:256–257.

49 Aḥmad b. Ḥanbal, *al-Zuhd*, 291–292; Beirut edition, 355–356.

50 Abū Nuʿaym, *Ḥilya*, 5:298.

51 See above, n. 41.

52 Al-Khaṭṭābī, *Maʿālim al-sunan*, ed. Muḥammad Rāghib al-Ṭabbākh (Aleppo, 1351–52/1932–34, repr. Beirut: al-Maktaba al-ʿIlmiyya, 1401/1981), 4:302–303; and ed. ʿAbd al-Salām ʿAbd al-Shāfī Muḥammad (Beirut: Dār al-Kutub al-ʿIlmiyya, 1416/1996), 4:279–280.

53 Ibn Ḥajar, *Fatḥ al-bārī bi-sharḥ Ṣaḥīḥ al-Bukhārī*, ad *k. faḍāʾil al-aṣḥāb* 7, *bāb manāqib ʿUthmān*, no. 3698, ed. ʿAbd al-ʿAzīz b. ʿAbdallāh Bāz Bāz (Beirut: Dār al-Fikr, 1428–9/2008), 7:325.

Bibliography

ʿAbd al-Razzāq. *al-Muṣannaf.* Edited by Ḥabīb al-Raḥmān al-Aʿẓamī, Min Manshūrāt al-Majlis al-ʿIlmī 39. 11 vols. Johannesburg: Majlis Ilmi, 1390–92/1970–72.

Abū Dāwūd al-Sijistānī. *Kitāb masāʾil al-imām Aḥmad.* Edited by Muḥammad Bahja al-Bayṭār. Cairo: Dār al-Manār, 1353/1934; repr. Beirut: Muḥammad Amīn Damj, n.d.

Abū Dāwūd al-Sijistānī. *al-Sunan.* Edited by Shuʿayb al-Arnaʾūṭ and Muḥammad Kāmil Qarah Balilī. 7 vols. Beirut: Dār al-Rasāʾil al-ʿĀlamiyya, 1430/2009.

Abū Dāwūd al-Ṭayālisī. *Musnad Abī Dāwūd al-Ṭayālisī.* Hyderabad: Maṭbaʿat Majlis Dāʾirat al-Maʿārif al-Niẓāmiyya, 1321; repr. Beirut: Dār al-Maʿrifa, n.d.

ʿAjīn, Asmāʾ Ibrāhīm Saʿūd. *Manhaj al-ḥāfiẓ ʿAbd al-Razzāq al-Ṣanʿānī.* Amman: al-Dār al-ʿUthmāniyya and Cairo: al-Maktaba al-Islāmiyya, 1429/2008.

al-Bukhārī. *al-Jāmiʿ al-musnad al-ṣaḥīḥ al-mukhtaṣar.* In Ibn Ḥajar, *Fatḥ al-bārī bi-sharḥ Ṣaḥīḥ al-Bukhārī*, edited by ʿAbd al-ʿAzīz b.ʿAbdallāh b. Bāz. 15 vols. Beirut: Dār al-Fikr, 1428–29/2008.

Cook, Michael. "Activism and Quietism in Islam: The Case of the Early Murji'a." In *Islam and Power*, edited by Alexander S. Cudsi and Ali E. Hillal Dessouki, 15–23. Croom Helm ser. on the Arab world. London: Croom Helm, 1981.

Crone, Patricia. "ʿUthmāniyya." In *Encyclopaedia of Islam*, new ed., edited by P. J. Bearman, Th. Bianquis, C. E. Bosworth, E. van Donzel, and W. P. Heinrichs, 10:952–954. Leiden: Brill, 2000.

Crone, Patricia, and Martin Hinds. *God's Caliph: Religious Authority in the First Centuries of Islam.* University of Cambridge Oriental Publications 37. Cambridge: Cambridge University Press, 1986.

al-Dhahabī. *Tārīkh al-islām.* Edited by ʿUmar ʿAbd al-Salām Tadmurī. 52 vols. Beirut: Dār al-Kitāb al-ʿArabī, 1407–21/1987–2000.

van Ess, Josef. "Political Ideas in Early Islamic Religious Thought." *British Journal of Middle Eastern Studies* 28 (2001): 151–164.

van Ess, Josef. *Theologie und Gesellschaft im 2. und 3. Jahrhundert Hidschra.* 6 vols. Berlin: Walter de Gruyter, 1991–95.

Ibn Abī ʿĀṣim. *al-Sunna.* Edited by Muḥammad Nāṣir al-Dīn al-Albānī. 2 vols. Beirut: al-Maktab al-Islāmī, 1400/1980.

Ibn Abī ʿĀṣim. *al-Sunna.* Beirut: Dār Ibn Ḥazm, 1424/2004.

Ibn Abī Ḥātim. *Kitāb al-jarḥ wa-l-taʿdīl.* 9 vols. Hyderabad: Jamʿiyyat Dāʾirat al-Maʿārif al-ʿUthmāniyya, 1360–71; repr. Beirut: Dār Iḥyāʾ al-Turāth al-ʿArabī, n.d.

Ibn Abī Shayba. *al-Muṣannaf*. Edited by Ḥamad ʿAbdallāh al-Jumʿa and Muḥammad Ibrāhīm al-Luḥaydān. 16 vols. Riyadh: Maktabat al-Rushd, 1425/2004.

Ibn Abī Shayba. *al-Muṣannaf*. Edited by Muḥammad ʿAwwāma. 26 vols. Jedda: Dār al-Qibla and Damascus: Muʾassasat ʿUlūm al-Qurʾān, 1427/2006.

Ibn Abī l-Wafāʾ. *al-Jawāhir al-muḍiyya fī ṭabaqāt al-ḥanafiyya*. Edited by ʿAbd al-Fattāḥ Muḥammad al-Ḥulw. 5 vols. Cairo: Dār Iḥyāʾ al-Kutub al-ʿArabiyya, 1398–1408/1978–88; repr. Giza: Hajr, 1413/1993.

Ibn ʿAdī l-Qaṭṭān. *al-Kāmil fī ḍuʿafāʾ al-rijāl*. Edited by ʿĀdil Aḥmad ʿAbd al-Mawjūd and ʿAlī Muḥammad Muʿawwaḍ. 9 vols. Beirut: Dār al-Kutub al-ʿIlmiyya, 1418/1997.

Ibn Ḥajar. *Fatḥ al-bārī bi-sharḥ Ṣaḥīḥ al-Bukhārī*. Edited by ʿAbd al-ʿAzīz b. ʿAbdallāh b. Bāz. 15 vols. Beirut: Dār al-Fikr, 1428–9/2008.

Ibn Ḥanbal, ʿAbdallāh b. Aḥmad. *al-Sunna*. Edited by ʿAbdallāh b. Ḥasan b. Ḥusayn. Mecca: al-Maṭbaʿa al-Salafiyya, 1349.

Ibn Ḥanbal, ʿAbdallāh b. Aḥmad. *al-Sunna*. Edited by Abū Hājir Muḥammad Saʿīd b. Basyūnī Zaghlūl. Beirut: Dār al-Kutub al-ʿIlmiyya, 1405/1985.

Ibn Ḥanbal, Aḥmad. *Kitāb al-ʿilal wa-maʿrifat al-rijāl*. Edited by Waṣī Allāh b. Muḥammad ʿAbbās. 4 vols. Beirut: al-Maktab al-Islāmī, 1988.

Ibn Ḥanbal, Aḥmad. *Kitāb al-ʿilal wa-maʿrifat al-rijāl*. Edited by Muḥammad Ḥusām Bayḍūn. 2 vols. Beirut: Muʾassasat al-Kutub al-Thaqāfiyya, 1410/1990.

Ibn Ḥanbal, Aḥmad. *al-Musnad*. 6 vols. Cairo: al-Maṭbaʿa al-Maymaniyya, 1313/1895.

Ibn Ḥanbal, Aḥmad. *al-Musnad*. Edited by Shuʿayb al-Arnaʾūṭ et al. 50 vols. Beirut: Muʾassasat al-Risāla, 1413–21/1993–2001.

Ibn Ḥanbal, Aḥmad. *al-Zuhd*. Edited by ʿAbd al-Raḥmān b. Qāsim. Mecca: Maṭbaʿat Umm al-Qurā, 1357; reprinted with new pagination: Beirut: Dār al-Kutub al-ʿIlmiyya, 1403/1983.

Ibn Ḥanbal, Ṣāliḥ b. Aḥmad. *Masāʾil al-imām Aḥmad b. Ḥanbal*. Edited by Ṭāriq b. ʿAwaḍ Allāh b. Muḥammad. Riyadh: Dār al-Waṭan, 1420/1999.

Ibn Hānī. *Masāʾil al-imām Aḥmad b. Ḥanbal*. Edited by Zuhayr al-Shāwīsh. 2 vols. Beirut: al-Maktab al-Islāmī, 1400.

Ibn Māja. *al-Sunan*. Edited by Bashshār ʿAwwād Maʿrūf. 6 vols. Beirut: Dār al-Jīl, 1418/1998.

Ibn al-Nadīm. *Kitāb al-fihrist*. Edited by Gustav Flügel with Johannes Roediger and August Müller. Leipzig: F. C. W. Vogel, 1872.

Ibn Saʿd. *Kitāb al-ṭabaqāt al-kabīr*. Edited by Eduard Sachau et al. 9 vols in 15. Leiden: E. J. Brill, 1904–40.

Ibn Saʿd. *al-Ṭabaqāt al-kubrā*. 9 vols. Beirut: Dār Ṣādir, 1957–68.

Judd, Steven C. *Religious Scholars and the Umayyads*. Culture and Civilization in the Middle East 40. London: Routledge, 2014.

al-Khaṭṭābī. *Maʿālim al-sunan*. Edited by Muḥammad Rāghib al-Ṭabbākh. 4 vols in 3. Aleppo, 1351–52/1932–34; repr. Beirut: al-Maktaba al-ʿIlmiyya, 1401/1981.

al-Khaṭṭābī. *Maʿālim al-sunan*. Edited by ʿAbd al-Salām ʿAbd al-Shāfī Muḥammad. 4 vols in 2. Beirut: Dār al-Kutub al-ʿIlmiyya, 1416/1996.

al-Kirmānī, Ḥarb. *Masāʾil al-imām Aḥmad b. Muḥammad b. Ḥanbal wa-Isḥāq b. Rāhūyah*. Edited by Nāṣir b. Saʿūd b. ʿAbdallāh al-Salāma. Riyadh: Maktabat al-Rushd, 1425.

Laoust, Henri. "Le role de 'Ali dans la *sira* chiite." *Revue des études islamiques* 30 (1963): 7–26.

Madelung, Wilferd. *Der Imam al-Qāsim ibn Ibrāhīm und die Glaubenslehre der Zaiditen*. Studien zur Sprache, Geschichte und Kultur des islamischen Orients, n.F. 1. Berlin: Walter de Gruyter, 1965.

al-Mardāwī, ʿAlī b. Sulaymān. *al-Inṣāf fī maʿrifat al-rājiḥ min al-khilāf*. Edited by Muḥammad Ḥāmid al-Fiqī. 12 vols. Cairo: Maṭbaʿat al-Sunna al-Muḥammadiyya, 1955–58; repr. N.p.: Dār Iḥyāʾ al-Turāth al-ʿArabī, 1419/1998.

Melchert, Christopher. "A Response to Saud al-Sarhan's "The Creeds of Aḥmad ibn Ḥanbal."" In *Books and Bibliophiles: Studies in Honour of Paul Auchterlonie*, edited by Robert Gleave, 45–50. N.p.: Gibb Memorial Trust, 2014.

Murād, Ḥasan Qāsim. "'Umar II's View of the Patriarchal Caliphs." *Hamdard Islamicus* 10/1 (1987): 31–56.

Muslim. *Ṣaḥīḥ Muslim bi-sharḥ al-Nawawī*. 18 vols. Cairo: al-Maṭbaʿa al-Miṣriyya, 1347–9/1929–30; repr. 19 vols. Beirut: Dār al-Kutub al-ʿIlmiyya, 1415/1995.

al-Nasāʾī. *al-Mujtabā = Sunan al-Nasāʾī l-ṣughrā*. Edited by Ṣāliḥ b. ʿAbd al-ʿAzīz b. Muḥammad b. Ibrāhīm Āl al-Shaykh. Riyadh: Dār al-Salām, 1420/1999.

al-Nasāʾī. *al-Sunan al-kubrā*. Edited by ʿAbd al-Ghaffār Sulaymān al-Bundārī and Sayyid Kisrawī Ḥasan. 7 vols. Beirut: Dār al-Kutub al-ʿIlmiyya, 1411/1991.

al-Tirmidhī. *al-Jāmiʿ al-kabīr*. Edited by Bashshār ʿAwwād Maʿrūf. 6 vols. Beirut: Dār al-Gharb al-Islāmī, 1996.

Wensinck, A. J. *The Muslim Creed*. Cambridge: Cambridge University Press, 1932; repr. New Delhi: Oriental Books Reprint Corp., 1979.

4

"Patience in Our Situation is Better than Sedition": The Shift to Political Quietism in the Sunnī Tradition

Saud al-Sarhan

Scholars have noted that political quietism lies at the heart of Sunnī political doctrine and particularly that of the Ḥanbalīs.[1] This chapter argues that until the second half of the third/ninth century, two trends coexisted among early Islamic traditionalists,[2] one arguing for political activism and one for quietism. It was thanks to Aḥmad b. Ḥanbal that quietism eventually became the formal doctrine of the Sunnīs. In this chapter, I also examine the methods that Ibn Ḥanbal used to support quietism and to undermine Islamic traditions that seemed to endorse activism. Finally, I consider the differing reports about Ibn Ḥanbal's relationship with the authorities in his time and address the question of whether or not he collaborated with the rulers.

The roots of quietism in Sunnī jurisprudence

We can identify several individuals in Islamic history as key actors in the shift to quietism in the Sunnī tradition. The first was the Companion Ibn ʿUmar (d. 74/693), whose view on quietism is essential to understanding the Sunnī doctrine; as Sufyān al-Thawrī (d. 161/778) states, "We adhere to ʿUmar's opinion in times of unity, and to that of his son in times of division."[3] Keeping out of internal fights between Muslims was a fundamental aspect of Ibn ʿUmar's thought; when al-Ḥusayn b. ʿAlī (killed 61/680) and Ibn al-Zubayr (killed 73/692) left Medina after refusing to declare allegiance to Yazīd I in 60/680, they met with Ibn ʿUmar, who warned them not to divide the Muslim community.[4] Ibn ʿUmar also cautioned people against fighting on either side of the civil war, as neither the rebels nor the rulers were fighting for religious reasons.[5] During the war between Ibn al-Zubayr and al-Ḥajjāj (d. 95/714), a man asked Ibn ʿUmar which party he should fight with, and Ibn ʿUmar answered, "If you fought and were killed, you would burn in hell [*laẓā*], whichever party you fought with."[6]

After Ibn ʿUmar, the Basran successor Muṭarrif b. al-Shikhkhīr (d. 95/713–4) played an important role at the time of the rebellion of Ibn al-Ashʿath (81–3/700–2). Muṭarrif vociferously urged people to steer clear of rebellion.[7] In addition to emphasizing communal unity and warning of the harmful consequences of *fitna* (sedition), he noted that rebellion was without merit for the people, regardless of who might win. It was reported that when Ibn al-Shikhkhīr was informed about Ibn al-Ashʿath's revolt, he said: "If he [Ibn al-Ashʿath] were victorious, he would not stand with the doctrine of God's religion. And if he were defeated, they [Ibn al-Ashʿath and his army] would be servile [under the Umayyads' control] until the day of resurrection."[8]

After the disastrous end of Ibn al-Ashʿath's rebellion, the balance among the Sunnīs shifted from activism to quietism. While the majority of Sunnīs became quietists, activism also continued. Some Sunnīs took part in, or at least supported, the rebellions of Muḥammad b. al-Ḥasan (al-Nafs al-Zakiyya) and his brother Ibrāhīm. These Sunnīs included Abū Ḥanīfa, Mālik b. Anas, and some of Aḥmad b. Ḥanbal's teachers, such as Yazīd b. Hārūn and Hushaym b. Saʿīd.[9] Al-Shāfiʿī was also reported to be an activist.[10]

Aḥmad b. Ḥanbal's quietist doctrine

It was most likely Aḥmad b. Ḥanbal who definitively established quietism as the formal Sunnī doctrine. To achieve this, he employed a variety of methods. These included the following.

1. Ibn Ḥanbal strongly supported the doctrines of quietism. His pupil al-Marrūdhī (d. 275/888) reported that Ibn Ḥanbal demanded a halt to bloodshed and rebellion,[11] since such civil unrest was unsafe for the people. Thus, he argued, being patient and submitting to rulers was better for one's religion and security.[12]

2. By the beginning of the third/ninth century, two types of prophetic traditions could be found among traditionalists: some supported the doctrines of quietism, while others advocated activism. Ibn Ḥanbal's method, as noted by al-Khallāl (d. 311/923), was to accept the traditions that condemned rebellion and called for saving Muslims' blood, and to reject the opposing traditions that

endorsed revolution against unjust or sinful rulers. Ibn Ḥanbal was asked about a tradition attributed to the Prophet, which said: "Stand up for the Quraysh as long as they stand up for you. If they do not, put your swords upon your shoulders and destroy them all." According to several reports, Ibn Ḥanbal rejected this tradition because it contradicted other sound traditions, such as "Listen and obey, even if [your ruler] is a black slave" and "Listen [to your rulers] and obey [them], as long as they perform prayers."[13]

Another example is a tradition accepted as sound by many traditionalists (including al-Bukhārī and Muslim) that quoted the Prophet as saying: "This people of Quraysh will destroy my nation." The Companions asked him: "What, then, do you order us to do?" The Prophet replied: "People should retreat from them."[14] Al-Marrūdhī claimed that Ibn Ḥanbal dismissed this as "a bad tradition," adding that "these Muʿtazilīs rely on it" as justification for not attending Friday prayers.[15] Interestingly, this tradition was included in Ibn Ḥanbal's *Musnad*,[16] but ʿAbdallāh b. Aḥmad claimed that "on his deathbed, my father ordered me to 'omit this tradition, because it contradicts other prophetic traditions.' He meant [the Prophet's] saying: 'Listen, obey and stand patient.'"[17] Apparently, ʿAbdallāh did not follow his father's instructions.

3. Ibn Ḥanbal also criticized activist *salaf* and traditionalists. He disagreed with Saʿīd b. Jubayr (d. 95/714), a famous activist successor who was executed as a result of his involvement in Ibn al-Ashʿath's revolt.[18] When Ibn Ḥanbal was asked about a Zaydī activist, al-Ḥasan b. Ḥayy (d. 167/783), he said, "He [i.e., Ibn Ḥayy] believes in [using] the sword [against unjust rulers(?)], and this is not accepted; we prefer Sufyān [al-Thawrī] over him."[19] It became commonplace for quietist traditionalists to criticize activists by accusing them of "believing in [using] the sword."[20]

4. In addition, Ibn Ḥanbal sought to rewrite the revolutionary aspect of Sunnī history by omitting or at least minimizing it. Along with other quietist traditionalists, Ibn Ḥanbal attempted to downplay the number of Companions and successors who were involved in the first civil war[21]; at the same time he criticized traditionalists, recalled the events of the *fitna*, and named the Companions and the successors who had been involved in these events.[22] The famous (Shāfiʿī?) jurisprudent al-Ḥusayn al-Karābīsī (d. 248/862) wrote *al-Mudallisūn* [The distorters] during Ibn Ḥanbal's lifetime; in the book, al-Karābīsī attacked al-Aʿmash (d. 148/765–6) and defended al-Ḥasan b. Ḥayy. When Ibn Ḥanbal was asked about this book and especially about the part on Ibn Ḥayy, in which al-Karābīsī had written, "If you say al-Ḥasan b. Ṣāliḥ [Ibn Ḥayy] believed in the Khārijī doctrine, [we will say] here is Ibn al-Zubayr, who revolted," Ibn

Ḥanbal commented: "This [man] supports our adversaries in what they cannot do for themselves. Warn [people] of this [book]."[23]

Another example of Ibn Ḥanbal's views can be found in the works of the famous traditionalist Nuʿaym b. Ḥammād al-Marwazī (d. 228/843), whose book *al-Fitan* includes a chapter with the title "What is narrated regarding the regret of the Companions and others at the time of the *fitna* and after it."[24] The chapter contains a number of reports from eminent Companions such as ʿAlī b. Abī Ṭālib, ʿĀʾisha, Ṭalḥa, al-Zubayr, and ʿAmmār b. Yāsir; these reports state that they regretted their involvement in the *fitna*. One of these reports claims that al-Ḥasan b. ʿAlī told Sulaymān b. Ṣurad: "I saw [my father] ʿAlī during the fighting; he came to me and said: 'O Ḥasan! I wish I had died twenty years before this.'"[25]

5. In practice, Ibn Ḥanbal refused to join revolutionary movements. In 231/846, during the "inquisition" (*miḥna*) in the reign of the caliph al-Wāthiq (r. 227–32/842–7), some Sunnīs in Baghdad led by Aḥmad b. Naṣr al-Khuzāʿī (killed 231/846), one of the leaders of the Muṭawwiʿa movement,[26] planned to take over the city. Some scholars (*fuqahāʾ*) who had joined the rebels visited Ibn Ḥanbal in order to convince him to join the revolt. They told him, "O Abū ʿAbdallāh [Aḥmad], this issue [i.e., the belief in the creation of the Qurʾān, the subject of the inquisition] has spread and been exacerbated." According to another report, their greatest concern was with the state's proposal to compel the teaching of this doctrine to schoolchildren. Ibn Ḥanbal asked, "So what do you want to do?" They replied: "We would like to consult you, as we do not accept his [i.e., al-Wāthiq's] rule or sovereignty." Ibn Ḥanbal argued with them for a while, saying,

> You should rather condemn [this heresy] in your hearts, but do not remove your hand from obedience, divide the unity of the Muslims or shed your blood and Muslim blood with yours. Look at the consequences of your actions! You should wait until the pious rest [by their death] or the sinful [i.e., the caliph] are made to rest.[27]

Others among the group of rebel scholars exclaimed, "We are concerned about our children, as they will only know this [false doctrine of the created Qurʾān], and consequently Islam will be expunged." But Ibn Ḥanbal retorted, "No. God supports His religion, and this matter has God to support it, and Islam remains influential and impregnable." Ultimately, neither side could convince the other, and the rebels left Ibn Ḥanbal, who subsequently relayed his disagreement with the rebels to his family. Ibn Ḥanbal stated that rebellion was wrong because it contradicts the traditions that command people to be patient in response to unjust rulers, and he quoted the Prophet's statement "If [the ruler] beats you, you should remain patient; if he deprives you, you should remain patient … "[28]

Ibn Ḥanbal also advised one of his students against joining the rebels, saying: "Glory be to God; [shedding] blood! [shedding] blood! I do not consent, nor do I command it; observing patience in our situation is better than sedition (*fitna*), which leads to bloodshed, that causes the shedding of blood, the plundering of wealth, and violations of prohibitions [i.e., raping women]." Ibn Ḥanbal then asked his student: "Do you remember what people were [suffering from] at the time of the *fitna* [i.e., in Baghdad after the caliph al-Amīn was killed and before the new caliph al-Maʾmūn arrived]?" His student asked again: "[But what about] people now, are they not in a state of *fitna*?" Clearly, the student meant the inquisition and the threat it posed to people's beliefs. Ibn Ḥanbal explained to him that the inquisition was a *fitna* in a specific matter, but if violence were used, the *fitna* would become generalized and collective security would be lost. Ibn Ḥanbal concluded by recommending that the student be patient for the good of his religion.[29]

We should note two important points here. First, the security of the common people was obviously a crucial factor behind the Sunnī doctrine of quietism, as is very clear in the case of Aḥmad b. Ḥanbal. It is surprising that Ibn Ḥanbal rejected or modified his view of the authenticity of some prophetic traditions that supported activism. He also sought to obscure the history of activist Companions, successors, and traditionalists, thus implying that the safety of the Muslim community was more important than following some of the pious predecessors (*al-salaf al-ṣālih*). Second, the doctrine of quietism not only promoted obedience to rulers but encouraged people not to focus on the politics that arose between the rulers and the people.

Quietism versus collaboration

Sunnī scholars were accused of following kings because of their quietist views.[30] But in fact, Ibn Ḥanbal and other traditionalists did admonish the rulers for certain actions, though they were wary of being in a position of weakness vis-à-vis those in power (and thus unable to command or forbid them) or, worse, flattering them and eating at their table. Aḥmad b. Shabbawayh (d. 229/843) traveled from Marw to Baghdad in order to rebuke the caliph. Ibn Shabbawayh consulted with Aḥmad b. Ḥanbal, who discouraged him from pursuing his mission because Ibn Ḥanbal feared he would not be able to carry it out.[31]

In other reports, Ibn Ḥanbal's uncle Isḥāq b. Ḥanbal (d. 253/867) urged him to take advantage of his involuntary presence at the court of al-Mutawakkil

(r. 232–47/847–61) to command the caliph to do right and forbid him from doing wrong, because the caliph would accept his advice. Ibn Ḥanbal refused. Isḥāq b. Ḥanbal then invoked the example of Isḥāq b. Rāhawayh (d. 238/853), whom he described as acting in this manner at Ibn Ṭāhir's court; but Ibn Ḥanbal declined to recognize his conduct as normative and said, "You invoke Isḥāq? I do not agree with him. There is no good for him [i.e., the caliph] in seeing me, nor for me in seeing him."[32] Ibn Ḥanbal was afraid of being in a position of weakness in front of the caliph and could not confront him with the truth. When Ibn al-Mubārak's cousin encouraged Ibn Ḥanbal to go to the caliph, Ibn Ḥanbal replied, "Your uncle i.e., Ibn al-Mubārak said 'Do not go to them; but if you go, you have to tell them the truth.' And I am afraid I will not be able to tell them the truth."[33]

It is important to note that for the early quietists (such as Ibn ʿUmar and Ṭalḥa b. al-Shikhkhīr), the main argument against rebellion was the need to save the Muslim community (i.e., the "unity versus division" paradigm). Although he insisted on the importance of adherence to the Muslim community, Ibn Ḥanbal's main argument was the community's need for safety (i.e., "safety versus insecurity" as the guiding principle). This shift in priorities probably reflects the fact that the concerns of Ibn Ḥanbal, and that of the people who followed him, were more social than political; in addition, it perhaps shows that Ibn Ḥanbal and those around him had lost their faith in the prospect of restoring a true Muslim state and were focused on the needs of the people rather than on the state.

Quietism in practice: Aḥmad b. Ḥanbal's relationship with authority

A striking feature of the sociopolitical history of early Islam is the way in which pious scholars chose not to work for, assist, or even have any kind of interaction with their rulers. Some scholars see this as a mark of the influence of Jewish, Christian, and pre-Islamic tribal customs on Islamic thought.[34] Others see a Shīʿī influence.[35] However, it is more logical to regard this as a natural expression of condemnation by pious people toward an impious government. Goldziher points out that this kind of "passive" resistance started during the Umayyad dynasty[36]; other scholars note that pious individuals also refused to associate themselves with the government during the ʿAbbāsid era.[37] Throughout his life, Aḥmad b. Ḥanbal also kept his distance from the rulers, to the greatest extent possible.

Ḥanbalī literature confirms that Ibn Ḥanbal neither worked for the rulers nor accepted any request to do so. However, reports differ on his opinion about the permissibility of working for rulers. Below, I list the various opinions from those most resistant to the idea to those most open to it. In one account, a friend of Ibn Ḥanbal's asked him, "I am in debt. Do you recommend that I work for these [rulers] until my debt is paid?" Ibn Ḥanbal rejected the idea and suggested that his friend should rather die indebted than work for rulers.[38] In another report, Ibn Ḥanbal agreed that whoever worked for the rulers would inevitably be involved in bloodshed.[39] Ibn Ḥanbal was also reported to have said, "I do not like anyone to [work] in the judiciary."[40]

Ibn Ḥanbal's attitude toward working for the rulers is presented in a dramatically different way in a report that depicts him as endorsing work as a judge: "Muslims must have a *ḥākim* [judge], [otherwise] people will lose their rights."[41] However, caution is warranted with respect to this last report, as it was related by al-Marrūdhī, who claimed to have heard it from Ibn Ḥanbal. But it contradicts what al-Marrūdhī narrates in his extant writings. The exact report is found in al-Marrūdhī's book *Akhbār al-shuyūkh*, but there, it is not related to the authority of Aḥmad b. Ḥanbal; instead, it is ascribed to Ḥafṣ b. Ghiyāth.[42] This suggests that the report may have been attributed to Ibn Ḥanbal later, in order to justify the work of later Ḥanbalīs in the judiciary.

Three early sources record Ibn Ḥanbal's relationship with the state. The authors of these reports were eyewitnesses or heard the accounts they describe from eyewitnesses. The three sources are Ibn Ḥanbal's son Ṣāliḥ, his cousin Ḥanbal b. Isḥāq, and his disciple Abū Bakr al-Marrūdhī. Besides these contemporary sources, I also consider some later sources.

Ḥanbal b. Isḥāq and Ṣāliḥ provide full details on the inquisition and Ibn Ḥanbal's attitude toward the caliphs (i.e., a Ḥanbalī perspective). Although the two agree on most details, they disagree on certain points.

After Ibn Ḥanbal rejected the caliph's doctrine of the creation of the Qurʾān, al-Maʾmūn ordered Isḥāq b. Ibrāhīm, his governor in Baghdad, to bring Aḥmad b. Ḥanbal and Muḥammad b. Nūḥ, in chains, to his camp in Ṭarsūs. When the two prisoners arrived in Adana[43] on their way to the caliph's court, they met a man who told them that the caliph had died. Ibn Ḥanbal commented that this was wonderful news and that he had begged God that he not have to see al-Maʾmūn. On this point, Ṣāliḥ and Ḥanbal b. Isḥāq provide different explanations as to why Ibn Ḥanbal did not want to see al-Maʾmūn. Ṣāliḥ quotes the following statement from his father, on the authority of Maymūn b.

Muhāran: "Do not test yourself with three [things]. Do not go to a *sulṭān*, even though you say, 'I will command him to obey God.'"[44]

This indicates that Ibn Ḥanbal did not want to see al-Maʾmūn because the latter was a *sulṭān* and he feared being tested. However, Ḥanbal b. Isḥāq gives another version of the story, according to which Ibn Ḥanbal was afraid to see al-Maʾmūn because the latter had promised that once he saw Ibn Ḥanbal he would cut him into pieces (*la-uqaṭṭiʿannah^{u} irba^{n} irba^{n}*).[45]

Another interesting point of divergence concerns an anecdote in which the caliph al-Muʿtaṣim appointed two men to debate with Ibn Ḥanbal for three days. During this time, the caliph sent food and drink to them. Ṣāliḥ reports his father's claim that he did not eat with the men during these three days and instead tried to occupy himself (*yataʿallal*) with something else in order to forget his hunger.[46] But in Ḥanbal b. Isḥāq's account, Ibn Ḥanbal ate only the minimum amount necessary to prevent death and considered himself to have been compelled (*muḍṭarr*) to do so.[47] A final story about Ibn Ḥanbal during the inquisition took place after Ibn Ḥanbal had been flogged, when al-Muʿtaṣim gave him clothes before releasing him. When he arrived home, Ibn Ḥanbal took off these garments, sold them, and distributed the proceeds of their sale to the poor.[48]

Interestingly, Ibn Ḥanbal's conviction that rulers should be avoided did not change when he became a favorite of the caliph. At the end of the inquisition, the caliph al-Mutawakkil enticed certain traditionists to stay in Sāmarrāʾ and expelled other parties, such as the Jahmīs and Muʿtazilīs, from his court.[49] The caliph then invited Ibn Ḥanbal to visit his camp and gave him 10,000 dirhams as a gift. Ibn Ḥanbal first refused to take the money but was warned that the caliph might become suspicious of him if he refused to take the offering. So he accepted it, but according to reports, he did not even look at the coins, but instead covered the money with a basin.[50] That night, Ibn Ḥanbal woke his family (sons, uncle, and cousin) and informed them that he was sleepless because accepting the money from the caliph had troubled him greatly. Weeping, he told his son Ṣāliḥ: "I have successfully preserved myself from these [i.e., the caliphs] for such a long a time, until at the end of my life I am troubled by them."[51]

Ibn Ḥanbal decided not to spend the money he had received and instead to give it away as alms. In the early dawn, he gathered his family and some of his friends and distributed the money to the descendants of the Muhājirūn and the Anṣār, poor scholars and poor people in Baghdad, until he had given away the entire sum he had received, including the bag that had held the money.[52]

Finally, when al-Mutawakkil asked Ibn Ḥanbal to visit him, Ibn Ḥanbal refused because he was not well. Ibn Ḥanbal did not suffer from a disease, but his body was very weak due to continuous fasting. However, despite his efforts to avoid dealing with the rulers, he had to obey some of the caliph's requests. He visited the caliph's son and allowed the caliph's messengers to dress him according to the customs of the court (Patton supposes that Ibn Ḥanbal would not have put on the garments himself),[53] but when he returned home, he took the clothes off and asked his son Ṣāliḥ to send them to Baghdad to be sold and to give the profits to the poor. Ibn Ḥanbal also expressed regret that he had not been able to evade this visit.[54]

In sum, Ibn Ḥanbal made great efforts to distance himself from the rulers, and made his interactions with them as infrequent as possible. In addition, the differences in the reports about Ibn Ḥanbal's actions in Sāmarrā ʾ show that the Ḥanbalī literature sought to edit reports about Ibn Ḥanbal to present him as stronger and purer than he was.[55]

Ibn Ḥanbal also criticized his friends and traditionalist colleagues who had established relationships with the state or accepted money from rulers. According to one account, Ibn Ḥanbal stopped writing to Isḥāq b. Rāhawayh after the latter showed Ibn Ḥanbal's letter to Ibn Ṭāhir, the governor of Khurasan.[56] When Ibn Ḥanbal was in Sāmarrāʾ, as noted earlier, his uncle Isḥāq tried to convince him to visit the caliph and invoked the example of Isḥāq b. Rāhawayh to support his case, but Ibn Ḥanbal rejected both the example and the entreaty.[57]

Finally, some Shāfiʿī sources claim that the caliph Hārūn al-Rashīd (r. 170–93/786–809) asked al-Shāfiʿī to nominate someone for the position of judge of Yemen. Al-Shāfiʿī offered the position to Ibn Ḥanbal, but the latter replied with a sharp and insulting retort: "I visit you only to learn asceticism (*al-ʿilm al-muzahhid fī l-dunyā*), and you bid me to take [the position of] a judge? Were it not for knowledge I would not speak to you after today." The response embarrassed al-Shāfiʿī.[58] Although Hurvitz trusts the story's authenticity, Melchert rightly doubts it, suggesting that it is less likely to have been an actual incident in Ibn Ḥanbal's life than a later fiction intended to illustrate Ibn Ḥanbal's piety and al-Shāfiʿī's respect for him.[59] We know that al-Shāfiʿī visited Baghdad in 184/800[60] when Ibn Ḥanbal was only twenty years old, and there is no evidence that Ibn Ḥanbal met him then. However, al-Shāfiʿī visited Baghdad again in 195/810–1, during the rule of the caliph al-Amīn,[61] at a time when Ibn Ḥanbal was busy seeking traditions and traveling to study with traditionalists; on that occasion, he and al-Shāfiʿī did meet in Baghdad. The story was noted in later Ḥanbalī sources, but the caliph was al-Amīn, not Hārūn al-Rashīd.[62]

Ibn Ḥanbal's relationships with his friends and family also suffered as a consequence of his dissociation from the rulers. According to one story, after his sons began to accept money from the caliph, Ibn Ḥanbal steadfastly refused to eat anything at his sons' houses or to eat food that had been prepared in their houses. Another story recounts that Ibn Ḥanbal found himself in a difficult financial situation and, as a result, he and his household went without food for three days. At that point, he borrowed some flour from a friend. The flour was processed and baked, and when the bread was placed in Ibn Ḥanbal's hands, he asked: "How did you do it? [How] did you bake it so quickly?" He was informed that the oven in Ṣāliḥ's house had already been heated, and so the bread had been baked in it. On hearing this, Ibn Ḥanbal ordered the loaf to be taken away and refused to eat it.[63] Prior to this incident, Ibn Ḥanbal had already stopped talking to his sons and uncle, blocked up the doorways between his own and his sons' houses, and ceased praying with his uncle, the imam of the neighborhood mosque, choosing instead to walk to a mosque much further away.[64] This pattern continued with the second generation of Ḥanbalīs, whose idea of piety closely resembled that of the Ḥanbalīs of Baghdad.

Conclusion

The story of Sunnī Islam's shift to quietism demonstrates that for Ibn Ḥanbal, the historical experience of the Muslim state and the interests of the common people had a greater influence on his thought than the traditions did. For the quietists, safety took priority over justice, and concerns over the security of individual Muslims and the community as a whole formed the basis of Ibn Ḥanbal's scholarly approach. With regard to the rulers themselves, the Umayyad caliphs supported quietism for their own benefit. Not all quietists were supportive of the rulers; for many quietists, withdrawing from involvement in politics was their way of expressing their dissatisfaction with impious and unjust rulers. As the example of Ibn Ḥanbal shows, this passive approach had far-reaching consequences for the Ḥanbalīs, but rarely obstructed the agendas of their rulers, just or otherwise.

Notes

1 Cook, "Activism and Quietism in Islam," in *Islam and Power*, ed. Alexander S. Cudsi and Ali E. Hillal Dessouki (London: Croom Helm, 1981), 22; Crone, *God's Rule: Government and Islam* (New York: Columbia University Press, 2004), 135–139; Zaman, *Religion and Politics Under the Early ʿAbbāsids: The Emergence of the Proto-Sunnī Elite* (Leiden: Brill, 1997), 73.

2 By traditionalist, I am referring to one of the *ahl al-ḥadīth* who adheres to the traditional authority in dogma, as against the claim of rationalists (*ahl al-kalām*); by contrast, the term "traditionist" refers to a *muḥaddith*, one who transmits *ḥadīth*.

3 Al-Khallāl, *al-Sunna*, ed. ʿAṭiyya al-Zahrānī (Riyadh: Dār al-Rāya, 1989–2000), 1:138.

4 Ibn Saʿd, *al-Ṭabaqāt* (Tehran: Muʾassasat al-Naṣr, 1970), 5:360; al-Ṭabarī, *Tārīkh al-rusul wa-l-mulūk*, ed. Muḥammad Abū l-Faḍl Ibrāhīm (Cairo: Dār al-Maʿārif, 1967), 5:343.

5 Al-Baghawī, *Maʿālim al-tanzīl*, ed. Muḥammad al-Nimr et al. (Riyadh: Dār Ṭayba, 1989), 1:214:
قال رجل لابن عمر: كيف ترى في قتال الفتنة؟ فقال [ابن عمر]: هل تدري ما الفتنة؟ كان محمد ... يقاتل المشركين، وكان الدخول عليهم فتنة، وليس بقتالكم على الملك.

6 Muḥammad b. Muḥammad al-Ḥākim al-Nīsābūrī, *al-Mustadrak ʿalā l-Ṣaḥīḥayn* (Riyadh: Maktabat wa-Maṭbaʿat al-Naṣr al-Ḥadītha, 1968), 4:471.

7 For Ibn al-Shikhkhīr's position against Ibn al-Ashʿath's revolt, see ʿAlī al-Ṣayyāḥ, *Min siyar ʿulamāʾ al-salaf ʿind al-fitan: Muṭarrif b. ʿAbdallāh b. al-Shikhkhīr namūdhaj*[an] (Riyadh: Madār al-Waṭan, 2012).

8 Ibn Abī Shayba, *al-Muṣannaf*, ed. Ḥamad al-Jumʿa and Muḥammad al-Luḥaydān (Riyadh: Maktabat al-Rushd, 2004), 6:206:
والله لقد رابني أمران: لئن ظهر [ابن الأشعث] لا يقوم لله دين. ولئن ظُهِرَ عليه لا يزالون أذلة إلى يوم القيامة.

9 For a list of people who joined or supported these rebellions, see al-Iṣbahānī, *Maqātil al-ṭālibiyyīn*, ed. Aḥmad Ṣaqr (Cairo: Dār Iḥyāʾ al-Kutub al-ʿArabiyya, 1949), 244–261, 304–329. See also Elad, "Rebellion of Muḥammad b. ʿAbdallāh b. al-Ḥasan," in *ʿAbbāsid Studies: Occasional Papers of the School of ʿAbbāsid Studies, Cambridge 6–10 July 2002*, ed. James E. Montgomery (Leuven: Peeters, 2004), 147–199; Zaman, *Religion and Politics*, 73–74.

10 Ibn al-Nadīm, *al-Fihrist*, edited by Riḍā Tajaddud (Tehran: Amir Kabir, 1987), 263; see also Zaman, *Religion and Politics*, 78 n. 32.

11 Al-Khallāl, *al-Sunna*, 1:133, 140.

12 Ibid., 1:140.

13 Al-Khallāl, *al-Sunna*, 1:126–130; Ibn Qudāma al-Maqdisī, *al-Muntakhab min al-ʿIlal li-l-Khallāl*, ed. Ṭāriq ʿAwaḍ Allāh (Riyadh: Dār al-Rāya, 1998), 163.

14 Al-Bukhārī, *al-Jāmiʿ al-ṣaḥīḥ*, kitāb al-fitan, bāb qawl al-nabī … : "Halāk ummatī ʿalā yaday ughaylima sufahāʾ," no. 7058, ed. Muḥibb al-Dīn al-Khaṭīb et al. (Cairo: al-Maṭbaʿa al-Salafiyya, 1980), 4:313; Muslim, *al-Jāmiʿ al-ṣaḥīḥ*, kitāb al-fitan wa-ashrāṭ al-sāʿa, Taqtul^{u} ʿAmmār^{an} al-fiʾa al-bāghiyya, no. 2917, ed. Muḥammad Fuʾād ʿAbd al-Bāqī (Beirut: Dār al-Kutub al-ʿIlmīyya, 1991), 6:2236.

15 Al-Marrūdhī, *al-Waraʿ*, ed. Samīr al-Zuhayrī (Riyadh: Maktabat al-Maʿārif, 2001), 42–43:

وذُكر لأبي عبد الله حديث ... "لو أن الناس اعتزلوهم". قال: هو حديث رديء. أُراه قال: هؤلاء المعتزلة يحتجون به. يعني: في ترك حضور الجمعة.

16 Ibn Ḥanbal, *al-Musnad* (Beirut: al-Maktab al-Islāmī, 1969), 2:301.

17 Ibid.; see also Ibn Qudāma, *al-Muntakhab*, 163.

18 Al-Khallāl, *al-Sunna*, 1:131.

19 Ibid., 1:135–136; Ibn Abī Yaʿlā, *Ṭabaqāt al-Ḥanābila*, ed. ʿAbd al-Raḥmān al-ʿUthaymīn (Riyadh: al-Amāna al-ʿĀmma li-l-Iḥtifāl bi-Murūr Miʾat ʿĀm ʿalā Taʾsīs al-Mamlaka, 1999), 1:142. For al-Ḥasan b. Ḥayy and his opinions on activism, see Cook, *Commanding Right and Forbidding Wrong in Islamic Thought* (Cambridge: Cambridge University Press, 2000), 51.

20 See, for example, ʿAbdallāh b. Aḥmad b. Ḥanbal, *Kitāb al-sunna*, ed. Muḥammad b. Saʿīd al-Qaḥṭānī (Riyadh: Dār ʿĀlam al-Kutub, 1996), 1:182.

21 See Saud Saleh al-Sarhan, "Early Muslim Traditionalism: A Critical Study of the Works and Political Theology of Aḥmad Ibn Ḥanbal" (PhD thesis, University of Exeter, 2011), 130.

22 Ibid., 131.

23 Ibn Rajab, *Sharḥ ʿIlal al-Tirmidhī*, ed. Hammām ʿAbd al-Raḥīm Saʿīd (N.p.: Maktabat al-Manār, 1987), 2:806–807:

قال المروذي: مضيت إلى الكرابيسي، وهو إذ ذاك مستور يذب عن السنة، ويظهر نصرة أبي عبد الله، فقلت له: إن كتاب المدلسين يريدون أن يعرضوه على أبي عبد الله، فأظهِرْ أنك قد ندمتَ حتى أخبر أبا عبد الله. فقال لي: إن أبا عبد الله رجل صالح مثله يوفق لإصابة الحق، وقد رضيت أن يعرض كتابي عليه، وقال: قد سألني أبو ثور وابن عقيل، وحبيش أن أضرب على هذا الكتاب فأبيتُ عليهم، وقلت: بل أزيد فيه. ولج في ذلك، وأبى أن يرجع عنه، فجيء بالكتاب إلى أبي عبد الله وهو لا يدري من وضع الكتاب، وكان في الكتاب الطعن على الأعمش، والنصرة للحسن بن صالح، وكان في الكتاب إن قلتم: إن الحسن بن صالح كان يرى رأي الخوارج، فهذا ابن الزبير قد خرج! فلما قرىء على أبي عبد الله قال: قد هذا جمع للمخالفين ما لم يحسنوا أن يحتجوا به حذروا عن هذا، ونهى عنه

24 Al-Marwazī, *al-Fitan*, ed. Samīr Amīn al-Zuhayrī (Cairo: Maktabat al-Tawḥīd, 1991), 78–94.

25 Ibid., 80.

26 On this movement, see Lapidus, "The Separation of State and Religion in the Development of Early Islamic Society," *International Journal of Middle East Studies* 6, no. 4 (1975): 372–374; Madelung, "Vigilante Movement of Sahl b. Salāma and the Origins of Ḥanbalism Reconsidered," *Journal of Turkish Studies* 14 (1990): 331–337; van Ess, *Theologie und Gesellschaft* (Berlin: Walter de Gruyter, 1991–97), 3:173–175, 448.

27 Ḥanbal b. Isḥāq b. Ḥanbal, *Dhikr miḥnat al-imām Aḥmad Ibn Ḥanbal*, ed. Muḥammad Naghsh (N.p.: n.p., 1983), 70–72; al-Khallāl, *al-Sunna*, 1:133–134.

28 This story was narrated by Ḥanbal b. Isḥāq, who was an eyewitness. However, we have two versions of Ḥanbal's report: Ḥanbal b. Isḥāq b. Ḥanbal, *Dhikr*, 70–72; and al-Khallāl, *al-Sunna*, 1:133–134.

29 Al-Khallāl, *al-Sunna*, 1:132–133:

سألت أبا عبد الله في أمر كان حدث ببغداد، وهم قوم بالخروج، فقلت: يا أبا عبد الله، ما تقول في الخروج مع هؤلاء القوم؟ فأنكر ذلك عليهم، وجعل يقول: سبحان الله! الدماء الدماء! لا أرى ذلك، ولا آمر به. الصبر على ما نحن فيه خير من الفتنة، يسفك فيها الدماء، ويستباح فيها الأموال، وينتهك فيها المحارم. أما علمت ما كان الناس فيه -يعني: أيام الفتنة-؟. قلت: والناس اليوم، أليس هم في فتنة يا أبا عبد الله؟ قال: وإن كان، فإنما هي فتنة خاصة، فإذا وقع السيف عمت وانقطعت السبل الصبر على هذا ويسلم لك دينك خير لك.

30 Al-Nawbakhtī, *Firaq al-Shīʿa*, ed. Hellmut Ritter (Istanbul: Staatsdruckerei, 1931), 6.

31 Ibn Abī Yaʿlā, *Ṭabaqāt*, 1:109–111. It is claimed that Ibn Ḥanbal told Ibn Shabbawayh: "Innī akhāf ʿalayk an lā taqūm[a] bi-dhālik." It is clear that Ibn Ḥanbal was worried that Ibn Shabbawayh might not be able to complete his mission. However, Cook (*Commanding Right*, 101) interprets this to mean that Ibn Ḥanbal discouraged him on the grounds of the risks he would be running. I believe this is a mistranslation.

32 Al-Marrūdhī, *Akhbār al-shuyūkh wa-akhlāquhum*, ed. ʿĀmir Ḥasan Ṣabrī (Beirut: Dār al-Bashāʾir al-Islāmīyya, 2004), 41–42; Ibn Abī Yaʿlā, *Ṭabaqāt*, 1:299; Ibn al-Jawzī, *Manāqib al-imām Aḥmad b. Ḥanbal*, ed. ʿAbdallāh al-Turkī (Egypt: Maktabat al-Khānjī, 1979), 504–505.

33 Al-Marrūdhī, *Akhbār al-shuyūkh*, 42; Ibn Abī Yaʿlā, *Ṭabaqāt*, 1:280; Ibn al-Jawzī, *Manāqib*, 505.

34 Wensinck, "Refused Dignity," in *A Volume of Oriental Studies Presented to E. G. Browne*, ed. T. W. Arnold and R. A. Nicholson (Cambridge: Cambridge University Press, 1922), 491–495; Goitein, "Attitudes towards Government," in *Studies in Islamic History and Institutions*, 197–213 (Leiden: Brill, 1966), 210.

35 Van Ess, *Theologie und Gesellschaft*, 1:224.

36 Goldziher, *Muslim Studies*, trans. and ed. S. M. Stern and C. R. Barber (London: Allen and Unwin, 1967–71), 2:47.

37 Coulson, "Doctrine and Practice in Islamic Law: One Aspect of the Problem," *Bulletin of the School of Oriental and African Studies* 18 (1956), 212.

38 Ibn Abī Yaʿlā, *Ṭabaqāt*, 2:123–124.

39 Ibid., 1:355.

40 Abū Yaʿlā b. al-Farrāʾ, *al-Aḥkām al-sulṭāniyya*, ed. Muḥammad Ḥāmid al-Fiqī (Cairo: Muṣṭafā l-Bābī l-Ḥalabī, 1966), 70.

41 Ibid., 71.

42 Al-Marrūdhī, *Akhbār al-shuyūkh*, 116.

43 This is Ṣāliḥ's narrative; in Ḥanbal b. Isḥāq's account, Ibn Ḥanbal heard about al-Maʾmūn's death when he arrived in Ṭarsūs.

44 Ṣāliḥ b. Aḥmad b. Ḥanbal, *Sīrat al-imām Aḥmad b. Ḥanbal*, ed. Fuʾād ʿAbd al-Munʿim Aḥmad (Riyadh: Dār al-Salaf, 1995), 49–50.

45 Ḥanbal b. Isḥāq b. Ḥanbal, *Dhikr*, 39.

46 Ṣāliḥ b. Aḥmad b. Ḥanbal, *Sīrat al-imām*, 57, 59, 62, 64.

47 Ḥanbal b. Isḥāq b. Ḥanbal, *Dhikr*, 48.

48 Ibid., 60.

49 Melchert, "Religious Policies of the Caliphs from al-Mutawakkil to al-Muqtadir, AH 232–295/AD 847–908," *Islamic Law and Society* 3 (1996): 322–326.

50 Interestingly, Ṣāliḥ claimed that his father asked him to cover the money with the basin (*Sīrat al-imām*, 92), whereas Ḥanbal b. Isḥāq b. Ḥanbal claimed that he had been the one who covered the money with the basin (*Dhikr*, 85). There are also other differences between the accounts of Ṣāliḥ and Ḥanbal.

51 Ṣāliḥ b. Aḥmad b. Ḥanbal, *Sīrat al-imām*, 92.

52 Ḥanbal b. Isḥāq b. Ḥanbal, *Dhikr*, 85–86; Ṣāliḥ b. Aḥmad b. Ḥanbal, *Sīrat al-imām*, 92–93.

53 Walter Melville Patton, *Aḥmad Ibn Ḥanbal and the Miḥna: A Biography of the Imām Including an Account of the Moḥammedan Inquisition Called the Miḥna, 218–234 A.H.* (Leiden: Brill, 1897), 143.

54 Ṣāliḥ b. Aḥmad b. Ḥanbal, *Sīrat al-imām*, 97–98; Patton, *Aḥmad Ibn Ḥanbal*, 143–144.

55 Hurvitz, *The Formation of Hanbalism: Piety into Power* (London: RoutledgeCurzon, 2002), 6.

56 Ṣāliḥ b. Aḥmad b. Ḥanbal, *Sīrat al-imām*, 42.

57 Al-Marrūdhī, *Akhbār al-shuyūkh*, 41–42; Ibn Abī Yaʿlā, *Ṭabaqāt*, 1:299; Ibn al-Jawzī, *Manāqib*, 458.

58 Al-Bayhaqī, *Manāqib al-Shāfiʿī*, ed. Aḥmad Ṣaqr (Cairo: Dār al-Turāth, 1970), 1:154; Ibn ʿAsākir, *Tārīkh madīnat Dimashq wa-dhikr faḍlihā wa-tasmiyat man ḥallahā min al-amāthil aw ijtāza bi-nawāḥīhā min wāridīhā wa-ahlihā*, ed. ʿUmar b. Gharāma al-ʿAmrī (Beirut: Dār al-Fikr, 1995), 5:273–274; Ibn Kathīr, *al-Bidāya wa-l-nihāya*, ed. ʿAbdallāh al-Turkī (Cairo: Dār Hajar, 1997), 14:387. Ibn Kathīr took the story from al-Bayhaqī, presumably from the latter's book *Manāqib Aḥmad*. See also Hurvitz, *Formation of Hanbalism*, 85.

59 Melchert, *Aḥmad ibn Ḥanbal* (Oxford: Oneworld, 2006), 4.

60 Ibn Kathīr, *al-Bidāya wa-l-nihāya*, 14:133.

61 Al-Khaṭīb al-Baghdādī, *Tārīkh madīnat al-Salām wa-akhbār muḥaddithīhā wa-dhikr quṭṭānihā l-ʿulamāʾ min ghayr ahlihā wa-wāridīhā*, ed. Bashshār ʿAwwād Maʿrūf (Beirut: Dār al-Gharb al-Islāmī, 2001), 2:409.

62 Ibn al-Jawzī, *Manāqib*, 361–362.

63 Abū Nuʿaym al-Iṣfahānī, *Ḥilyat al-awliyāʾ wa-ṭabaqāt al-aṣfiyāʾ* (Beirut: Dār al-Kutub al-ʿIlmiyya, 1988), 9:177. In another account, the bread was baked in the

house of ʿAbdallāh (Aḥmad's other son); see Ibn al-Jawzī, *Manāqib*, 302; Hurvitz, *Formation of Hanbalism*, 69.

64 Ṣāliḥ b. Aḥmad b. Ḥanbal, *Sīrat al-imām*, 108.

Bibliography

Abū Nuʿaym al-Iṣbahānī, Aḥmad b. ʿAbdallāh. *Ḥilyat al-awliyāʾ wa-ṭabaqāt al-aṣfiyāʾ*. 10 vols. Beirut: Dār al-Kutub al-ʿIlmiyya, 1988.

Abū Yaʿlā b. al-Farrāʾ, Muḥammad b. al-Ḥusayn. *al-Aḥkām al-sulṭāniyya*. Edited by Muḥammad Ḥāmid al-Fiqī. Cairo: Muṣṭafā l-Bābī l-Ḥalabī, 1966.

al-Baghawī, al-Ḥusayn b. Masʿūd. *Maʿālim al-tanzīl*. Edited by Muḥammad al-Nimr et al. 8 vols. Riyadh: Dār Ṭayba, 1989.

al-Bayhaqī, Aḥmad b. al-Ḥusayn. *Manāqib al-Shāfiʿī*. Edited by Aḥmad Ṣaqr. 2 vols. Cairo: Dār al-Turāth, 1970.

al-Bukhārī, Muḥammad b. Ismāʿīl. *al-Jāmiʿ al-ṣaḥīḥ*. Edited by Muḥibb al-Dīn al-Khaṭīb et al. 4 vols. Cairo: al-Maṭbaʿa al-Salafiyya, 1980.

Cook, Michael. "Activism and Quietism in Islam." In *Islam and Power*, edited by Alexander S. Cudsi and Ali E. Hillal Dessouki, 15–22. London: Croom Helm, 1981.

Cook, Michael. *Commanding Right and Forbidding Wrong in Islamic Thought*. Cambridge: Cambridge University Press, 2000.

Coulson, N. J. "Doctrine and Practice in Islamic Law: One Aspect of the Problem." *Bulletin of the School of Oriental and African Studies* 18 (1956): 211–226.

Crone, Patricia. *God's Rule: Government and Islam*. New York: Columbia University Press, 2004.

Elad, Amikam. "Rebellion of Muḥammad b. ʿAbdallāh b. al-Ḥasan (known as al-Nafs al-Zakīya) in 145/762." In *ʿAbbāsid Studies: Occasional Papers of the School of ʿAbbāsid Studies, Cambridge 6–10 July 2002*, edited by James E. Montgomery, 147–198. Leuven: Peeters, 2004.

Goitein, S. D. "Attitudes towards Government in Judaism and Islam." In *Studies in Islamic History and Institutions*, 197–213. Leiden: Brill, 1966.

Goldziher, Ignác. *Muslim Studies*. Translated and edited by S. M. Stern and C. R. Barber. 2 vols. London: Allen and Unwin, 1967–71.

Hurvitz, Nimrod. *The Formation of Hanbalism: Piety into Power*. London: RoutledgeCurzon, 2002.

Ibn Abī Shayba, ʿAbdallāh b. Muḥammad. *al-Muṣannaf*. Edited by Ḥamad al-Jumʿa and Muḥammad al-Luḥaydān. 16 vols. Riyadh: Maktabat al-Rushd, 2004.

Ibn Abī Yaʿlā, Muḥammad b. Muḥammad. *Ṭabaqāt al-Ḥanābila*. Edited by ʿAbd al-Raḥmān al-ʿUthaymīn. 3 vols. Riyadh: al-Amāna al-ʿĀmma li-l-Iḥtifāl bi-Murūr Miʾat ʿĀm ʿalā Taʾsīs al-Mamlaka, 1999.

Ibn ʿAsākir, ʿAlī b. al-Ḥasan. *Tārīkh madīnat Dimashq wa-dhikr faḍlihā wa-tasmiyat man ḥallahā min al-amāthil aw ijtāza bi-nawāḥīhā min wāridīhā wa-ahlihā*. Edited by ʿUmar b. Gharāma al-ʿAmrī. 80 vols. Beirut: Dār al-Fikr, 1995.

Ibn Ḥanbal, ʿAbdallāh b. Aḥmad. *Kitāb al-sunna*. Edited by Muḥammad b. Saʿīd al-Qaḥṭānī. 2 vols. Riyadh: Dār ʿĀlam al-Kutub, 1996.

Ibn Ḥanbal, Aḥmad. *al-Musnad*. 6 vols. Beirut: al-Maktab al-Islāmī, 1969.

Ibn Ḥanbal, Ḥanbal b. Isḥāq. *Dhikr miḥnat al-imām Aḥmad b. Ḥanbal*. Edited by Muḥammad Naghsh. N.p.: n.p., 1983.

Ibn Ḥanbal, Ṣāliḥ b. Aḥmad. *Sirat al-imām Aḥmad b. Ḥanbal*. Edited by Fuʾād ʿAbd al-Munʿim Aḥmad. Riyadh: Dār al-Salaf, 1995.

Ibn al-Jawzī, ʿAbd al-Raḥmān b. ʿAlī. *Manāqib al-imām Aḥmad b. Ḥanbal*. Edited by ʿAbdallāh al-Turkī. Egypt: Maktabat al-Khānjī, 1979.

Ibn Kathīr, Ismāʿīl b. ʿUmar. *al-Bidāya wa-l-nihāya*. Edited by ʿAbdallāh al-Turkī. 21 vols. Cairo: Dār Hajar, 1997.

Ibn al-Nadīm, Muḥammad b. Isḥāq. *Kitāb al-fihrist*. Edited by Riḍā Tajaddud. Tehran: Amir Kabir, 1987.

Ibn Qudāma al-Maqdisī, ʿAbdallāh b. Aḥmad. *al-Muntakhab min al-ʿIlal li-l-Khallāl*. Edited by Ṭāriq ʿAwaḍ Allāh. Riyadh: Dār al-Rāya, 1998.

Ibn Rajab, ʿAbd al-Raḥmān b. Aḥmad. *Sharḥ ʿIlal al-Tirmidhī*. Edited by Hammām ʿAbd al-Raḥīm Saʿīd. 2 vols. N.p.: Maktabat al-Manār, 1987.

Ibn Saʿd, Muḥammad. *al-Ṭabaqāt al-kubrā*. 10 vols. Tehran: Muʾassasat al-Naṣr, 1970.

al-Iṣbahānī, Abū l-Faraj ʿAlī b. al-Ḥusayn. *Maqātil al-ṭālibiyyīn*. Edited by Aḥmad Ṣaqr. Cairo: Dār Iḥyāʾ al-Kutub al-ʿArabiyya, 1949.

al-Khallāl, Aḥmad b. Muḥammad. *al-Sunna*. Edited by ʿAṭiyya al-Zahrānī. 5 vols. in 7 parts. Riyadh: Dār al-Rāya, 1989–2000.

al-Khaṭīb al-Baghdādī, Aḥmad b. ʿAlī. *Tārīkh madīnat al-Salām wa-akhbār muḥaddithīhā wa-dhikr quṭṭānihā l-ʿulamāʾ min ghayr ahlihā wa-wāridīhā*. Edited by Bashshār ʿAwwād Maʿrūf. 17 vols. Beirut: Dār al-Gharb al-Islāmī, 2001.

Lapidus, Ira. "The Separation of State and Religion in the Development of Early Islamic Society." *International Journal of Middle East Studies* 6, no. 4 (1975): 363–385.

Madelung, Wilferd. "Vigilante Movement of Sahl b. Salāma al-Khurāsānī and the Origins of Ḥanbalism Reconsidered." *Journal of Turkish Studies* 14 (1990): 331–337.

al-Marrūdhī, Aḥmad b. Muḥammad. *Akhbār al-shuyūkh wa-akhlāquhum*. Edited by ʿĀmir Ḥasan Ṣabrī. Beirut: Dār al-Bashāʾir al-Islāmiyya, 2004.

al-Marrūdhī, Aḥmad b. Muḥammad. *al-Waraʿ*. Edited by Samīr al-Zuhayrī. Riyadh: Maktabat al-Maʿārif, 2001.

al-Marwazī, Nuʿaym b. Ḥammād. *al-Fitan*. Edited by Samīr Amīn al-Zuhayrī. Cairo: Maktabat al-Tawḥīd, 1991.

Melchert, Christopher. *Aḥmad ibn Hanbal*. Oxford: Oneworld, 2006.

Melchert, Christopher. "Religious Policies of the Caliphs from al-Mutawakkil to al-Muqtadir, AH 232–295/AD 847–908." *Islamic Law and Society* 3 (1996): 316–342.

Muslim = al-Nīsābūrī, Muslim b. al-Ḥajjāj. *al-Jāmiʿ al-ṣaḥīḥ*. Edited by Muḥammad Fuʾād ʿAbd al-Bāqī. 5 vols. Beirut: Dār al-Kutub al-ʿIlmiyya, 1991.

al-Nawbakhtī, al-Ḥasan b. Mūsā. *Firaq al-Shīʿa*. Edited by Hellmut Ritter. Istanbul: Staatsdruckerei, 1931.

al-Nīsābūrī, Muḥammad b. ʿAbdallāh al-Ḥākim. *al-Mustadrak ʿalā l-Ṣaḥīḥayn*. 4 vols. Riyadh: Maktabat wa-Maṭbaʿat al-Naṣr al-Ḥadītha, 1968.

Patton, Walter Melville. *Aḥmad Ibn Ḥanbal and the Miḥna: A Biography of the Imām Including an Account of the Moḥammedan Inquisition Called the Miḥna, 218–234 A.H.* Leiden: Brill, 1897.

Al-Sarhan, Saud Saleh. "Early Muslim Traditionalism: A Critical Study of the Works and Political Theology of Aḥmad Ibn Ḥanbal." PhD thesis, University of Exeter, 2011.

al-Ṣayyāḥ, ʿAlī. *Min siyar ʿulamāʾ al-salaf ʿind al-fitan: Muṭarrif b. ʿAbdallāh b. al-Shikhkhīr namūdhaj[an]*. Riyadh: Madār al-Waṭan, 2012.

al-Ṭabarī, Muḥammad b. Jarīr. *Tārīkh al-rusul wa-l-mulūk*. Edited by Muḥammad Abū l-Faḍl Ibrāhīm. 10 vols. Cairo: Dār al-Maʿārif, 1967.

van Ess, Josef. *Theologie und Gesellschaft im 2. und 3. Jahrhundert Hidschra: Eine Geschichte des religiösen Denkens im frühen Islam*. 6 vols. Berlin: Walter de Gruyter, 1991–97.

Wensinck, A. J. "Refused Dignity." In *A Volume of Oriental Studies Presented to E. G. Browne*, edited by T. W. Arnold and R. A. Nicholson, 491–499. Cambridge: Cambridge University Press, 1922.

Zaman, Muhammad Qasim. *Religion and Politics Under the Early ʿAbbāsids: The Emergence of the Proto-Sunnī Elite*. Leiden: Brill, 1997.

5

Quietism and Political Legitimacy in Imāmī Shīʿī Jurisprudence: al-Sharīf al-Murtaḍā's *Treatise on the Legality of Working for the Government* Reconsidered

Robert Gleave

Imāmism and quietism

In Twelver (*Ithnā ʿAsharī*, sometimes also Imāmī) Shīʿism, historical reflection on the disputes around the succession to the Prophet Muḥammad led to the doctrine that there would always be a clear designation (*naṣṣ*) of a sinless leader (*imām maʿṣūm*) as Muḥammad's successor.[1] The notion of "designation" derives from the Shīʿī belief in the Prophet's own explicit designation of ʿAlī[2]; the notion of sinlessness also emerges from the early Shīʿī belief that this quality was somehow transferred from the Prophet to members of his family. In history, for Shīʿīs generally, these principles have been realized in the rightful leadership of ʿAlī and his offspring. Arguments about the identity of the Imam and his role have resulted in a fissiparous movement; the Imāmīs (the subject of this chapter) are only one strand of Shīʿism extant from the early period until today. Mainstream Imāmī-Ithnā ʿAsharī belief holds that the twelfth Imam is in occultation (*ghayba*) to escape oppression. The Imam is concealed (*mastūr*) from normal human perception and has been given a messianic promise of his reappearance or manifestation (*ẓuhūr*) at some future time. These theological doctrines create a theoretical problem for any government other than that of the Imam himself, since religious legitimacy belongs, at least in the first instance, to the government of the Imam. These doctrines lay the foundation for the so-called Imāmī "quietism," the assumption being that since political power in the absence of the Imam is illegitimate, there is a religious obligation to detach oneself from all political activity (both from seeking political office and from cooperating with illegitimate political structures) and instead turn to piety and the internal operations of the "saved sect" (i.e., the Imāmī Shīʿa).[3] In the secondary literature, there is an argument, implicit at times and explicit at other times, that the quietism of the Imāmiyya came at the price of a compromise on a fundamental element of Shīʿī dogma—namely, that only the Imam from the House of the Prophet has the right to rule.[4] The treatise by al-Sharīf al-Murtaḍā that I (re)analyze in this chapter is viewed as an important piece of evidence in this process of accommodating political structures into Twelver Shīʿī religious belief. Al-Sharīf al-Murtaḍā's treatise argues that governments other than that of the Imam can be described as "just," and working for them is not problematic for ordinary Shīʿīs. In this chapter, I argue, first, that this interpretation of al-Murtaḍā's treatise is faulty, since it does not consider the wider legal discussions in which al-Murtaḍā was participating. Second, I argue that if one limits the definition of quietism as only the refusal to allow rebellion against an unjust ruler, then al-Murtaḍā's position can, indeed, be described as "quietist." However, the treatise actually promotes a politically engaged and pragmatic form of quietism, in which the individual Shīʿī, by working for the unjust ruler, can implement the *sharīʿa* without recognizing the ruler as morally good or as a rightful ruler. We might say, tentatively, that this was the position in most premodern Imāmī legal works.[5] What is clear, however, is that Imāmī quietism did not rest on a concession over the legitimacy of government.[6] The legal tradition maintained the Imāmī rejection of rebellion, I argue, without compromising on the exclusive right of the hidden, sinless Imam to rule the Muslim community.

The secondary literature regularly mentions that the Imāmīs are understood as "quietist," and that this distinguishes them from other more "activist" Shīʿī (or Sunnī) traditions. This quietism is often linked to the withdrawal from political activity associated with the later Imams, recognized by the Imāmī Shīʿī Imams, from Imam Muḥammad al-Bāqir (d. 144/733) onward. The quietism of the Imams became "the central Twelver tradition" in later years.[7] Even before the occultation of the twelfth Imam (in 329/940–1), Crone states, "the Imāmīs can be defined as those Shiʿites who renounced political action."[8] Numerous secondary sources propose a contrast between "activist" (e.g., Zaydī, Ismāʿīlī) and "quietist" (primarily the Imāmiyya) strands of Shīʿism.[9]

Naturally, whether the Imāmī tradition more generally is accurately described as "quietist-and-not-activist" depends, among other things, on (first) the criteria one uses to define quietism and (second) what the Imāmiyya are said to be refusing to be involved in. Looking at the field of Islamic political thought more generally, the term "quietist" has been used in various accounts of contemporary Islamic political thought, including some branches of Salafism, sometimes associated with Nāṣir al-Dīn al-Albānī (d. 1999) and the followers of al-Albānī's pupil Rabīʿ al-Madkhalī (b. 1931, his followers are known as Madkhalīs). Wagemakers uses "quietist" to refer to radical Salafī theorists of *jihād,* such as the Jordanian Abū Muḥammad al-Maqdisī, who do not align themselves with particular *jihādī* movements and do not promote actual campaigns of *jihād.*[10] "Quietist" is also used to refer to certain Sufi trends (e.g., the Moroccan Budshīshiyya order) that advocate a contemplative attitude to religious doctrine, an absence of formal engagement in social and political action, and a pietistic attitude to religious ritual and belief.[11] While there is clearly a shared emphasis on withdrawal from political *opposition* (or more strongly, *rebellion*) in all these movements, there is not a uniform refusal to engage in political *activity* per se. Al-Maqdisī is quietist because he does not support particular "activist" *jihādī* movements; the Madkhalīs are "quietist" because they tend to accept the legitimacy of the Saudi political order; the Budshīshiyya are "quietist" because they withdraw from society (including all involvement with political power) and focus purely on inner spiritual perfection. Despite its regular usage, the application of the term is rarely discussed in the literature on Islamic thought, and, when applied to the Imāmiyya (and other traditions as well), "quietist" appears to have entered the academic discussion without much theoretical reflection. Clearly, it is often associated with movements and thinkers who refuse to countenance rebellion against the current political system. In this sense, the whole Sunnī tradition can be considered quietist, in that rebelling against the political leader (*imam, sulṭān*) is not encouraged by any of the so-called orthodox Sunnī schools, except in very limited circumstances.[12] Any ruler would be satisfied with these forms of quietism, since none of these groups constitutes a threat to his power. However, to think of the whole of the established Sunnī legal tradition as well as the Imāmiyya as all, similarly, "quietist" rather limits further research into this category. In this chapter, I cautiously propose a typology of quietism with reference to early Islamic political thought. By doing so, I aim to bring a little more nuance to the use of the term as an analytical tool.

One of the few to discuss the appropriateness of the term "quietist" for Islamic intellectual history is Michael Cook, who specifically discusses the "quietism" of Ibn Ḥanbal (d. 241/855). He notes, "I have not in general sought to distinguish political quietism (i.e. quietism in relation to the state) and social quietism (i.e. quietism in relation to the surrounding society). The two naturally tend to go together, but they need not always do so."[13] Here Cook identifies two forms of quietism, "political" and "social," though he does not elaborate extensively on their characteristics. The former does not rebel against the state (thus, it accepts the state's existence); the latter withdraws from society more generally and, perhaps in a reclusive fashion, focuses on personal spirituality. For Cook, the key element of both types of quietism appears to be the refusal to rebel against the state,[14] even if the quietists in question see it as illegitimate or irrelevant to the implementation of the *sharīʿa*. It could be argued that tying quietism exclusively to the refusal to rebel (as Cook and other commentators have done) ignores other elements of quietism, such as detachment from political engagement or withdrawal from society more generally.

In light of the case of the Imāmiyya (and in particular the treatise of al-Sharīf al-Murtaḍā that I analyze in this chapter), I would propose an adjustment to Cook's typology. Cook's category of political (as opposed to social) quietism conflates at least three subcategories of "political" quietists that we find in the elaboration of several groups in the early Islamic period. These groups were all prompted to reject rebellion for different reasons and proposed different attitudes toward political power as a result.

(1) One group views the state as illegitimate and therefore refuses to engage with it in any form.
(2) One group views the state as legitimate and therefore has no (or few) reservations about engaging with it.
(3) One group views the state as illegitimate, or avoids pronouncing an opinion about its legitimacy, but is willing to engage with it for strategic reasons.

It might be argued that the first is represented by some strands of early Ḥanbalīs and the second by certain groups of Ḥanafīs.[15] I argue below that in the third form, we can locate the Imāmiyya in their form of "pragmatic political quietism," which they shared with some other strands of early Islamic political thinkers. As we see, the level of interaction and engagement with political power that al-Sharīf al-Murtaḍā envisages (at least in his treatise on the topic) might make one hesitate to describe the Imāmiyya as advocating "political quietism." Al-Murtaḍā advocates extensive activity, perhaps even collaboration, with political power. To term it "quietist" or even "politically quietist" requires a little elaboration; this elaboration can most properly be undertaken through an examination of al-Murtaḍā's treatise against the backdrop of wider discussions by early Muslims on the question of "working for the government."

Political legitimacy in Imāmī jurisprudence

The literature of Islamic jurisprudence (*fiqh*) rarely addresses the issue of political theory generally (and specifically where legitimate power might lie). Generally speaking, this issue is not the primary concern of the writers of these compendium-like legal texts. This is not to say political theory did not exist; rather that the explicit exposition of the questions of authority, legitimacy, and governmental organization is not routinely addressed in works of *fiqh*, which concern jurisprudence, not politics. However, there are clear political questions underpinning specific legal questions, and these can be used to explore an underlying vision of the legitimacy of political power within the system of jurisprudence. In studies of the Imāmī legal tradition, this has been a common method of discerning Imāmī political theory. For example, when discussing the distribution of the alms tax (*zakāt*), the Imāmī doctrine that this is the responsibility of the Imam unavoidably drifts into a discussion of political power during the Imam's absence. The solutions to this issue proposed by Imāmī jurists over the centuries are multifarious.[16] The answers of the various Imāmī writers reveal varying levels of acceptance of existing political structures, the construction of alternative authority structures, and, therefore, underlying political attitudes that might be combined to construct an Imāmī political theory. Aside from *zakāt*, a number of issues can be used to tease out where Imāmī jurists might locate political authority during the Imam's occultation.[17] In addition to the collection of the religious *zakāt* tax, other relevant issues include

(1) the collection and distribution of the *khums* (lit., "fifth") tax;
(2) the legality of certain forms of land tax (*kharāj* being the most obvious example);
(3) the validity of Friday prayer (without an Imam to lead it);
(4) the implementation of certain legal provisions (including establishing the prescribed punishments or *ḥudūd*);
(5) the treatment of rebels (*bughāt*);
(6) the legitimacy of military action, and specifically whether this action might be termed a *jihād*; and

(7) the acceptability of taking posts in political structures other than those led by a rightful Imam.

It is the last of these issues (i.e., working for the government, expressed as *al-ʿamal maʿa l-sulṭān* or similar locutions) that forms the focus of this chapter.

While recent secondary literature (including some of my own work) uses the treatment of these issues in Imāmī *fiqh* works as test cases for a (post-occultation) Imāmī political theory, the results have not, however, led to unanimity among commentators. There is much dispute over whether (and if so, how much) legitimacy Imāmī jurists accorded political structures during the occultation. In large part, the various positions adopted by scholars in the secondary literature (summarized on p. 112) are reflections on (and developments of) the findings of Wilferd Madelung, who, in an important article, edits and analyzes the treatise of al-Sharīf al-Murtaḍā (d. 436/1044) on the issue of "working for the government."[18] In this chapter, my purpose is to reexamine this treatise (and Madelung's analysis of it), compare it with treatments of the issue of "working for the government" in early Islam, and thereby explore what I have termed above as the "pragmatic political quietism" of the Imāmī tradition.

The question of "working for the government" in the legal context

Al-Sharīf al-Murtaḍā was not the first jurist to discuss whether or not (and if so, under what circumstances and in what roles) one should work for the government. There is extensive evidence of legal disputes, both in *ḥadīth* literature and in early *fiqh* writings, that there were ongoing discussions concerning the issue. These discussions draw a fundamental distinction (on occasions implicitly and often explicitly) between oppressive (*ẓālim*) and just (*ʿadl*) rulers. In much of the discussion found in early Islamic literature, there appears to be an implicit assumption that working for a just ruler is not problematic legally (and may even be encouraged or obligatory in certain circumstances). An individual is at least permitted (and perhaps expected) to provide services to a ruler who is just (such as the Prophet). The issue becomes more complicated when the ruler is unjust.

In the early *ḥadīth* literature, the focus is on working for an unjust or oppressive political authority. Implicitly, a legal or moral (or more broadly religious) issue only emerges when the ruler is unjust (or oppressive).[19] For example,

> Kaʿb b. ʿUjra said, the Messenger of God came out to us, and … said, "Listen! Have you heard that after me there will be leaders? Those who visit them and declare their lies to be truth, and help them with their oppression are not of me, and I am not of them, and they will not enter *ḥawḍ*. Those who do not visit them, and do not help them in their oppression, and do not declare their lies to be truth, they are of me, and I am of them; they will enter *ḥawḍ*."[20]

Clearly, the report here is part of a polemic against those who support the (allegedly) oppressive leaders who will come after the Prophet. There are more pithy expressions of the same sentiment: "The people of injustice (*jawr*) and their helpers are in hellfire." And, "the oppressors (*al-ẓalama*) and their helpers are in hellfire."[21]

In these reports, the implicit argument is that it is the injustice of the ruler that makes working for him legally problematic. Like most *ḥadīth* reports, these can be, first and foremost, taken as evidence that the issue was debated in the period before the emergence of defined legal schools and the composition of *fiqh* literature.

Reports of the early legal authorities and their views also demonstrate that the problematic factor is the unjust nature of the ruler, not working for the ruler per se. The famous report attributed to Sufyān al-Thawrī (d. 161/778) represents perhaps the most restrictive position in early Islamic legal discourse: "A tailor came to Sufyān al-Thawrī and said, 'I make garments for the *sulṭān*—do you think I am one of those who help the oppressors?' Sufyān said to him, 'Rather you are one of the oppressors—those who help the oppressors sell you the needles and the cloth.'"[22] In this case, working for the ruler who is oppressive makes one an oppressor. The distinction between the categories of oppressor and the one who assists the oppressor shifts, such that anyone who directly helps an oppressor is an oppressor, but anyone who sells to the one who helps the oppressor (now redefined as an oppressor himself) is a "helper." The helpers are, of course, partly culpable and have transgressed, but they are not themselves oppressors.[23]

For Sufyān, then, one is tainted by oppression even if one sells materials to those who manufacture goods that the *sulṭān* uses. This strict doctrine of association implies that one becomes corrupt simply by providing goods to an unjust ruler. The early legal literature, though, reveals more ambivalence on the matter. In the *Muwaṭṭaʾ*, Ibn al-Qāsim is asked about an unjust ruler who demands that an individual take part in carrying out the specified punishments (*ḥudūd*—such as amputation or stoning). While Mālik does not appear to have ruled on this, Ibn al-Qāsim's answer is that one only obeys when one knows the judgment has been passed correctly. That is, the injustice of the ruler does not necessarily mean that the implementation of just and proper punishment on offenders should be prevented. "As for those who know [the *imam*] to be unjust (*jawr*), then if it is clear to you that he rules justly according to God's limits, and correctly in terms of evidence from just people who stand up—then do [what they order]."[24] That is, an unjust ruler can give legally valid rules, which deserve obedience. Ibn al-Qāsim is also asked about a just governor "who knows the *sunna*" who orders the *ḥudūd* (punishments for crimes in which the form of punishment is stipulated in revelation). In this case, also, the order is obeyed, but, in contrast to the case of the unjust ruler, there is no need to verify the procedure whereby the rule was created. Here, the discussion reveals an awareness of the tension between, on the one hand, a rule being valid because it was issued by a legitimate power and, on the other hand, it being valid because it is appropriate and fair, given the evidence. Regarding the legal literature (including *ḥadīth*, *fiqh*, and biographical sources), this is the earliest nuanced discussion of the question of these different forms of legal validity; here it is applied to the issues of, first, whether one should participate in any system of government (just or unjust) and, second, whether an unjust ruler can issue a valid, just edict that deserves obedience. The fact that the former issue was discussed here could indicate the emergence of the opinion that one should not even cooperate with a just ruler.

These isolated examples, however, conflate a number of issues that later jurists disaggregated. The first concerns the question of working for (or with) any *sulṭān*, whether just or unjust (cf. the *Muwaṭṭa'* discussion); the second addresses the legality of offering support (or help) to an oppressive *sulṭān* (cf. the *ḥadīth* texts); the third is a discussion over whether one can be paid for this support, assuming it is allowed; the fourth concerns the issue of what counts as "support" (cf. Sufyān and the tailor, in which providing an oppressive *sulṭān* with cloth makes one an oppressor); and fifth, are there different rules and regulations for taking up positions of judge, or governor, or lower level jobs (such as a tailor).

It was some time before a full description of the various opinions and their arguments was laid out. In many works, the legality of working for a legitimate ruler appears to be taken for granted and is hardly discussed. Regarding "taking up office" for an unjust ruler, an early exposition can be found in the *Naṣīḥat al-mulūk* of pseudo-Māwardī (dated by some commentators to the early fourth/tenth century and erroneously attributed to the well-known Abū l-Ḥasan al-Māwardī [d. 448/1058]). It is not clear what is excluded from "taking up office," but pseudo-Māwardī offers an inclusive list: "acting as a secretary, judge, and being a market inspector and such tasks." His final phrase substantially widens the scope.

While essentially a work from the "mirrors for princes" (*naṣīḥat al-mulūk*) genre, a review of the views on working for an unjust ruler reveals that they are clearly derived from *fiqh* discussions:

> The scholars (*ʿulamāʾ*) have disputed over taking office with an unjust king (*al-malik al-jāʾir*) and an oppressive ruler (*al-sulṭān al-ẓālim*).[25] A large number forbid it; another group disapproves of it, and the rest permit it as along as the ruler does not order the one working for him to perform an injustice, and force him to commit an act of oppression. When he does so order, then it is forbidden to take office in [the ruler's] employment, unless he is forced to do so, unwillingly and in fear that he will be killed or tortured beyond what he could bear.
>
> A large number of [scholars] distinguish between these acts, and forbid some—namely all those acts that involve illegally taking someone's wealth, and spilling blood without justification, or imprisoning or punishing [someone]. They permit acting as a secretary, judge, being a market inspector, and such tasks.
>
> Those who forbid this refer to God's statement, "Do not make contracts with the oppressors," and the prophetic statement, "There is no obedience of a created being in disobedience to the Creator." They say, "How can you permit taking up office and assisting [the ruler] when he has no legitimacy or covenant with God?"
>
> The others say, "If he does not order you to disobey [God], and permits you to rule in accordance with the orders of God, then it is recommended that you do this in order to uphold the truth, to enhance the rule [of the divine law], to reject falsehood and to repel oppression."[26]

The intricacies of the positions outlined in this passage are worth discussing. Here, I outline the four views on the topic of taking up office for the unjust imam (although at first glance there appear to be only three):

(1) It is forbidden under all circumstances.
(2) It is discouraged (without elaboration of the legal effects).
(3) It is permitted (but with conditions).
(4) It is recommended (under specific circumstances).

It is not clear which opinion the author of the *Naṣīḥat al-mulūk* affirms, but it is notable that he gives more space to the third and fourth opinions (which may actually be combined into "permitted with conditions" or under certain circumstances recommended). The "conditions" for permission are that one does not perform injustice or violence. The "circumstances" that indicate that it might be recommended are when the rule issued by the unjust ruler is clearly correct, and he does not order the individual to transgress God's law.

These are not the only early (i.e., before al-Sharīf al-Murtaḍā's treatise was composed) examples of legal discussions that assess the issue of working for a ruler; there are in fact numerous references.[27] All these discussions involve, of course, imprecise notions (what does injustice mean, and what counts as transgressing God's law); whatever the range of opinions and caveats applied to them, they create the legal backdrop against which one can evaluate subsequent discussions. As I demonstrate, al-Sharīf al-Murtaḍā's treatise, titled *Masʾala fī ʿamal maʿa l-sulṭān* ["The issue of working for the government"], is best seen as a continuation of these legal discussions, exemplified by the *ḥadīth* texts, the discussions in the *Muwaṭṭaʾ*, and the summary of juristic differences (*khilāf*) laid out in the *Naṣīḥat al-mulūk* and in many other texts before al-Sharīf al-Murtaḍā wrote his treatise. Al-Murtaḍā's form of argument, the options he entertains, and his modes of expression are all drawn from more general discussions; clearly, this was not an issue that only concerned the Twelver Shīʿa, even though al-Murtaḍā's answers were, in some ways, characteristic of the broader Shīʿī perspective.

Al-Sharīf al-Murtaḍā's treatise on working for the government

Al-Sharīf al-Murtaḍā is well known as a Shīʿī theologian and jurist; in particular, he is recognized for his exploitation of Basran Muʿtazilī ideas in an Imāmī framework.[28] Detailed academic expositions of his thought are now available and provide a useful background to his thought and influence. While in many areas he is considered a maverick, his treatment of the legal question of whether or not one is permitted to work for the government is the first comprehensive attempt to outline the Imāmī position on the issue.

The Imams made numerous statements clarifying their generally negative stance toward working for an unjust ruler.[29] For example, Imam Jaʿfar al-Ṣādiq condemned those who work for the Umayyads:

> [Al-Ṣādiq] said, "if the Banū Umayya had not found someone to write for them, collect their taxes and fight for them, lead their prayers, when at the same time they usurped our right (*ḥaqqanā*), then if the people had abandoned them, they would have had nothing other than what their own hands possessed …"[30]

Similarly, Muḥammad b. ʿUdhāfir tells of his father's encounter with Jaʿfar al-Ṣādiq. ʿUdhāfir asks whether he should be considered someone who helps the oppressors because he did business with Abū Ayyūb and Rabīʿ b. Yūnus (who both played roles in the ʿAbbāsid court). The Imam replied that he is indeed a helper of the oppressors.[31] These views can be seen as similar in tone and position as the reports given above from contemporary Sunnī sources. However, many of these reports imply that the rulers' injustice is not a result of their actions in office (i.e., whether, once they acquired power, they acted fairly and in accordance with the *sharīʿa*). Rather, their injustice is a result of their usurping the Imams' legitimate right to rule. These reports form the background for al-Sharīf al-Murtaḍā's discussion, but like most so-called sources of jurisprudence, they do not control his discussion. As we see, for him the oppressive nature (*ẓulm*) of the ruler is primarily because of the way in which he behaves; his legitimacy (i.e., whether he is *muḥiqq* or *mubṭil*) is a linked, but separate issue, and not al-Murtaḍā's primary concern.

Al-Sharīf al-Murtaḍā's treatise on working for the government first came to the notice of Western academic scholars in an article published by Wilferd Madelung in 1980. In that article, Madelung introduced his edited and translated version of Majlis MS5187 (Tehran), attributed to al-Sharīf al-Murtaḍā.[32] It is quite a late manuscript (dated 1818, nearly 800 years after al-Murtaḍā's death), though Madelung states that he has no reason to doubt its authenticity. There may be other copies of the text, not least the collection of treatises used by Aḥmad al-Ḥusaynī for his 1405/1985 four-volume collection, *Rasāʾil al-Sharīf al-Murtaḍā*.[33] Al-Ḥusaynī's version of the treatise appears to have been in Ayatollah Muṣṭafā Ṣafāʾī l-Khwānṣārī's private collection in Qum. Al-Ḥusaynī's edition of the text varies from that of Madelung's at certain points; al-Ḥusaynī, though, appears to know Madelung's edition (or at least knows of one of the Iranian reprints of it), as he refers to the "published version" (*al-maṭbūʿ*) of the text (which corresponds to Madelung's edition) without giving its full reference. We should also note that both Madelung and al-Ḥusaynī suggest various corrections to what are presumably copyists' errors in the manuscript. In general, al-Ḥusaynī's emendations are certainly possible alternatives, but, in the main, I would argue that Madelung's variants appear equally, perhaps more, plausible. These differences, though, rarely change the meaning in a substantial way, as far as I can tell, and the variants need not detain us further here.

In the treatise itself, there is a brief introduction providing the background to its writing. Abū l-Qāsim al-Maghribī (ʿAbbāsid vizier, agent provocateur, and author of the well-known mirror for princes, *Kitāb al-siyāsa*) discussed the issue in 415/1024, and this is what prompted al-Murtaḍā to compose this treatise. Al-Murtaḍā divides the government (*sulṭān*) into legitimate and just (*muḥiqq wa-ʿādil*) and illegitimate, unjust, and usurpatory (*mubṭil ẓālim mutaghallib*). As in the *ḥadīth* literature, and in the early *fiqh* discussions recorded in pseudo-Māwardī, there is little exploration of the permissibility of working (or "being appointed to a position of authority"—*al-walāya min qibal al-sulṭān*) for a "just" and "legitimate" government. Al-Murtaḍā simply states that it is permitted and sometimes may actually be obligatory when such a government asks for it. As we see, Madelung makes much of this brief statement, which I return to below.

Al-Murtaḍā's treatise goes into much more detail about how to justify working for an unjust *sulṭān*, a fact that, in itself, might indicate that this was either a common occurrence or a disputed element. In any case, he clearly pays particular attention to it. In the rest of the treatise, following this opening categorization of rulers into two types, al-Murtaḍā embarks on a detailed justification for taking up office, even though working for an oppressive government is, to use the Muʿtazilī definition, essentially wrong (*qabīḥ*). The term he uses here, and throughout the treatise, for the unjust ruler is *ẓālim*. However, it is clear that al-Murtaḍā sees this term as synonymous with another common term for someone who is "unjust," namely, *jāʾir*, as in the passage:

> How can it be known that the person who appears to be holding office on behalf an "unjust" ruler (*al-sulṭān al-jāʾir*) is [in fact] legitimately doing so, such that it is not permitted to oppose or contradict him? He appears to be an appointee of a rebellious oppressor, against whom it is permitted to fight *jihād*, and whose orders it is improper to implement?[34]

The difference between *jāʾir* and *ẓālim* might be parsed as follows: the *jāʾir* is "illegitimate" and the *ẓālim* is both illegitimate and oppressive, though this proposition requires further evidence. For al-Murtaḍā, this distinction does not seem relevant—since legitimacy (having the "right" to rule) is summed up in the term he uses only once in the treatise—that is, *muḥiqq*. Al-Murtaḍā is defending a position that affirms that even though working for an unjust ruler is an essentially bad act, such work might still be legally assessed as obligatory or permitted if it brings about good. The broader issue here is the problematic Muʿtazilī correlation between the moral categorizations (*taḥsīn* and *taqbīḥ*) and the legal categorizations (*aḥkām*). Can morally bad acts sometimes be legally obligatory? This, as we know, was a matter of some debate and controversy.[35] Here I restrict myself to summarizing al-Murtaḍā's assessment of the legal categories (obligatory, permitted, forbidden).

As al-Murtaḍā lays out in the rest of the treatise, taking up office for an unjust ruler or political authority might fall into one of three legal categories: obligatory, permitted, or forbidden. How it is categorized depends on the circumstances. It might be obligatory if the individual recognizes that by taking the job he can promote adherence to the *sharīʿa*. For this, there may be no compulsion involved, simply that the individual seeks out or is offered employment, and in assessing whether to accept it, decides he can do some good by taking up the post. However, for al-Murtaḍā, this is not the only way in which it might be obligatory. The individual might be forced, on pain of death, to take up the post. If he is so threatened, he must undertake the work, because not doing so would be a transgression of the rationally established "requirement to preserve life." However, al-Murtaḍā appears to distinguish between being forced to take up the post (but having the freedom when doing it to promote adherence to the *sharīʿa*) and when being forced to take up the post (and being unable to promote the *sharīʿa*). In the latter case, one is assuming *taqiyya* (dissimulation), that is, the legal agent (*mukallaf*) can transgress the law and will not face a penalty (in the next life) for failing to abide by the rules of the *sharīʿa*. In this last case only, it appears that the individual is not permitted to do anything that brings about physical harm to another individual, *safk al-dimāʾ* (lit., "the spilling of blood").[36] In the other areas of the law, the individual can harm others legally, it seems; but when under *taqiyya*, this is not permitted. From this, I surmise that there are three ways in which taking up office for an unjust/illegitimate *sulṭān* can become obligatory.

With regard to the permission to take up office, al-Murtaḍā specifies only one context, namely, when there is a threat to his property (but not to his person). In these cases, the *mukallaf* can choose whether to accept the risk of damage to property or to carry out the work. Al-Murtaḍā does not appear to express a preference between taking up the office or refusing to do so—both are permitted. The circumstances in which taking up office is forbidden are not explicitly laid out but are apparent through the difference "issues" (*masāʾil*) al-Murtaḍā tackles. If one is not compelled, and one can see no way in which one can do good (i.e., promote adherence to the *sharīʿa*), and can only see ways in which one can do harm (i.e., transgress the *sharīʿa*), then it is forbidden to take up the office. It is important to note that in all these decisions, the individual is inevitably uncertain about what the outcome of his actions might be. He therefore must follow signs (*amārāt*), which might enable him to come to the opinion (*ẓann*) that this or that is likely to happen. It is on this basis that the individual can determine the appropriate course of action.[37]

The various rules can be represented in a tabular form as follows[38]:

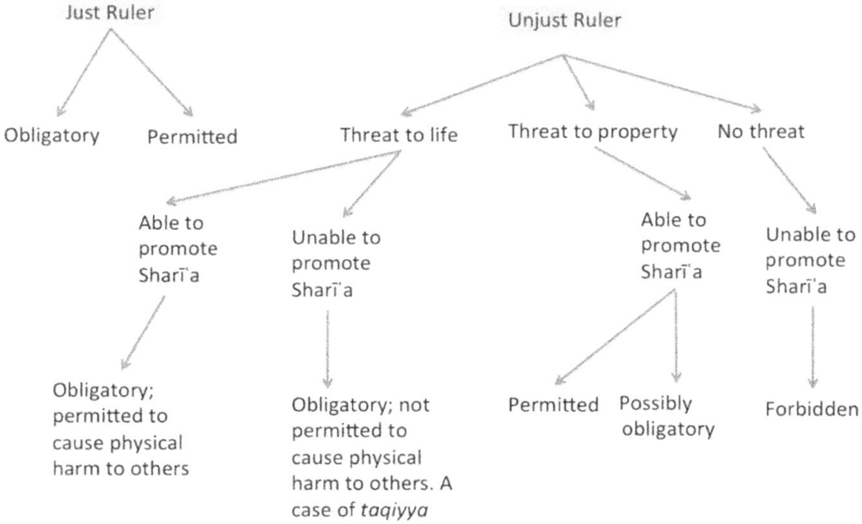

I believe that these regulations and rulings for particular circumstances indicate that al-Murtaḍā was looking for ways in which the individual might work with and for the various rulers during the occultation, even though they were far from perfect, and are not legitimate in the sense of being, even in derivative form, the government of the Imam.

The whole treatise, with its focus on working for an unjust ruler, clearly draws on the wider juristic discussions in the generation of scholars before al-Murtaḍā and outlined in the previous section (from Mālik onward). In that context, al-Murtaḍā's exposition is certainly flavored with Shīʿī elements. In particular, when he draws on the theory of *taqiyya* and *safk al-dimāʾ*, he gives the treatise a Shīʿī emphasis (notwithstanding the fact that these notions were not entirely absent from Sunnī discussions). However, the treatise is more clearly a development of the various positions recorded in, for example, *Naṣīḥat al-mulūk* ("advice for princes" literature) rather than any internal, exclusively Shīʿī discussion.

The academic scholarship on al-Sharīf al-Murtaḍā's treatise

Madelung's exposition of al-Murtaḍā's treatise from his 1980 article following his edition and translation focuses almost entirely on the phrase in the introductory section of the treatise, where al-Murtaḍā divides government into two types:

> Know that the ruler may be of two kinds: legitimate (*muḥiqq*) and just, or illegitimate (*mubṭil*), unjust and usurpatory. There is no question in regard to holding office on behalf of the legitimate, just ruler since it is permissible and may even be obligatory, if the ruler commands it as a duty and makes acceptance incumbent.[39]

This passage, in Madelung's view, establishes that for al-Murtaḍā, the legitimate just *sulṭān* is not only the rule of the sinless Imam who is in occultation. There are numerous problems with this deduction, which I outline below. In Madelung's analysis, this passage indicates that the legitimate just ruler can, for al-Murtaḍā and for subsequent Shīʿī jurists, be "any ruler of government acting in the [Imam's] name and in accordance with Imāmī law ..."[40] The decisive evidence for Madelung is that this position was elaborated by al-Murtaḍā's pupil, Muḥammad b. Ḥasan al-Ṭūsī (d. 460/1067). Madelung states that al-Ṭūsī's discussion of the question (in his *Kitāb al-nihāya*) is clearly a reference to just rulers in general and not exclusively to the sinless Imams; rather, there is no reason to believe that this was also the view of al-Murtaḍā.[41] Madelung continues:

> The question deserves particular notice since some Western scholars have sometimes expressed the opinion that according to Imāmī belief all government in the absence of the *Imām* is necessarily and inescapably illegitimate. This is clearly not the case. It is true that primary legitimacy belongs only to the *Imām*. In the absence of the *Imām*, however, any ruler or government acting in his name and in accordance with Imāmī law acquires a derivative, functional legitimacy and can command not only the sincere obedience, but also the loyal support of the faithful.[42]

This seems, to me, a rather hasty conclusion on the basis of the evidence presented here. First, even Madelung recognizes that al-Murtaḍā's statement, taken in isolation, does not clearly imply that the legitimate just ruler is someone other than the sinless Imam. This is why he turns to al-Ṭūsī's passage in the *Kitāb al-nihāya* to elucidate al-Murtaḍā's (less explicit) notion of the "just, legitimate ruler." Second, al-Murtaḍā and al-Ṭūsī do not agree on all topics in jurisprudence, and there is no reason to use a passage in al-Ṭūsī to determine what al-Murtaḍā might have meant in this treatise. Third, al-Ṭūsī's passage in the *Kitāb al-nihāya* (as employed by Madelung) is, for me at least, far from explicit on the question of whether this term applies to a ruler other than the sinless Imam.[43]

Returning to what al-Murtaḍā actually states in his treatise (rather than what al-Ṭūsī might have meant in a separate work), we can see a clear distinction between the just legitimate ruler (*ʿādil muḥiqq*) and the unjust illegitimate usurpatory rulers (*ẓālim mubṭil mutaghallib*). Al-Murtaḍā's own binary categorization would seem to undermine Madelung's interpretation here. The unjust, invalid ruler is also *mutaghallib* (usurpatory), that is, he has taken power by force rather than by right. The term distinguishes such a ruler from the properly invested ruler (i.e., the Shīʿī Imam who was explicitly designated as sinless). In the historical context, all actual rulers in al-Murtaḍā's contemporary context gained power on the basis of military success rather than directly by pure right. Even if such a ruler is just and fair in the daily administration of the state, he is still *mutaghallib*. From this, one can justifiably conclude that any ruler other than the sinless Imam himself is *mutaghallib*, and that al-Murtaḍā is clearly referring to the sinless Imam.

Notwithstanding these Shīʿī elements of the discussion, it is clear that al-Murtaḍā is participating in the wider Muslim legal discussion around the issue of working for the government. The terminology, the questions and issues he addresses, and the answers he entertains are all drawn from previous *fiqh* discussions outlined in the previous section. Those discussions (which are not exclusively Shīʿī) use a basic set of categories employed by jurists, often without explicit definition and almost always without reference to specific real-world instances of the phenomena classified in a category. These terms, I would argue, include *imām, sulṭān, jāʾir, ẓālim*, and *ʿādil*.[44] Therefore, when al-Murtaḍā refers to *al-sulṭān al-ʿādil* (or a later jurist uses the term *al-imām al-ʿādil*), they are employing a legal category rather than spelling out which people may or may not fulfill the criteria for inclusion in this category. The legal discussions can (and do) proceed without naming any *sulṭān* or *imām* who is *ʿādil*. Conclusions about the legitimacy or otherwise of a government other than that of the sinless Imam are inappropriate here. Rather, the fact that works of *fiqh* do not employ real-world referents enabled Shīʿī jurists to participate in the broader Muslim legal discourse without embarking on extended theological discussions about the nature and character of the Imam.

It is also clear that it is difficult to untangle the two notions of justice and legitimacy in the juristic literature. Al-Murtaḍā combines justice and legitimacy into a single category and contrasts this category with another (in which he combines injustice and illegitimacy). This, I would argue, is generally a trend among Shīʿī juristic writers, though there is much nuance in their schemas. Other writers, implicitly or explicitly, might make a distinction: an illegitimate ruler could, perhaps, act justly. For the Twelver Shīʿa, it is almost axiomatic (given their foundational narrative) that the simple fact of holding power does not establish the legitimacy of that individual's rule; this was certainly not true for all Shīʿī strands and certainly not across the legal and political spectrum of early Islam. As outlined below, the situation is further complicated by the observation of some researchers that the term *al-sulṭān al-jāʾir* ("the unjust ruler") in many Shīʿī writings means not an unjust but an illegitimate ruler.[45]

Turning to subsequent scholarship on al-Murtaḍā's treatise, we find that in the academic literature, Madelung's edition (and his characterization of al-Sharīf al-Murtaḍā's principal message in the treatise) has become a central reference point in an intense debate about the nature of political authority in Twelver Shīʿī thought. The debate was, primarily, a response to the need to understand Iran's post-revolutionary government and its claims to legitimacy. Much subsequent academic comment has focused on Madelung's concluding remarks: namely, that al-Murtaḍā's thesis demonstrates (for him) that for the Shīʿa, a just and legitimate government during the occultation need not be confined to that of the hidden sinless Imam.

Madelung's view (namely, that premodern Shīʿī jurists considered political legitimacy to refer generally to just rulers, and not merely to the sinless Imams) has been much cited in Western scholarship. One of the principal hypotheses of Said Amir Arjomand's approach, including his 1984 monograph *The Shadow of God and the Hidden Imam*, is that Shīʿī jurists regularly accorded political legitimacy to governments other than that of the sinless Imam.[46] In *The "Just Ruler" (al-sulṭān al-ʿādil) in Shīʿite Islam* (published in 1988), Abdulaziz Sachedina argues that the term *al-sulṭān al-ʿādil* in Shīʿī works of law (explicitly in relation to al-Shaykh al-Mufīd, al-Ṭūsī, and al-ʿAllāma al-Ḥillī) is not restricted to the sinless Imams but also can refer to a just ruler who enforces the *sharīʿa* and "enjoins the good and prohibits the evil."[47] Sometimes, he remarks, the phrase is left unqualified, and hence this gives rise to an ambiguity that is clarified by subsequent authors; sometimes the ambiguity is understood as deliberate, as the writer may have been composing his work under circumstances that required dissimulation (*taqiyya*).[48] Khaled Abou El Fadl, in his monograph *Rebellion and Violence in Islamic Law*, discusses the Shīʿī view and remarks in a note: "Madelung ['Treatise'] argues that after the fifth/eleventh century not every illegitimate ruler was considered unjust. I think his argument is persuasive."[49] Madelung's view confirms Abou El Fadl's own position: namely, that a ruler's legitimacy was distinct from his justice in later Imāmī writings. This meant that Imāmīs were no longer forced to take up an inherently oppositional stance to any rule other than that of the sinless Imam; for Abou El Fadl, this is what had characterized earlier Shīʿī discussions.

Arjomand, Sachedina, and Abou El Fadl, then, all maintain Madelung's line of argumentation, namely, that Shīʿī legal discussions, particularly after the formative period, extended justice (and also some form of legitimacy) beyond the rule of the sinless Imams to other supposedly "just" rulers (in the more general sense of the term).

However, there has been another reaction to Madelung's important article. In relation to this question generally, and Madelung's work in particular, Hossein Modarressi writes:

> An ordinary ruler is considered to be an unjust ruler and his rule regarded as illegitimate, according to a prevailing view in Shīʿī law. The term "unjust" here is not used in its general sense, but rather refers to the injustice this sort of ruler perpetrated against the Imāms and their legitimate successors [namely the jurists] by usurping their rights. All rulers, except the *Imām* and his legitimate successors are to be regarded as unjust rulers according to the above statements.[50]

In Shīʿī law, it is, Modarressi states,

> an offence to help an "unjust ruler" ... It is strictly forbidden to associate with unjust rulers, to defend them against their enemies and to hold office on their behalf unless one holds office with the intention of supporting what is right, and of taking care of coreligionists affairs in matters such as the reduction of their taxes.[51]

Modarressi acknowledges, but considers atypical, those scholars—both in Shīʿī history and in Western academia—who consider rulers other than the sinless Imams potentially "just."[52]

Norman Calder's various comments take a similar, but more strident, vein, first in his dissertation (completed in 1979, a year before Madelung published his edition and analysis of al-Murtaḍā's treatise) and then more explicitly in an article on political legitimacy in the legal thought of the Safavid jurist Muḥammad Bāqir al-Sabzawārī published in 1987. In his much-cited thesis, Calder argues that "[t]he relationship between the sacred community (the *dār al-īmān*) and the profane power, as depicted in juridical works, underwent little or no change from Buyid to Safavid times. The ruler was always *ẓālim/ jāʾir*. The Shīʿī community, if they submitted to his power, did not concede his authority."[53] In reference to the specific citation of al-Ṭūsī to support the view on al-Murtaḍā's use of the term *al-sulṭān al-ʿādil*, Calder explicitly disagrees:

> The just sultan is he who is *ʿādil* who orders the *maʿrūf* [the good] and forbids the *munkar* [evil] who puts things in their places etc. That this is the *imām* seems to me inevitable though the context in isolation may [deliberately?] permit of other interpretations. Later discussion of the same problem indicated that the *sulṭān ʿādil* was the *imām al-aṣl*. Shahīd II[54] whose remarks on the

> general problem of taking up official posts betray his considerable concern and interest, relates those remarks entirely to the *sulṭān jāʾir*; he displays no interest in the *sulṭān ʿādil*. It would appear that for all the Imāmī *fuqahāʾ* the *sulṭān ʿādil* was the *imām* and remarks about service with him were of merely formal interest. Ṭūsī's assertion that service with him is permissible, desirable maybe indeed *wājib* was generally confirmed and prompted minimal elaboration.[55]

The general point underlying Calder's presentation concerns the absence of elaboration or discussion in the *fiqh* literature (as with al-Ṭūsī's position), and the likelihood that this is evidence (indirect perhaps, but nonetheless evidence) that the matter is of little practical interest. In his later article, and in specific reference to Madelung's comments on al-Murtaḍā's treatise, Calder writes,

> As it happens, I believe that terms of the type *al-sulṭān al-muḥiqq al-ʿādil*, when used in a work of *fiqh*, including the treatise of Murtaḍā, refer only to the *Imām*. In other respects, however, the interpretation given to Murtaḍā's work by Madelung is a possible one; and in view of his conception of "primary and inherent legitimacy" as belonging to the *Imām*, it may be that he and I do not differ very much. I do nevertheless wish to argue that the systematic elaboration of the Imāmī juristic tradition was such as to preclude the possibility of any secular governor being the legitimate agent of the *sharīʿa*, except in a number of secondary and derived senses.[56]

I could add additional references here, but these, I hope, demonstrate that Madelung's 1980 article established al-Murtaḍā's text as an important (perhaps defining) contribution to any "political theory" in Imāmī law. But what, precisely, it indicated was a matter of some dispute, and Madelung's own interpretation has not been universally accepted as an accurate account of al-Murtaḍā's treatise itself or as representative of the Imāmī position more generally.

With regard to the term *al-sulṭān al-ʿādil* in the treatise, my own position is broadly in line with that of Calder and Modarressi. The phrase is, at the very least, imprecise (possibly deliberately so, as Calder appears to argue), but this is an aside. I would argue that al-Murtaḍā's choice of words and phrasing is not aimed at resolving the question of political legitimacy during the occultation as much as it is a contribution to the legal discussions about working for an *unjust* ruler. This question occupies nearly all of his treatise, and it is with this question that he is most concerned. This, in itself, could indicate that working for an unjust *sulṭān* was the most pressing issue. His approach is highly pragmatic: though a *sulṭān* may be unjust, or even illegitimate (understanding *jāʾir* to have both meanings, as was the norm in later Imāmī *fiqh*), one could work for him, and this need not be under conditions of *taqiyya*. Instead, for the Shīʿa, there may be conditions that call for political tolerance and openness; in his thesis, al-Murtaḍā recognizes that one can, by working with an unjust ruler, do good even if working for him is, essentially, bad.

Conclusions

With regard to the depiction of the Imāmiyya as "quietist," how does al-Sharīf al-Murtaḍā's treatise on working for the government qualify such a characterization? The quietism displayed here is certainly not a withdrawal from all political structures, combined with a refusal to rebel—it is not a pietistic quietism that one might find (among certain early Ḥanbalīs for example). Al-Sharīf al-Murtaḍā permits (and in some circumstances, obligates) the individual to work for a government. He therefore encourages engagement with political structures, whatever the government's moral character (*ʿādil, jāʾir, ẓālim*); and this position is quietist in the sense that it does not promote rebellion. It is, if it is not a contradiction in terms, a politically engaged quietism that is essentially pragmatic. If one wishes to stipulate a disengagement with politics (and not simply the refusal to rebel, even when the ruler is manifestly unjust) as the hallmark of quietism, then al-Murtaḍā is not "quietist" at all. Similarly, subsequent Imāmī writers (who, until the contemporary period, broadly affirm al-Murtaḍā's position) are not quietist.

There is, though, an imprecise link between the ruler's legitimacy and quietism in early Imāmī legal thinking specifically and in Islamic law more generally. Some quietist traditions clearly refuse to countenance political opposition because they consider that the ruler, irrespective of his moral character, has the right to rule (one might say he has "legitimacy"; this has been the characteristic of some Ḥanafī writers). The Imāmī *ḥadīth* literature, and legal discussions before al-Murtaḍā's treatise, appears to recommend (and even obligate) a political disengagement, since all rulers are unjust (*ẓālim* or *jāʾir*). As noted, Modarressi argues that this injustice is not related to their cruelty to their subjects or their disregard of the *sharīʿa*, but rather they are unjust to the Imams (who alone have the legitimate right to rule). Here injustice is very close to usurpation (*taghallub*), a term al-Murtaḍā himself uses. The Sunnī material appears to be more accepting of an unjust ruler, and therefore it permits working for him. Al-Murtaḍā's treatise moves the debate forward in Imāmī jurisprudence by working within the context of the existing legal debate on working for an unjust ruler, and focusing on the ruler's moral character, rather than on his usurpation of power from the Imams. For al-Murtaḍā, injustice, illegitimacy, and usurpation (*ẓulm, ibṭāl, taghallub*) go together, but they are distinct characteristics of an immoral ruler. In investigating the legality of employment with him, the most significant of these are his injustice and oppression. Al-Murtaḍā argues that even if the ruler is evil, the individual—if they can see good coming from service to the *ẓālim*—should take up office with him.

There are, for al-Murtaḍā, multiple ways in which the individual thinking of taking up office with the illegitimate and unjust *sulṭān* can work with the government for the general good, even if it comes to enforcing *ḥudūd* punishments. The prime example of this is probably the position of judge, but it might also apply to working for the police (*shurṭa*) or market inspector (*muḥtasib*). If one wanted to speak to al-Murtaḍā's immediate historical context, the ruling set out in the treatise examined here could also be applied to positions of ministers or clerks in the emerging (Sunnī-dominated) polity. In all this, though, al-Murtaḍā appears quite clear—the ruler is still immoral, usurpatory, and illegitimate. This quietism, if it can be called that, might promote political involvement, but it does not cede principal and primary legitimacy to rulers other than the sinless Imams. Al-Murtaḍā's treatise demonstrates that his form of Imāmī quietism requires political engagement with the unjust ruling power, while not implying its political legitimacy. This is the central reason I refer to it as "pragmatic political quietism."

In arguing in this way, al-Murtaḍā's position, and those of subsequent Imāmī scholars, was not so different in practice from many Sunnī legal writers. Positions can be taken; judgments enforced. Al-Murtaḍā's position differed in the sense that, as the argument emerged in later Imāmī jurisprudence, in acting as a judge for an unjust *sulṭān*, enacting the *sharīʿa* as best one can, one is not, in reality, working for this *sulṭān*; in fact, one is working for the true, sinless, hidden, Imam.[57] The ruling power may gain a cooperative worker, but this worker is not servile and does not recognize the ruler's authority. This was, it seems, al-Murtaḍā's position, one that proved remarkably resilient to legal modification, even when overtly Shīʿī political powers, such as the Safavids, came to power. Given the permissions, and even the encouragement, given by Shīʿī jurists to those who wished to work with and for the government, it seems rather inappropriate simply to characterize the Imāmīs as "quietist" without outlining the caveats and qualifications detailed in al-Murtaḍā's treatise and expanded on in later Imāmī *fiqh*.

Notes

The research for this chapter was partially funded by the ERC Project "Law, Learning and Authority in Imami Shiʿite Islam" (695245). I am grateful for all the support of the KCFRIS, particularly Saud al-Sarhan and his team. Very useful comments were provided by colleagues in the Centre for the Study of Islam, IAIS, Exeter (namely, Wissam Halawi, Mustafa Baig, Omar Anchassi, Suha Taji-Farouki, Istvan Kristo-Nagy, and Sajjad Rizvi). I particularly thank my colleague, Paul Gledhill, who made extensive comments that motivated me to rethink certain elements of the chapter. I also presented some of the ideas in this chapter at a seminar at Columbia University in November 2017 and benefited from the comments of the audience there.1 See Rodrigo Adem, "Classical *Naṣṣ* Doctrines in Imāmī Shīʿism: On the Usage of an Expository Term," *Shii Studies Review* 1 (2017): 42–71.

2 See W. Madelung, *The Succession to Muhammad* (Cambridge: Cambridge University Press, 1996), 1–27.

3 See Sajjad Rizvi, "Authority in Absence? Shiʿi Politics of Salvation from the Classical Period to Modern Republicanism," *Studies in Christian Ethics* 29 (2016): 204–212.

4 See the references below, particularly those in p. 112.

5 For a preliminary investigation, see Crone, *Medieval Islamic Political Thought* (Edinburgh: Edinburgh University Press, 2004), 110–125.

6 See below, p. 112.

7 Denis McEoin "Aspects of Militancy and Quietism in Imami Shiʿism," *Bulletin (British Society for Middle Eastern Studies)* 11, no. 1 (1984): 19.

8 Crone, *Medieval Islamic Political Thought*, 123.

9 Fāṭimid Ismāʿīlī "activism" is contrasted to Imāmī "quietism" (A. Black, *A History of Islamic Political Thought* (Edinburgh: Edinburgh University Press, 2001), 45); Cook refers to "Imāmī quietism" on occasion, for example, see *Commanding Good and Forbidding Wrong* (Cambridge: Cambridge University Press, 2010), 52 and 262; Bayhom-Daou refers to al-Mufīd as part of a "quietist and legalist current" in T. Bayhom-Daou, *Shaykh Mufid* (Oxford: Oneworld, 2005); we have Nikki Keddie's book devoted to how Shīʿism became activist with the Iranian revolution: *Religion and Politics in Iran Shiʿism from Quietism to Revolution* (New Haven: Yale University Press, 1983); and Katrin Jomaa, "Quietism and Activism," in *The Princeton Encyclopedia of Islamic Political Thought*, ed. Gerhard Böwering et al. (Princeton, NJ: Princeton University Press, 2013), 446: "In premodern history, both Sunni and Twelver Shiʿi attitudes toward illegitimate authorities were predominantly quietist." These references include numerous references to Imāmī quietism.

10 J. Wagemakers, *A Quietist Jihadi: The Ideology and Influence of Abu Muhammad al-Maqdisi* (Cambridge: Cambridge University Press, 2015).

11 Marta Dominguez Diaz, *Women in Sufism* (London: Routledge, 2014), 27ff.

12 See Khaled Abou El Fadl, *Rebellion and Violence in Islamic Law* (Cambridge: Cambridge University Press, 2002), 96–99, for a discussion of quietism.

13 See Cook, *Commanding Good*, 106–107; McEoin "Aspects of Militancy"; J. Van Ess, "Political Ideas in Early Islamic Religious Thought," *British Journal of Middle Eastern Studies* 28, no. 2 (2001): 151–164; and even earlier, Bernard Lewis, "On the Quietist and Activist Traditions in Islamic Political Writing," *Bulletin of the School of Oriental and African Studies* 49, no. 1 (1986), 141–147.

14 It might be argued that using the term "state" to describe medieval political entities is anachronistic; hence, an Islamic state is a misnomer, or even impossible (see W. Hallaq, *The Impossible State: Islamic, Politics and Modernity's Moral Predicament* [New York: Columbia University Press, 2013]). I do not find this usage problematic, but in order to avoid confusion, I refer here to "ruler," "political power," or "systems of government" (or "governance") rather than the "state."

15 Hence the term "quietist" has become associated with the Qadarī or the Māturīdī theological trends in early Islam. Michael Cook, "*Activism and Quietism* in Islam: The Case of the Early Murji'a," in *Islam and Power*, ed. A. Cudsi and A. E. Dessouki (London: Croom Helm, 1981), 15–23.

16 Norman Calder, "Zakāt in Imāmī Shīʿī Jurisprudence, from the Tenth to the Sixteenth Century A.D.," *Bulletin of the School of Oriental and African Studies* 44, no. 3 (1981): 468–480.

17 See, for example, Norman Calder, "Khums in Imāmī Shīʿī Jurisprudence, from the Tenth to the Sixteenth Century A. D.," *Bulletin of the School of Oriental and African Studies* 45, no. 1 (1982): 39–47; Andrew Newman, "Fayd al-Kashani and the Rejection of the Clergy/State Alliance: Friday Prayer as Politics in the Safavid Period," in *The Most Learned of the Shi'a*, ed. Linda Walbridge (Oxford: Oxford University Press, 2000): 34–52; Robert Gleave, "Public Violence, State Legitimacy: The *Iqāmat al-Ḥudūd* and the Sacred State," in *Public Violence in Islamic Societies*, ed. C. Lange and M. Fierro (Edinburgh: Edinburgh University Press, 2009), 256–275.

18 Wilferd Madelung, "A Treatise of the Sharīf al-Murtaḍā on the Legality of Working for the Government '(Mas'ala fī 'l-'amal ma'a 'l-sulṭān),'" *Bulletin of the School of Oriental and African Studies* 43, no. 1 (1980): 18–31. We should bear in mind that the term *sulṭān* did mean not just the individual but a more general sense of "power" or "authority"; see the useful introduction to the term by D. Tor, "Sultan," in *The Princeton Encyclopedia of Islamic Political Thought*, ed. Böwering et al. (Princeton, NJ: Princeton University Press, 2013), 352–354.

19 The terms used here are *jāʾir* and *ẓālim*, with the latter appearing to be more serious than the former. This was discussed in later Shīʿī jurisprudence, and distinctions between the two were made, but it would be far-fetched to think that there is a clear distinction in the *ḥadīth* literature.

20 This *ḥadīth* can be located in many references; see Muḥammad b. ʿĪsā l-Tirmidhī, *Jāmiʿ al-Tirmidhī*, ed. Aḥmad Shākir, Muḥammad Fuʾād ʿAbd al-Bāqī, and Ibrāhīm ʿAṭwa ʿAwaḍ (Beirut: Dār Iḥyāʾ al-Turāth al-ʿArabī, n.d.), "Abwāb al-fitan," book 33, *ḥadīth* no. 2259. The *ḥawḍ* is the pool, which, according to Muslim eschatology, links heaven and earth and from where believers will enter paradise.

21 *Ahl al-jawr/al-ẓalama wa-aʿwānuhum fī l-nār*: al-Ḥākim al-Nīsābūrī, *al-Mustadrak ʿalā l-Saḥīḥayn* (Cairo: Dār al-Ḥaramayn li-l-Ṭibāʿa wa-l-Nashr wa-l-Tawzīʿ, 1997), 4:891. Here I translate *jawr* as "injustice" and *al-imām al-jāʾir* as the unjust imam; I use "oppression" and "oppressor" for *ẓulm* and *ẓālim,* respectively. The terms appear interchangeable in the early *ḥadīth* literature (as these variants demonstrate). Later Shīʿī *fiqh* appears to distinguish between these, giving *jawr* more a sense of someone who is illegitimate and *ẓālim* more specifically the moral quality of an oppressor. How this divergence occurred requires further investigation.

22 Muḥammad Shams al-Dīn al-Dhahabī, *al-Kabāʾir* (Cairo: Dār al-Nadwa al-Jadīd, 1980), 112.

23 A similar story (a Ḥanbalī adaptation, one might say) can be found in the *Manāqib Aḥmad*, where he calls his jailer an oppressor and those who (among other things) buy and sell from him "oppressors." Ibn Jawzī, *Manāqib Aḥmad b. Ḥanbal* (Cairo: Maktabat al-Khānjī, 1979), 231.

24 Ibn al-Qāsim, *al-Mudawwana* (Cairo: Dār al-Kutub, n.d.), 4:509–510.

25 At this stage at least, there does not appear to be a distinction between the terms *ẓālim* and *jāʾir*.

26 Abū l-Ḥasan al-Māwardī (attrib.), *Naṣīḥat al-mulūk* (Kuwait: Maktabat al-Falāḥ, 1403/1983), 292; for a detailed discussion of this work, see Louise Marlow, *Counsel for Kings: Wisdom and Politics in Tenth-Century Iran*. Vol. 1: *The Nasihat al-muluk of Pseudo-Mawardi: Contexts and Themes*. Vol. 2: *The Nasihat al-muluk of Pseudo-Mawardi: Texts, Sources and Authorities* (Edinburgh: Edinburgh University Press, 2016).

27 See, for example, Abū Bakr al-Jaṣṣāṣ, *Aḥkām al-Qurʾān* (Beirut: Dār al-Kitāb al-ʿArabī, 1978), 1:86.

28 Devin Stewart, "al-Sharīf al-Murtaḍā (d. 436/1044)," in *Islamic Legal Thought: A Compendium of Muslim Jurists*, ed. Oussama Arabi, David S. Powers, and Susan A. Spectorsky (Leiden: Brill, 2013), 167–210; and now Hussein Abdulsater, *Shiʿi Doctrine, Mu'tazili Theology: al-Sharif al-Murtada and Imami Discourse* (Edinburgh: Edinburgh University Press, 2017), particularly Chapter 1.

29 Ali-Rida Rizek has completed a useful and detailed study of the reports in al-Kulaynī's collection on working for the government: "The Lawfulness of Working for the Unjust Ruler in Early Imami Thought and Literature" (PhD dissertation, American University of Beirut, 2014), though I am not sure whether his suggestion about the progression of positions (from prohibition to conditional permissibility) between the Imams is correct.

30 Muḥammad b. Yaʿqūb al-Kulaynī, *al-Kāfī* (Tehran: Dār al-Kutub al-Islāmiyya, 1388/1968–9), 5:106.

31 al-Kulaynī, *al-Kāfī*, 5:105. ʿUdhāfir is dumbstruck. The Imām adds, "I only wish to frighten you with what God himself has frightened me." Muḥammad b. ʿUdhāfir adds that his father remained depressed and concerned until his death following this conversation. The last section may be a rollback from the total prohibition (and perhaps an amendment to the tradition) on working for, and therefore helping, the government. The similarity with the Sufyān/Kaʿb b. ʿUjra reports discussed above is clear.

32 The catalogue reference is given by Madelung, "A Treatise," 20, n. 14.

33 al-Sharīf al-Murtaḍā, *Rasāʾil al-Sharīf al-Murtaḍā* (Qum: Dār al-Qurʾān al-Karīm, 1405/1985); the treatise can be found at 2:87–98.

34 Madelung, "A Treatise," 23; for his translation, see 28; the translation here is mine. Note that Madelung translates *al-sulṭān al-jāʾir* as "unjust ruler" and *al-ẓālim al-bāghī* also as "unjust ruler." Clearly, he considers both *jāʾir* and *ẓālim* to mean "unjust." Elsewhere he consistently translates *ẓālim* as "unjust."

35 The debate became an element of the Akhbārī-Uṣūlī conflict in later Imāmī jurisprudence; see my *Scripturalist Islam: The History and Doctrines of the Akhbārī School of Shiʿite Thought* (Leiden: Brill, 2007), 114.

36 There is much debate about the reference of *safk al-dimāʾ* and whether it refers to those occasions in which blood is spilled (i.e., injury less than death) or whether it is a metaphor for "killing." See, for example, Yūsuf al-Baḥrānī, *al-Ḥadāʾiq al-nādira* (Qum: Muʾassasat al-Nashr al-Islāmī, n.d.), 18:134–135.

37 There is a wider debate here, which al-Murtaḍā hints at, in which signs (*amārāt*) in texts or based on reason bring an opinion to the jurist's mind (*ẓann*); this could be an indication (*dalīl*), stronger than a "sign," and thus indicates a conclusion closer to certainty.

38 My colleague Paul Gledhill took my original diagram and transformed it into something much more useful—this is what you see here.

39 Madelung's translation, "A Treatise," 24.

40 Madelung, "A Treatise," 30.

41 With regard to the passage referred to here by Madelung, it is true that it does not explicitly include (or exclude) any particular individual from holding the position of *al-sulṭān al-ʿādil*, but this does not necessarily mean that anyone could hold that position. These are descriptions of what a just ruler does, not who that ruler might legitimately be. Madelung's comment does not consider the use of these terms in juristic literature more broadly. As I have argued, the discussions of al-Murtaḍā (and for that matter al-Ṭūsī) are continuations of the legal discussions beyond the Shīʿī tradition. In the *fiqh* literature, references to *al-imām al-ʿādil* and *al-sulṭān al-ʿādil* (and *al-imām al-jāʾir* and *al-sulṭān al-jāʾir*) are standard locutions. The discussion of whether this or that ruler qualifies as *al-imām al-ʿādil*

is a separate legal discussion than whether one is obligated to work for such an *imām* when he commands it. The jurists could discuss whether the obligation exists without committing to the view that this or that ruler is *al-imām al-ʿādil*. It is this phenomenon that we encounter in the texts of both al-Murtaḍā and al-Ṭūsī, rather than an acceptance of just and legitimate government beyond that of the sinless, hidden Imam. Whether there is a significance to the use of *sulṭān* rather than *imām* requires further investigation; I suspect they both simply refer to "ruler" (or even more broadly "government").

42 Madelung, "A Treatise," 30.

43 A full exposition of al-Ṭūsī's juristic position would require a separate treatment. However, Madelung refers to al-Ṭūsī's phrase that the just ruler is one who "orders what is proper, forbids what is reprehensible and places things in their proper place" (Madelung, "A Treatise," 30). From this "it is clear" for Madelung that this is not an exclusive referent to the sinless Imam and could refer to any ruler who does good. We must be aware of how these terms are used in juristic discussions: the category of just ruler (*al-sulṭān al-ʿādil*) is simply a description of a legal category, not an individual occupant of the role; it is likely a less politically charged variant of *al-imām al-ʿādil*, a term that is found more regularly in Muḥammad b. Ḥasan al-Ṭūsī, *Nihāyat al-aḥkām* (Qum: Intishārāt-i Quds-i Muḥammadī, 1980), 133, 143, 171, 290. For more on al-Ṭūsī's terminology, see Norman Calder, "Legitimacy and Accommodation in Safavid Iran: The Juristic Theory of Muhammad Bāqir al-Sabzawārī (d. 1090/1679)," *Iran: Journal of the British Institute of Persian Studies* 25 (1987): 104, n. 22.

44 The term *muḥiqq* may also be technical, though I have not found it regularly employed in *fiqh* works with regard to the *mukallaf's* responsibilities before the government. Madelung chooses to translate this as "legitimate" and *jāʾir* as "unjust." Of course, this is precisely the point of dispute: Is *jāʾir* a descriptive term of the moral character of the ruler? Or is it a technical term relating to the legitimacy of that ruler holding a position of power? Calder and Modarressi understand it to be a reference to legitimacy and not a characterization of the moral character of the individual ruler (see above, and Hossein Modarressi, "The Just Ruler or the Guardian Jurist: An Attempt to Link Two Different Shiʿite Concepts," *Journal of the American Oriental Society* 111, no. 3 (1991): 556: "The term 'unjust' [*jāʾir* or *ẓālim*] ... does not mean 'oppressor,' rather it means 'illegitimate'"). They would argue, one suspects, that while *jāʾir* was a description of the moral character of the ruler in some Sunnī works of law, in Shīʿī works it came to mean simply "illegitimate," even if the ruler is not particularly oppressive. Later Shīʿī jurists may have distinguished between *jāʾir* and *ẓālim*, with the former meaning illegitimate and the latter meaning actually oppressive (I have heard this, but not yet found an explicit reference). The application of the terms is fluid and not stable. It may well be the case that the ambiguity was part of the discourse—or a tactic in their presentation, and Shīʿī jurists, at least in *fiqh* works, felt no need to be explicit here.

45 See below, n. 53.

46 Said Amir Arjomand, *The Shadow of God and the Hidden Imam: Religion, Political Order, and Societal Change in Shiʿite Iran from the Beginning to 1890* (Chicago: Chicago University Press, 1984).

47 Abdulaziz Abdulhussein Sachedina, *The Just Ruler (al-sultān al-ʿādil) in Shīʿite Islam: The Comprehensive Authority of the Jurist in Imamite Jurisprudence* (New York: Oxford University Press, 1988).

48 Ibid., 100–105.

49 Abou El Fadl, *Rebellion*, 301, n. 18. The point that occasioned Abou El Fadl's reference to Madelung is Abou El Fadl's argument that the increased use of the indefinite "a just ruler" (*imām ʿādil*, rather than "*the* just ruler") is the jurists' attempt to be deliberately ambiguous and therefore include rulers other than the sinless Imam in the category. This is a rather heavy burden for the indefinite article to carry, in my view, and fails to recognize that the Imāmī jurists are referring to the category (for which the indefinite is perfectly natural in certain circumstances) rather than deliberately opening the door to just rulers apart from the sinless Imam.

50 Hossein Modarressi Ṭabāṭabāʾī, *Kharāj in Islamic Law* (London: Ithaca Press, 1983), 158.

51 Modarressi, *Kharāj*, 159–160.

52 Modarressi references Madelung here. In an appendix "The unjust ruler in Islamic literature," Modarressi mentions that Shīʿī law "does not give any legitimacy to rulers who seize power by force" (Modarressi, *Kharāj*, 214—Modarressi adds the note: "See *all* Shīʿī theological works" (my emphasis)), as opposed to Sunnī theological works. Once again, he acknowledges that there were attempts (he mentions sources from the Safavid and Qajar periods) to create an equivalence between the "true rule" (*dawlat al-ḥaqq*—predicted as an element in the messianic and apocalyptic narratives) and the reign of these dynasties. However, these are once again seen as marginal, and their interpretations are novel and appear to be a "breach of the consensus and against the Shīʿī doctrine." These are careful remarks and indicate that while there may have been some jurists who, in some works, give a sort of de facto legitimacy to the ruling dynasty, the weight of Shīʿī tradition supports the notion that all rulers, irrespective of their individual character or behavior, are "unjust" since they have usurped a position that should, properly, only be held by the sinless Imams.

53 Norman Calder, "The Structure of Authority in Imāmī Shīʿī Jurisprudence" (PhD dissertation, University of London, 1980), 146.

54 al-Shahīd al-Thānī Zayn al-Dīn al-ʿĀmilī (d. 965/1558).

55 Calder, "The Structure," 90–91.

56 Calder, "Legitimacy and Accommodation," 91. In response to this, Said Amir Arjomand wrote, "In a good illustration of orientalist bias for 'Islami' explanations,

the late Norman Calder totally ignored this explicitly political treatise of nearly 900 printed pages and devoted an entire article to a few paragraphs of abstruse and tortuous legal reasoning, buried in another thick book on jurisprudence by Sabzawārī, to prove the allegedly inescapable *de jure* illegitimacy of monarchy in Shiʿism." S. A. Arjomand, "Political Ethic and Public Law in the Early Qajar Period," in *Religion and Society in Qajar Iran*, ed. R. Gleave (London: Routledge, 2005), 36, n. 18.

57 Robert Gleave, "Two Classical Shīʿī Theories of *qaḍāʾ*," in *Studies in Islamic and Middle Eastern Texts and Traditions in Memory of Norman Calder*, ed. J. Mojaddedi, A. Samely, and G. Hawting (Oxford: Oxford University Press, 2001), 105–121.

Bibliography

Abdulsater, Hussein. *Shiʿi Doctrine, Mu'tazili Theology: al-Sharif al-Murtada and Imami Discourse*. Edinburgh: Edinburgh University Press, 2017.

Abou El Fadl, Khaled. *Rebellion and Violence in Islamic Law*. Cambridge: Cambridge University Press, 2002.

Adem, Rodrigo. "Classical *Naṣṣ* Doctrines in Imāmī Shīʿism: On the Usage of an Expository Term." *Shii Studies Review* 1 (2017): 42–71.

Arjomand, S. A. "Political Ethic and Public Law in the Early Qajar Period." In *Religion and Society in Qajar Iran*, edited by R. Gleave, 21–40. London: Routledge, 2005.

Arjomand, Said Amir. *The Shadow of God and the Hidden Imam: Religion, Political Order, and Societal Change in Shiʿite Iran from the Beginning to 1890*. Chicago: Chicago University Press, 1984.

al-Baḥrānī, Yūsuf. *al-Ḥadāʾiq al-nādira*. Qum: Muʾassasat al-Nashr al-Islāmī, n.d.

Bayhom-Daou, T. *Shaykh Mufid*. Oxford: Oneworld, 2005.

Black, A. *A History of Islamic Political Thought*. Edinburgh: Edinburgh University Press, 2001.

Calder, Norman. "Khums in Imāmī Shīʿī Jurisprudence, from the Tenth to the Sixteenth Century A. D." *Bulletin of the School of Oriental and African Studies* 45, no. 1 (1982): 39–47.

Calder, Norman. "Legitimacy and Accommodation in Safavid Iran: The Juristic Theory of Muhammad Bāqir al-Sabzawārī (d. 1090/1679)." *Iran: Journal of the British Institute of Persian Studies* 25 (1987): 91–105.

Calder, Norman. "The Structure of Authority in Imāmī Shīʿī Jurisprudence." PhD dissertation, University of London, 1980.

Calder, Norman. "Zakāt in Imāmī Shīʿī Jurisprudence, from the Tenth to the Sixteenth Century A.D." *Bulletin of the School of Oriental and African Studies* 44, no. 3 (1981): 468–480.

Cook, Michael. "Activism and Quietism in Islam: The Case of the Early Murji'a." In *Islam and Power*, edited by A. Cudsi and A. E. Dessouki, 15–23. London: Croom Helm, 1981.

Cook, Michael. *Commanding Good and Forbidding Wrong*. Cambridge: Cambridge University Press, 2010.

Crone, P. *Medieval Islamic Political Thought*. Edinburgh: Edinburgh University Press, 2004.

al-Dhahabī, Muḥammad Shams al-Dīn. *al-Kabāʾir*. Cairo: Dār al-Nadwa al-Jadīd, 1980.

Dominguez Diaz, Marta. *Women in Sufism*. London: Routledge: 2014.

Gleave, Robert. "Public Violence, State Legitimacy: The *Iqāmat al-Ḥudūd* and the Sacred State." In *Public Violence in Islamic Societies*, edited by C. Lange and M. Fierro, 256–275. Edinburgh: Edinburgh University Press, 2009.

Gleave, Robert. *Scripturalist Islam: The History and Doctrines of the Akhbārī School of Shiʿite Thought*. Leiden: Brill, 2007.

Gleave, Robert. "Two Classical Shīʿī Theories of *Qaḍāʾ*." In *Studies in Islamic and Middle Eastern Texts and Traditions in Memory of Norman Calder*, edited by J. Mojaddedi, A. Samely, and G. Hawting (eds.), 105–121. Oxford: Oxford University Press, 2001.

al-Ḥākim al-Nīsābūrī. *Mustadrak ʿalā l-Saḥīḥayn*. Cairo: Dār al-Ḥaramayn li-l-Ṭibāʿa wa-l-Nashr wa-l-Tawzīʿ, 1997.

Hallaq, W. *The Impossible State: Islamic, Politics and Modernity's Moral Predicament*. New York: Columbia University Press, 2013.

Ibn Jawzī. *Manāqib Aḥmad Ibn Ḥanbal*. Cairo: Maktabat al-Khānjī, 1979.

Ibn al-Qāsim. *al-Mudawwana*. Cairo: Dār al-Kutub, n.d.

al-Jaṣṣāṣ, Abū Bakr. *Aḥkām al-Qurʾān*. Edited by ʿAbd al-Salām Muḥammad ʿAlī Shāhīn. 3 vols. Beirut: Dār al-Kitāb al-ʿArabī, 1978.

Jomaa, Katrin. "Quietism and Activism." In *The Princeton Encyclopedia of Islamic Political Thought*, edited by Gerhard Böwering et al., 446–449. Princeton, NJ: Princeton University Press, 2013.

Keddie, Nikki. *Religion and Politics in Iran: Shiʿism from Quietism to Revolution*. New Haven: Yale University Press, 1983.

al-Kulaynī, Muḥammad b. Yaʿqūb. *al-Kāfī*. Tehran: Dār al-Kutub al-Islāmiyya, 1388/1968–69.

Lewis, Bernard. "On the Quietist and Activist Traditions in Islamic Political Writing." *Bulletin of the School of Oriental and African Studies* 49, no. 1 (1986): 141–147.

Madelung, Wilferd. *The Succession to Muhammad*. Cambridge: Cambridge University Press, 1996.

Madelung, Wilferd. "A Treatise of the Sharīf al-Murtaḍā on the Legality of Working for the Government '(Mas'ala fī 'l-'amal ma'a 'l-sulṭān).'" *Bulletin of the School of Oriental and African Studies* 43, no. 1 (1980): 18–31.

Marlow, Louise. *Counsel for Kings: Wisdom and Politics in Tenth-Century Iran*. Vol. 1: *The Nasihat al-muluk of Pseudo-Mawardi: Contexts and Themes*. Vol. 2: *The Nasihat al-muluk of Pseudo-Mawardi: Texts, Sources and Authorities*. Edinburgh: Edinburgh University Press, 2016.

al-Māwardī, Abū l-Ḥasan (attrib.). *Naṣīḥat al-mulūk*. Kuwait: Maktabat al-Falāḥ, 1403/1983.

McEoin, Denis. "Aspects of Militancy and Quietism in Imami Shiʿism." *Bulletin (British Society for Middle Eastern Studies)* 11, no. 1 (1984): 18–27.

Modarressi [Ṭabāṭabāʾī], Hossein. "The Just Ruler or the Guardian Jurist: An Attempt to Link Two Different Shiʿite Concepts." *Journal of the American Oriental Society* 111, no. 3 (1991): 549–562.

Modarressi Ṭabāṭabāʾī, Hossein. *Kharāj in Islamic Law*. London: Ithaca Press, 1983.

Newman, Andrew. "Fayd al-Kashani and the Rejection of the Clergy/State Alliance: Friday Prayer as Politics in the Safavid Period." In *The Most Learned of the Shi'a*, edited by Linda Walbridge, 34–52. Oxford: Oxford University Press, 2000.

Rizek, Ali-Rida. "The Lawfulness of Working for the Unjust Ruler in Early Imami Thought and Literature." PhD dissertation, American University of Beirut, 2014.

Rizvi, Sajjad. "Authority in Absence? Shiʿi Politics of Salvation from the Classical Period to Modern Republicanism." *Studies in Christian Ethics* 29 (2016): 204–212.

Sachedina, Abdulaziz Abdulhussein. *The Just Ruler (al-sultān al-ʿādil) in Shīʿite Islam: The Comprehensive Authority of the Jurist in Imamite Jurisprudence*. New York: Oxford University Press, 1988.

al-Sharīf al-Murtaḍā. *Rasāʾil al-Sharīf al-Murtaḍā*. Qum: Dār al-Qurʾān al-Karīm, 1405/1985.

Stewart, Devin. "al-Sharīf al-Murtaḍā (d. 436/1044)." In *Islamic Legal Thought: A Compendium of Muslim Jurists*, edited by Oussama Arabi, David S. Powers, and Susan A. Spectorsky, 167–210. Leiden: Brill, 2013.

al-Tirmidhī, Muḥammad b. ʿĪsā. *Jāmiʿ al-Tirmidhī*. Edited by Aḥmad Shākir, Muḥammad Fuʾād ʿAbd al-Bāqī, and Ibrāhīm ʿAṭwa ʿAwaḍ. Beirut: Dār Iḥyāʾ al-Turāth al-ʿArabī, n.d. [reprint of Cairo 1938 edition].

Tor, D. "Sultan." In *The Princeton Encyclopedia of Islamic Political Thought*, edited by Gerhard Böwering et al., 352–354. Princeton, NJ: Princeton University Press, 2013.

al-Ṭūsī, Muḥammad b. Ḥasan. *Nihāyat al-aḥkām*. Qum: Intishārāt-i Quds-i Muḥammadī, 1980.

Van Ess, Josef. "Political Ideas in Early Islamic Religious Thought." *British Journal of Middle Eastern Studies* 28, no. 2 (2001): 151–164.

Wagemakers, J. *A Quietist Jihadi: The Ideology and Influence of Abu Muhammad al-Maqdisi*. Cambridge: Cambridge University Press, 2015.

Part Three

Political Quietism in Modern and Contemporary Islamic Thought

6

"I'm Only a Village Farmer and a Dervish": Between Political Quietism and Spiritual Leadership: Early Modern Shīʿī Sufism and the Challenge of Modernity

Alessandro Cancian

In public discourse, and in the media, it has become common to identify the roots of late-twentieth- and early-twenty-first-century political Islam with the rise of Khomeini's ideology of the Islamic government (*wilāyat-i faqīh*) and its success in establishing the Islamic Republic of Iran. Such a common presumption enables popular yet ill-informed pundits to explain the emergence of late-twentieth-century Islamic political activism with the transformation of Shīʿism from a quietist tradition to a militant religion. While there is a temporal connection between this phenomenon and the Islamization of the political discourse in the Middle East, a closer scrutiny of the political, social, and historical circumstances that made possible the elaboration of Khomeini's theory of an Islamic government shows the absurdity of such a connection.

In this chapter, I address alternative views on the subject of a religious government as formulated by various voices in modern Shīʿism. In particular, I focus on the approach of the masters of the influential and hitherto understudied Niʿmatullāhī order to political and social activism, specifically in the nineteenth and twentieth centuries. In doing so, I demonstrate how the Sufis negotiated the traditional Shīʿī quietist position in order to claim spiritual authority and religious legitimacy, on the one hand, and to adapt to the challenges posed by the need of the religious classes to reposition themselves in the new political landscape generated by the appearance of modern political categories that originated in the West, on the other hand.

By demonstrating this, I show how these views are a world apart from modernist-inspired theories and practices of political activism, yet how they also represent a counter-discourse that carries progressive elements entirely absent from the forms of Islamist political activism currently under the international spotlight.

Political quietism in Shīʿism

An examination of a variety of sources shows that the imams recognized by Twelver Shīʿism largely adopted a quietist attitude in matters of politics, that is, they opted for isolation from political power. This attitude seems to have prevailed in particular after the tragedy of Karbalāʾ, when Ḥusayn b. ʿAlī, the third Shīʿī imam, and his followers, died at the hands of the army of the Umayyad caliph Yazīd I in 61/680.[1] The word used to define this attitude is *quʿūd* (lit., "remaining seated"), from which the term *al-qāʿid* ("the seated") was attributed to the imams, as opposed to *al-qāʾim* ("the standing"), which characterized the twelfth and last imam, the only one whose authority allows him to "rise" as the Mahdī—an "insurgent" (*qiyām, khurūj*) against oppression.[2] As Amir-Moezzi puts it,

> The impression that emerges from the earliest corpus of Imami sources is that after Karbalāʾ the period of understanding between spiritual and temporal power had forever changed. The imams, based on traditions that are attributed to them, seem to have concluded that henceforth "the religion of truth" (*din al-ḥaqq*), i.e., Shiʿism and temporal power had become two poles forever irreconcilable: "Forever" since "the ideal city," governed by a just ruler, can only be realized at the end of time, with the Mahdi, the eschatological savior as the only truly just sovereign (*al-solṭān al-ʿādel*). He is the only being authorized to legitimately fight the unjust, the only one able to avenge the oppressed and establish a world of knowledge and justice.[3]

One tradition, repeated by several of the imams, is particularly relevant here and looms large in any discussion about the legitimacy of secular power in the absence of the imam: "The carrier of any banner raised before the uprising of the *qāʾim* is an oppressor (*ṭāghūt*)."[4] From then until the end of time (*ākhir al-zamān*), it was believed that the world would be ruled by unjust and illegitimate rulers, and any attempt to reinstate a just and legitimate government would be doomed to fail and become injustice itself. The traditions from the imams attesting this fate for any who rebel are numerous.[5] It is from this stance that the Shīʿa are enjoined by the imams to be patient and assume a tolerant attitude when facing adversities—an attitude that Henry Corbin aptly labeled *desperatio fiducialis*: a desperation for the injustice ruling the world, but an indefectible faith in the return of the imam and the restoration of justice at the end of time. An entire section of *Kitāb al-īmān wa-l-kufr* (the book of faith and infidelity) in the seminal Shīʿī collection of traditions by al-Kulaynī, the *Uṣūl min al-Kāfī*, is devoted to traditions advising the Shīʿī believers against pursuing leadership (*riʾāsa*), be it religious or political.[6] While foundational texts are clear about the matter, reality placed the Shīʿa in a position where compromise was necessary, and collaboration with unjust rulers could not be eluded. But the main paradox is one in which a religion that is presented as essentially initiatory and esoteric was transformed, over the course of history, by its religious scholars, into a force not just able to claim direct political power, but one that established a political ideology and urged the class of the jurist-theologians to assume political power. The establishment of Khomeini's theory and practice of Islamic government is the result of a long and steady process in which the rationalist camp among Shīʿī jurists expanded the remit of the *ʿulamāʾ* in society. This coincided with the beginning stage of the Islamization of the political discourse in the Middle East. While there is a temporal connection between this phenomenon and the Islamization, a closer scrutiny of the political, social, and historical circumstances that made the elaboration of Khomeini's theory of an Islamic government possible shows that establishing a causal connection between Khomeini and this phenomenon (i.e., that Khomeini's theory generated the Islamization of the political discourse in the Middle East) is all but absurd.

While it is correct to affirm that the experience of Iran "set an example to subsequent Islamist challengers to the west since Khomeini emphasized self-assertion against over-whelming might, as well as the use of modern technology, organization and propaganda,"[7] it would be an exaggeration to say that it was Khomeini who inspired those challengers. What remains of Khomeini's experience in the larger Middle Eastern stage is his success in challenging the secular state, although the development of the Islamic Republic in the twenty-first century shows that any claim by the government that it has made a clear division between its own ideology and the secular organization of the state is indeed feeble.

The background in Iran

In the nineteenth century, Iran fell behind the rest of the Middle East in terms of political, social, and economic development.[8] The Qajar monarchy attempted reforms, relying on foreign forces, but in the process also antagonized the clergy and the business owners/traders in the bazaars, who opposed the centralizing policies and Western influence and resisted the destabilizing effects of the reforms. The Constitutional Revolution (1906) was, in part, also a result of this struggle and was an opportunity for Iran to introduce new concepts and institutions, and to consolidate public participation in state decision-making. After the failure of the constitutional movement and the bombing of the parliament in 1908 by order of the Qajar king Muḥammad ʿAlī Shāh, a former official of the Cossack Brigade of the Qajar army, Reza Shah Pahlavi, rose to power in 1925 with the goal of restoring Iran's power and prestige. The king and founder of the new dynasty, however, was overly dependent on the army and eventually renounced political reform and development. The same policy was continued under the rule of his son, Mohammad Reza Pahlavi (ruled 1944–79). His rule relied heavily on a secularist ideology as a basis for progress and development and resorted to a nativist nationalism rooted in the myth of the Aryan origin of Iran[9] while allowing Western powers to block any balanced political progress by dictating the political agenda and alienating the clergy with a systematic policy of unmediated modernization.[10]

Meanwhile, in the Arab world, a form of socialism emerged that, albeit far from democratic, conferred upon the state a measure of legitimacy. This form of modernization was lost in Iran, given the suppression of the Left under the Pahlavi regime, which also suppressed participative nationalism with the coup d'état that toppled the democratically elected prime minister Mohammad Mosaddegh in 1953. The void was filled by the Shīʿī clerics, who were simply the faction within society that could represent popular instances and had the highest degree of organization and mobilizing power, codified in centuries of independence. Despite its traditional outlook, the clergy was able to rely on two other forms of organization: one modeled on the educational and welfare societies not unlike those organized by the Muslim Brotherhood in Egypt; and the other, a network established in the bazaars throughout Iran, ultimately influenced by Marxist mobilization methods. The whole structure was coherent, detailed, and efficient enough for the clergy to emerge as the more reliable leadership among the opposition to the regime. Ayatollah Khomeini, who maintained a cautious stance until the death of the widely respected Ayatollah Sayyid Ḥusayn Burūjirdī (d. 1961), respectful of the unwritten etiquette in place within the Twelver Shīʿī religious hierarchies, capitalized on this structure as soon as the powerful senior religious character passed away.

His rise to the leadership of the opposition movement did not come in a vacuum but went hand in hand with a vast and effective work of ideology-building from other key characters. To appeal to middle-class youth, the Shīʿī Islamic ideology had to counter rival ideologies *en vogue* in the area, namely, Marxism and liberal democracy.[11] Khomeini's main aid in this field was Morteza Motahhari (d. 1979), who sought to develop an alternative system based on faith, but also on philosophy, science, and knowledge. Khomeini's idea of an Islamic state found a complementary philosophical buttress in the influential works of Motahhari, in a system in which individual freedom and human agency were made to coincide with divine inspiration and religious responsibility. Motahhari's main concern was to defend Islam from Western modernism and to develop an Islamic ideology that could respond to modern challenges while at the same time remaining faithful to the "essence" of Islam. To do so, he devised an ideological system whereby modernity, and the inevitable progress of humanity, would be Islamized, rather than the other way around, in a harmonious way that encompassed an element of democracy.[12]

Khomeini, even by the time of the revolution, did not appear to have had a specific vision of the Islamic state. His objective was a general one that functioned like an ideology; his goal was a government based on Islam. The first instance of this ideology was developed by Khomeini in his *Kashf al-asrār*, a 1943 work, written—quite tellingly—as a response to ʿAlī Akbar Hakimzāda's *Asrār-i hizārsāla*, a book with a somewhat modernist, militant inspiration.[13] It is curious that Khomeini's first foray in political thought came as a reaction to a work by a Muslim reformist that was shaped as a defense of traditional Shīʿism and contained a scathing attack against modernism and Iranian intellectuals like Aḥmad Kasravī and Ḥasan Sharīʿat Sangalajī who incorporated some modernist elements into their thought. From the *Kashf* onward, however, Khomeini's political thought showed a development, namely, in a gradual increase of the role of the ʿ*ulamā*ʾ in the state—from a supervisory role to one of actual rule.

Khomeini's vision certainly resembles, in some ways, that of other Islamist movements. In particular, in both cases, Islam was reified and seen as a perfect system able to provide guidance and objectives to the Muslim community on how to run a state.[14] The *sharīʿa* is seen as a full package, something given by God in its final form, ready to put in practice for the orderly running of a complex, modern society. Khomeini's Islam, however, left space for areas vaguely covered by Shīʿī jurisprudence and engaged with the issues of the time, in the language of the time: it was anti-imperialist and third-worldist in its rejection of Western hegemony, modernist in its engagement with technology and progress, and classless in its rebuttal of political parties and the call to unity. What is specific to Khomeini's vision is, however, the way it introduced elements of traditional

Shīʿī juristic culture into the Islamic state; these rendered it more pluralistic and flexible than the structures envisaged by, for example, Ḥasan al-Bannā and Sayyid Quṭb.

Three elements are crucial in Khomeini's idea of the state: the first is the idea of a moral community, in which the power of the state reposes mainly in a leader of outstanding qualities (the supreme leader, *walī l-faqīh*)—an idea that draws on the platonic idea of the Republic and al-Fārābī's "virtuous city"; the second is the idea of a legal state defined by laws, the blueprint of which can be found in the reified idea of Islam; and the third is that of a modern, strong, and developed state, well organized and defended, centralized in power and authority, but with a strong popular legitimacy.

Mysticism, Sufism, and politics

ʿIrfān, a modern Persian word that indicates both the generic mysticism present in all religions and the specific gnosis of Islam and in particular Shīʿī Islam,[15] influenced Khomeini from his early years.[16] The particular form of Shīʿī gnosis originated in what Henry Corbin defines as the Neoplatonism of Islam, as developed by the school of Ibn ʿArabī and disseminated in Shīʿī Persia through the school of Mullā Ṣadrā Shīrāzī in Safavid times. *ʿIrfān* is important for the understanding of Khomeini's political activity, his concept of leadership and authority, and his view of the state: "*ʿIrfān* inspired him with particular spiritual objectives and led him to inspire others. Through its ethics and stress on self-knowledge, it also provided a means of reaching and mobilizing ordinary people."[17] However important mysticism may be in Shīʿī Iran, the form of mysticism preferred by the religious class is unorganized and informal, and not related to a specific Sufi order (*ṭarīqa*); rather, it was known by the word *ʿirfān*.

Organized Sufism, on the other hand, no matter how popular and influential, is still subject to the stigma of heterodoxy and is a challenging force for traditional Shīʿī authorities. While today Sufism is alternatively denounced as a form of *ghuluww*, superstition, and a quietist foreign-inspired antipolitical movement,[18] mainstream Shīʿī critiques of it during Safavid times preferred to accuse mystics of being crypto-Sunnīs. Sufis were denounced as substantially alien, if not enemies, then beyond the sphere of the *ahl al-bayt*: the "Sunnīs in disguise" argument was a powerful polemical tool in the hands of the puritan *ʿulamāʾ* in a subtle struggle for authority among mystics, philosophers, theologians, and jurists. It is no surprise then that in early modern and contemporary times,

Shīʿī Sufis of Iran developed a very different approach to politics and their engagement with it. In the paragraphs that follow, I focus on the late nineteenth and early twentieth centuries, and limit my overview to the Niʿmatullāhiyya, the most influential of the Iranian Sufi orders.[19]

Although individual Sufis, even high-ranking ones, have taken part in the political life of modern and contemporary Iran, there is no systematic Niʿmatullāhī "political thinking" in the order's work.[20] Since their comeback in Iran in the eighteenth century under the suspicion of seeking political power, the masters have steered away from politics, lest they be accused of making claims to any kind of authority that went beyond the spiritual realm. However, one can draw an outline of the order's approach to politics from scattered references in the works of Niʿmatullāhī masters. In the early twentieth century, one master of the Gunābādī branch of the Niʿmatullāhī Sufi order, Nūr ʿAlī Shāh II (d. 1918), allegedly wrote a booklet in which he invited Iranians to unite under the banner of Sufism, to put an end to the fragmentation of the country that occurred in the years of the civil war that followed the Constitutional Revolution.[21]

In the monumental work of the preceding master and father of Nūr ʿAlī Shāh II, Sulṭān ʿAlī Shāh Gunābādī (d. 1909) urged his followers to assume responsibility and take an active role in managing their social and political affairs. To be sure, he never provided details on how this activism should occur. It is safe to conclude from reading his works that he stood with the traditional Shīʿī approach, according to which, in the absence of the imam, no political power is fully legitimate, but, since society must function in an orderly way, it is necessary to compromise with the illegitimate powers that rule society.

The position of the Niʿmatullāhī Sufis on the constitutional movement, when it was at its peak, ranged from indifference to support.[22] When today's Gunābādīs confronted the master on his position, Sulṭān ʿAlī Shāh replied to constitutionalist villagers in Baydukht and said that he was "only a village farmer and a dervish, and I do not know what 'constitutionalism' and 'despotism' mean." He continued, "We have nothing to do with these things and we will obey the orders of the government, regardless of it being constitutional or despotic."[23] By contrast, there are reports that Sulṭān ʿAlī Shāh publicly targeted the wrongdoings of the Qajar monarchy and even stated that he prayed to God that He might expedite the death of Nāṣir al-Dīn Shāh, predicted by Saʿādat ʿAlī Shāh to happen in 1318/1901, and anticipate it by five years.[24] Apparently, it emerged from his correspondence and advice to disciples that his neutrality was genuine.[25] Although no precise political agenda was affirmed in the works of the masters, it is safe to argue that Sulṭān ʿAlī Shāh was unhappy with the autocratic rule of the Qajars, and though not opposed to monarchy in itself as a system, he did not refrain from attacking the court (though without making accusations) in one of the final chapters of his celebrated *Wilāyat-nāma*.[26]

Even more interesting is the fact that throughout his work, Sulṭān ʿAlī Shāh affirmed that Islam is different than *īmān*, in that the former only serves to "preserve the blood and property of the people." We find this argument throughout his work, to the point that we can consider it one of the pillars of his intellectual building.[27] In other words, Islam is seen as a set of social rules that exist to guarantee the orderly life of the community. However, by affirming this, he seems to empty exoteric religion, which he says is intended as a set of practical rules for running society, of its social normativity and immanent sacred nature. Thus, he sees the authentically immutable essence of Islam as *īmān*, while the rest is something exoteric, which is not immutable: he seems to suggest that what counts is that society works, subsists, and prospers, regardless of the actual form of law that allows this.

However, affirming that Sulṭān ʿAlī Shāh implied that any law that provided social stability was acceptable may be going a bit too far in my interpretation, as the circumstances in which he lived did not allow him to bring his premises to these conclusions. The recent history of the order, however, allows me to put forward the hypothesis that this might have been the case. In spite of one apparently conservative move, manifested in the form of an attack on the Universal Declaration of Human Rights penned by one of the masters of the Gunābādīs,[28] in the twentieth century the flexibility of the order's position on the matter of politics allowed its masters to accommodate the Islamic Republic and its tenets, at least in the first two decades, and simultaneously to emerge as vocal critics of the injustice and oppression of the same republic, in particular—and perhaps through channels that allow it to subsist—at the beginning of the new millennium. The Niʿmatullāhī order maintains a clear stance against oppression and in favor of freedom, and advocates that its members take responsibility for their own political destiny, without detailing the direction this activism should take. It is a sort of an apolitical advocacy of personal responsibility in politics, which, while flirting with reformism, does not restrict the range of the possible political engagements.

These views must be considered within the tradition of pluralism typical of Shīʿī jurisprudence and are clearly a world apart from modernist theories and practices of political activism. With various nuances, and given the limits of the Iranian revolutionary experience, they represent a counter-discourse and carry within themselves progressive elements entirely absent in the forms of violent activism currently in the international spotlight.

Notes

1 Mohammad Ali Amir-Moezzi, *The Divine Guide in Early Shiʿism: The Source of Esotericism in Islam*, trans. David Streight (Albany: State University of New York Press, 1994), 61–69. The eighth imam, ʿAlī l-Riḍāʾ (d. 203/818), made an exception to this rule (in part), when he reluctantly accepted an invitation from the ʿAbbāsid caliph al-Maʾmūn to succeed him to the caliphate in 201/816.

2 Mohammad Ali Amir-Moezzi, "Islam in Iran, x: The Roots of Political Shiʿism," in *Encyclopaedia Iranica*, online: http://www.iranicaonline.org/articles/islam-in-iran-x-the-roots-of-political-shiisms.

3 Ibid.

4 Muḥammad b. Yaʿqūb al-Kulaynī, *al-Rawḍa min al-Kāfī*, ed. H. al-Rasūlī Maḥallātī (Tehran, 1389/1969), 2:121–122.

5 A saying attributed to the imam Jaʿfar al-Ṣādiq states: "Dust always falls upon him who raises it." And "any revolt from one among us will be no more than more suffering for us and our believers" (Ibn Abī Zaynab al-Nuʿmānī, *Kitāb al-ghayba*, ed. ʿA. A. Ghaffārī [Tehran, 1397/1977], 244, 248, 283, 286, 291).

6 Amir-Moezzi, "Islam in Iran."

7 Vanessa Martin, *Creating an Islamic State: Khomeini and the Making of a New Iran* (London: I.B. Tauris, 2000), ix.

8 On Iran's economy in the nineteenth century, see Willem Floor, *Guilds, Merchants and Ulama in Nineteenth Century Iran* (Washington, DC: Mage, 2009).

9 On the rise of Iranian nationalism and the myth of Aryanism that sustained it, see Reza Zia-Ebrahimi, *The Emergence of Iranian Nationalism: Race and the Politics of Dislocation* (New York: Columbia University Press, 2016).

10 Akhavi Shahrough, *Religion and Politics in Contemporary Iran: Clergy-State Relations in the Pahlavi Period* (Albany: State University of New York Press, 1980); Hamid Algar, "The Oppositional Role of the ʿUlama in Twentieth Century Iran," in *Scholars, Saints, and Sufis*, ed. Nikki Keddie (Berkeley and Los Angeles: University of California Press, 1972), 231–255.

11 See Farzin Vahdat, *God and Juggernaut: Iran's Intellectual Encounter with Modernity* (Syracuse, NY: Syracuse University Press, 2002). See also Hamid Dabashi, *Theology of Discontent: The Ideological Foundation of the Islamic Revolution in Iran* (New York: New York University Press, 1993).

12 Mahmood Davari, *The Political Thought of Ayatollah Murtaza Mutahhari: An Iranian Theoretician of the Islamic State* (London: Routledge, 2005).

13 Vanessa Martin, "Religion and State in Khumaini's 'Kashf-i Asrar,'" *Bulletin of the School of Oriental and African Studies* 56, no. 1 (1993): 34–45.

14 On Khomeini's ideology, see Ervand Abrahamian, *Khomeinism: Essays on the Islamic Republic* (Berkeley: University of California Press, 1993). For a useful

sample of Khomeini's own voice, see Hamid Algar, *Islam and Revolution: Writings and Declarations of Imam Khomeini (1941–1980)* (Berkeley: Mizan Press, 1981).

15 On the rise of the concept and the term in Safavid Iran and its consolidation in early modern Iran, see Ata Anzali, "Safavid Shiʿism, the Eclipse of Sufism and the Emergence of ʿIrfān" (PhD dissertation, Rice University, 2012).

16 On Khomeini's mysticism, see Yahya Christian Bonaud, *L'Imam Khomeyni, un gnostique méconnu du XXe siècle* (Beirut: al-Bouraq, 1997).

17 Martin, *Creating an Islamic State*, xi.

18 See Alessandro Cancian, "In between Reform and Bigotry: The Gunābādī *Silsila* in Two Early Twentieth-Century Anti-Sufi Works," in *Sufis and Mullahs: Sufis and Their Opponents in the Persianate World*, ed. Leonard Lewisohn and Reza Tabandeh (Irvine: University of California Press, forthcoming).

19 On the Niʿmatullāhiyya, see Nasrollah Pourjavady and Peter Lamborn Wilson, *Kings of Love: The Poetry and History of the Ni'matullahi Sufi Order* (Tehran: Imperial Academy of Philosophy, 1978). On its Indian period and its resurgence in Iran, see Leonard Lewisohn and David Morgan (eds.), *The Heritage of Sufism III: Late Classical Persianate Sufism (1501–1750)* (Oxford: Oneworld, 1999); Leonard Lewisohn, "An Introduction to the History of Modern Persian Sufism, Part II: A Socio-Cultural Profile of Sufism, from the Dhahabi Revival to the Present Day," *Bulletin of the School of Oriental and African Studies* 62 (1999): 36–59; Leonard Lewisohn, "An Introduction to the History of Modern Persian Sufism, Part I: The Nimatullahi Order: Persecution, Revival and Schism," *BSOAS* 61, no. 3 (1998): 437–464; Alessandro Cancian, "Translation, Authority and Exegesis in Modern Iranian Sufism: Two Iranian Sufi Masters in Dialogue," *Journal of Persianate Studies* 7 (2014): 88–106; Cancian, "Incontro con il maestro della Neʿmatollâhiyya Gonâbâdiyya, Nûr ʿAlî Tâbandeh 'Majzûb ʿAlî Shâh,'" in *Con I dervisci: otto incontri sul campo*, ed. Giovanni De Zorzi (Milan: Mimesis, 2013), 155–172; Oliver Scharbordt, "The Quṭb as Special Representative of the Hidden Imam: The Conflation of Shiʿi and Sufi *Vilāyat* in the Niʿmatullāhī Order," in *Shiʿi Trends and Dynamics in Modern Times (XVIIIth–XXth Centuries)/Courants et dynamiques chiites à l'époque modern (XVIIIe–XXe siècles)*, ed. Denis Hermann and Sabrina Mervin (Beirut: Ergon Verlag, 2010), 33–49; Fabrizio Speziale, "À propos du renouveau *Ni'matullāhī*: Le centre de Hyderabad au cours de la première modernité," *Studia Iranica* 42, no. 1 (2013): 91–118; Matthijs van Den Bos, *Mystic Regimes: Sufism and the State in Iran, from the Late Qajar Era to the Islamic Republic* (Leiden: Brill, 2002).

20 However, about the eponymous master of the Gunābādī branch, see Matthijs van Den Bos, "Conjectures on Solṭānʿalīshāh, the *Valāyat-nāme* and Shiite Sufi Authority," *Sociology of Islam* 3 (2015): 190–207. For a reply to van Den Bos, see Reza Tabandeh, "Mīrzā Muḥammad Maʿṣūm Shīrāzī: A Sufi and a Constitutionalist," *Studia Islamica* 112 (2017): 99–130.

21 The only confirmation of this booklet is William M. Miller, "Shi'ah Mysticism' (The Sufis of Gonabad)," *Moslem World* 13 (1923): 343–363. Miller arrived in Khurasan five years after Nūr ʿAlī Shāh II's death, but did not have the opportunity to meet the then master of the order, Ṣāliḥ ʿAlī Shāh. His main firsthand informant was the grandson of Mullā Ḥādī Sabzawārī, Ḥājjī ʿImād al-Dīn, who was appointed shaykh by Nūr ʿAlī Shāh II and presided over a sizeable community of Sufis in the town of Sabzawār. We have no further evidence of Nūr ʿAlī Shāh having written such a book, although his unusually voluminous written production remains to be thoroughly studied. The Intishārāt al-Riḍāʾ have recently published a monumental series of forty volumes by Nūr ʿAlī Shāh II: *Qulzum: Uqiyānūs-i bī-karān-i maʿārif-i Ahl-i Bayt* (Mashhad, 1392/2013–14); this encyclopedic work touches on subjects as diverse as universal history, biography, theology, mysticism, magic, ethics, *ḥadīth,* etc.

22 For the background, see Reza Tabandeh, "Mīrzā Muḥammad Maʿṣūm Shīrāzī."

23 "Mā yak nafar-i zāriʿ-i dahātī-yi darwīsh-īm wa namīdānam mashrūṭiyyat ya istibdād cha maʿnī dārad. Mā ba īn chīz-hā kārī nadārīm wa muṭīʿ-i amr-i dawlat mībāshīm khwāh mashrūṭa wa khwāh mustabidd"; see Sulṭān Ḥusayn Tābanda Gunābādī "Riḍā ʿAlī Shāh," *Nābigha-yi ʿilm wa ʿirfān dar qarn-i chahārdahum: Sharḥ-i ḥāl-i marḥūm Ḥājj Mullā Sulṭān Muḥammad Gunābādī Sulṭān ʿSul Shāh* (Tehran: Ḥaqīqat, 1384), 145.

24 Ibid., 138.

25 Though this does not mean that he remained silent before blatant oppression and violence.

26 Sulṭān Muḥammad Sulṭān ʿAlī Shāh Gunābādī, *Wilāyat-nāma* (Tehran: N.p., 1363/1984–85).

27 On this point and the instances in which this device is deployed, see Alessandro Cancian, "Faith as Territory: *Dār al-islām* and *dār al-ḥarb* in Modern Shiʿi Sufism," in *Dār al-islām/Dār al-ḥarb: Territories, People, Identities*, ed. Giovanna Calasso and Giuliano Lancioni (Leiden: Brill, 2017), 295–312.

28 Sulṭān Ḥusayn Tābanda Gunābādī "Riḍāʾ ʿAlī Shāh," *Naẓar-i madhhabī ba iʿlāmiyya-yi ḥuqūq-ī bashar* (N.p.: n.p., 1354/1975–76).

Bibliography

Abrahamian, Ervand. *Khomeinism: Essays on the Islamic Republic.* Berkeley: University of California Press, 1993.

Akhavi, Shahrough. *Religion and Politics in Contemporary Iran: Clergy-State Relations in the Pahlavi Period.* Albany: State University of New York Press, 1980.

Algar, Hamid. *Islam and Revolution: Writings and Declarations of Imam Khomeini (1941–1980).* Berkeley: Mizan Press, 1981.

Algar, Hamid. "The Oppositional Role of the ʿUlama in Twentieth Century Iran." In *Scholars, Saints, and Sufis*, edited by Nikki Keddie, 231–255. Berkeley and Los Angeles: University of California Press, 1972.

Amir-Moezzi, Mohammad Ali. *The Divine Guide in Early Shiʿism: The Source of Esotericism in Islam*. Translated by David Streight. Albany: State University of New York Press, 1994.

Amir-Moezzi, Mohammad Ali. "Islam in Iran, x: The Roots of Political Shiʿism." In *Encyclopaedia Iranica*. Online: http://www.iranicaonline.org/articles/islam-in-iran-x-the-roots-of-political-shiisms.

Anzali, Ata. "Safavid Shiʿism, the Eclipse of Sufism and the Emergence of ʿIrfān." PhD dissertation. Rice University, 2012.

Bonaud, Yahya Christian. *L'Imam Khomeyni, un gnostique méconnu du XXe siècle*. Beirut: al-Bouraq, 1997.

Cancian, Alessandro. "Faith as Territory: *Dār al-islām* and *dār al-ḥarb* in Modern Shiʿi Sufism." In *Dār al-islām/Dār al-ḥarb: Territories, People, Identities*, edited by Giovanna Calasso and Giuliano Lancioni, 295–312. Leiden: Brill, 2017.

Cancian, Alessandro. "In Between Reform and Bigotry: The Gunābādī *Silsila* in Two Early Twentieth-Century Anti-Sufi Works." *In Sufis and Mullahs: Sufis and Their Opponents in the Persianate World*, edited by Reza Tabandeh and Leonard Lewisohn. Irvine: Samuel Jordan Center for Persian Studies and Culture at the University of California Press (forthcoming, 2019).

Cancian, Alessandro. "Incontro con il maestro della Neʿmatollâhiyya Gonâbâdiyya, Nûr ʿAlî Tâbandeh 'Majzûb ʿAlî Shâh.'" In *Con I dervisci: otto incontri sul campo*, edited by Giovanni De Zorzi, 155–172. Milan: Mimesis, 2013.

Cancian, Alessandro. "Translation, Authority and Exegesis in Modern Iranian Sufism: Two Iranian Sufi Masters in Dialogue." *Journal of Persianate Studies* 7 (2014): 88–10.

Dabashi, Hamid. *Theology of Discontent: The Ideological Foundation of the Islamic Revolution in Iran*. New York: New York University Press, 1993.

Davari, Mahmood. *The Political Thought of Ayatollah Murtaza Mutahhari: An Iranian Theoretician of the Islamic State*. London: Routledge, 2005.

Floor, Willem. *Guilds, Merchants and Ulama in Nineteenth Century Iran*. Washington, DC: Mage, 2009.

al-Kulaynī, Muḥammad b. Yaʿqūb. *al-Rawḍa min al-Kāfī*. Edited by H. al-Rasūlī Maḥallātī. Tehran: Nashr-i ʿIlmiyya Islāmiyya, 1389/1969.

Lewisohn, Leonard. "An Introduction to the History of Modern Persian Sufism. Part I: The Nimatullahi Order: Persecution, Revival and Schism." *Bulletin of the School of Oriental and African Studies* 61, no. 3 (1998): 437–464.

Lewisohn, Leonard. "An Introduction to the History of Modern Persian Sufism. Part II: A Socio-Cultural Profile of Sufism, from the Dhahabi Revival to the Present Day." *BSOAS* 62, no. 1 (1999): 36–59.

Lewisohn, Leonard, and David Morgan (eds.). *The Heritage of Sufism III: Late Classical Persianate Sufism (1501–1750)*. Oxford: Oneworld, 1999.

Martin, Vanessa. *Creating an Islamic State: Khomeini and the Making of a New Iran.* London: I.B. Tauris, 2000.

Martin, Vanessa. "Religion and State in Khumaini's 'Kashf-i Asrar.'" *Bulletin of the School of Oriental and African Studies* 56, no. 1 (1993): 34–45.

Miller, William M. "'Shi'ah Mysticism' (The Sufis of Gonabad)." *Moslem World* 13 (1923): 343–363.

al-Nuʿmānī, Ibn Abī Zaynab. *Kitāb al-ghayba.* Edited by ʿA. A. Ghaffārī. Tehran: Ṣadūq, 1397/1977.

Nūr ʿAlī Shāh II. *Qulzum: Uqiyānūs-i bī-karān-i maʿārif-i Ahl-i Bayt.* 40 vols. Mashhad: Intishārāt al-Riḍāʾ, 1392/2013–14.

Pourjavady, Nasrollah, and Peter Lamborn Wilson. *Kings of Love: The Poetry and History of the Ni'matullahi Sufi Order.* Tehran: Imperial Academy of Philosophy, 1978.

Scharbordt, Oliver. "The Quṭb as Special Representative of the Hidden Imam: The Conflation of Shiʿi and Sufi *Vilāyat* in the Niʿmatullāhī Order." In *Shiʿi Trends and Dynamics in Modern Times (XVIIIth–XXth Centuries)/Courants et dynamiques chiites à l'époque modern (XVIIIe–XXe siècles)*, edited by Denis Hermann and Sabrina Mervin, 33–49. Beirut: Ergon-Verlag, 2010.

Speziale, Fabrizio. "À propos du renouveau *Ni'matullāhī*: Le centre de Hyderabad au cours de la première modernité." *Studia Iranica* 42, no. 1 (2013): 91–118.

Sulṭān ʿAlī Shāh Gunābādī, Sulṭān Muḥammad. *Wilāyat-nāma.* 3rd ed. Tehran: N.p., 1363/1984–85.

Tābanda Gunābādī "Riḍāʾ ʿAlī Shāh," Sulṭān Ḥusayn. *Nābigha-yi ʿilm wa ʿirfān dar qarn-i chahārdahum: Sharḥ-i ḥāl-i marḥūm Ḥājj Mullā Sulṭān Muḥammad Gunābādī Sulṭān ʿAlī Shāh.* Tehran: Ḥaqīqat, 1384.

Tābanda Gunābādī "Riḍāʾ ʿAlī Shāh," Sulṭān Ḥusayn. *Naẓar-i madhhabī ba iʿlāmiyya-yi ḥuqūq-ī bashar.* 2nd ed. N.p.: n.p., 1354/1975–76.

Tabandeh, Reza. "Mīrzā Muḥammad Maʿṣūm Shīrāzī: A Sufi and a Constitutionalist." *Studia Islamica* 112 (2017): 99–130.

Vahdat, Farzin. *God and Juggernaut: Iran's Intellectual Encounter with Modernity.* Syracuse, NY: Syracuse University Press, 2002.

van Den Bos, Matthijs. "Conjectures on Solṭānʿalīshāh, the *Valāyat-nāme* and Shiite Sufi Authority." *Sociology of Islam* 3 (2015): 190–207.

van Den Bos, Matthijs. *Mystic Regimes: Sufism and the State in Iran, from the Late Qajar Era to the Islamic Republic.* Leiden: Brill, 2002.

Zia-Ebrahimi, Reza. *The Emergence of Iranian Nationalism: Race and the Politics of Dislocation.* New York: Columbia University Press, 2016.

7

Legal Discourses on *Hijra* in the Caucasus after the Fall of the Caucasus Imamate: *al-Risāla al-Sharīfa* by the Dagestani Scholar ʿAbd al-Raḥmān al-Thughūrī

Magomed Gizbulaev

The nineteenth century marked a major turning point in the history of the Caucasus. The long and fierce struggle of the Caucasus imamate against the Russian advance in the north Caucasus ended in victory for the Russian Empire. The annexation of Dagestan, Chechnya, in 1859 and the subsequent conquest of the whole territory of Circassia in 1864 brought a large Muslim population under Russian rule. Governing this population, which was composed of a number of different communities, presented particular difficulties, and the imposition of the colonial administration from 1861, called *voenno-narodnoe upravlenie* (military people's administration), and the persecution of Muslims provoked a number of local uprisings in the region. The consequences of these failed uprisings against the tsarist efforts to prohibit the practice of the *sharīʿa* led to the *hijra* (migration) of native populations (the 1860s to the 1880s) from the north Caucasus, an area that is famous for the many persecutions its people have suffered. Some Dagestani legal works give the impression that the issue of *hijra* was widely discussed.

In this chapter, I hope to contribute to our knowledge of the development of legal discourse on the *hijra* after Russia's incorporation of the Caucasus by undertaking an analysis, as well as a comparative and textual study, of the formerly unexamined treatise *al-Risāla al-sharīfa* by ʿAbd al-Raḥmān al-Thughūrī (d. 1882), a work that I discovered in the course of my research as a visiting Fulbright scholar at Princeton University in 2010/2011. From a historical point of view, the study of *al-Risāla al-sharīfa* should give us some insight into

Figure 7.1 Sogratl after it was burned to the ground in November 1877. Material from Wikimedia Commons: https://commons.wikimedia.org/wiki/File:Сожженный_Согратль.jpg

the development of juristic discourse on the enforced Muslim emigration from the Caucasus to the lands of the Ottoman Empire and about the practice and understanding of Islamic international law in Dagestan, in which the notions of *dār al-kufr* and *dār al-islām* were used.

The history of Islamic culture in the Caucasus

Dagestan is situated in the northern Caucasus and bordered on its eastern side by the Caspian Sea. The process of Islamization in Dagestan was uneven; it lasted for more than one thousand years and was distinguished by several stages. By the end of the sixteenth century, Islam had ousted pagan beliefs, Zoroastrianism, Judaism, and Christianity from the region and became the official religion of the numerous independent polities (Avar khanate, *shamkhalate* of Ghazi-Qumuq, *utsmiate* of Qaytaq) and more than sixty alliances of rural communities (ʿAndalal, Hidatle, ʿAndi, Antsukh, Dido, Aqusha, Akhti-Pari, etc.).[1] Dagestan's first encounter with Islam is associated with the Prophet Muḥammad's Companions—in the period of the rightly guided caliphs (*al-khulafāʾ al-rāshidūn*)—under the leadership of Salmān b. Rabīʿa. Their successors—in the period of Umayyad rule—Abū ʿUbayda al-Jarrāh b. ʿAbdallāh, Maslama b. ʿAbd al-Malik, and Marwān b. Muḥammad b. Marwān incorporated the coastal part of Dagestan (Bāb al-Abvāb, Lakz, Tabasaran, Samandar) into the caliphate. A considerable Muslim community of 24,000 Arab *ribāṭ*s was established in Bāb al-Abvāb (Derbend); from there, Muslims undertook a number of campaigns (*ghazawāt*) against infidels in the mountains up to the end of the ninth century.[2] In addition, external campaigns (by the Saljūqs and Tīmūr) and internal activities (by *du'at*s, or those inviting others to Islam, and by local scholars) of the eleventh to sixteenth centuries brought about the conversion of the peoples of Dagestan to Islam.

The Dagestani intellectual revival in the late seventeenth to the early twentieth century represents one of the most important periods in the history of Arabic literature and culture in the Caucasus. Islamic education brought with it new perceptions of the traditional culture and attempts at adaptation to new conditions and realities.[3] The Russian academician Krachkovskii notes that "Dagestani scholars from the seventeenth to nineteenth centuries had already acquired and mastered expertise in the whole Arabic literary heritage … their academic interests included, in equal measure, Arabic grammar, mathematics, and astronomy. Dagestanis created original works in legal, historical and philosophical scholarship."[4] For instance, in the nineteenth century, Dagestan developed a particularly widespread historical genre; local authors, mostly connected with the local *ʿulamāʾ*, wrote chronicles and bio-bibliographical works, including texts on the history of the Islamization of Dagestan, the Caucasus imamate, the Russia–Caucasus wars, and postwar political and social events. To date, many of the chronicles are noted for the high quality of their research; they represent a reliable source for the study of the history of Dagestan. The list of historical texts provides a good illustration of the historical literature: *Bāriqat al-suyūf al-jabāliyya fī baʿḍ ghazāwāt al-shāmiliyya* of Muḥammad Ṭāhir al-Qarākhī (d. 1880)[5], *Kitāb al-tadhkira* of ʿAbd al-Raḥmān al-Ghāzī Qumūqī (d. 1901)[6], *Āthār al-Dāgistān* of Ḥasan al-Qadārī (d. 1910)[7], *Tārīkh al-aʾimma al-thalātha* of Khaidar-Bek al-Ghinichutlī (d. 1873)[8], and at least thirty other titles of Dagestani historical works. A significant part of the Dagestan literary corpus focused on logic and rhetoric. A dozen works in this genre were written by Dagestani logicians, including books such as *Sharḥ al-Muṭawwal* of Ḥasan al-Kudalī (d. 1795) and *Fatḥ al-ghālib* of ʿUmārjhan al-Kudalī (d. 1801).[9]

My objective in this chapter is to further develop our knowledge of the long-standing Caucasian Muslim Arabic textual practices, a field of study that has not received the attention that it deserves in Islamic studies outside Dagestan.

The intensive cultural exchange between Dagestan and other Muslim regions resulted in the enrichment of its distinct culture. Muslim students from Dagestan continued their academic pursuits at educational centers in the Hijaz, Yemen, Shirvan, Cairo, and Aleppo. For example, Ḥasan al-Qadārī's chronicle *Āthār al-Dāghistān* describes Muḥammad b. Mūsā l-Quduqī's (d. 1717) efforts to inculcate the practice of *ijtihād* among his fellow Dagestanis; al-Quduqī was introduced to this form of legal reasoning during his studies with the Yemeni shaykh Ṣāliḥ al-Maqbalī (1638–97).[10] The creative heritage of the seventeenth-century scholars contributed significantly to the evolution, development, and establishment of Dagestani scholarship in the eighteenth and nineteenth centuries. I refer, in particular, to a number of representatives of the science of the period, including Dāwūd al-Kudalī, ʿAlī b. Ḥajjī b. ʿAbd al-Karīm al-Chūkhī, ʿĪsā l-Shanghūdī, Shaʿbān al-ʿUbūdī (d. 1667), Malla-Muḥammad al-Ghūlūdī, ʿAlī Kelebskī, Ḥasan al-Kudalī (d. 1700), Ṭayyib al-Kharakhī, and more.[11] I suggest that, following this period in Dagestani learning, there transpired a significant production of commentaries, legal discourses, and *fatāwā* in related topics of Islamic jurisprudence.

It is noteworthy that the development of Muslim law and judicial institutions, and the gradual transformation of the norms of customary law (*ʿādāt*) in Dagestan, was a result of the efforts of local scholars. Their scholarly activity produced Islamic legal treatises and tracts like those of Muḥammad b. Salmān al-Kudalī and Ibrāhīm-ḥajjī l-Hidatlī (d. 1770), who wrote *fatāwā* on the obligatory nature of resisting the invasion of Nādir Shah (i.e., the Safavids) into Dagestan in 1741[12]; the *Iʿlām al-tilmīz bi-aḥkām al-nabīz* of Abū Bakr al-ʿAymakī (d. 1791)[13]; the *Nikāḥ al-mutʿa* of Saʿīd al-Harakānī (d. 1834)[14]; and Ghāzī Muḥammad al-Ghimrī, the first imam of Dagestan (1829–32), a poet and expert of Arabic literature, and the organizer of numerous military campaigns against Russian imperial forces in the Caucasus. He is the author of *Iqāmat al-burhān ʿalā irtidād ʿurafāʾ al-Dāghistān*, a treatise on the implementation of *sharīʿa* and the replacement of customary law (*ʿādāt*) in Dagestan, addressed to the rulers of Dagestani principalities and the alliances of rural communities like the Avar khanate and *shamkhalate* of Tarqi.[15] Clarifying each problem, the jurists refer to citations from the Qurʾān, prophetic traditions, and opinions given by acknowledged experts on Islamic law.

The nineteenth century was a turning point in the history of Caucasus. The Caucasian Muslims, from the 1820s until 1864, in 1877, and from 1918 until 1925, under the five imams—Ghāzī Muḥammad al-Ghimrāwī (d. 1832), Ḥamzat-Bek (d. 1834), Shāmil al-Ghimrāwī (d. 1871), Ḥājjī Muḥammad al-Thughūrī

(d. 1877), and Najhmudīn al-Ḥutsī (d. 1925)—struggled for independence from Russian encroachment. Dagestan was, increasingly, separated from its traditional orientation toward the Muslim world as it encountered Russian and more generally Western civilization; in addition, the Cyrillic alphabet was established as a result of Russian education in the Caucasus. Many legendary Caucasian personalities in this period—young and old, prominent and unknown—were martyred for their faith and the freedom of their homeland. These martyrs included ʿAlī-Bek Khiriyasulav (d. 1839), Akhberdilav Muḥammad (d. 1843), Batuko, Qebed-Muḥammad, Idrīs al-Ghirghibilī (d. 1837), Buk Muḥammad (d. 1851), Muḥammad Amīn al-Avarī (d. 1899)—the leader of Circassia's struggle against Russian aggression in the west Caucasus—Daniyal-Bek (d. 1872), and Ḥājjī-Murād (d. 1856). The latter, Daniyal-Bek and Ḥājjī-Murād, were courageous politicians and members of the Elisu sultanate and the Avar khanate ruling family; they were the trusted *nāʾib*s of the imamate and organizers of swift guerrilla tactics that inflicted heavy casualties on Russian troops.[16]

After the fall of the Caucasian imamate in 1859 and the failed uprisings in 1877, a number of Shāfiʿī jurists in Dagestan began to invoke the Qurʾānic concept of *hijra* in order to encourage Muslims to migrate from the Islamic territory conquered by Orthodox Russians to Islamic territories, particularly the Ottoman Empire. One of the most prominent figures in this group was Shāmil's *nāʾib*, a Sufi shaykh and Islamic scholar named ʿAbd al-Raḥmān b. Aḥmad al-Thughūrī (1792–1882), a scholar with great influence in Dagestan who continued to opt for *jihād*, though this was crushed by the Russian army in 1877. Notably, in the large-scale uprising that broke out throughout Dagestan and Chechnya, Muḥammad-ḥājjī, a son of ʿAbd al-Raḥmān al-Thughūrī, was elected as a leader (*imām*). Later the Russians executed him, along with many other leaders of the uprising, but because of his advanced age, ʿAbd al-Raḥmān was only exiled to the village of Nizhnee Kazanishe, where he died in 1882.[17]

According to al-Thughūrī, when a Muslim territory falls to non-Muslim rule, such that Muslims cannot fulfill their religious obligations, it is obligatory for them to leave the land of *dār al-ḥarb* and migrate to the *dār al-islām*. Indeed, many of his followers emigrated to the *dār al-islām*, among them, for example, the Avar shaykhs Muḥammad b. ʿUthmān al-Kikunī (d. 1914), who moved to Istanbul,[18] and Muḥammad al-ʿUbudī (d. 1890), who moved to Medina.[19] Moreover, long before the aforementioned uprising took place, ʿAbd al-Raḥmān's elder son Ḥājjī-Muḥammad encountered injustice and faced ongoing repression by the tsarist Russian authorities and migrated to Ottoman lands. He settled in the province of Kars, where he died in 1870.[20] Many Dagestanis chose migration, on the grounds that justice could not

Figure 7.2 The first picture of Imam Shāmil was made by I. G. Nostitz in September 1859 in Chiryurt. Material from Wikimedia Commons: https://commons.wikimedia.org/wiki/File:Имам_Шамиль.jpg?uselang=ru

prevail in their homeland at the time. For example, "some 500 families of the Avar community of Salataviya in Dagestan applied to the Russian colonial administration [in Tiflis], seeking permission to resettle in the Ottoman lands."[21]

The conceptual categories through which Muslim jurists divided the world: *Dār al-islām* and *dār al-ḥarb*

The beginning of the regional Islamic discourse on Muslim/non-Muslim interactions and *hijra* was linked to a legal treatise: *al-Zājir ʿan muwālāt al-kuffār* by the renowned Dagestani jurist Abū Bakr al-ʿAymakī. In it, he discussed topics concerning mutual relations between Muslims and non-Muslims. This work appeared in the second half of the eighteenth century; it was written in response to military and political circumstances: during the reign of Catherine II (1762–96), Russia resumed its colonial encroachment in the Caucasus.[22] The judge (*qāḍī*) Murtaḍā ʿAlī l-ʿUradī (d. 1865) of the Caucasian imamate broadened this debate in his treatise *al-Murghim*, which utilized legal sources to substantiate Imam Shāmil's claim to power in the imamate and to provide a better understanding of the notion of *hijra*. He demanded that in order to carry out a *jihād*, every Muslim living in Russian-controlled territories must emigrate to the lands of Shāmil's government (i.e., not to foreign lands).[23] During the war against tsarist Russia, the imamate was supported by other Muslim Caucasians, and eventually it amalgamated parts of Dagestan (especially the territory with the population of Avars) and Chechnya; the Circassian people fell under the control of the imamate during Shāmil's rule as well. The conventional portrayal of the imamate as a theocratic institution and Sufi brotherhood is misleading. Mirza Kazem-bek was the first to state that *muridizm* was a Sufi order.[24] Among others, Anna Zelkina also argues that the imamate was a theocratic Sufi state.[25] In fact, the imamate was a result of the political mobilization of northern Caucasian Muslims who were committed to securing their cultural and physical survival against dangers posed by Russian imperial ambitions.

It is noteworthy that the Shāfiʿī *madhhab* prevailed among Ḥanafī and Shīʿī Muslim legal discourses in Dagestan. We know very little about the practical application of Islamic legal rulings in the Dagestani polities in the early stage of Islamization. According to Muslim travelers, historians, and geographers, among them Abū Ḥāmid al-Gharnāṭī, who visited southern Dagestan in 1191, and his successor Zakariyyā al-Qazwīnī (d. 1283), jurists used Shāfiʿī texts in the colleges, *madrasas*, and academic gathering (*majlis*).[26] The most popular legal works were *Minhāj al-ṭālibin* of Muḥyī l-Dīn al-Nawawī (d. 1277), *Jāmiʿ al-jawāmiʿ* of al-Subkī (d. 1370), *al-Anwār ʿalā aʿmāl al-abrār* of Yūsuf al-Ardabīlī (d. 1396), *Kanz al-rāghibīn* of Jalāl al-Dīn al-Maḥallī (d. 1459), *Tuḥfat al-muḥtāj fī sharḥ al-Minḥāj* of Ibn Ḥajar al-Haytamī (d. 1567), and *al-Bahjāt* by Aḥmad al-Qalyūbī (d. 1659). It was in these classical legal works that local jurists found their inspiration, functional models, and source material.

A number of types of works were highly valued in Dagestan, namely, compendiums, abridgements, and *fatwā*s in Islamic law. Driven by the desire to render the *sharīʿa* rulings adaptable to the complex demands of contemporary Dagestani life, local scholars were particularly interested in the spheres of public relations. The development of Islamic law and judicial institutions and the gradual transformation of the norms of community law (*ʿādāt*) in Dagestan resulted from the efforts of local scholars and Arab jurists. For instance, an al-Azhar University scholar and Shāfiʿī jurist Aḥmad al-Yamānī (d. 1450), who settled in the town Ghāzī-Qumūq, stands out as a key figure in the development of the *sharīʿa* in central and northern Dagestan. His successor ʿAlī l-Kabīr al-Ghāzī Qumūqī (d. 1538) was the author of the popular legal work *al-Mukhtaṣar*, which was an abridgment that provided important additional information about the aforementioned legal work. While in the course of my research, I discovered a commentary on it in the Princeton University library; it is entitled *Sharḥ ʿalā l-Mukhtaṣar al-Dāghistān*[27] of the Egyptian writer and scholar ʿAbdallāh b. Ḥijāzī b. Ibrāhīm al-Sharqawī (d. 1812).

To understand the nature of the relationship between the Muslims of the north Caucasus and the Orthodox Russian Empire, we must grasp the conceptual categories through which Muslims understood the world. Muslim jurists divided the world into conceptual divisions: *dār al-islām* and *dār al-ḥarb*. When the territories of *dār al-islām* (north Caucasus) were annexed to *dār al-ḥarb* (Russia), this raised the question of whether *hijra* (emigration) was obligatory, forbidden, or recommended.

Islamic jurists identify the territory of *dār al-islām* by three criteria. First, the renowned scholars and founders of schools of law, imams Mālik, Shāfiʿī, and Ibn Ḥanbal, define it as the territory in which Islamic law (*sharīʿa*) is applied. It is also defined as a territory in which the *aḥkām* (rules or practices of Islam) exist or, at a minimum, a region in which Muslims can freely proclaim their belief in Islam and perform the prayers.[28] Others "even believe that a country remains *dār al-islām* so long as a single provision (*ḥukm*) of the Muslim law is kept in force there."[29] Second, al-Shawkānī maintains that "a territory can be considered *dār al-islām*, even if it is not under Muslim rule, as long as a Muslim can reside there in safety and freely fulfil his religious obligations."[30] Third, for Abū Ḥanīfa, *dār al-islām* is a territory in which Islamic law is applied and Muslims and the *ahl al-dhimma* (non-Muslim citizens of the *dār al-islām*) are safe.[31]

It follows that *dār al-ḥarb* refers to territories in which these criteria are lacking. According to the first definition, it is a territory where Islamic law (*sharīʿa*) is not applied or where it is not safe to profess belief in Islam or perform prayers.[32] According to the second definition, *dār al-ḥarb* is a territory ruled by non-Muslims,[33] while, according to the third definition, it is a territory in which the laws of Islam cannot be applied or exist and in which Muslims and *ahl al-dhimma* are not safe.[34] Thus, the classifications of *dār al-ḥarb* and *dār al-islām* refer to the existence or nonexistence of safety and peace, and specifically, the freedom of Muslims to apply and practice Islamic law.[35]

It is worth adding here that if Muslims are not safe to profess their belief in Islam, fulfill their religious obligations, and their lives are imperiled, it is obligatory for them to emigrate (undertake the *hijra*) from the *dār al-ḥarb* to the *dār al-islām*; however, if Muslims are unable because of weakness, illness, and incapacity, then the *hijra* is not obligatory upon them.

The notion of *hijra* (lit., "to abandon" or "to migrate") is central to Islamic collective memory. The Prophet Muḥammad's forced migration from Mecca to Medina, where in 622 he founded an Islamic society, is the event that begins the Islamic calendar. Thus, it signifies the first opportunity Muslims had to enjoy freedom of religion as a community and to face the common challenges confronting them. The Qur'ān and sunna emphasize the utmost importance of the *hijra* and do not limit it by time or by place.[36] There are two circumstances in which *hijra* should be made. First, *hijra* is obligatory from lands in which people are forced to commit wrongdoing (*ẓulm*). Second, specific Qur'ānic verses connect *hijra* with the duty to fight (*jihād*) against nonbelievers, as this is an act of commitment to the community of believers. The Qur'ān exempts from the *hijra* only those who are truly incapable of migrating. Alan Verskin's book and Jocelyn Hendrickson's PhD thesis have made available in English a significant body of *fatwā*s issued by Muslim jurists across a wide range of historical and geographical contexts; these rulings deal specifically with the legality of residence under non-Muslim rule, the question of the obligation to emigrate, and the status of territory in which Muslims reside. These works thus represent a significant contribution to the field.[37]

Hijra appeared in early Islam when Muslims were a persecuted minority, then faded in importance once Muslims came to possess political power. It became widespread in response to Christian territorial gains during the Reconquista, when Muslims fled Andalusia, then rose to prominence again, in the nineteenth century, with the Russian encroachment in the Caucasus, the French and British incursions in the Maghrib and India, and then in the postcolonial period it faded from discussions when the borders between Christian and Muslim lands became more stable. In these cases, scholars felt free to determine when and how to invoke the concept of *hijra* in response to the needs of their societies.

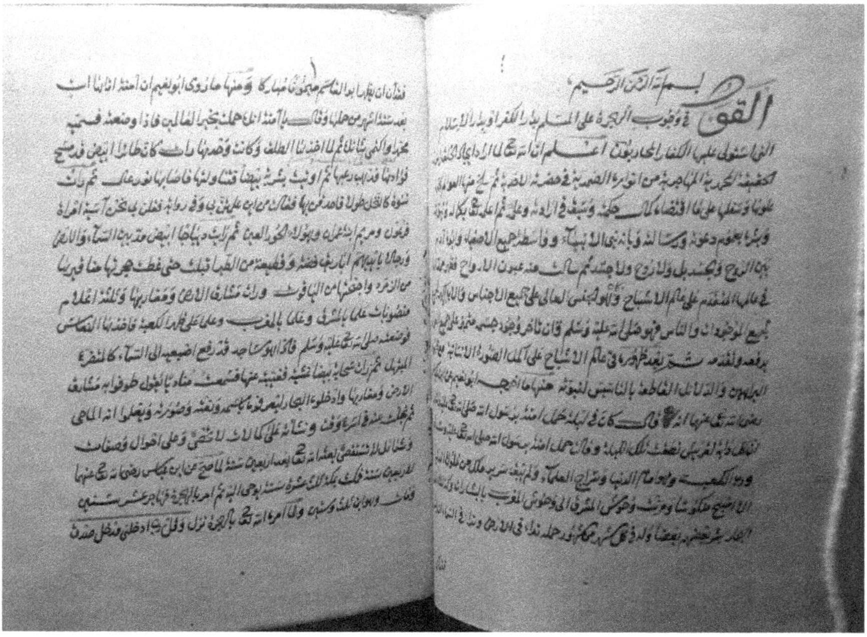

Figure 7.3 *al-Risāla al-sharīfa*. Firestone Library, Princeton University, MS Garrett Yahuda 2867/Mach 2034

The concept of *hijra* in ʿAbd al-Raḥmān al-Thughūrī's *al-Risāla al-sharīfa*

I now turn to the references to *hijra* in the Dagestani legal treatise entitled *al-Risāla al-sharīfa*. The manuscript is 215 × 170; 155 × 120 mm, with sixteen lines per page; it comprises four folios and can be found in the volume of distinctive titles kept at the Princeton University Firestone Library: MS Garrett Yahuda 2867/Mach 2034. The textual sources for *al-Risāla al-sharīfa* are the Qurʾān, *ḥadīth*, and the opinions of the Shāfiʿī authorities of *fiqh*. After quoting the Qurʾān and *ḥadīth*, al-Thughūrī introduces the debate on whether the obligation of *hijra* has been abrogated. The resolution of this question was naturally of great importance to Dagestani jurists who wished to introduce *hijra* into the legal tradition when the territories of *dār al-islām* (Muslim Caucasus) were annexed to *dār al-kufr* (Orthodox Russia). He quotes two *ḥadīth*s on the issue of whether or not *hijra* had been abrogated.

The first says, "There is no *hijra* after the liberation [of Mecca]."[38] The second says, "*Hijra* will not end until repentance ends, and repentance will not end until the sun rises in the West."[39]

How, one may ask, can the two *ḥadīth*s, one of which declares that *hijra* is abrogated and the other that it can never be abrogated, be reconciled? In response, al-Thughūrī explains:

> When the Prophet (may God bless him and grant him peace) immigrated to Medina, that *hijra* became obligatory for Muslims. They were ordered to move to where he was in order to be together with him to make common cause in times of difficulty (*jihād*), to help one another, and to study and come to understand religious matters. When Mecca was liberated, the obligation to migrate to Medina was abrogated, since the former became part of *dār al-islām*.[40]

He argues that "*hijra* from *dār al-ḥarb* always has been and always will be obligatory."[41]

For al-Thughūrī, therefore, the two *ḥadīth*s on *hijra* do not conflict; they merely refer to different circumstances. This meant that when the early Muslims were politically weak, the positive spirit of *hijra*, with its destabilizing effect on the status quo, could be enthusiastically employed. However, with greater Muslim power, the disadvantages of *hijra* became quickly apparent and it was abrogated.

In general, Sunnī jurists accepted the validity of the tradition abrogating the *hijra*, although some still regarded *hijra* as legitimate under extreme circumstances of political weakness in which Muslims are not free to practice Islam.[42] It is noteworthy that after 1859, two branches of the Sufi Khālidiyya emerged in the north Caucasus:

> one in Central Dagestan under sheikh ʿAbd al-Raḥmān al-Thughūrī, who tried to continue the heritage of *jihād*, and a new branch [called the] *Maḥmūdiyya* [founded by shaykh Maḥmūd Afandī l-Almalī, d. 1877] coming from Shirwan to Dagestan which was outspokenly against *jihād* and promoted a political quietism [in opposition to the group of shaykh ʿAbd al-Raḥmān al-Thughūrī].[43]

The rivalry between the two branches became manifest during the *jihād* of 1877 and 1919–21. In his *Risāla*, al-Thughūrī attempts to provide a more adequate understanding of the notion of *hijra*, which was often misperceived and neglected by his contemporaries. His doctrine of *hijra* was based on his experience of the Russian encroachment into the Caucasus. Russians saw it as their divinely inspired right to expand across the region, based on the policies of "wanton destruction of property, mass deportation, and indiscriminate killing—all committed in the name of bringing true freedom and enlightenment to backward tribal peoples."[44] The main objective of the Russian authorities was to eliminate the local Muslim populations; this resulted in a most dramatic loss for the Avars, Chechens, Circassian ethnic groups, Crimean Tatars, and Nogays. In other words, the Russian authorities, in fact, supported this *hijra* movement, and this resulted in a huge exodus, especially of Circassians.

In this regard, al-Thughūrī argues that "disbelievers' intention (*qaṣd*) toward Muslims always has been and always will be their extermination or their admission to the military service in order to struggle against [Muslim leader]."[45]

Al-Thughūrī called for Muslims to refuse to serve in the imperial Russian army; his call was directed against the growing number of Caucasians in the imperial Russian army, which was engaged in wars against Muslims and was a result of his belief that association with the Russians led Caucasians to accept features of the Russian lifestyle. The Dagestan irregular cavalry, for example, was formed in 1852 as a division of the imperial Russian Army. It was composed of volunteers from diverse communities. It took part in the Caucasus war until the fall of Shāmil's imamate in 1859; in putting down uprisings in Unkratl (Dagestan) and Argun District (Chechnya) in 1861; in military campaigns in the Zakatala District in 1863 and Qaitaq-Tabasaran District (Dagestan) in 1866; in conquering Manghishlak (Kazakhstan) in 1870 and Khiva (Uzbekistan) in 1873; and in the Russian–Ottoman war in 1877–78. Russia's subjugation of the Caucasus, the "putting aside the arrows of war" as Alexander Pushkin termed it, rendered invalid the Circassians' (Caucasians)

Figure 7.4 Officers and non commissioned officers of the Dagestan irregular cavalry division in 1871 (see Kozubskii, "History of the Dagestan Cavalry Division"). Material from forum WW1 Daily Pic: https://www.coh2.org/topic/35335/ww1-daily-pic/page/2

purpose as a nation and made them another subject under Russian imperial rule.[46] This narrative was perpetuated in tsarist Russia, even though it ran contrary to historical fact.

Having thus established that there are two kinds of *hijra*, only one of which was abrogated, al-Thughūrī discussed whether *hijra* from the following lands is obligatory. He says,

> As for a Muslim who is residing in the land of the disbelievers (*dār al-kufr*) or in the land of the believers (*dār al-islām*) conquered by the disbelievers, [and] where he is unable to manifest his religion (*dīn*) or fears corruption (*fitna*) in his religion, it is obligatory for him to perform *hijra*.[47]

Al-Thughūrī continues, "if he stays there while having the ability to migrate, then he wrongs himself and commits a sin."[48] The Qurʾān exempts from *hijra* only those "oppressed, be they men, women, or children, who cannot devise something (*ḥīla*) and are not guided to a way" (4:98), that is, those who are truly unable to migrate. Thus, Dagestani jurists maintained that *hijra* is not required from a territory merely because it is governed by non-Muslims, rather, *hijra* is applicable only under a very limited set of circumstances.

Other sources also affirm the importance of *hijra*. The Mālikī jurist Aḥmad b. Yaḥyā l-Wansharīsī (d. 1508), for example, gives an expansive outline of the meaning of *hijra* and its application to the situation of his Muslim contemporaries in al-Andalus at the end of the fifteenth century. He says, "For living with infidels, without [their being] subject tributaries (*ahl al-dhimma*), is not permitted or allowed for even one hour of one day because of the pollutions, the filth, and the religious and worldly corruptions to which this gives rise, throughout their lives … "[49]

The Qurʾān frequently emphasizes that *hijra* is a religious obligation of the utmost importance. In his treatise, al-Thughūrī speaks of *hijra* as a divinely ordained act:

> Verily, as for those whom the angels take [in death] while they are wronging themselves [as they stayed among the disbelievers even though emigration was obligatory for them], they [the angels] say: "In what [condition] were you?" They reply: "We were weak and oppressed on the earth." They [the angels] say: "Was not the earth of God spacious enough for you to emigrate therein?" Such men will find their abode in Hell—what an evil destination! (4:97)

This verse, he comments, was revealed regarding some Muslims living in Mecca, who did not emigrate. At that time, *hijra* was obligatory and one of the conditions of accepting Islam. Whoever embraced Islam should join the Prophet in Medina.[50]

But, as noted above, Muslims who were unable because of weakness, illness, or incapacity were exempt from the obligation to undertake the *hijra*. After the fundamental condition of ability is met, residing in the land of disbelief and the land of Islam conquered by the non-Muslims falls into the following categories. To support his argument in this case, al-Thughūrī refers to the authority of the Shāfiʿī legal school:

> According to Ibn Ḥajar, he [a Muslim] resides there [in the land of disbelief, i.e., the land of Islam conquered by non-Muslims] in order to seek *maṣlaḥa* (public interest), for example, Ibn ʿAbbās did not perform the *hijra* and continued to correspond with the Prophet (may God bless him and grant him peace), but [al-Thughūrī states that] if he is able to openly manifest Islam [and is not prevented from performing the outward acts of Islam], to abstain [from grave sins], and to migrate, then this residence [in the aforementioned lands] remains obligatory for him.[51]

For al-Thughūrī, however, these conditions on residence (*iqāma*) were rarely observed in his time, especially by those who had participated in the 1877 anticolonial uprising, which was, for the most part, supported by a coalition of old supporters of *jihād* and the local aristocracy, who had recently lost the remainder of their former political power as a result of a Russian administrative reform. Therefore, he reached the conclusion that "if the Muslim is living in one of the aforementioned lands and is facing some difficulties in practicing his *dīn*, then *hijra* is recommended (*mustaḥabba*) in his case."[52]

The argument al-Thughūrī used is based on the writings of Shāfiʿī scholars, particularly, Muḥyī l-Dīn al-Nawawī (d. 1277), who held that emigration is recommended, rather than obligatory, for those protected by their high rank; applied to Dagestanis (and Caucasian Muslims in general), this would mean that if they felt protected by the sheer number of their community, which thus lent it status, they would not be obligated to emigrate. But then he says "it is *mustaḥabb* [recommended] for one with the ability to make the *hijra*."[53]

In sum, Islamic legal discourse in Dagestan on the issue of *hijra* demonstrates the significant dynamism of scholars who responded to the challenges of living under non-Muslim rule. Al-Thughūrī's argument for the continuing validity of *hijra* was not without precedent in the works of previous classical Shāfiʿī jurists. His principle contribution to the discourse is *al-Risāla al-sharīfa*, in which he gathered a number of legal discussions on the topic into a single reference work.

Islamic arguments and polemics against residence in the Russian Empire

There was no precise precedent in Dagestan for jurists to address the issue of *hijra*; rather, it was the nineteenth-century political events that compelled local jurists to deal with this issue. They saw Russian colonial expansion as a threat to Islam; these scholars supported the *jihād* movement of the Caucasian imams, the most famous of which was that of the third Imam Shāmil (1834–59). When this *jihād* was eventually crushed by the Russians, some Dagestani scholars encouraged Caucasian Muslims to move to Ottoman lands, because implementation of Islamic law under non-Muslim rule was a contradiction in terms. Many of these migrants settled in the Ottoman Empire, especially in what is now Turkey, Syria, and Jordan; thus, the Chechen, Circassian, and Dagestani diasporas were created.[54] However, a majority of the Dagestanis remained in their homeland with new status as imperial Russian subjects. Dagestani jurists continued, periodically, to address the legal subjects of life under non-Muslim rule. Among those jurists who discussed the subject, for example, are Muḥammad ʿAlī l-Chukhī and Murtaḍā ʿAlī l-ʿUradī.

In response to a query about whether *hijra* was obligatory or abrogated at the time, the Dagestani scholar Muḥammad ʿAlī l-Chukhī (d. 1888) fully endorsed it: "the obligation of *hijra* from the lands where the believer cannot practice his religion fully … " is considered in a "category of *farḍ al-ʿayn* which remains obligatory until the day of resurrection."[55]

His interest in *hijra* was a product of his residence in Dagestan when it was subject to occupation by the Russians. Although he does not explicitly address Russian policies toward the practice of Islam in Dagestan, he says that a territory remains Muslim, and in the *dār al-islām*, regardless of who rules it, provided that the Muslims who live there are able to practice their religion. Thus, we can deduce from the form of his argument that he does not consider "*hijra* from the *dār al-islām* to the *dār al-islām* to be applicable."[56] He does not deny the obligation of *hijra* but counsels against it being applied too broadly. Prior to this lenient ruling of the Dagestani scholar, a similar position had been adopted by the distinguished classical Shāfiʿī jurist al-Māwardī (d. 1058), who held that if Muslims living in the land of disbelievers could practice their religion, then that territory becomes part of *dār al-islām*.[57] Al-Māwardī even argued that residence in such a territory is preferable to migration because of the hope of winning converts to Islam. Then al-Chukhī states that "there is another kind of *hijra*, which is to migrate from a land in which grave sins (*maʿāṣī*) are prevalent, to a land in which there is [more] obedience (*hijra min al-maʿāṣī ilā l-ṭāʿa*)." The Dagestani jurist mentioned that this kind of migration is obligatory, because "staying in such a land may lead one to be among those who may be inflicted with torment because of their evil deeds."[58]

We must bear in mind that Muḥammad ʿAlī l-Chukhī was not a *qāḍī*, and his legal statements are merely the private views of a Muslim scholar and do not represent the views of official Islamic institutions in the Russian Empire or the *sharīʿa* courts that operated within the framework of the Russian administration.

In a similar vein, the *qāḍī* of the Caucasian imamate, Murtaḍā ʿAlī l-ʿUradī, in his treatise *al-Durra al-nafīsa*, lists the opinions of *sharīʿa* authorities, classifies the territories, and also defines the social circumstances that were factors in his legal argument in favor of *hijra*. He says that

> a Muslim, male or female, is allowed to postpone *hijra* from the land of the disbelievers (*dār al-kufr*) or the land of the believers (*dār al-islām*) conquered by disbelievers, if he does not fear for his/her life, dignity and property, [or if] a leader (*imām*) orders him/her to make migration, or [he/she] is able to openly practice *sharīʿa* rulings (*aḥkām*).[59]

In his work, al-ʿUradī states that emigration is only obligatory if it is not possible to practice Islam, and then he refers his reader to the commentaries of Shāfiʿī scholars like Ibn Ḥajar al-ʿAsqalānī (d. 1449). He thus maintains that it is only under specific circumstances that a person is obliged to emigrate. These scholars were responding to circumstances characterized by colonial rule throughout the Islamic world.

Overall, Muslim scholars in Dagestan under imperial Russian rule maintained the principles of classical Islamic law to maintain the idea that they still lived in a Muslim society. In daily life, the role of *sharīʿa* was largely reduced to issues of personal status, that is, to registering marriages and divorces, inheritance, etc.

The geographical location, the natural curiosity of scholars and their thirst for knowledge, their Islamic orientation, their ability to subsist, and the existence of established traditions and educational centers all indicate that we should consider the population of Dagestan a highly educated one at that time. This Dagestani Islamic academic tradition flourished in the Caucasus until it fell under the dominance of the Russian Empire and its successor Soviet Russia.

As in Dagestan, Tatar Muslim legal scholars at the end of the eighteenth and beginning of the nineteenth centuries also debated on a number of politically relevant issues. Thanks to Michael Kemper's in-depth work on Volga-Ural *fiqh* in Tatar history and his analyses of a number of *fatwā*s issued by Tatar jurists, we are aware of these works. The scholars of Dagestan and the Volga-Ural region followed different schools of law, namely, the Shāfiʿī and the Ḥanafī, respectively. Behind all this stood the broader question of whether Muslims living in the Russian Empire still belonged to *dār al-islām*, or whether their position, as part of Russia, meant that they should regard their status as one of living in the *dār al-ḥarb*. The Tatar scholar Mulla Murtaḍā b. Ḥusayn al-Buralī produced a short treatise titled *Risāla fī dār al-ḥarb*. In it he refers to *al-Multaqit*,[60] which mentions that the [Muslim] lands that find themselves in the hands of the disbelievers (*kuffār*) are without any doubt still part of *dār al-islām*, and are not part of *dār al-ḥarb*, as long as these lands are not ruled by the legislation of unbelief (*kufr*), and as long as they have Muslim *qāḍī*s and scholars who only obey [the disbelievers] because it is necessary for the Muslims.[61] This Ḥanafī position thus expressed the situation of the Muslims of the Volga-Ural region, where Muslims were encouraged to obey non-Muslims for the sake of necessity, as long as they could maintain their Islamic identity and obey Islamic legal regulations, and have their acknowledged representatives.

By comparing the different positions on *hijra* held by Dagestani Shāfiʿīs and Tatar Ḥanafīs, one can see that they adopted positions that they believed were appropriate to the needs of their communities. I believe that the appearance of *al-Risāla al-sharīfa* can be seen as the product of two factors. First, the instability caused by the Orthodox Russian annexation of Muslim Caucasus during and after the period of the Caucasus imamate forced Muslims to consider the issue of migration as a defensive strategy. Second, I suggest that the practice of *hijra* in Dagestan and the northern Caucasus, in general, was justified from a legal point of view. At the very least, the results of this chapter greatly enrich researchers' understanding of the peculiarities of Dagestani Arabic legal texts as important historical documents for the study of the social, political, and intellectual history of the Caucasus. I also hope to further my research work on *al-Durra al-nafīsa*, which I believe will make a similar contribution, and then undertake a more in-depth comparative research on the treatises of ʿAbd al-Raḥmān al-Thughūrī and Murtaḍā ʿAlī l-ʿUradī, to gain some insight into the question of whether *hijra* was obligatory, forbidden, or recommended after the Russian conquest that culminated in the annexation of Caucasus in 1864.

This chapter has traced the development of the concept of *hijra* as a basis for a Muslim's obligation to leave the territory of *dār al-ḥarb*. Despite the centrality of the concept in Islamic thinking, jurists felt relatively free to decide when it should be applied and when it could be taken as a recommendation only. In his *al-Risāla al-sharīfa*, al-Thughūrī confirms his own position that emigration is only obligatory for those who cannot practice their religion and are capable of emigrating. In support of this position, he cites the opinions of a number of adherents of the Shāfiʿī school, who held that emigration is only obligatory if Muslims cannot practice Islam. Moreover, it is clear that after 1877, the group surrounding ʿAbd al-Raḥmān al-Thughūrī continued to promote *hijra* in Dagestan and Chechnya. Thus, the failure of the uprisings led to the emigration of many Caucasians to the Ottoman Empire.

Notes

1 Sh. Shikhaliev, "Islamizatsia Dagestana v X–XVI vv," PhD dissertation (Makhachkala, 2007).

2 M. Gizbulaev, "Ta'rikh by Khalifa ibn Khayyat kak istochnik po istorii Dagestan v VII–VIII vv," *VESTNIK of the Saint Petersburg State University* 13, no. 4 (2016): 22–27.

3 M.-S. Saidov, *Dagestanskaya literatura XVIII–XIX vv. na Arabskom yazike*, in *Proceedings of 25th International Congress of the Orientalists* (Moscow, 1963); I. Krachkovskii, *Arabskaya literatura na Severnom Kavkaze*, in *Izbraniye Sochineniya* (Moscow, 1960), 6:551.

4 Krachkovskii, *Arabskaya literatura*, 6:615.

5 Muhammad-Tahir al-Qarakhi, *Khronika Mukhammeda Takhira al-Karakhi o dagestanskikh voinakh v period Shamilia*, trans. Barabanov, ed. Krachkovskii (Moscow and Leningrad, 1941).

6 A. R. Shikhsaidov and Kh. A. Omarov (eds.), *Abdurakhman iz Gazikumukha. Kniga vospominaniia*, trans. M.-S. Saidov (Makhachkala: Dagestanskoe knijhnoe izdatelstvo, 1997).

7 Al-Qadari, *Asari Dagestan. Istoricheskie svedeniya o Dagestane*, trans. Ali Gasanov (Makhachkala: Izdanie Dagestanskogo nauchno-issledovatelskogo instituta, 1929).

8 Khaidar-Bek al-Ghinichutlī, *Tārīkh al-aʾimma al-thalātha.* [*Istoriko-biographicheskie i istoricheskie ocherki Khaidarbeka Genichutlinskogo*], trans. and ed. T. M. Aytberov (Makhachkala: Tipographiya DNS RAN, 1992).

9 M. Gizbulaev, "Khasan al-Kabir iz Kudali—'Alim 18 veka na Kavkaze," *VESTNIK of the Institute of History, Archaeology and Ethnography* 1 (2013): 8–14; M. Gizbulaev, "Umarjan iz Kudali—verkhovnii qadii v Shamkhalestve Tarkovskoe," *VESTNIK of the Institute of History, Archaeology and Ethnography* 2 (2014): 31–34.

10 Al-Qadari, *Asari Dagestan*, 137.

11 For more on the tradition of Islamic scholarship in Dagestan, see Nazir al-Durgeli, *Nuzkhat al-azkhān fī tarādzhim "ulamā" Dāgistān: Uslada umov v biografiiākh dagestanskikh uchenykh: dagestanskie uchenye X–XX vv. i ikh sochineniiā,* trans.

and ed. A. R. Shikhsaidov, M. Kemper, and A. Bustanov (Moscow: Izdatel'skiĭ dom Mardzhani, 2012); ʿAlī l-Ghumūqī, *Tarājim ʿulamā-yi Dāghistān*, Rukopisnii fond, Daghestan Institute for History, Archeology, and Ethnography, MS Fond 25/Opis 1:1 (Azeri).

12 M. Gizbulaev, "Istochnikovedcheskii analis dagestanskogo pravovogo istochnika XVIII v. Fetwa Ibn Salmana al-Kudali," *Sovremenniye problemi nauki I obrazovaniya* 4 (2013), online: www.science-education.ru/110-9906.

13 M. Gizbulaev, "Istochnikovedcheskii analis sochineniya *'I'lam at-Tilmidh bi Ahkam an-Nabidh*,'" *VESTNIK of the Saint Petersburg State University*, 13, no. 4 (2013): 9–15.

14 M. Gizbulaev, "Vzglyd na 'vremennii brak'v kontekste izucheniya dagestanskogo araboyazichnogo pravovogo zaklycheniya Saida Arakanskogo," *Jurnal Islamovedeniye* 3 (2014): 72–77.

15 M. Kemper, "Ghazi Muhammad's Treatise against Daghestani Customary Law," in *Islam and Sufism in Daghestan*, ed. Moshe Gammer (Helsinki: Academia Scientiarum Fennica, 2009), 95; M. Kemper, *Herrschaft, Recht und Islam in Daghestan* (Wiesbaden: Ludwig Reichert Verlag, 2005), 219–224.

16 Kh. Donogo, *Shahidi Kavkazskoy voyni* (Makhachkala: Epokha, 2008).

17 For more biographical detail on the uprising of al-Thughūrī in 1877, see Z. A. Magomedova, "Mesto i rol Abdurakhmana-khadji as-Sughuri v istorii Naqshobandiskogo tariqata v Dagestane XIX v." (PhD dissertation, Institute of History, Archaeology and Ethnography, Dagestan Scientific Center of the Russian Academy of Sciences, Makhachkala, 2008).

18 Nazir al-Durgeli, *Nuzkhat al-azkhān fī tarādzhim "ulamā" Dāgistān*, trans. and ed. Shikhsaidov, Kemper, and Bustanov (Moscow: Izdatel'skiĭ dom Mardzhani, 2012), 209.

19 Shuʿayb al-Bākinī, *Ṭabaqāt al-khwājagān al-Naqshbandiyya* (Damascus: Dār al-Nuʿmān li-l-ʿUlūm, 2003), 365.

20 Al-Durgeli, *Nuzkhat al-azkhān*, 122.

21 Z. Ibragimova, "Problema mukhajhirstva v dagestanskikh pamytnikakh epistolyrnogo jhanra kontsa 19- nach.20 vv," online: www.gazavat.ru/history3.php?rub=19&art=632 (accessed December 20, 2017).

22 M. Gizbulaev, "Azājir ʿan muwālāt al-Kuffār: kak istochnik po istorii razvitii musulmanskogo mejdunarodnogo prava v Dagestane XVIII v. Azājir ʿan muwālāt al-Kuffār," *Sovremenniye problemi nauki I obrazovaniya* 5 (2014), online: http://www.science-education.ru/119-14628.

23 M. Kemper, "The Daghestani Legal Discourse on the Imamate," *Central Asian Survey* 21, no. 3 (2002): 265–278.

24 Kazem-bek Mirza, "Muridizm i Shamil," *Russkoe slovo* 12 (1859): 182–256.

25 A. Zelkina, *In Quest for God and Freedom: Sufi Responses to the Russian Advance in the North Caucasus* (London: Hurst and Co., 2000).

26 A. Shikhsaidov, "The Political History of Dagestan in the Tenth–Fifteenth Centuries," in *Dagestan and the World of Islam*, ed. Moshe Gammer and David J. Wasserstein (Helsinki: Academia Scientiarum Fennica, 2006), 51–52.

27 For more, see M. Gizbulaev, "From the Caucasus to USA: Dagestani Islamic Manuscripts in Princeton University," *Journal of Islamic Thought and Civilization* 4, no. 1 (Spring 2014): 31–45.

28 Khaled Abou El Fadl, "Islamic Law and Muslim Minorities: The Juristic Discourse on Muslim Minorities from the Second/Eighth to the Eleventh/Seventh Centuries," *Islamic Law and Society* 1, no. 2 (1994), 161; Dandal Jabr, *Dār al-ḥarb: Dār al-islām, al-bilād al-islāmiyya, dār al-silm wa-l-amān, dār al-ʿahd, al-mustaʾmanūn, al-muʿāhadāt* (Amman: Dār ʿAmmār, 1425/2004), 11.

29 A. Abel, "Dār al-Ḥarb," in *Encyclopaedia of Islam*, 2nd ed. (Leiden: Brill, 1965), 2: 126.

30 H. M. Zawati, *Is Jihad a Just War? War, Peace, and Human Rights Under Islamic and Public International Law* (Lewiston, NY: Edwin Mellen Press, 2001), 50.

31 Abou El Fadl, "Islamic Law and Muslim Minorities," 162; Yūsuf al-Qaraḍāwī, *Fiqh al-jihād: Dirāsa muqārana li-aḥkāmih wa-falsafatih fī ḍawʾ al-Qurʾān wa-l-sunna* (Cairo: Maktabat al-Wahba, 2009), 2: 889.

32 Wahba al-Zuḥaylī, *Āthār al-ḥarb fī l-islām: Dīrāsa muqārana* (Damascus: Dār al-Fikr, 1419/1998), 170.

33 M. Parvin and M. Sommer, "Dar al-Islam: The Evolution of Muslim Territoriality and Its Implications for Conflict Resolution in the Middle East," *International Journal of Middle East Studies* 11, no. 1 (February 1980), 3.

34 ʿAbdulḤamīd AbūSulaymān, *Towards an Islamic Theory of International Relations: New Directions for Islamic Methodology and Thought* (Herndon, VA: International Institute of Islamic Thought, 1987), 20.

35 al-Zuḥaylī, *Āthār al-ḥarb fī l-islām*, 172.

36 See Qurʾān 23:69, 74:5, 19:46, 4:34; Sulaymān b. al-Ashʿath Abū Dāwūd, *Sunan Abī Dāwūd*, ed. Muḥammad Muḥyī l-Dīn ʿAbd al-Ḥamīd (N.p.: Dār al-Fikr, n.d.), 2:234, *ḥadīth* number 1933.

37 Alan Verskin, *Oppressed in the Land? Fatwās on Muslims Living Under Non-Muslim Rule from the Middle Ages to the Present* (Princeton, NJ: Markus Wiener Publishers, 2013), 96–108; Jocelyn N. Hendrickson, "The Islamic Obligation to Emigrate: Al-Wansharisi's *Asnā al-matājir* Reconsidered," PhD dissertation, Emory University, 2009.

38 Muḥammad b. Ismāʿīl al-Bukhārī, *al-Jāmiʿ al-ṣaḥīḥ al-mukhtaṣar*, ed. Muṣṭafā Dīb al-Baghā. Damascus and Beirut: Dār Ibn Kathīr (1987/1407), 3:1076, *ḥadīth* number 2783.

39 ʿAbd al-Raḥmān al-Thughūrī, *al-Risāla al-sharīfa*, Firestone Library, Princeton University, MS Garrett Yahuda 2867/Mach 2034, fol. 93. Al-Thughūrī cites a *ḥadīth* of Abū Dāwūd; see Abū Dāwūd, *Sunan Abī Dāwūd*, 3:7, *ḥadīth* number 2479. The

reference to the sun rising in the West is a sign of the apocalypse; thus, the *ḥadīth* indicates that the *hijra* will not end until the end of time.

40 al-Thughūrī, *al-Risāla al-sharīfa*, fol. 93.

41 Ibid.

42 Abou El Fadl, "Islamic Law and Muslim Minorities," 144.

43 M. Kemper, "Khalidiyya Networks in Daghestan and the Question of Jihad." *Die Welt des Islams* 42, no. 1 (2002): 43.

44 Ch. King, *The Ghost of Freedom: A History of the Caucasus* (New York: Oxford University Press, 2008), 45.

45 al-Thughūrī, *al-Risāla al-sharīfa*, fol. 93.

46 Susan Layton, "Nineteenth-Century Russian Mythologies of Caucasian Savagery," in *Russia's Orient*, ed. Daniel R. Brower and Edward J. Lazzerini (Bloomington: Indiana University Press, 2001), 81.

47 al-Thughūrī, *al-Risāla al-sharīfa*, fol. 93.

48 Ibid.

49 On this, see Hendrickson, "The Islamic Obligation to Emigrate," appendix B: Translation of the Marbella Fatwa, 384.

50 Al-Thughūrī, *al-Risāla al-sharīfa*, fol. 94.

51 Ibid.

52 Ibid., fol. 95.

53 Muḥyī l-Dīn b. Sharaf al-Nawawī, *al-Majmū*ʿ*: Sharḥ al-Muhadhdhab*, ed. Maḥmūd Matirajī (Beirut: Dār al-Fikr, 2000), 21:37.

54 On these migrations, see Karpat Kemal, "The Status of the Muslim under European Rule: The Eviction and Settlement of the Cerkes," *Journal of the Institute of Minority Affairs* 1, no. 2 (1979): 7–27; Berat Yildiz, "Emigrations from the Russian Empire to the Ottoman Empire: An Analysis in the Light of the New Archival Materials" Master's thesis (Department of International Relations, Bilkent University Ankara, 2006); A. Magomeddadaev, *Emigratsia dagestantsev v Osmanskuyu imperiyu*, Makhachkala: Izdatelstvo Dagestanskogo nauchnogo centra, 2001.

55 Fourteen years after Muḥammad ʿAlī l-Chukhī's death, his son Muḥammad Mirzā Mavraev compiled his father's scattered correspondence and published it. See under Muḥammad ʿAlī l-Chukhī, *Fatāwā l-Chukhī* (Temirkhan-Shura: al-Maṭbaʿa al-Islāmiyya, 1908), 472.

56 Ibid.

57 On al-Māwardī's opinion, see Abou El Fadl, "Islamic Law and Muslim Minorities," 150.

58 Al-Chukhī, *Fatāwā l-Chukhī*, 478.

59 Murtaḍā ʿAlī l-ʿUradī, *al-Durra al-nafīsa*, Firestone Library, Princeton University, MS Garrett Yahuda 2867/Mach 2034, fol. 98.

60 By Naṣr al-Dīn al-Samarqandī (d. 1160).

61 For a full discussion of this point, see M. Kemper, "Imperial Russia as Dar al-Islam? Nineteenth-Century Debates on Ijtihad and Taqlid among the Volga Tatars," *Islamic Law and Society: A Global Perspective* 6 (Fall 2015), 114.

Bibliography

Abel, A. "Dār al-Ḥarb." In *Encyclopaedia of Islam*, new ed., edited by P. J. Bearman, Th. Bianquis, C. E. Bosworth, E. van Donzel, and W. P. Heinrichs, 2:126. Leiden: Brill, 1965.

Abou El Fadl, Khaled. "Islamic Law and Muslim Minorities: The Juristic Discourse on Muslim Minorities from the Second/Eighth to the Eleventh/Seventh Centuries." *Islamic Law and Society* 1, no. 2 (1994): 141–187.

Abū Dāwūd, Sulaymān b. al-Ashʿath. *Sunan Abī Dāwūd*. Edited by Muḥammad Muḥyī l-Dīn ʿAbd al-Ḥamīd. N.p.: Dār al-Fikr, n.d.

AbūSulaymān, ʿAbdulḤamīd. *Towards an Islamic Theory of International Relations: New Directions for Methodology and Thought*. Herndan, VA: International Institute of Islamic Thought, 1987.

al-Bākinī, Shuʿayb. *Ṭabaqāt al-khwājagān al-Naqshbandiyya*. Damascus: Dār al-Nuʿmān li-l-ʿUlūm, 2003.

al-Bukhārī, Muḥammad b. Ismāʿīl. *al-Jāmiʿ al-ṣaḥīḥ al-mukhtaṣar*. Edited by Muṣṭafā Dīb al-Baghā. Damascus and Beirut: Dār Ibn Kathīr, 1987/1407.

al-Chukhī, Muḥammad ʿAlī. *Fatāwā l-Chukhī*. Temirkhan-Shura: al-Maṭbaʿa al-Islāmiyya, 1908.

Donogo, Kh. *Shahidi Kavkazskoy voyni* [Martyrs of the Caucasus war]. Makhachkala: Epokha, 2008.

al-Durgeli, Nazir. *Nuzkhat al-azkhān fī tarādzhim "ulamā" Dāgistān: Uslada umov v biografii͡akh dagestanskikh uchenykh: dagestanskie uchenye X–XX vv. i ikh sochinenii͡a* [Journey of the minds through the biographies of the Islamic scholars of Daghestan: Dagestani scholars of the tenth–twentieth centuries and their works]. Translated and edited by A. R. Shikhsaidov, M. Kemper, and A. Bustanov. Moscow: Izdatel'skiĭ dom Mardzhani, 2012.

al-Ghinichutlī, Khaidar-Bek. *Tārīkh al-aʾimma al-thalātha: Istoriko-biographicheskie i istoricheskie ocherki Khaidarbeka Genichutlinskogo*. Translated and edited by T. M. Aytberov. Makhachkala, 1992.

al-Ghumūqī, ʿAlī. *Tarājim ʿulamā-yi Dāghistān*. Rukopisnii fond, Daghestan Institute for History, Archeology, and Ethnography, MS Fond 25/Opis 1:1 (Azeri).

Gizbulaev, M. "Azājir ʿan muwālāt al-Kuffār: kak istochnik po istorii razvitii musulmanskogo mejdunarodnogo prava v Dagestane XVIII v. Azājir ʿan muwālāt al-Kuffār." [The source on history of Islamic international law development in Dagestan in the eighteenth century.] *Sovremenniye problemi nauki I obrazovaniya* 5 (2014); online: http://www.science-education.ru/119–14628.

Gizbulaev, M. "From the Caucasus to USA: Dagestani Islamic Manuscripts in Princeton University." *Journal of Islamic Thought and Civilization* 4, no. 1 (Spring 2014): 31–45.

Gizbulaev, M. "Istochnikovedcheskii analis dagestanskogo pravovogo istochnika XVIII v. 'Fetwa Ibn Salmana al-Kudali.'" [Source analysis of the Dagestani legal source of the eighteenth century: "Ibn Salman al-Kudali's Fatwa."] *Sovremenniye problemi nauki I obrazovaniya* no. 4 (2013). Online: http://www.science-education.ru/110-9906.

Gizbulaev, M. "Istochnikovedcheskii analis sochineniya '*I'lam at-tilmidh bi ahkam an-nabidh*'" [Source analysis of the Dagestani manuscript, *Iʿlam al-tilmidh bi-aḥkām al-nabidh*]. *VESTNIK of the Saint Petersburg State University* 13, no. 4 (2013): 9–15.

Gizbulaev, M. "Khasan al-Kabir iz Kudali—'Alim 18 veka na Kavkaze" [Hassan al-Kabir from Kudali—the eighteenth-century *ʿālim* in the Caucasus]. *VESTNIK of the Institute of History, Archaeology and Ethnography* 1 (2013): 8–14.

Gizbulaev, M. "Ta'rikh by Khalifa ibn Khayyat kak istochnik po istorii Dagestan v VII-VIII vv." [*Tārīkh* by Khalīfa b. Khayyāt as a source for Dagestan history in the seventh–eighth centuries]. *VESTNIK of the Saint Petersburg State University* 13, no. 4 (2016): 22–27.

Gizbulaev, M. "Umarjan iz Kudali—verkhovnii qadii v Shamkhalestve Tarkovskoe" [Umarjan from Kudali—the grand *qāḍī* in the *shamkhalate* of Tarkovskoe]. *VESTNIK of the Institute of History, Archaeology and Ethnography* 2 (2014): 31–34.

Gizbulaev, M. "Vzglyd na 'vremennii brak'v kontekste izucheniya dagestanskogo araboyazichnogo pravovogo zaklycheniya Saida Arakanskogo" [A view on the "short-term marriage" in the context of exploring the Dagestani Arabic legal work by Said Arakanskii]. *Jurnal Islamovedeniye* 3 (2014): 72–77.

Hendrickson, J. "The Islamic Obligation to Emigrate: Al-Wansharīsī's *Asnā al-matājir* Reconsidered." PhD dissertation. Emory University, 2009.

Ibragimova, Z. "Problema mukhajhirstva v dagestanskikh pamytnikakh epistolyrnogo jhanra kontsa 19- nach.20 vv" [*Hijra* issue in the Dagestan epistolary monuments of the late nineteenth to early twentieth centuries]. Online: www.gazavat.ru/history3.php?rub=19&art=632. Accessed December 20, 2017.

Jabr, Dandal. *Dār al-ḥarb: Dār al-islām, al-bilād al-islāmiyya, dār al-silm wa-l-amān, dār al-ʿahd, al-mustaʾmanūn, al-muʿāhadāt*. Amman: Dār ʿAmmār, 1425/2004.

Karpat, Kemal. "The Status of the Muslim under European Rule: The Eviction and Settlement of the Cerkes." *Journal of the Institute of Minority Affairs* 1, no. 2 (1979): 7–27.

Kemper, M. "The Daghestani Legal Discourse on the Imamate." *Central Asian Survey* 21, no. 3 (2002): 265–278.

Kemper, M. "Ghazi Muhammad's Treatise against Daghestani Customary Law." In *Islam and Sufism in Daghestan*, edited by Moshe Gammer, 85–100. Helsinki: Academia Scientiarum Fennica, 2009.

Kemper, M. *Herrschaft, Recht und Islam in Daghestan*. Wiesbaden: Ludwig Reichert Verlag, 2005.

Kemper, M. “Imperial Russia as Dar al-Islam? Nineteenth-Century Debates on Ijtihad and Taqlid among the Volga Tatars.” *Islamic Law and Society: A Global Perspective* 6 (Fall 2015): 95–124.

Kemper, M. “Khalidiyya Networks in Daghestan and the Question of Jihad.” *Die Welt des Islams* 42, no. 1 (2002): 42–71.

King, Ch. *The Ghost of Freedom: A History of the Caucasus*. New York: Oxford University Press, 2008.

Kozubskii, E. I. “History of the Dagestan Cavalry Division.” In *Istoriya Dagestanskogo konnogo polka*, edited by E. I. Kozubskii. Petrovsk: Izdatelstvo Polka, 1909.

Krachkovskii, I. *Arabskaya literatura na Severnom Kavkaze* [Arabian literature in the North Caucasus]. In *Izbraniye Sochineniya*. Vol. 6. Moscow, 1960.

Layton, Susan. “Nineteenth-Century Russian Mythologies of Caucasian Savagery.” In *Russia's Orient*, edited by Daniel R. Brower and Edward J. Lazzerini, 80–100. Bloomington: Indiana University Press, 2001.

Magomeddadaev, A. *Emigratsia dagestantsev v Osmanskuyu imperiyu* [The emigration of Dagestanis to the Ottoman Empire]. Makhachkala: Izdatelstvo Dagestanskogo nauchnogo centra, 2001.

Magomedova, Z. A. “Mesto i rol Abdurakhmana-khadji as-Sughuri v istorii Naqshobandiskogo tariqata v Dagestane XIX v.” [ʿAbd al-Raḥmān al-Thughūrī's role in the history of the Naqshbandī *ṭarīqa* in nineteenth-century Dagestan]. PhD dissertation. Institute of History, Archaeology and Ethnography, Dagestan Scientific Center of the Russian Academy of Sciences, Makhachkala, 2008.

Mirza, Kazem-bek. “Muridizm i Shamil.” *Russkoe slovo* 12 (1859): 182–256.

al-Nawawī, Muḥyī l-Dīn b. Sharaf. *al-Majmūʿ: Sharḥ al-Muhadhdhab*. Edited by Maḥmūd Matirajī. Beirut: Dār al-Fikr, 2000.

Parvin, M., and M. Sommer. “Dar al-Islam: The Evolution of Muslim Territoriality and Its Implications for Conflict Resolution in the Middle East.” *International Journal of Middle East Studies* 11, no. 1 (February 1980): 1–21.

al-Qadari. *Asari Dagestan. Istoricheskie svedeniya o Dagestane*. Translated by Ali Gasanov. Makhachkala, 1929.

al-Qaraḍāwī, Yūsuf. *Fiqh al-jihād: Dirāsa muqārana li-aḥkāmih wa-falsafatih fī ḍawʾ al-Qurʾān wa-l-sunna*. Cairo: Maktabat al-Wahba, 2009.

al-Qarakhi, Muhammad-Tahir. *Khronika Mukhammeda Takhira al-Karakhi o dagestanskikh voinakh v period Shamilia*. Translated by Barabanov. Edited by Krachkovskii. Moscow and Leningrad: Nauka, 1941.

Saidov, M.-S. “Dagestanskaya literatura XVIII–XIX vv. na Arabskom yazike” [Dagestan literature in Arabic in the nineteenth and twentieth centuries]. In *Proceedings of 25th International Congress of the Orientalists*. Moscow: Vostochnaya literatura, 1963.

Shikhaliev, Sh. “Islamizatsia Dagestana v X–XVI vv.” [Islamization of Dagestan in the tenth to sixteenth centuries]. PhD dissertation. Makhachkala, 2007.

Shikhsaidov, A. "The Political History of Dagestan in the Tenth–Fifteenth Centuries." In *Dagestan and the World of Islam*, edited by Moshe Gammer and David J. Wasserstein, 51–52. Helsinki: Academia Scientiarum Fennica, 2006.

Shikhsaidov, A. R., and Kh. A. Omarov (eds.). *Abdurakhman iz Gazikumukha. Kniga vospominaniia*. Translated by M.-S. Saidov. Makhachkala: Dagestanskoe knijhnoe izdatelstvo, 1997.

al-Thughūrī, ʿAbd al-Raḥmān. *al-Risāla al-sharīfa*. Firestone Library, Princeton University, MS Garrett Yahuda 2867/Mach 2034, fols. 93–96.

al-ʿUradī, Murtaḍā ʿAlī. *al-Durra al-nafīsa*. MS Garrett Yahuda 2867/Mach 2034, fol. 98.

Verskin, Alan. *Oppressed in the Land? Fatwās on Muslims Living Under Non-Muslim Rule from the Middle Ages to the Present*. Princeton, NJ: Markus Wiener Publishers, 2013.

Yildiz, Berat. "Emigrations from the Russian Empire to the Ottoman Empire: An Analysis in the Light of the New Archival Materials." Master's thesis. Department of International Relations, Bilkent University, Ankara, 2006.

Zawati, H. M. *Is Jihad a Just War? War, Peace, and Human Rights Under Islamic and Public International Law*. Studies in Religion and Society. Vol. 53. Lewiston, NY: Edwin Mellen Press, 2001.

Zelkina, A. *In Quest for God and Freedom: Sufi Responses to the Russian Advance in the North Caucasus*. London: Hurst and Co., 2000.

al-Zuḥaylī, Wahba. *Āthār al-ḥarb fī l-islām: Dirāsa muqārana*. Damascus: Dār al-Fikr, 1419/1998.

8

Constitutionalism as Quietist Strategy: The Case of Tunisia

Jeremy Kleidosty

> If we consider the competition of nations in the fields of civilization and the keen rivalry of even the greatest among them to achieve what is most beneficial and helpful, it becomes clear we can properly distinguish what is most suitable for us only by having knowledge of those outside our own group … Further, if we consider the many ways which have been created in these times to bring men and ideas closer together, we will not hesitate to visualize the world as a single, united country peopled by various nations who surely need each other … Whoever considers these two undoubtedly true principles and who according to his religion knows that the Islamic sharī'a is a guarantor for the two worlds will necessarily recognize that secular organization is a firm foundation for supporting the religious system.
>
> Khayr al-Dīn al-Tūnisī, *The Surest Path*[1]

In the introduction, or *muqaddima*, to his *Aqwam al-masālik fī ma'rifat aḥwāl al-mamālik*, translated as *The Surest Path to Knowledge Concerning the Conditions of Countries* (hereafter referred to as *The Surest Path*), the statesman, theorist, and author of Tunisia's 1861 constitution Khayr al-Dīn al-Tūnisī sets out a discourse one might expect to see from any nineteenth-century European reformist. Namely, that improved governance is essential to the well-being of a people and that this improvement can be achieved by studying what are now called best practices from other states and by emulating them. Of course, what makes this text notable is not the originality of its content but the originality of its context. This father of an explicitly Islamic and equally modern constitutionalism, whose influence remains palpable in Tunisian politics today, is not a North American or European reformer, but a Maghribi governmental official who rose through the ranks of power from *mamlūk* clerk to prime minister of Tunisia and eventually to grand vizier of the Ottoman Empire. Despite being relatively unknown outside the Maghrib and scholarly circles, al-Tūnisī's influence on modern Tunisia is still significant. His founding of Sadiqi College in 1875 marked a turning point in state–mosque relations, as it became the primary educational institution for training the country's elites and ended the dominance of the *ʿulamāʾ* over education. Unsurprisingly, it also produced reformist leaders who largely adopted the parliamentarian and constitutionalist positions of their school's founder.[2]

Furthermore, the Tunisian case of the 1860s was one of dual imperial entanglements—officially, as part of the Ottoman Empire; and practically, under the sphere of influence and domination of an assertive France. Taking what might be called, colloquially, an "if you can't beat them, join them" approach, he asserted that the only way for Tunisia to escape their colonial straightjacket was to develop their own national consciousness, institutions, and economy in a manner that is compatible with both European norms and Islamic law.

In this way, al-Tūnisī's work can also be said to assert a dual quietism with regard to foreign policy while simultaneously rejecting quietism, at least in its most despotism-friendly forms, in terms of domestic politics and development. In this chapter, I use an exegetical reading of his only work of political theory, *The Surest Path*, to analyze the extent to which his redefinition of the meaning and proper sphere of state involvement in religion, which might now be an important element in a discourse of political quietism, reshaped the Tunisian, and perhaps Ottoman, understanding of the relationship between Islam and the modern state. Subsequently, I briefly overview his personal history and role in developing the modern Tunisian state and its constitutional traditions in order to illuminate the way in which he translated this theory into practice. Finally, I turn to the implications for present constitutionalist discourses: how might they likewise grapple with the effects of religious piety, colonialism (albeit from a postcolonial rather than a soon-to-be-colonized perspective), given their need to create stability and genuine representation in contexts which are pluralist, inherently volatile, and demand adherence to international customs and local mores. Just as Tunisia led the way in inaugurating both modern Islamic constitutionalism and the Arab Spring, so too its political thought might serve as a starting point for reimagining the role of quietism in Muslim-majority states from the perspectives of both domestic and foreign policies, and advocating a constitutional approach to governance as the surest path to a stable and representative state.

On "Islamic" constitutionalism

The question of a distinctly Islamic constitutional tradition is one that is infused with a number of theological and political controversies, nearly all of which fall outside the purview of this discussion. However, it is important to briefly define what, exactly, is meant by constitutionalism for the purposes of this chapter and what is further implied by the phrase "Islamic constitutionalism." Numerous scholars, me among them, trace the tradition of Islamic constitutionalism back to the foundation of Islam itself. Although clearly not a constitution in the modern sense, what has come to be known as Muḥammad's "constitution of Medina" is nonetheless the type of foundational document that can serve as a model of contractual obligations and community relations in a diverse polity. In it, a number of Islamic and Jewish tribes submit to Muḥammad's role as supreme political judge while still maintaining their own internal power structures and patriarchal leadership traditions. This first social contract between Muslims and their allied co-occupants of Medina is very much in the vein of the social contract constitutional thought that did not appear in the realm of divinely ordained European kings for several hundred years.

The characterization of the "constitution of Medina," as reported by its chronicler Ibn Isḥāq, is revealing. "The apostle wrote a document concerning the emigrants and the helpers in which he made a friendly agreement with the Jews and established them in their religion and their property, and stated the reciprocal obligations."[3] The idea of a social contract is not one that requires abstraction in this instance; the language of a contract is clear. Here we have words such as "agreement," "property," and "reciprocal obligations." These terms later developed into the more systematic classification of society, into a Muslim *umma* and co-occupant monotheist *dhimmī* peoples. Interestingly, in what might be called the first iteration of an Islamic state, the *umma* initially covered everyone under the jurisdiction of the city of Medina and the judgment of Muḥammad. As Frederick Denny notes,

> The *ummah* of the Constitution is made up of believers and Muslims … All the kinship groups mentioned are subsumed under this *ummah* idea, a very significant fact. But why are the believers distinguished from the Muslims? … This preponderance of *mu'min* may indicate an early date for much of the Constitution, before *muslim* was used as the name for the followers of Muhammad, or at least before it gained a clear technical sense limited to the followers of Muhammad. Of course, it had a deep religious sense before the time of the Constitution, describing the human approach to God pre-scribed in the Revelation.[4]

While Denny is concerned mainly with the philological issue of what is meant by the terms *believer* and *Muslim*, from a political theory perspective, it is noteworthy that even a person who may not accede to Muḥammad's prophetic claims could nonetheless submit to his judgeship and rulership, and be a *Muslim* in the sense of social practice and political conduct, even if they were not *Muslim* in religious belief. This has incredibly important implications for the question of quietism in Islam, as it suggests that even in the very earliest Islamic polity there was ample room for private religious belief, so long as public order and judgments were respected. It also acknowledges the multilayered identities of the people who lived under this regime. They may have been both believers in Muḥammad's message and, likewise, members of particular Arab tribes, which were Jewish or formerly polytheist. What mattered most in the contractual arrangement of this text were the principles of social cohesion and mutual defense. Although not directly relevant to the conversation surrounding constitutionalism in the time of Khayr al-Dīn and his successors, which is clearly a much more formalized legal process, this brief examination of Muḥammad's political arrangements at Medina demonstrates both the legitimacy of the concept of a religiously pluralist Muslim state and a continuity in the use of contractual language to establish rights and obligations between rulers, the ruled, and between diverse communities within the larger society.

For the purposes of this chapter, it is necessary to expand somewhat upon this rudimentary contractualism to include additional key aspects of constitutionalism, namely, the document must explicitly represent its people in some way via relevant institutions and political representatives, create a rule of law that is applied to all citizens under its jurisdiction, and set limits on the powers of various government organs and personages, establishing a limit on what the state can or should do at the same time as it empowers it to make and enact law within a given scope. This basic set of premises is sufficient for establishing a *thin constitutionalism* that allows for extensive diversity in institutional and cultural arrangements in order to conform to local needs and histories while also allowing a given state to meet its international obligations should it wish to be part of the many conventions and institutions that help legitimize states as international actors in the modern era.[5] Proceeding from this set of basic premises, I now turn to *The Surest Path* and the constitutional solutions Khayr al-Dīn offers to meet the particular needs of a Muslim-majority polity, solutions that cover the rule of law, representation, and the limitation/definition of power. In turn, I assess these solutions for their impact on the disposition of the citizenry and their tendency toward quietist positions and/or postures in politics.

The rule of law

> It is related that a Jew came to ʿUmar ibn al-Khattab, may God be pleased with him, making a demand against ʿAli, may God honor him. ʿAli was at ʿUmar's side, and ʿUmar said to him, "Get up, O Father of Hasan, and sit with your opponent." He saw anger rise on the face of ʿAli. When the lawsuit had been decided, ʿUmar asked him, "Why were you angry at the demand that you be put on the same footing as your opponent?" ʿAli replied, "I did not get angry about that, but I did not like your calling me by my familiar name in the presence of my opponent."[6]

In this brief anecdote, Khayr al-Dīn communicates a number of important points about his views on the rule of law and its absolute necessity to good governance. Referring back to a story from the early days of Islam, he begins by noting that this particular court case involved ʿAlī and a Jew. In direct contradiction to the Ottoman *millet* system, in which each religious community lived under more or less autonomous and separate judicial orders, this tale invokes a unified legal system for both Jewish and Muslim litigants.[7] Rather than dealing with religious pluralism via segregation, the account here is one of integration. Perhaps even more striking, this account shows that Jewish and Muslim participants shared the same legal status before their judge, ʿUmar, despite the well-known position of non-Muslim monotheists as *dhimmīs*, and in a number of senses, politically inferior people. Indeed, this absolute equality is confirmed twice.

First, there is the request that ʿAlī "sit with his opponent," rather than maintaining his position at ʿUmar's side. If he had remained in his initial position, his closeness with ʿUmar would literally have been on display and brought the impartiality of any subsequent judgment into question. The anger apparent on ʿAlī's face is interpreted by ʿUmar as a protestation to this equalizing move, which would be a reasonable assumption. However, Khayr al-Dīn tells us that the anger actually stemmed from him calling him "father of Hasan" (Abū Ḥasan). Why should this be a problem, given that the paternity of his son was public knowledge. Put simply, this form of familiar address revealed their close relationship and undermined the very impartiality ʿUmar sought to establish by asking him to sit next to his opponent. This story speaks to an anxiety present in Khayr al-Dīn's time that Europeans or other non-Muslims living or working in a Muslim state would be subjected to the *sharīʿa* and necessarily disadvantaged in these courts. It was deemed impossible that they could be treated fairly under the rule of this religious-based law.[8]

In dealing with these European objections, Khayr al-Dīn turns them on their head and writes that European objections to unitary law being practiced in states like Tunisia were one of the primary obstacles to instituting exactly the type of rule of law they claimed to advocate. He writes that achieving *tanzimat*, or reform, is problematic "in all Islamic countries" because of

> the reluctance of European countries to let their subjects be judged by the laws of the Muslim countries in which they reside ... They rely on old agreements no longer appropriate to this time. In fact, they should not be called agreements for they are built upon what violates an agreement.[9]

This passage is a thinly veiled rebuke of the imperialist mindset of European powers in their dealings with Muslim countries. Agreements that are built upon threat or force are not agreements but coerced concessions. They are, as Khayr al-Dīn says, "built upon what violates an agreement." Herein lies another point relevant to considerations of quietism in Muslim politics, particularly in the multitude of states that are both Muslim-majority and postcolonial. We must ask whether or not the political quietism they experienced is as likely a reflection of this history of domination as it is any quality supposedly inherent to Islamic governance, particularly given the extent to which these states suffered coercive and repressive relationships with the European governments.

Although more of a precolonial thinker than a postcolonial one, Khayr al-Dīn was careful to note the potential outcomes for Tunisia, as it moved from the Ottoman periphery to a French sphere of influence. As early as 1867, he responded to this provocative attitude of legal superiority by making the elegantly plain point that

> these Europeans do not stick to the text (of prior agreements), but they extract from them non-existent provisions which are contrary to the laws of equality among nations and to the laws that territorial sovereignty extends to all who appear on it, i.e., he who enters a certain kingdom must necessarily be subject to its laws.[10]

Rather than arguing for a quietist attitude of subjection to domestic law out of religious duty, Khayr al-Dīn used the principle of domestic equality before the law, and its complementary principle of internal territorial sovereignty, to reclaim a more balanced stance of equality between nations.

Upon reflection, it is clear that the relationship of quietism and the rule of law in Khayr al-Dīn's thought is multilayered and complex, perhaps even paradoxical. On the one hand, he was concerned that territorial sovereignty be respected and that one set of law apply to all people within a given domain. This is a traditional rule of law account that remains active in ongoing disputes over when it is or is not appropriate to intervene in the domestic affairs of another state. Khayr al-Dīn argued for an assumption of fairness and impartiality in his work, a stance that might indicate tacit approval of a quietist acceptance of domestic rulings within a given state. However, unlike popular conceptions of quietism that equate it with a type of passivity, Khayr al-Dīn felt compelled to provide logical reasons that this approach might benefit all parties involved; he specifically notes that "without this support of the population one cannot hope to attain any results."[11]

The populace is thus actively involved in making equality under the law a reality, and they do so by supporting reform and government efforts to make the state more fair and efficient. Perhaps as, or even more, important in his consideration of equality before the law is his rejection of special privileges for European citizens and coerced concessions to European powers. People within the state, but also states acting in a system of international sovereigns with no superior power, are equal before a fundamental law of equality. His scathing critique of European hypocrisy in advocating political reform in their own states while thwarting it or claiming it as unsuitable for Muslim states indicates that he was by no means quietist in his resistance to colonial domination.[12] In this scheme of constitutional republicanism, the rule of law serves the dual function of promoting domestic stability and preventing weakness in international relations and domination by foreign powers.

Representation

The matter of representation in Khayr al-Dīn's thought is somewhat more difficult to describe in a traditional constitutionalist discourse centered on institutions, elections, and the like. In lighting a path to institutional stability or indicating any preference for particular modes of government, *The Surest Path* is astonishingly light on detail. We must remember that Khayr al-Dīn was acting and writing within the limitations of his biography as a person who had spent his entire life in the service of a monarchy that was also under Ottoman suzerainty and within the limitations of his political exile, which necessitated a diplomatic caution in advocating state reform. Here it is necessary to draw upon more ancient conceptions of the constitution, as one that reflects both the Greek *politeia* and the Latin *constituere*, something that is fundamentally of a people and that is also enacted and consciously constructed by them.[13] Khayr al-

Dīn redefined and reimagined terms from classical Islam and put them to more modern purposes. This is clear from his frequent references to the *umma*, or people, of his state. Their Muslim faith is presumed but not explicitly prescribed in his text. Likewise, he makes a strong case for the complete compatibility of a timeless and perfect *sharīʿa* with a contingent and effective constitutional modern law. Building upon this, he revives the practice of *shūrā* as a value-based norm native to Islamic tradition and a practice that can be transmogrified into representative opportunities to partake in advising and shaping the government. In this section, I look at his uses of each of these terms, with an eye to their relationship to a quietist or activist approach to politics, especially in what he regarded as obligatory or permitted under religious law.

The term *umma* appears throughout *The Surest Path* and is used almost exclusively in discussions about the citizens/subjects of a given Muslim state. It takes on both a universalist sense, as a global community of believers, and a local sense, as a Muslim population that live in a given territory. He begins the book by making the following rather bold assertion about the *umma*:

> After I had long contemplated the causes of progress and backwardness of nations generation after generation, relying on the Islamic and European histories I was able to examine what the authors of both groups have written concerning the Islamic *umma*, its attributes and its future … I decided to assert what I believe no intelligent Muslim will contradict and no one who has been shown the evidence will oppose: If we consider the competition of nations in the fields of civilization and the keen rivalry of even the greatest among them to achieve what is most beneficial and helpful, it becomes clear that we can properly distinguish what is most suitable for us only by having knowledge of those outside our own group. [14]

This passage establishes that his target audience was his fellow Muslims, especially those who may have been in positions of power in society and the state. Furthermore, he appeals directly to the idea of a global *umma*, rather than simply his fellow Tunisians or Ottomans. He moves on to a discussion of generic nations, without reference to their respective religious makeup. He thus clearly shows that the purpose of his book was to provide information beneficial to any Muslim state while at the same time drawing upon scholarship and experience from any state that has achieved a high degree of success relative to its international rivals. He explicitly (and repeatedly) rejects the idea that Muslim societies can only look to their own history or the time of the Prophet and rightly guided caliphs for inspiration and instead states that no "intelligent Muslim" will be able to disagree with his premise that determining what government and social reforms will most benefit a Muslim state can *only* be achieved by "having knowledge of those outside our own group."

By positioning Muslims as a unique community, but one that exists among others that it can learn from, he is then free to use Islamic history and terminology in combination with European norms and institutions to achieve a number of goals simultaneously. First among these is establishing that it is completely acceptable to imitate or borrow from non-Muslims wherever it benefits the *umma* and is not in contradiction to the *sharīʿa*.[15] Second, he states that in many instances, it is actually Europeans who first borrowed from Muslims, making the problem of imitating non-Muslims effectively moot.[16] Having established these points, he is free to draw upon Muslim history to give his own account of the significance and potential application of *shūrā*.

> Among the most important of the *shariʿa* principles is the duty of consultation with which God charged his impeccable Prophet ... although Muhammad could have dispensed with this since he received inspiration directly from God and also because of the many perfections which God had placed in him. The underlying reason for this obligation upon the Prophet was that it should become a tradition incumbent upon later rulers.[17]

He goes on to cite a number of authorities from Abū Bakr Ibn al-ʿArabī (d. 543/1148), a notable traditionist who calls *shūrā* "one of the foundations of the religion and God's rule for the two worlds," to ʿAlī, who says "there can be no right behavior when consultation is omitted," to al-Ghazālī's (d. 505/1111) claim that Muslim rulers "want to be refuted even if they should be in the pulpit."[18] This exercise in legitimation quickly turns into a lesson on comparative politics, where Khayr al-Dīn notes that in Muslim states it is the *ʿulamāʾ* and "the notables of the *umma*" who must resist any evil they see in the king or government, whereas in European states, they have established "councils and have given freedom to the printing presses." The result in both systems is that in "the Islamic *umma* the kings fear those who resist evil just as the kings of Europe fear the councils and the opinions of the masses that proceed from them and from the freedom of the press."[19] In both cases, the goal of such accountability is to ensure that the state is upright in its conduct, "even if the roads leading to this end may differ."[20]

What is interesting about Khayr al-Dīn's approach to consultation, or *shūrā*, is that its obligatory nature is not simply divinely ordered but also stems from its functionality in creating governments that work for the people. He lauds the European value of holding rulers to account but does so by claiming its origins in Islamic sources and by replacing a free press and parliament with a central role for clerics and nobility. He clearly did not advocate democracy or mass politicization, but he was advocating a far more active role for elements that already exist in most Muslim states. Thus, while the subjects of a king are supposed to take on a role of obedience, and hence a quietist nature, their interests are supposed to be protected by the clerical class who ensure that even the ruler is compliant with the letter and spirit of *sharīʿa*. Their prosperity and well-being are further guarded by the people who actually run the various bureaucracies and ministries in the state, who, in striving to govern wisely and efficiently, will in turn increase the prosperity and stability of those below them in the social hierarchy. In support of this point, he says that it "is God's custom in His world that justice, good management and an administrative system duly complied with be the causes of an increase in wealth, peoples and property." This echoes Muḥammad's maxim that "Justice brings glory to the religion, probity to constituted authority and strength to all orders of the people, high and low."[21]

Quietism with respect to political representation is seen as a highly desirable outcome, yet one that is conditional upon the *ʿulamāʾ* and nobles actually serving and protecting the people well. Although he does not provide mechanisms for revoking authority from rulers who abuse their power, he uses Ibn Khaldūn to provide a powerful motivation for upright rule, noting that according to Ibn Khaldūn's extensive study of history, oppression always foreshadows the destruction and ruin of a society. He mentions Ibn Khaldūn again to argue that abuses in power lead to the rise of resistance and group feeling (*ʿaṣabiyya*) in the populace, and these, in turn, "[lead] to turmoil and fighting."[22]

Restricting/defining power

We have already discussed the restriction of a ruler's power in terms of both rule of law and representation. In Khayr al-Dīn's constitutional theory, the ruler (in his case both the local bey of Tunisia and the Ottoman *sulṭān*) is restricted by the *sharīʿa* from committing acts that are forbidden or otherwise immoral, the *ʿulamāʾ* enforce such compliance and sustain domestic tranquility through their support for the government and its legitimizing effects, and key nobles and ministers are tasked with actually running the daily workings of the government. Each of these roles is crucial in his discussions of law and representation, but the subjects and aims of these spheres of influence overlap.

This relationship among the ruler, the administrative state, the clerics, and the people is very much in keeping with the vision of constitutional power as separated into competing branches with overlapping purviews in works like *The Federalist Papers.* The monarch, the clerics, and the "notables" have functions similar to that of the executive, judicial, and legislative branches in European constitutionalism.

Although it is unclear if Khayr al-Dīn had read such documents, it is reasonable to believe he may have been familiar with the idea of branches of government and the separation of powers, given his extensive time in France and his study of European governments. This is explicit in his chapter entitled "The Necessity of Cooperation Between the Statesmen and the *'Ulama* in Bringing About What Is Good for the *Umma* and Warding Off What Will Corrupt." Here he takes on a distinctly moderate tone with regard to the relationship between the state and religion. On the one hand, he notes that it is difficult for those running the state to know whether or not their actions are compliant with *sharīʿa*, and this requires that clerics and specialists in Islamic law "examine the politics of their countries, consider the imperfections occurring in domestic and foreign affairs and assist the political leaders in the organization of their *tanzimat*," or reforms.[23] However, on the other hand, he also suggests that care should be taken to chart a moderate course between too much distance between the religious and political leaders, which can lead to a separation between the principles of laws that comply with the *sharīʿa* and the actual conduct of the state, and too little distance, which could lead the *ʿulamāʾ* to favor the interests of the ruling classes and identify with it themselves.[24] This careful balancing of power leads to an effectively quietist populace who benefit from efficient governance and laws that conform to universal and timeless moral requirements. Following Khayr al-Dīn's contention that this type of just and moral rule necessarily leads to increased prosperity and contentment, this quietism was seen as a simple by-product of a happy and well-governed people, rather than an intentional or even consciously sought outcome.

Ongoing relevance

It is no coincidence that the political movement known as the Arab Spring began in the birthplace of Islamic constitutionalism, Tunisia. To this day, Khayr al-Dīn's legacy, though often unacknowledged or unknown outside his homeland, remains highly influential in the work of scholars, political reformists, and activists. His identification of the *ʿulamāʾ* as key legitimators of power and as vessels through which political ideas can be mediated in a culturally and religiously appropriate way is echoed in works like Noah Feldman's *The Fall and Rise of the Islamic State*. Similarly, Khayr al-Dīn's early identification of *shūrā* as a crucial aspect of a truly Islamic constitutional tradition has been built upon by thinkers like Abdullahi Ahmed An-Na'im, whose book *African Constitutionalism and the Role of Islam* advocates the use of *shūrā* as a concept vital to the establishment of democratically accountable legislatures, complemented with the notion of *bayʿa*, or allegiance, as indicative of an indigenous social contract and election tradition. In Feldman's and An-Na'im's recent interpretations of Islamic constitutionalism, the presence of a quietist discourse is notably absent. These authors assume the right of people to elect, criticize, and replace their governments. However, they share the ultimate aims of earlier writers like Khayr al-Dīn, who saw good governance, observance of religion, and increasing prosperity as part of a virtuous cycle that ensures a naturally quietist populace who are confident that their institutions and rulers are spiritually upright representatives. This serves as a powerful alternative discourse and rebuke to those who represent Islamic politics as extremist, revolutionary, or violent and simultaneously rejects the justification of old tropes of Oriental despotism and submissive quietist masses in Muslim countries.

Notes

1 Khayr al-Dīn al-Tūnisī, *The Surest Path to Knowledge Concerning the Conditions of Countries*, trans. L. Carl Brown (Cambridge: Harvard University Press, 1967), 71–72.

2 For more on Sadiqi College and its influence, see Lisa Andersen, *The State and Social Transformation in Tunisia and Libya: 1830–1980* (Princeton, NJ: Princeton University Press, 2014).

3 Ibn Isḥāq, *The Life of Muhammad: A Translation of Isḥāq's Sīrat Rasūl Allāh* (London: Oxford University Press, 1955), 231.

4 Frederick Denny, "Ummah in the Constitution of Medina," *Journal of Near Eastern Studies* 36, no. 1 (1977), 43.

5 For a much more detailed account of constitutionalism and the idea of *thin constitutionalism* as outlined above, see Kleidosty, *The Concert of Civilizations: The Common Roots of Western and Islamic Constitutionalism* (Surrey: Ashgate, 2015), 1–43.

6 Al-Tūnisī, *Surest Path*, 121.
7 Khayr al-Dīn discusses the drawbacks of the millet system directly in al-Tūnisī, *Surest Path*, 117–118.
8 This particular anxiety remains a notable presence in any number of Islamophobic and xenophobic political movements in non-Muslim states. The institution of *sharīʿa* is often raised as a call to arms to resist the normalization or integration of Islamic customs and/or Muslim people in these states. For more on Khayr al-Dīn's opinion of this matter, see al-Tūnisī, *Surest Path*, 119–120.
9 Ibid., 118–119.
10 Ibid., 119.
11 Ibid., 119–120.
12 He follows up his discussion of the necessity of judicial equality by claiming that "these Europeans are not content with obstructing the implementation of these laws by their own refusal. Some of them even turn the subjects of certain Islamic kingdoms against accepting the *tanzimat* their rulers wish to establish. They proclaim to them, 'These *tanzimat* are not appropriate for your situation and it is preferable for you to return to your previous condition.'" In other words, Europeans assume Muslim states are incapable of independent and fair judiciaries and successful constitutional reforms; they then impede reform efforts and block their successful implementation by making use of the fact that Europeans "own most of the industry and commerce," and this dooms reform efforts to failure, thus proving correct their claim of the unsuitability of constitutional republican government in Islamic states (see 121–122).
13 For more on this, see Graham Maddox, "A Note on the Meaning of 'Constitution,'" *American Political Science Review* 76, no. 4 (1982): 805–806.
14 Al-Tūnisī, *Surest Path*, 71.
15 For an example of this line of argument, see his account of Salman the Persian, al-Tūnisī, *Surest Path*, 75–76.
16 See ibid., 97–111.
17 Ibid., 82.
18 Ibid., 82–83.
19 Ibid., 84.
20 Ibid.
21 Ibid., 81.
22 Ibid., 81–82, 84.
23 Ibid., 125. Lest non-Muslim readers find this suggestion overly problematic, it is worth noting that in Britain's House of Lords, bishops from the official Church of England can and do suggest amendments to legislation, in line with what they deem to be suitable to Christian values.
24 Ibid., 128–129.

Bibliography

Andersen, Lisa. *The State and Social Transformation in Tunisia and Libya: 1830–1980.* Princeton, NJ: Princeton University Press, 2014.

Denny, Frederick. "Ummah in the Constitution of Medina." *Journal of Near Eastern Studies* 36, no. 1 (1977): 39–47.

Feldman, Noah. *The Fall and Rise of the Islamic State.* Princeton, NJ: Princeton University Press, 2008.

Hamilton, Alexander, James Madison, and John Jay. *The Federalist Papers.* Edited by Jacob Ernest Cooke. Middletown, CT: Yale University Press, 1961.

Ibn Isḥāq, Muḥammad. *The Life of Muhammad: A Translation of Isḥāq's Sīrat Rasūl Allāh.* Introduction and notes by A. Guillaume. London: Oxford University Press, 1955.

Kleidosty, Jeremy. *The Concert of Civilizations: The Common Roots of Western and Islamic Constitutionalism.* Surrey: Ashgate Publishing, 2015.

Maddox, Graham. "A Note on the Meaning of 'Constitution.'" *American Political Science Review* 76, no. 4 (1982): 805–809.

Na'im, Abdullahi. *African Constitutionalism and the Role of Islam.* Philadelphia, PA: University of Pennsylvania Press, 2007.

al-Tūnisī, Khayr al-Dīn. *The Surest Path: The Political Treatise of a Nineteenth Century Muslim Statesman.* Translated by L. Carl Brown. Harvard Middle Eastern Monographs, 16. Cambridge, MA: Harvard University Press, 1967.

9

"Dropping a Thick Curtain of Forgetting and Disregard": Modern Shīʿī Quietism beyond Politics

Rainer Brunner

The past more than three and a half decades of Middle Eastern history have been characterized by a dramatic advance in the significance of religion in general and of fundamentalist movements in particular. The key year was 1979, and although there were two other major events in that year (the Soviet invasion of Afghanistan and the assault on the Great Mosque in Mecca), the one event that has remained in everyone's head is, of course, the revolution in Iran that brought, for the first time in modern history, a decidedly Islamic/Islamist regime into power. It also thoroughly changed the image of Islam, especially that of Shīʿī Islam, in the rest of the world, and while the two basic tendencies of activist and quietist thinking have long existed side by side, it raised the question of whether or not Shīʿī Islam, even more than other currents in Islam, is an intrinsically activist religion, even a revolutionary ideology.[1] As Khomeini became an icon as popular (at least in some parts of the world) as Ché Guevara or Ho Chi Minh, in other parts of the world, the question about Shīʿī Islam and quietism was and is, understandably, a pertinent concern, although we should remember that "what is" questions are problematic with regard to religions, particularly when viewed from the outside.[2]

Religions, like other intellectual activities, are a product of time and space, influenced by the respective political, social, and economic circumstances—which then, in turn, may be influenced by religious developments. Islam is by no means an exception to this rule, and Shīʿī history, in particular, is a striking example of this observation. The current in Shīʿism that is by far dominant today is generally known as Twelver Shīʿism (*al-shīʿa al-ithnā ʿashariyya*), and this is probably the reason the depiction of Shīʿism in Muslim and non-Muslim historiography more often than not comes across as remarkably teleological, as if Shīʿī history, from its outset, was Twelver history in the making and as if all the other factions—Zaydiyya, Kaysāniyya, Ismāʿīliyya, Nuṣayriyya/ʿAlawiyya, etc.—were more or less only splinter groups that split from this, so to speak, "orthodox" lineage. Nothing could be further from reality. On the contrary, as Hassan Ansari has convincingly stated, it does not make much sense to draw artificial demarcation lines between the diverse Shīʿī tendencies during the first three centuries. Instead of speaking of "Shīʿī currents," we should, rather, speak of "Ecoles de différentes cités et/ou régions formées autour de personnalités notoires."[3] With regard to what was later called Twelver Shīʿism, it resulted from a long process, during the course of which basic doctrinal tenets were repeatedly reworked and broad genealogical claims of succession to Muḥammad as leader of the community were increasingly narrowed down.[4] The path led from the Hāshimīs (who were in favor of the Banū Hāshim in general) to the ʿAlids (who supported only ʿAlī), to the Ḥusaynids (who followed the latter's son Ḥusayn), to the Imāmīs (who molded the very specific theory of the Imams); it was only in the late third/ninth and early fourth/tenth centuries that this path gave way to the nascent Twelver Shīʿīs who eventually and authoritatively limited the number of legitimate imams to the significant number twelve.[5]

With regard to activist and quietist phases, this development, which took place over several centuries, was characterized by intense periods of back and forth, ebb and flow. While in the beginning, in the first/seventh century, the events between Ṣiffīn and Karbalāʾ were of a decidedly activist nature, the theory of the imamate as it was conceived mostly during the tenures of the fifth and sixth imams, Muḥammad al-Bāqir (d. around 115/733) and Jaʿfar al-Ṣādiq (d. 148/765), was a lesson in quietism.[6] As the central institution of religious guidance, the imamate was separated from power, which was embodied in the political caliphate. Henceforward, it was possible to be imam without being caliph at the same time. In view of the fact that Shīʿīs had, until then, been fighting against the Umayyads in a way that was as relentless as it was futile, and, also, in view of the fact that they were quickly ousted by the ʿAbbāsids after the latter's victory over the Umayyads, this "quietist" revolution was a makeshift solution and, quite simply, a survival strategy. The defeat on the battlefield was compensated for by the assurance that they were the chosen community and by their exaltation of the figure of the imam, as the theory rests upon the conviction that the world—past, present, and future—cannot exist without an imam.[7] And since he is divinely appointed, sinless, and omniscient, he cannot err, even if he is devoid of all mundane means to enforce his will. This is, needless to say, an ideal precondition for quietism: you do not need to have political power, you will be saved all the same. Indeed, Jaʿfar al-Ṣādiq himself, like most imams after Ḥusayn, distanced themselves from politics,[8] and two subsequent imams, Muḥammad al-Jawād (the ninth) and ʿAlī l-Hādī (the tenth), were minors when they assumed the imamate and thus could not but be quietist.

In 280/874, the eleventh imam, al-Ḥasan al-ʿAskarī, died, and the vast majority of his followers was unaware of the existence of a male successor.[9] The severe crisis that ensued and the impending decay of the imamate could only be settled by yet another compromise, one that was, in a sense, the completion of the previous development. In the course of the following decades, the idea gained acceptance that there was, in fact, a successor imam who had been taken by God into occultation.[10] At the end of this transitory period, when the greater occultation was proclaimed in the middle of the fourth/tenth century, not only was the number of imams limited to twelve, but the system was apparently stable enough to work in the imam's absence. Therefore, it comes as no surprise that al-Kulaynī, the compiler of the earliest of the canonical *ḥadīth* collections in Shīʿism, transmits a number of traditions, according to which every form of political rule in the absence of the imam is illegitimate; however, since "he who seeks leadership perishes" (*man ṭalaba l-riʾāsa halaka*), the believer must not revolt, but instead must endure the vicissitudes of life and patiently wait for the return of the imam at the end of time.[11] It is quite clear that this development, which may be regarded as a quietist freezing of the imams' genealogy, happened in a deliberate contradistinction to other Shīʿī groups[12]: both Zaydīs and (especially) Ismāʿīlīs/Fāṭimids continued their respective lines of living and present imams and were (at the time) much more activist and far more successful than the Imāmīs, who were only promoted during the rule of the Būyid dynasty (334–447/945–1055) though they did not exercise political power themselves.

Theoretically, this could have been the end of the story, and the (Twelver) Shīʿīs could have ended up as a slightly esoteric and messianic sect without further ambitions. But religious scriptures and traditions need constant interpretation to stand the test of time, and interpretation is an ongoing human preoccupation. Thus, a process was set in motion in Shīʿī intellectual history, one that went on for many centuries and that, arguably, may be described as the "clericalization" of Shīʿī religious scholars—which went hand in hand with a far-reaching rejection by the nascent stratum of Shīʿī jurists of their own tradition, aptly called "tradition originelle ésotérique non-rationnelle."[13] First, some eminent scholars of the fifth/eleventh century, such as al-Shaykh al-Mufīd

(d. 413/1022), al-Sharīf al-Murtaḍā (d. 436/1044), and Muḥammad b. al-Ḥasan al-Ṭūsī, surnamed "Shaykh al-ṭā'ifa" (d. 460/1067), declared it permissible, even necessary, to collaborate with the political powers that be, if it helped the cause of Shīʿism[14]; later, the juristic method of individual reasoning (*ijtihād*), which had been strictly prohibited by the imams during their presence, was permitted and eventually was even incumbent on the scholars during the continued absence of the imams. Finally, starting from the tenth/sixteenth century, during the rule of the Ṣafavid dynasty in Iran, scholars began to appropriate several of the most important prerogatives of the imam: collecting religious taxes, exercising jurisdiction, leading the communal Friday prayer, and finally, in the nineteenth century, calling for *jihād*. The preliminary result of this development—which we can only depict here in its most condensed and rudimentary form—was the stratification of the class of scholars and the emergence of a hierarchy with (ideally) one supreme scholar/jurist at the top, the *marjaʿ al-taqlīd*, the source of emulation.[15]

All this is not to say that Shīʿism was thoroughly politicized such that Khomeini only had to throw a lever in order to switch on Shīʿī activism. By far most Shīʿī scholars in premodern times understood themselves as the collective representatives and gatekeepers of the hidden imam, but they did not have any ambition of their own to assume power, let alone to establish a Shīʿī theocracy. Neither the *fatwā* issued by the *marjaʿ al-taqlīd* Mīrzā Ḥasan al-Shīrāzī (d. 1895) that triggered the famous tobacco revolt in 1891/92, nor, in fact, the active participation of several leading *ʿulamā'* in the constitutional revolution from 1905 onward was intended to lead to a government run by the clergy.[16] However, it is true that the extensive framework of the Shīʿī jurist's authority time and again inspired individual scholars to step forward with somewhat bolder claims. Examples of this can be found in actions of Aḥmad al-Narāqī (d. 1829), who was the first to speak of "the sovereignty of the jurist" (*wilāyat al-faqīh*),[17] or Shaykh Faḍlallāh Nūrī (d. 1909), the most outspoken clerical opponent of constitutionalism in Iran.[18] And it is also true that without this development, Khomeini would have had a much more difficult time in getting his theory across. And yet, it would be misleading to walk into another teleological trap and read Shīʿī history of the post-occultation period as an inevitable run-up to Khomeini.[19] Even for the twentieth century, this would be an overemphasis of the latter's significance. Khomeini's star only began to rise after the mid-1970s, and even following the revolution, consent to his political theory of Shīʿism was far from unanimous. It is not without good reason that his eventual successor, Khamenei, found it rather difficult to be installed as the new "leader of the revolution" in 1989. Shīʿī critics of the *wilāyat al-faqīh* abound, both within Iran and beyond, and Iraqi clerics are often less than enthusiastic about their famous Iranian peer.[20]

But this is not the place for such a discussion; instead, I would like to focus on another realm, one that has been far less analyzed than the political debate proper, though it may, however, add an important aspect to our understanding of quietism. So far, activism and quietism have been considered as largely political terms: the activists are those who strive for political authority and power, the quietists are those who do not. It goes without saying that this is correct to a large extent. But beyond this, one of the standard arguments of the quietist faction gives us a hint: it is preferable, they say, to obey a despotic government for 60, 70, or 100 years than to suffer chaos or civil war for even one day.[21] The term for "chaos," which is often used in this context, is *fitna*. This, of course, immediately brings to mind the first civil war in Islam, after the killing of ʿUthmān, and the deep split of the community that resulted thereof.[22] According to this reading, those who seek to avoid *fitna* are quietist, while those who do not care about *fitna* or who keep turning their knives in this wound by insulting the other side and composing polemical treatises are activist. Seen from this perspective, the question of quietism is also closely related to the problem of how to deal with history.

Ideological governments and compliant historiography go hand in hand—this is a truism; every ideology needs its fuel, and the fuel usually comes from the past. With regard to Shīʿism, we need only think of the skirmish of Karbalāʾ and Imam Ḥusayn's death in 61/680, and the usefulness this event had before and during the revolution in 1979: "Every day is ʿ*āshūrā*ʾ, every land is Karbalāʾ," was a highly popular slogan at the time. What is astonishing, however, is how late this transformation of Karbalāʾ happened: a former student of Khomeini's, Niʿmatullāh Ṣāliḥī Najafābādī (d. 2006), whose book *The Eternal Martyr* came out in 1968, was the first to reinterpret the traditional view of Karbalāʾ in a more politically activist light,[23] and it was ʿAlī Sharīʿatī (d. 1977) who coined this slogan in the 1970s.[24] But the revision came at a price: for many centuries (though not unanimously backed by early sources), the image of Ḥusayn was more quietist in nature; it was molded by Wāʿiẓ Kāshifī in the ninth/fifteenth century and rested on the assumption that Ḥusayn knew beforehand of his impending martyrdom, which was preordained by God and which he thus accepted without hesitation or bitterness. According to the revised view, when Ḥusayn rebelled against the Umayyads—an important example of the activist call for resistance against unjust rule—he did not have any foreknowledge of his fate at Karbalāʾ. This loss of Ḥusayn's omniscience was accepted as a sort of collateral consequence and critical change to the original belief.[25]

Karbalāʾ is an obvious example of a quietist historical myth turned into activist ideology. There are other areas in which dealing with history, and with controversial history in particular, played a decisive role, but on a more subtle and at the same time more fundamental level. Among these, we must count the initiatives of Sunnī and Shīʿī scholars in the twentieth century to come to terms with one another and to reach a kind of ecumenical rapprochement (*taqrīb*) between Sunnism and Shīʿism. For approximately one and a half decades, between 1947 and 1961, there existed in Cairo a pan-Islamic association, Jamāʿat al-Taqrīb Bayn al-Madhāhib al-Islāmiyya, whose declared aim was to establish a permanent forum for exchange between Shīʿī and Sunnī scholars and thus enable a learned debate beyond a polemical and presumptuous attitude.[26] The Sunnī participants came mostly (although not exclusively) from the ranks of al-Azhar University,[27] while on the Shīʿī side a number of eminent scholars, mostly from Iraq and Lebanon, were involved. The Shīʿīs—among whom we might mention Muḥammad al-Ḥusayn Āl Kāshif al-Ghiṭāʾ (d. 1954), ʿAbd al-Ḥusayn Sharaf al-Dīn (d. 1957), and Muḥammad Jawād Mughniyya (d. 1979), to name but a few—acted mostly as long-distance members who seldom came to Cairo.[28] On the other hand, however, the general secretary of the organization, a young Iranian scholar by the name of Muḥammad Taqī Qummī (d. 1979), acted on behalf of the supreme *marjaʿ al-taqlīd* of the time, the Iranian Ayatollah Ḥusayn Burūjirdī (d. 1961), who was the *éminence grise* of this institution.[29]

Throughout its regular existence, the ecumenical society published its own journal, *Risālat al-islām*.[30] When sifting through the articles, one quickly notes its decidedly quietist approach, in the way it prioritized the avoidance of every possible *fitna*. It is not surprising that there was no detailed and thorough discussion, for instance, of the legitimacy of the caliphate, of the trustworthiness of the Companions of the Prophet, or the authenticity of the traditions they transmitted—all topics that were the roots of countless mutual polemics, both classical and modern.[31] To be more precise, there was *no* discussion whatsoever of these issues; the few voices, mostly of Sunnī historians, suggesting that the study of history should not be neglected, were quickly and vehemently rejected both by Shīʿī authors and by the editors of the journal. Instead, this appeal for deliberate forgetfulness was the central thread that ran through the journal's pages from the beginning. For example, the Iraqi Shīʿī scholar Muḥammad Ṣādiq al-Ṣadr stated (in the first year of the journal) that since it was impossible to undo the past, the problem of the caliphate would be best forgotten, or at least they ought to pretend to overlook it (*an natanāsā l-māḍī*).[32] And when the renowned Egyptian historian Aḥmad Amīn published his book on the Mahdī and mahdist thinking (outside the Jamāʿat al-Taqrīb),[33] Muḥammad Taqī Qummī severely criticized him for digging up the dark sides of enmity and hate, and passionately called for letting the reasons for antagonism disappear behind a "thick curtain of forgetting and disregard" (*sitār ghalīẓ min al-nisyān wa-l-ihmāl*).[34] It is precisely for this reason that the editors of the journal also vehemently abstained from offering any forum for their readers to debate the issues. In contrast to many other religious journals, such as the Lebanese *al-ʿIrfān* or Muḥammad Rashīd Riḍā's classical *al-Manār*,[35] *Risālat al-islām* did not accept letters to the editor or requests for *fatwā*s. Fearing that such a forum would focus on controversial issues and thus emphasize sectarian disagreement, the editors' apologetic reasoning again centered on casting a "cloak of forgetting" (*thawb al-nisyān*) to overlook many of the inherited controversies and polemics.[36]

The question of how to deal with controversial issues was, however, not unanimously answered by this call for intentional, feigned amnesia.[37] In the face of their opponents' unrelenting attacks, but also following their own standardized protestation to enhance mutual knowledge among Sunnīs and Shīʿīs, some authors from time to time decided to directly address matters that, for a long time, had been objects of mutual polemics. It goes without saying that it was primarily the Shīʿī scholars who had a keen interest in addressing these points of contention, but they did not do this by simply writing counter-polemics; rather, they tried to "rectify" what they perceived to be the incorrect views of Sunnī authors, both within the ecumenical movement and beyond. Given the need by the minority Shīʿīs to defend themselves against the Sunnī reproaches, it should come as no surprise that their way of treating controversial topics was inevitably apologetic.[38]

When dealing with the differences, we can distinguish three basic perspectives: the first and most straightforward way was simply to declare specific contentious points obsolete. The mostly Shīʿī authors claimed that the circumstances that had caused these issues in the distant past, and later contributed to their role in polemical disputes, had since ceased to exist. Therefore, the controversies themselves, which were regarded as no longer valid, could not be an obstacle to rapprochement. In this manner, for example, Muḥammad Jawād Mughniyya de-emphasized controversial practices, such as *taqiyya* or temporary marriage (*mutʿa*).[39] Although theoretically still valid, after defending them in great detail, he insisted that they were no longer used in daily life and were even disapproved of by modern Shīʿīs.[40]

The second approach was of a more legalistic nature, and was somewhat more demanding, inasmuch as it consisted of drawing a distinction between the fundamental obligations of the religion (*dīn*) on the one hand and those of the legal school (*madhhab*) on the other. This approach was not entirely new: already in the 1930s, the al-Azhar rector Muḥammad Muṣṭafā l-Marāghī (d. 1945) and the Iraqi Shīʿī scholar ʿAbd al-Karīm al-Zanjānī (d. 1968) had met in Cairo and later corresponded in order to fathom the chances for sectarian rapprochement.[41] As far as I am aware, they were the first, in the context of Sunnī-Shīʿī dialogue, to divide the categories of religious law into three types: the indisputable *uṣūl al-dīn*, which were restricted to just three points—(1) belief in the unity of God (*tawḥīd*), in Muḥammad's prophethood (*nubuwwa*), and in the hereafter (*maʿād*); (2) the inoffensive legal norms (*furūʿ al-dīn*), which were open to legitimate *ijtihād* and about which unity was therefore not considered a prerequisite; and, finally, (3) the "principle of the legal schools" (*aṣl madhhabī*). The latter point was reserved, more or less exclusively, for the institution of the (Shīʿī) imamate, which was thus rendered innocuous, since—although it was certainly more than merely a secondary and derivative matter—it did not touch on the very foundations of Islamic religiosity. Thus, according to this logic, whoever rejected the imamate, but accepted the three overriding principles, was not a Shīʿī, but could absolutely be considered a Muslim.[42] In the context of the *taqrīb* debate of the 1950s, it was once again Muḥammad Jawād Mughniyya who adopted this principle and thus described the imamate as a "principle of the Shīʿī *madhhab*" (*aṣl li-madhhab al-tashayyuʿ*).[43]

The third approach was to a certain extent the most risky one, as it consisted of reinterpreting contentious points in such a way that they were compatible with the Sunnī point of view, without denying their existence or their significance out of hand. This was, for instance, the approach of the two Iraqi scholars, Tawfīq al-Fukaykī (d. 1969) and Ayatollah Abū l-Qāsim al-Khūʾī (d. 1992), in their respective articles on the thorny issue of the alleged falsification of the Qurʾānic text (*taḥrīf*).[44] In many premodern Shīʿī sources—above all in al-Kulaynī's compilation *al-Kāfī*—there are traditions to the effect that the Sunnī compilers of the scripture intentionally omitted all references and hints to ʿAlī and the imams (which were supposed to have been included in the original revelation) in order to reject any divine backing of the Shīʿī claim for leadership of the *umma*.[45] Al-Fukaykī, however, after quoting a number of classical and modern scholars, concluded that all the *ḥadīth*s in which the authenticity of the Qurʾān is questioned were themselves undoubtedly forged. According to him, al-Kulaynī had quoted these traditions only "in order to depreciate those who uphold such an absurd claim."[46] Al-Khūʾī went further than that—he basically accepted the authenticity of the traditions in question and did not flatly dispute the theoretical possibility of additions in ʿAlī's version of the Qurʾān. But he emphasized that these additions could easily be explained as exegetical (*taʾwīl*) explanations or as (non-Qurʾānic) "revelations sent down by God in order to clarify the meaning of individual passages."[47]

Beyond these three defensive approaches to history, there were a number of more or less standardized arguments about the self-image of the Jamāʿat al-Taqrīb and its main goals, and these arguments revealed a decidedly quietist attitude. The most important evidence in this context was the protestation that the main task of the association was to bring about a rapprochement of the legal schools, but not to strive for their unification, let alone their elimination.[48] Therefore, the question was not about converting Sunnīs to Shīʿism or vice versa, but rather to establish Shīʿism as a fifth *madhhab* alongside the four Sunnī schools of law. This was a remarkable contrast from an earlier attitude among Shīʿī scholars in this regard: when Nādir Shāh held his famous conference in Najaf in 1743 and tried to subdue the Shīʿī clergy, he attempted to achieve this by persuading the Ottomans to recognize Shīʿism as a fifth *madhhab*. The Shīʿī scholars understood that the underlying motive was to do away with their principles, and they refused to cooperate.[49] The same idea was brought forward by the Shīʿīs themselves 200 years later and was reinterpreted as the noblest goal of ecumenical thought in Islam. It came to fruition in the summer of 1959, in the famous *fatwā* issued by Maḥmūd Shaltūt, the al-Azhar rector, in which he fully acknowledged Shīʿism as a fifth *madhhab*, on a par with the Sunnī schools; he even allowed mutual conversions. Until today, it is hailed by ecumenically minded ("quietist," so to speak) Sunnī and Shīʿī scholars alike as the most remarkable step toward reaching a sectarian accord, its rather short-lived success and rather abrupt failure on the ground notwithstanding.[50]

Yet, by calling this approach (and in fact ecumenical endeavors in general) "quietist," we must bear in mind that many of those who finally did convert—usually from Sunnism to Shīʿism, as there seem to be far more converts in this direction than the reverse—tended to end up writing the kind of literature that is rather typical of new converts. These treatises, which aim at proselytizing others and helping them "to see the light" (the technical term in Shīʿism denoting converts is, rather characteristically, *mustabṣirūn*),[51] are more often than not distinctly polemical. By expressing their bias against their former convictions, these authors show much more "activist" leanings.[52] This, then, draws our attention to the fact that the identification of any course of action as quietist or activist cannot and should not be separated from its wider context, that is, from the more general and overarching intentions of the respective actors. This means that the above-mentioned Shīʿī scholars did not participate in the *taqrīb* movement because the ecumenical idea, as such, was necessarily quietist. Rather, Mughniyya or al-Khūʾī had a distinctly quietist outlook on religion and thus, apparently, found it easy to contribute to an association whose primary goal was to foster mutual understanding, while refraining from political claims.[53] The *taqrīb* idea could also be used on the firm basis of a thoroughly activist regime, a point that was later demonstrated by the Iranian government, which—significantly after Khomeini's death in 1989—promoted the foundation of the "World Association for the Rapprochement of the Islamic Schools of Law."[54] While for more than twenty-five years the activist post-1979 regime has been using the ecumenical idea as a vehicle for the propagation of the Iranian revolution, their quietist predecessors in the 1950s and 1960s aimed at defusing sectarian tensions between the main groups in Islam; yet both found ecumenism a viable tool for their principal disposition.

It comes as no surprise that, throughout its existence, the Jamāʿat al-Taqrīb vehemently emphasized its intention to remain aloof from politics, which was blamed for causing the split between Shīʿīs and Sunnīs in the first place, for fear of being swept away by it. It seems rather ironic that this is precisely what ultimately happened when the association fell victim to the political struggle between the Egyptian president Nasser and the Iranian shah in the summer of 1960.[55] Its sad ending notwithstanding, the sheer existence of the ecumenical society may be considered evidence that a defensive, careful, that is, quietist approach to history can and did exist in modern Shīʿism, and that the offensive, political, that is, activist approach is not necessarily the only logical outcome of history. Religion, like history in general, it must be remembered, is what people make of it; as the Greek philosopher Epictetus clearly recognized: "Men are disturbed not by things, but by the views which they take of things."[56] This is likely true of quietists and activists alike.

Notes

1 A short overview of these two basic currents of thought is given by Bernard Lewis, "On the Quietist and Activist Traditions in Islamic Political Writing," *Bulletin of the School of Oriental and African Studies* 49 (1986): 141–147; on the Shīʿī (and Persian) context specifically, see Saïd Amir Arjomand, "The Conception of

Revolution in Persianate Political Thought," *Journal of Persianate Studies* 5 (2012): 1–16; Denis Hermann, "Political Quietism in Contemporary Shīʿism: A Study of the *Siyāsat-i mudun* of the Shaykhī Kirmānī Master ʿAbd al-Riḍā Khān Ibrāhīmī," *Studia Islamica* 109 (2014): 274–302; a number of twentieth-century case studies are treated in Juan Cole and Nikki Keddie (eds.), *Shiʿism and Social Protest* (New Haven, CT: Yale University Press, 1986).

2 A recent (and widely discussed) book even has this in its title: Shahab Ahmed, *What Is Islam? The Importance of Being Islamic* (Princeton, NJ, and Oxford: Princeton University Press, 2016).

3 Hassan Ansari, *L'imamat et l'Occultation selon l'imamisme. Etude bibliographique et histoire des textes* (Leiden: Brill, 2017), x.

4 For a concise description of the many currents in early Islamic Iraq, especially in Kufa, which finally gave way to the beginnings of Twelver Shīʿism proper, see Josef van Ess, *Theologie und Gesellschaft im 2. und 3. Jahrhundert Hidschra. Eine Geschichte des religiösen Denkens im frühen Islam* (Berlin and New York: Walter de Gruyter, 1991–97), 1: 233–403; this volume is now also available in English translation: *Theology and Society in the Second and Third Centuries of the Hijra: A History of Religious Thought in Early Islam*, trans. John O'Kane (Leiden: Brill, 2017), 268–473; for the early phase of Shīʿism, see also Najam Haider, *The Origins of the Shīʿa: Identity, Ritual, and Sacred Space in Eighth-Century Kūfa* (Cambridge: Cambridge University Press, 2011). Heinz Halm's overview of Shīʿī history and the various branches of Shīʿism is still unsurpassed, see Halm, *Die Schia* (Darmstadt: Wissenschaftliche Buchgesellschaft, 1988), trans. Janet Watson and Marian Hill, as *Shiʿism* (New York: Columbia University Press, 2004).

5 Ansari, *L'imamat*, 12–119.

6 On Muḥammad al-Bāqir, see Arzina R. Lalani, *Early Shīʿī Thought: The Teachings of Imam Muḥammad al-Bāqir* (London and New York: I.B. Tauris, 2000); on Jaʿfar al-Ṣādiq, see Robert Gleave et al., "Jaʿfar al-Ṣādeq," *Encyclopaedia Iranica* 14: 349–366, online: www.iranicaonline.org/articles/jafar-al-sadeq; Ronald P. Buckley, "The Writings of Jaʿfar al-Ṣādiq," in *Books and Bibliophiles: Studies in Honour of Paul Auchterlonie on the Bio-Bibliography of the Muslim World*, ed. Robert Gleave (Exeter: Gibb Memorial Trust, 2014), 14–28.

7 Muḥammad b. Yaʿqūb al-Kulaynī, *Uṣūl al-kāfī* (Beirut 1428/2007), 1:103–104 (*bāb anna l-arḍ lā takhlū min ḥujja*). For the idea of Shīʿism as a religion of the "chosen community," see Etan Kohlberg, "In Praise of the Few," in *Studies in Islamic and Middle Eastern Texts and Traditions, in Memory of Norman Calder*, ed. G. R. Hawting et al. (Oxford: Oxford University Press, 2000), 149–162.

8 On "la vie 'politique' des imâms," see Mohammad Ali Amir-Moezzi, *Le guide divin dans le shîʿisme originel. Aux sources de l'ésotérisme en Islam* (Lagrasse: Verdier, 1992), 155–165.

9 Saïd Amir Arjomand, "Imam *Absconditus* and the Beginnings of a Theology of Occultation: Imami Shiʿism *circa* 280–90 A.H./900 A.D.," *Journal of the American Oriental Society* 117 (1997), 1–12, on 1 (reprinted in Arjomand, *Sociology of Shiʿite Islam: Collected Essays* (Leiden: Brill, 2016), 74–95).

10 While Abū l-Ḥasan ʿAlī b. al-Ḥusayn b. Mūsā b. Bābawayh al-Qummī (d. 329/940 or 941) in his *Kitāb al-imāma wa-l-tabṣira min al-ḥayra* avoids any clear statement concerning the exact number of the imams, his contemporary al-Kulaynī does quote several traditions to the effect that there are twelve imams; al-Kulaynī, *Uṣūl al-kāfī*, 1:337–343 (*bāb mā jāʾa fī l-ithnā ʿashar wa-l-naṣṣ ʿalayhim*); Muḥammad b. Ibrāhīm al-Nuʿmānī (d. *c.* 360/971) also quotes such traditions; on all these, see Ansari, *L'imamat*, 24, 35, 42.

11 Al-Kulaynī, *Uṣūl al-kāfī*, 2:173–174 (*bāb ṭalab al-riʾāsa*); on the transition from Imamite Shīʿism to Twelver Shīʿism, see Arjomand, *Sociology of Shiʿite Islam*, 42–120; Etan Kohlberg, "From Imāmiyya to Ithnā-ʿashariyya," *Bulletin of the School of Oriental and African Studies* 39 (1976), 521–534; on al-Kulaynī and his compilation in particular, see Mohammad Ali Amir-Moezzi and Hassan Ansari, "Muḥammad b. Yaʿqūb al-Kulaynī (m. 328 ou 329/939–40 ou 940–41) et son *Kitāb al-Kāfī*. Une introduction," *Studia Iranica* 38 (2009), 191–247.

12 Ansari, *L'imamat*, 11–17; on the Ismāʿīliyya, see Farhad Daftary, *The Ismāʿīlīs: Their History and Doctrines* (Cambridge: Cambridge University Press, 2007); on the evolution of Zaydī doctrine, see Wilferd Madelung, *Der Imam al-Qāsim ibn Ibrāhīm und die Glaubenslehre der Zaiditen* (Berlin: Walter de Gruyter, 1965); Najam Haider, *Shīʿī Islam: An Introduction* (Cambridge: Cambridge University Press, 2014), 103–122, 169–181; Patricia Crone, *Medieval Islamic Political Thought* (Edinburgh: Edinburgh University Press, 2004), 99–109 (and 197–218 on the Ismāʿīlīs).

13 Mohammad Ali Amir-Moezzi, Le Coran silencieux et le Coran parlant. *Sources scriptuaires de l'islam entre histoire et ferveur* (Paris: CNRS Editions, 2011), 190 n. 187, translated as *The Silent Qur'an and the Speaking Qur'an: Scriptural Sources of Islam between History and Fervor* (New York: Columbia University Press, 2015).

14 For the general background, see Crone, *Medieval Islamic Political Thought*, 110–124; on Mufid, see Tamima Bayhom-Daou, *Shaykh Mufid* (Oxford: Oneworld, 2005); for the (not totally undisputed) specific case of al-Sharīf al-Murtaḍā, see Wilferd Madelung, "A Treatise of the Sharīf al-Murtaḍā on the Legality of Working for the Government (*Mas'ala fī 'l-ʿamal maʿa 'l-sulṭān*)," *Bulletin of the School of Oriental and African Studies* 43 (1980), 18–31; on al-Ṭūsī, see Hassan Ansari and Sabine Schmidtke, "Al-Shaykh al-Ṭūsī: His Writings on Theology and Their Reception," in *The Study of Shiʿi Islam: History, Theology and Law*, ed. Farhad Daftary and Gurdofarid Miskinzoda (London: I.B. Tauris, 2014), 475–497.

15 Nowadays, literature on the development of Shīʿī political thought abounds; for general overviews, see Mohammad Ali Amir-Moezzi, "Islam in Iran, x: The Roots

of Political Shiʿism," *Encyclopaedia Iranica* 14: 146–154, online: http://www.iranicaonline.org/articles/islam-in-iran-x-the-roots-of-political-shiisms; Amir-Moezzi, "Réflexions sur une évolution du shiʿisme duodécimain: tradition et idéologisation," in *Les retours aux écritures. Fondamentalismes présents et passés*, ed. E. Patlagean and A. de Boulluec (Leuven: Peeters, 1993), 63–81; Saïd Amir Arjomand, *The Shadow of God and the Hidden Imam: Religion, Political Order and Societal Change in Shiʿite Iran from the Beginning to 1890* (Chicago and London: University of Chicago Press, 1984); Abdulaziz Abdulhussein Sachedina, *The Just Ruler in Shiʿite Islam: The Comprehensive Authority of the Jurist in Imamite Jurisprudence* (New York and Oxford: Oxford University Press, 1988); Rainer Brunner, "Shiʿite Doctrine, ii: Hierarchy in the Imamiyya," *Encyclopaedia Iranica*, online: www.iranicaonline.org/articles/shiite-doctrine-ii-hierarchy-emamiya.

16 On al-Shīrāzī and his *fatwā*—that he issued much against his will, mainly on the instigation of the well-known activist of Muslim reformism, Jamāl al-Dīn al-Afghānī (d. 1897)—see Werner Ende, "Der amtsmüde Ayatollah," in *Festschrift für Burkhart Kienast zu seinem 70. Geburtstage dargebracht von Freunden, Schülern und Kollegen*, ed. Gebhard Selz (Münster: Ugarit-Verlag, 2003), 51–63; Fatema Soudavar Farmanfarmaian, "Revisiting and Revising the Tobacco Rebellion," *Iranian Studies* 47 (2014), 595–625; Nikki R. Keddie, *Religion and Rebellion in Iran: The Tobacco Protest of 1891–1892* (London: Cass, 1966); on the Constitutional Revolution, one of the most well-researched areas of modern Iranian history before 1979, see Abbas Amamat et al., "Constitutional Revolution," *Encyclopaedia Iranica*, 6: 163–216, online: http://www.iranicaonline.org/articles/constitutional-revolution-index; Vanessa Martin, *Islam and Modernism: The Iranian Revolution of 1906* (Syracuse: Syracuse University Press, 1989); Martin, *Iran between Islamic Nationalism and Secularism: The Constitutional Revolution of 1906* (London: I.B. Tauris, 2013).

17 On al-Narāqī and his contribution to Shīʿī jurisprudence, see Arjomand, *Sociology of Shiʿite Islam*, 176–178; Arjomand, *The Shadow of God*, 232 and index, s.v.

18 On Nūrī, who was executed because of his radical stance, see Martin, *Islam and Modernism*, 165–200; Martin, "Nūrī, Fażl-Allāh," *Encyclopaedia Iranica*, online: http://www.iranicaonline.org/articles/nuri-fazl-allah.

19 Arjomand, *Sociology of Shiʿite Islam*, 361–390; on Khomeini's political theory and its impact, see Vanessa Martin, *Creating an Islamic State: Khomeini and the Making of a New Iran* (London: I.B. Tauris, 2007); on the gamut of Shīʿī political thought in the twentieth century, see Reza Hajatpour, *Iranische Geistlichkeit zwischen Utopie und Realismus. Zum Diskurs über Herrschafts- und Staatsdenken im 20. Jahrhundert* (Wiesbaden: Reichert, 2002).

20 On Khomeini's critics within Shīʿism, see Mariella Ourghi, "Shiite Criticism of the *welāyat-e faqīh*," *Asiatische Studien* 59 (2005), 831–844; Katajun Amirpur, "Aktuelle Aushandlungsprozesse des Verhältnisses von Religion, Staat und Politik: Eine Positionsbestimmung der heutigen Gegner und Befürworter der *velāyat-e faqīh* in

Iran und im Irak," *Asiatische Studien* 66 (2012), 521–564; on Shīʿī constitutional thought after 1979, cf. Arjomand, *Sociology of Shiʿite Islam*, 413–441.

21 Ulrich Haarmann, "'Lieber hundert Jahre Zwangsherrschaft als ein Tag Leiden im Bürgerkrieg'. Ein gemeinsamer Topos im islamischen und frühneuzeitlichen europäischen Staatsdenken," in *Gottes ist der Orient, Gottes ist der Okzident. Festschrift für Abdoljavad Falaturi zum 65. Geburtstag*, ed. Udo Tworuschka (Cologne and Vienna: Böhlau, 1991), 262–269; Crone, *Medieval Islamic Political Thought*, 135–137.

22 G. H. A. Juynboll, "The Date of the Great *fitna*," *Arabica* 20 (1973), 142–159; G. R. Hawting, "The Significance of the Slogan *lā ḥukma illā lillāh* and the References to the *ḥudūd* in the Traditions about the Fitna and the Murder of ʿUthmān," *Bulletin of the School of Oriental and African Studies* 41 (1978), 453–463; for modern ramifications (in the nineteenth century, *fitna* was also used for "revolution"), see Ami Ayalon, "From Fitna to Thawra," *Studia Islamica* 66 (1987), 145–174; Helga Rebhan, *Geschichte und Funktion einiger politischer Termini im Arabischen des 19. Jahrhunderts (1798–1882)* (Wiesbaden: Harrassowitz, 1986), 111–113.

23 Evan Siegel, "The Politics of *Shahīd-e Jāwīd*," in *The Twelver Shiʿa in Modern Times: Religious Culture and Political History*, ed. Rainer Brunner and Werner Ende (Leiden: Brill, 2001), 150–177.

24 Hans G. Kippenberg, "Jeder Tag ʿAshura, jedes Grab Kerbelaʾ. Zur Ritualisierung der Straßenkämpfe in Iran," in *Religion und Politik im Iran*, ed. K. Greussing and J.-H. Grevemeyer (Frankfurt 1981), 217–256. This deliberately political reading of the events of Karbalāʾ should not distract, however, from the general overwhelming significance that Ḥusayn's defeat had on the genesis and sectarian self-understanding of Shīʿism; Heinz Halm aptly described the skirmish of Karbalāʾ as "the 'big bang' that created the rapidly expanding cosmos of Shiʿism and brought it into motion": *Shiʿa Islam: From Religion to Revolution* (Princeton: Markus Wiener Publishers, 1997), 16.

25 On the evolution of the image of Karbalāʾ from Kāshifī to twentieth-century thinkers, see Kamran Scot Aghaie, *The Martyrs of Karbala: Shiʿi Symbols and Rituals in Modern Iran* (Seattle and London: University of Washington Press, 2004), 87–112.

26 For the history and intellectual background of this association, see Rainer Brunner, *Islamic Ecumenism in the 20th Century: The Azhar and Shiism Between Rapprochement and Restraint* (Leiden: Brill, 2004).

27 Among the founding members were the al-Azhar rectors Muṣṭafā ʿAbd al-Rāziq (d. 1947), ʿAbd al-Majīd Salīm (d. 1954), and Maḥmūd Shaltūt (d. 1963), who were also closely connected to various reformist endeavors within al-Azhar University; see also Wolf-Dieter Lemke, *Maḥmūd Šaltūt (1893–1963) und die Reform der Azhar. Untersuchungen zu Erneuerungsbestrebungen im ägyptisch-islamischen Erziehungssystem* (Frankfurt/Main: Peter Lang, 1980).

28 On Kāshif al-Ghiṭāʾ, see Silvia Naef, "Un réformiste chiite—Muḥammad Ḥusayn Āl Kāšif al-Ġitāʾ," *Die Welt des Orients* 27 (1996), 51–86; on Sharaf al-Dīn, see his own two-volume account of his family: *Bughyat al-rāghibīn fī silsilat Āl Sharaf al-Dīn*, I–II (Beirut 1411/1991); Sabrina Mervin, *Un réformisme chiite. Ulémas et lettrés du Ǧabal ʿĀmil (actuel Liban-Sud) de la fin de l'Empire ottoman à l'indépendance du Liban* (Paris 2000), 430 and index, s.v.; Brunner, *Islamic Ecumenism*, 51–81; on Mughniyya (occasionally spelled Maghniyya), see his autobiography *Tajārib Muḥammad Jawād Mughniyya* (Beirut 1400/1980); Chibli Mallat, *Shiʿi Thought from the South of Lebanon* (Oxford: Centre for Lebanese Studies, 1988), 16–25; Lynda Clarke, "ʿ*Aql* (Reason) in Modern Shiite Thought: The Example of Muḥammad Jawād Maghniyya (1904–79)," in *Essays in Islamic Philology, History, and Philosophy*, ed. Alireza Korangy et al. (Berlin and Boston: Walter de Gruyter, 2016), 281–311.

29 On Qummī, see Brunner, *Islamic Ecumenism*, index, s.v.; on Burūjirdī, ibid., 189–193, and Hamid Algar, "Borūjerdī, Ḥosayn Ṭabāṭabāʾī," *Encyclopaedia Iranica*, 4:376–379, online: http://www.iranicaonline.org/articles/borujerdi-hosayn-tabatabai.

30 The sixty issues of the journal (which appeared between 1949 and 1972) can now be consulted online: http://www.taghrib.org/?p=tex&gr=3; Brunner, *Islamic Ecumenism*, 143–149.

31 On details on the scope of topics and the modes of argumentation in the journal, see Brunner, *Islamic Ecumenism*, 208–248.

32 Muḥammad Ṣādiq al-Ṣadr, "Ilā Jamāʿat al-taqrīb," *Risālat al-islām* 1 (1949), 359.

33 Aḥmad Amīn, *al-Mahdī wa-l-mahdawiyya* (Cairo 1951). The small book is not restricted to Twelver Shīʿism but covers a whole range of mahdist thinking, including the former Būyid general Abū l-Ḥārith Arslān al-Basāsīrī (d. 452/1060), the Bābiyya and Bahāʾiyya, the Qādiyāniyya, the Sanūsiyya, and the Sudanese Mahdī in the nineteenth century.

34 Muḥammad Taqī Qummī, "al-Aqlām fī l-mīzān," *Risālat al-islām* 4 (1952), 148; the book sparked several Shīʿī counter-polemics, for example, Muḥammad ʿAlī l-Zuhaylī, *al-Mahdī wa-Aḥmad Amīn* (Najaf 1950); Muḥammad Amīn Zayn al-Dīn, *Maʿa l-duktūr Aḥmad Amīn fī ḥadīth al-mahdī wa-l-mahdawiyya* (Najaf 1951; new edition Beirut 1413/1992); on Aḥmad Amīn's (1886–1954) polemical exchanges with Shīʿī scholars over more than two decades and his complicated relationship with the ecumenical association, see Brunner, *Islamic Ecumenism*, 174–179; in general, see Emmanuelle Perrin, "Le creuset et l'orfèvre: le parcours d'Ahmad Amîn (1886–1954)," *Revue des mondes musulmans et de la Méditerranée* 95–98 (2002), 307–335, online: http://remmm.revues.org/index238.html.

35 On *al-ʿIrfān*, which was edited in Ṣaydā by Aḥmad ʿĀrif al-Zayn (1881–1960) from 1909 onward, see Silvia Naef, "Aufklärung in einem schiitischen Umfeld: Die libanesische Zeitschrift *al-ʿIrfān*," *Die Welt des Islams* 36 (1996), 365–378; Tarif

Khalidi, "Shaykh Ahmad ʿĀrif al-Zayn and *al-ʿIrfān*," in *Intellectual Life in the Arab East, 1890–1939*, ed. Marwan al-Buheiry (Beirut: American University of Beirut, 1981), 110–124. On Muḥammad Rashīd Riḍā (1865–1935) and his famous journal, see, for example, Umar Ryad, "A Printed Muslim 'Lighthouse' in Cairo: *al-Manār*'s Early Years, Religious Aspiration and Reception (1898–1903)," *Arabica* 56 (2009) 27–60; Stéphane Dudoignon et al. (eds.), *Intellectuals in the Modern Islamic World: Transmission, Transformation, Communication* (London, New York: Routledge, 2006), 1–158.

36 *Risālat al-islām* 3 (1951), 108–109; see, in detail, Brunner, *Islamic Ecumenism*, 210–211.

37 Aleida Assmann, *Formen des Vergessens* (Göttingen: Wallstein, 2016), 30–68, distinguishes seven modes of forgetting; in the context of the *taqrīb* debate, "constructive forgetting" ("Konstruktives Vergessen—*tabula rasa* im Dienste eines politischen oder biographischen Neubeginns," 57–64) probably comes closest to the intentions of those who participated in this discussion within the *Jamāʿat al-Taqrīb*.

38 For what follows, see Brunner, *Islamic Ecumenism*, 218–228.

39 On *taqiyya*, see Louis Medoff, "Taqiya, i: In Shiʿism," *Encyclopaedia Iranica*, online: http://www.iranicaonline.org/articles/taqiya-i-shiism; the different categorical aspects are dealt with by Yarden Mariuma, "Taqiyya as Polemic, Law and Knowledge: Following an Islamic Legal Term through the Worlds of Islamic Scholars, Ethnographers, Polemicists and Military Men," *Muslim World* 104 (2014), 89–108; in Sunnī Islam, *taqiyya* was mainly discussed in the context of the Moriscos's forced conversion to Christianity after the *reconquista* in the sixteenth century: Devin Stewart, "Dissimulation in Sunni Islam and Morisco *Taqiyya*," *al-Qanṭara* 34 (2013), 439–490. On temporary marriage, see, in general, Shahla Haeri, "Motʿa," *Encyclopaedia Iranica*, online: http://www.iranicaonline.org/articles/mota; on discussions in the twentieth century in particular, Werner Ende, "Ehe auf Zeit (*mutʿa*) in der innerislamischen Diskussion der Gegenwart," *Die Welt des Islams* 20 (1980), 1–43; a modern case study is Sabrina Mervin, "Normes religieuses et loi du silence: le mariage temporaire chez les chiites du Liban," in *Les métamorphoses du mariage au Moyen-Orient*, ed. Barbara Drieskens (Beirut: Presses de l'Ifpo, 2008), 47–58, online: http://ifpo.revues.org/452; on similar concepts in Sunnī Islam, see Roswitha Badry, "'Not macht erfinderisch' oder Sexualmoral im Umbruch? Die 'Genuss-Ehe' (*mut'a*) im sunnitischen Kontext," in *Die Grenzen der Welt. Arabica et Iranica ad honorem Heinz Gaube*, ed. Lorenz Korn et al. (Wiesbaden: Ludwig Reichert Verlag, 2008), 307–319.

40 Muḥammad Jawād Mughniyya, "al-Taqiyya bayn al-sunna wa-l-shīʿa," *Risālat al-islām* 14 (1963), 39–43; Mughniyya, "al-Mutʿa ʿind al-shiʿa," *al-ʿIrfān* 37, no. 10 (October 1950), 1095–1096; both articles are reprinted in his book *al-Shīʿa fī l-mīzān* (Beirut 1974), 48–52 and 373–374.

41 On these endeavors (and their ulterior failure), see Brunner, *Islamic Ecumenism*, 103–120.

42 Muḥammad Hādī al-Daftar, *Ṣafḥa min riḥlat al-imām al-Zanjānī wa-khuṭabihi fī l-aqṭār al-ʿarabiyya wa-l-ʿawāṣim al-islāmiyya* (Najaf 1366/1947; repr. Beirut 1417/1996), 46–50; see Brunner, *Islamic Ecumenism*, 109–110.

43 Muḥammad Jawād Mughniyya, "Ḍarūrāt al-dīn wa-l-madhhab ʿind al-shīʿa al-imāmiyya," *Risālat al-islām* 2 (1950), 389.

44 On the evolution of this debate, see Rainer Brunner, *Die Schia und die Koranfälschung* (Würzburg: Ergon, 2001).

45 Al-Kulaynī, *Uṣūl al-kāfī*, 1:347–350 (*kitāb faḍl al-Qurʾān—bāb al-nawādir*). One of the most important and key classical texts has recently been edited by Etan Kohlberg and Mohammad Ali Amir-Moezzi, *Revelation and Falsification: The* Kitāb al-qirāʾāt *of Aḥmad b. Muḥammad al-Sayyārī* (Leiden: Brill, 2009); on the general significance of the classical dispute and its implications for Islamic history in general, see Amir-Moezzi, *Le Coran silencieux*, 15–23, 63–100, 207–218.

46 "Fī tasfīh al-qāʾilīn bi-hādhihi l-daʿwā l-bāṭila": Tawfīq al-Fukaykī, "Fī sabīl al-tafāhum," *Risālat al-islām* 12 (1960), 67; al-Fukaykī also distinguished himself as an apologist of the *mutʿa*, see Ende, "Ehe auf Zeit," 18–21. See, in general, Karl-Heinrich Goebel, *Moderne schiitische Politik und Staatsidee nach Taufīq al-Fukaikī, Muḥammad Ǧawād Muġnīya, Rūḥullāh Ḫumainī (Khomeyni)* (Opladen: Leske + Budrich, 1984), 12–63.

47 "Al-tanzīl min Allāh sharḥ[an] li-l-murād": Abū l-Qāsim al-Khūʾī, "Ṣiyānat al-Qurʾān min al-taḥrīf," *Risālat al-islām* 10 (1958), 188; the article was an extract from a long chapter devoted to this issue in his book, Abū l-Qāsim al-Khūʾī, *al-Bayān fī tafsīr al-Qurʾān* (Najaf 1375/1955–56), 156–172, trans. A. A. Sachedina, *The Prolegomena to the Qurʾān* (New York and Oxford: Oxford University Press, 1988), 135–177; on al-Khūʾī's reasoning, see in more detail Brunner, *Die Schia und die Koranfälschung*, 88–92; on his biography, see Sachedina's introduction to the aforementioned translation.

48 Brunner, *Islamic Ecumenism*, 229–231, with a number of references.

49 On this episode, see, in detail, Ernest S. Tucker, *Nadir Shah's Quest for Legitimacy in Post-Safavid Iran* (Gainesville: University Press of Florida, 2006), 78–93.

50 On this *fatwā* in general, see Brunner, *Islamic Ecumenism*, 284–305.

51 See, for example, Ghulām Aṣghar Bajnūrī, *al-Mustabṣirūn* (Beirut: Dār al-Ṣafwa, 1414/1994); Khalid Sindawi, "*Al-Mustabṣirūn*, 'Those Who Are Able to See the Light': Sunnī Conversion to Twelver Shīʿism in Modern Times," *Die Welt des Islams* 51 (2011), 210–234.

52 An early representative of this tendency was Muḥammad Marʿī l-Amīn al-Anṭākī (d. 1963 or 1964) and his book *Li-mādhā ikhtart madhhab al-shīʿa, madhhab ahl al-bayt* (Beirut: Muʾassasat al-Aʿlamī li-l-Maṭbūʿāt, 1980); while

his tone (the book was written around 1960) was predominantly apologetic, the books of his successors since the 1980s (such as Muḥammad al-Tījānī l-Samāwī, Ṣāliḥ al-Wardānī, or Aḥmad Rāsim al-Nafīs) are tinged with polemics; on this phenomenon, see Rainer Brunner, "'Then I Was Guided': Some Remarks on Inner-Islamic Conversions in the 20th and 21st Centuries," *Orient* 50, no. 4 (2009), 6–15.

53 Mughniyya was an outspoken critic of Khomeini's theory of *wilāyat al-faqīh*; see Ourghi, "Shiite Criticism," 842; for al-Khūʾī's complicated relations with Khomeini, see Elvire Corboz, *Guardians of Shiʿism: Sacred Authority and Transnational Family Networks* (Edinburgh: Edinburgh University Press, 2015), 166–176.

54 Al-Majmaʿ al-ʿĀlamī li-l-Taqrīb Bayn al-Madhāhib al-Islāmiyya; on the early history of this institution, see Wilfried Buchta, "Teherans *Maǧmaʿ at-taqrīb*: Neubeginn islamischer Ökumene oder trojanisches Pferd Irans," in *Encounters of Word and Texts: Intercultural Studies in Honor of Stefan Wild on the Occasion of His 60th Birthday, March 2, 1997, Presented by His Pupils in Bonn*, ed. Lutz Edzard and Christian Szyska (Hildesheim: Georg Olms Verlag, 1997), 223–240; Buchta, *Die iranische Schia und die islamische Einheit 1979–1996* (Hamburg: Deutsches Orient-Institut, 1997), 245–344. It must be recalled that the founder of the Muslim Brotherhood, Ḥasan al-Bannā (d. 1949), was among the early (albeit not overly visible) participants of the Cairene association; see Brunner, *Islamic Ecumenism*, 180–183.

55 Brunner, *Islamic Ecumenism*, 305–337. The association continued to exist until well after the Iranian revolution, but it vanished from the public eye more or less completely; later attempts to reopen it (in 1992 and 2008) failed; cf. Rainer Brunner, "Interesting Times: Egypt and Shiism at the Beginning of the Twenty-First Century," in *The Sunna and Shia in History: Division and Ecumenism in the Muslim Middle East*, ed. Meir Litvak and Ofra Bengio (New York: Palgrave Macmillan, 2011), 223–241.

56 Thomas Wentworth Higginson (trans.), *The Works of Epictetus: Consisting of His Discourses, in Four Books, the Enchiridion, and Fragments* (Boston: Little, Brown, and Company, 1866), 377.

Bibliography

Aghaie, Kamran Scot. *The Martyrs of Karbala: Shiʿi Symbols and Rituals in Modern Iran*. Seattle and London: University of Washington Press, 2004.

Ahmed, Shahab. *What Is Islam? The Importance of Being Islamic*. Princeton, NJ, and Oxford: Princeton University Press, 2016.

Algar, Hamid. "Borūjerdī, Ḥosayn Ṭabāṭabāʾī." *Encyclopaedia Iranica* 4:376–379. Online: www.iranicaonline.org/articles/borujerdi-hosayn-tabatabai.

Amamat, Abbas et al., "Constitutional Revolution." *Encyclopaedia Iranica*, 6:163–216. Online: www.iranicaonline.org/articles/constitutional-revolution-index.

Amīn, Aḥmad. *al-Mahdī wa-l-mahdawiyya*. Cairo: Dār al-maʿārif li-l-ṭibāʿa wa-l-nashr, 1951.

Amir-Moezzi, Mohammad Ali. *Le Coran silencieux et le Coran parlant. Sources scriptuaires de l'islam entre histoire et ferveur*. Paris: CNRS Editions, 2011; English translation: *The Silent Qur'an and the Speaking Qur'an: Scriptural Sources of Islam between History and Fervor*. New York: Columbia University Press, 2015.

Amir-Moezzi, Mohammad Ali. *Le guide divin dans le shîʿisme originel. Aux sources de l'ésotérisme en Islam*. Lagrasse: Verdier, 1992.

Amir-Moezzi, Mohammad Ali. "Islam in Iran, x: The Roots of Political Shiʿism." *Encyclopaedia Iranica* 14:146–154. Online: www.iranicaonline.org/articles/islam-in-iran-x-the-roots-of-political-shiisms.

Amir-Moezzi, Mohammad Ali. "Réflexions sur une évolution du shiʿisme duodécimain: tradition et idéologisation." In *Les retours aux écritures. Fondamentalismes présents et passés*, edited by E. Patlagean and A. de Boulluec, 63–81. Leuven: Peeters, 1993.

Amir-Moezzi, Mohammad Ali, and Hassan Ansari. "Muḥammad b. Yaʿqūb al-Kulaynī (m. 328 ou 329/939–40 ou 940–41) et son *Kitāb al-Kāfī*. Une introduction." *Studia Iranica* 38 (2009): 191–247.

Amirpur, Katajun. "Aktuelle Aushandlungsprozesse des Verhältnisses von Religion, Staat und Politik: Eine Positionsbestimmung der heutigen Gegner und Befürworter der *velāyat-e faqīh* in Iran und im Irak." *Asiatische Studien* 66 (2012): 521–564.

Ansari, Hassan. *L'imamat et l'Occultation selon l'imamisme. Etude bibliographique et histoire des textes*. Leiden: Brill, 2017.

Ansari, Hassan, and Sabine Schmidtke. "Al-Shaykh al-Ṭūsī: His Writings on Theology and their Reception." In *The Study of Shiʿi Islam: History, Theology and Law*, edited by Farhad Daftary and Gurdofarid Miskinzoda, 475–497. London: I.B. Tauris, 2014.

al-Anṭākī, Muḥammad Marʿī l-Amīn. *Li-mādhā ikhtart madhhab al-shīʿa, madhhab ahl al-bayt*. Beirut, ca. 1980.

Arjomand, Saïd Amir. "The Conception of Revolution in Persianate Political Thought." *Journal of Persianate Studies* 5 (2012): 1–16.

Arjomand, Saïd Amir. "Imam *Absconditus* and the Beginnings of a Theology of Occultation: Imami Shiʿism *circa* 280–90 A.H./900 A.D." *Journal of the American Oriental Society* 117 (1997): 1–12; repr. in Saïd Amir Arjomand, *Sociology of Shiʿite Islam: Collected Essays*, 74–95. Leiden: Brill 2016.

Arjomand, Saïd Amir. *The Shadow of God and the Hidden Imam: Religion, Political Order and Societal Change in Shiʿite Iran from the Beginning to 1890*. Chicago and London: University of Chicago Press, 1984.

Arjomand, Saïd Amir. *Sociology of Shiʿite Islam: Collected Essays*. Leiden: Brill 2016.

Assmann, Aleida. *Formen des Vergessens*. Göttingen: Wallstein, 2016.

Ayalon, Ami. "From Fitna to Thawra." *Studia Islamica* 66 (1987): 145–174.

Badry, Roswitha. "'Not macht erfinderisch' oder Sexualmoral im Umbruch? Die 'Genuss-Ehe' (*mut'a*) im sunnitischen Kontext." In *Die Grenzen der Welt. Arabica et Iranica ad honorem Heinz Gaube*, edited by Lorenz Korn, 307–319. Wiesbaden: Ludwig Reichert Verlag, 2008.

Bajnūrī, Ghulām Aṣghar. *al-Mustabṣirūn*. Beirut: Dār al-Ṣafwa, 1414/1994.

Bayhom-Daou, Tamima. *Shaykh Mufid*. Oxford: Oneworld, 2005.

Brunner, Rainer. *Die Schia und die Koranfälschung*. Würzburg: Ergon, 2001.

Brunner, Rainer. "Interesting Times: Egypt and Shiism at the Beginning of the Twenty-First Century." In *The Sunna and Shia in History: Division and Ecumenism in the Muslim Middle East*, edited by Meir Litvak and Ofra Bengio, 223–241. New York: Palgrave Macmillan, 2011.

Brunner, Rainer. *Islamic Ecumenism in the 20th Century: The Azhar and Shiism Between Rapprochement and Restraint*. Leiden: Brill, 2004.

Brunner, Rainer. "Shi'ite Doctrine—ii: Hierarchy in the Imamiyya." *Encyclopaedia Iranica*. Online: www.iranicaonline.org/articles/shiite-doctrine-ii-hierarchy-emamiya.

Brunner, Rainer. "'Then I Was Guided': Some Remarks on Inner-Islamic Conversions in the 20th and 21st Centuries." *Orient* 50, no. 4 (2009): 6–15.

Buchta, Wilfried. *Die iranische Schia und die islamische Einheit 1979–1996*. Hamburg: Deutsches Orient-Institut, 1997.

Buchta, Wilfried. "Teherans *Maǧmaʿ at-taqrīb*: Neubeginn islamischer Ökumene oder trojanisches Pferd Irans." In *Encounters of Word and Texts: Intercultural Studies in Honor of Stefan Wild on the Occasion of His 60th Birthday, March 2, 1997, Presented by His Pupils in Bonn*, edited by Lutz Edzard and Christian Szyska, 223–240. Hildesheim: Georg Olms Verlag, 1997.

Buckley, Ronald P. "The Writings of Jaʿfar al-Ṣādiq." In *Books and Bibliophiles: Studies in Honour of Paul Auchterlonie on the Bio-Bibliography of the Muslim World*, edited by Robert Gleave, 14–28. Exeter: Gibb Memorial Trust, 2014.

Clarke, Lynda. "'*ʿAql* (Reason) in Modern Shiite Thought: The Example of Muḥammad Jawād Maghniyya (1904–79)." In *Essays in Islamic Philology, History, and Philosophy*, edited by Alireza Korangy et al., 281–311. Berlin and Boston: Walter de Gruyter, 2016.

Cole, Juan, and Nikki Keddie (eds.). *Shiʿism and Social Protest*. New Haven: Yale University Press, 1986.

Corboz, Elvire. *Guardians of Shiʿism: Sacred Authority and Transnational Family Networks*. Edinburgh: Edinburgh University Press, 2015.

Crone, Patricia. *Medieval Islamic Political Thought*. Edinburgh: Edinburgh University Press, 2004.

al-Daftar, Muḥammad Hādī. *Ṣafḥa min riḥlat al-imām al-Zanjānī wa-khuṭabihi fī l-aqṭār al-ʿarabiyya wa-l-ʿawāṣim al-islāmiyya*. Najaf 1366/1947; repr. Beirut 1417/1996.

Daftary, Farhad. *The Ismāʿīlīs: Their History and Doctrines*. Cambridge: Cambridge University Press, 2007.

Dudoignon, Stéphane et al. (eds.). *Intellectuals in the Modern Islamic World: Transmission, Transformation, Communication*. London and New York: Routledge, 2006.
Ende, Werner. "Der amtsmüde Ayatollah." In *Festschrift für Burkhart Kienast zu seinem 70. Geburtstage dargebracht von Freunden, Schülern und Kollegen*, edited by Gebhard Selz, 51–63. Münster: Ugarit-Verlag, 2003.
Ende, Werner. "Ehe auf Zeit (*mutʿa*) in der innerislamischen Diskussion der Gegenwart." *Die Welt des Islams* 20 (1980): 1–43.
Farmanfarmaian, Fatema Soudavar. "Revisiting and Revising the Tobacco Rebellion." *Iranian Studies* 47 (2014): 595–625.
al-Fukaykī, Tawfīq. "Fī sabīl al-tafāhum." *Risālat al-islām* 12 (1960): 65–73.
Gleave, Robert et al. "Jaʿfar al-Ṣādeq." *Encyclopaedia Iranica* 14:349–366. Online: http://www.iranicaonline.org/articles/jafar-al-sadeq.
Goebel, Karl-Heinrich. *Moderne schiitische Politik und Staatsidee nach Taufīq al-Fukaikī, Muḥammad Gawād Muġnīya, Rūḥullāh Ḫumainī (Khomeyni)*. Opladen: Leske and Budrich, 1984.
Haarmann, Ulrich. "'Lieber hundert Jahre Zwangsherrschaft als ein Tag Leiden im Bürgerkrieg'. Ein gemeinsamer Topos im islamischen und frühneuzeitlichen europäischen Staatsdenken." In *Gottes ist der Orient, Gottes ist der Okzident. Festschrift für Abdoljavad Falaturi zum 65. Geburtstag*, edited by Udo Tworuschka, 262–269. Cologne and Vienna: Böhlau, 1991.
Haeri, Shahla. "Motʿa." *Encyclopaedia Iranica*. Online: http://www.iranicaonline.org/articles/mota.
Haider, Najam. *The Origins of the Shīʿa: Identity, Ritual, and Sacred Space in Eighth-Century Kūfa*. Cambridge: Cambridge University Press, 2011.
Haider, Najam. *Shīʿī Islam: An Introduction*. Cambridge: Cambridge University Press, 2014.
Hajatpour, Reza. *Iranische Geistlichkeit zwischen Utopie und Realismus. Zum Diskurs über Herrschafts- und Staatsdenken im 20. Jahrhundert*. Wiesbaden: Reichert, 2002.
Halm, Heinz. *Die Schia*. Darmstadt: Wissenschaftliche Buchgesellschaft, 1988. Translated by Janet Watson and Marian Hill, *Shiʿism*. New York: Columbia University Press, 2004.
Halm, Heinz. *Shiʿa Islam: From Religion to Revolution*. Princeton, NJ: Markus Wiener Publishers, 1997.
Hawting, G. R. "The Significance of the Slogan *lā ḥukma illā lillāh* and the References to the *ḥudūd* in the Traditions about the Fitna and the Murder of ʿUthmān." *Bulletin of the School of Oriental and African Studies* 41 (1978): 453–463.
Hermann, Denis. "Political Quietism in Contemporary Shīʿism: A Study of the *Siyāsat-i mudun* of the Shaykhī Kirmānī Master ʿAbd al-Riḍā Khān Ibrāhīmī." *Studia Islamica* 109 (2014): 274–302.
Higginson, Thomas Wentworth (trans.). *The Works of Epictetus: Consisting of His Discourses, in Four Books, the Enchiridion, and Fragments*. Boston: Little, Brown, and Company, 1866.

Juynboll, G. H. A. "The Date of the Great *Fitna*." *Arabica* 20 (1973): 142–159.
Keddie, Nikki R. *Religion and Rebellion in Iran: The Tobacco Protest of 1891–1892*. London: Cass, 1966.
Khalidi, Tarif. "Shaykh Ahmad ʿĀrif al-Zayn and *al-ʿIrfān*." In *Intellectual Life in the Arab East, 1890–1939*, edited by Marwan al-Buheiry, 110–124. Beirut: American University of Beirut, 1981.
al-Khūʾī, Abū l-Qāsim. *al-Bayān fī tafsīr al-Qurʾān*. Najaf 1375/1955–56; translated by A. A. Sachedina as *The Prolegomena to the Qurʾān*. New York and Oxford: Oxford University Press, 1988.
al-Khūʾī, Abū l-Qāsim. "Ṣiyānat al-Qurʾān min al-taḥrīf." *Risālat al-islām* 10 (1958): 186–189.
Kippenberg, Hans G. "Jeder Tag ʿAshura, jedes Grab Kerbelaʾ. Zur Ritualisierung der Straßenkämpfe in Iran." In *Religion und Politik im Iran*, edited by K. Greussing and J.-H. Grevemeyer, 217–256. Frankfurt: Syndikat, 1981.
Kohlberg, Etan. "From Imāmiyya to Ithnā-ʿashariyya." *Bulletin of the School of Oriental and African Studies* 39 (1976): 521–534.
Kohlberg, Etan. "In Praise of the Few." In *Studies in Islamic and Middle Eastern Texts and Traditions, in Memory of Norman Calder*, edited by G. R. Hawting et al., 149–162. Oxford: Oxford University Press, 2000.
Kohlberg, Etan, and Mohammad Ali Amir-Moezzi (eds.). *Revelation and Falsification: The* Kitāb al-qirāʾāt *of Aḥmad b. Muḥammad al-Sayyārī*. Leiden: Brill, 2009.
al-Kulaynī, Muḥammad b. Yaʿqūb. *Uṣūl al-kāfī*. Beirut 1428/2007.
Lalani, Arzina R. *Early Shīʿī Thought: The Teachings of Imam Muḥammad al-Bāqir*. London and New York: I.B. Tauris, 2000.
Lemke, Wolf-Dieter. *Maḥmūd Šaltūt (1893–1963) und die Reform der Azhar. Untersuchungen zu Erneuerungsbestrebungen im ägyptisch-islamischen Erziehungssystem*. Frankfurt am Main: Peter Lang, 1980.
Lewis, Bernard. "On the Quietist and Activist Traditions in Islamic Political Writing." *Bulletin of the School of Oriental and African Studies* 49 (1986): 141–147.
Madelung, Wilferd. *Der Imam al-Qāsim ibn Ibrāhīm und die Glaubenslehre der Zaiditen*. Berlin: Walter de Gruyter, 1965.
Madelung, Wilferd. "A Treatise of the Sharīf al-Murtaḍā on the Legality of Working for the Government (*Mas'ala fī 'l-ʿamal maʿa 'l-sulṭān*)." *Bulletin of the School of Oriental and African Studies* 43 (1980): 18–31.
Mallat, Chibli. *Shiʿi Thought from the South of Lebanon*. Oxford: Centre for Lebanese Studies, 1988.
Mariuma, Yarden. "Taqiyya as Polemic, Law and Knowledge: Following an Islamic Legal Term through the Worlds of Islamic Scholars, Ethnographers, Polemicists and Military Men." *Muslim World* 104 (2014): 89–108.
Martin, Vanessa. *Creating an Islamic State: Khomeini and the Making of a New Iran*. London: I.B. Tauris, 2007.

Martin, Vanessa. *Iran between Islamic Nationalism and Secularism: The Constitutional Revolution of 1906*. London: I.B. Tauris, 2013.
Martin, Vanessa. *Islam and Modernism: The Iranian Revolution of 1906*. Syracuse: Syracuse University Press, 1989.
Martin, Vanessa. "Nūrī, Fażl-Allāh." *Encyclopaedia Iranica*. Online: http://www.iranicaonline.org/articles/nuri-fazl-allah.
Medoff, Louis. "Taqiya, i: In Shiʿism." *Encyclopaedia Iranica*. Online: http://www.iranicaonline.org/articles/taqiya-i-shiism.
Mervin, Sabrina. "Normes religieuses et loi du silence: le mariage temporaire chez les chiites du Liban." In *Les métamorphoses du mariage au Moyen-Orient*, edited by Barbara Drieskens, 47–58. Beirut: Presses de l'Ifpo, 2008. Online: http://ifpo.revues.org/452.
Mervin, Sabrina. *Un réformisme chiite. Ulémas et lettrés du Ǧabal ʿĀmil (actuel Liban-Sud) de la fin de l'Empire ottoman à l'indépendance du Liban*. Paris-Beyrouth-Damas: Karthala-CERMOCIFEAD, 2000.
Mughniyya, Muḥammad Jawād. "Ḍarūrāt al-dīn wa-l-madhhab ʿind al-shīʿa al-imāmiyya." *Risālat al-islām* 2 (1950): 387–389.
Mughniyya, Muḥammad Jawād. "al-Mutʿa ʿind al-shiʿa." *al-ʿIrfān* 37, no. 10 (October 1950): 1095–1096; repr. in *al-Shīʿa fī l-mīzān*, 373–374. Beirut 1974.
Mughniyya, Muḥammad Jawād. *Tajārib Muḥammad Jawād Mughniyya*. Beirut 1400/1980.
Mughniyya, Muḥammad Jawād. "al-Taqiyya bayn al-sunna wa-l-shīʿa." *Risālat al-islām* 14 (1963): 39–43; repr. in *al-Shīʿa fī l-mīzān*, 48–52. Beirut 1974.
Naef, Silvia. "Aufklärung in einem schiitischen Umfeld: Die libanesische Zeitschrift *al-ʿIrfān*." *Die Welt des Islams* 36 (1996), 365–378.
Naef, Silvia. "Un réformiste chiite–Muḥammad Ḥusayn Āl Kāšif al-Ġiṭāʾ." *Die Welt des Orients* 27 (1996): 51–86.
Ourghi, Mariella. "Shiite Criticism of the *welāyat-e faqīh*." *Asiatische Studien* 59 (2005): 831–844.
Perrin, Emmanuelle. "Le creuset et l'orfèvre: le parcours d'Ahmad Amîn (1886–1954)." *Revue des mondes musulmans et de la Méditerranée* 95–98 (2002): 307–335. Online: http://remmm.revues.org/index238.html.
Qummī, Muḥammad Taqī. "al-Aqlām fī l-mīzān." *Risālat al-islām* 4 (1952): 147–151.
Rebhan, Helga. *Geschichte und Funktion einiger politischer Termini im Arabischen des 19. Jahrhunderts (1798–1882)*. Wiesbaden: Harrassowitz, 1986.
Ryad, Umar. "A Printed Muslim 'Lighthouse' in Cairo: *al-Manār*'s Early Years, Religious Aspiration and Reception (1898–1903)." *Arabica* 56 (2009): 27–60.
Sachedina, Abdulaziz Abdulhussein. *The Just Ruler in Shiʿite Islam: The Comprehensive Authority of the Jurist in Imamite Jurisprudence*. New York and Oxford: Oxford University Press, 1988.
al-Ṣadr, Muḥammad Ṣādiq. "Ilā Jamāʿat al-taqrīb." *Risālat al-islām* 1 (1949): 358–364.

Sharaf al-Dīn, ʿAbd al-Ḥusayn. *Bughyat al-rāghibīn fī silsilat Āl Sharaf al-Dīn*. 2 vols. Beirut 1411/1991.

Siegel, Evan. "The Politics of *Shahīd-e Jāwīd*." In *The Twelver Shiʿa in Modern Times: Religious Culture and Political History*, edited by Rainer Brunner and Werner Ende, 150–177. Leiden: Brill, 2001.

Sindawi, Khalid. "*Al-Mustabṣirūn*, 'Those Who Are Able to See the Light': Sunnī Conversion to Twelver Shīʿism in Modern Times." *Die Welt des Islams* 51 (2011): 210–234.

Stewart, Devin. "Dissimulation in Sunni Islam and Morisco *Taqiyya*." *al-Qanṭara* 34 (2013): 439–490.

Tucker, Ernest S. *Nadir Shah's Quest for Legitimacy in Post-Safavid Iran*. Gainesville: University Press of Florida, 2007.

van Ess, Josef. *Theologie und Gesellschaft im 2. und 3. Jahrhundert Hidschra. Eine Geschichte des religiösen Denkens im frühen Islam*. Berlin and New York: Walter de Gruyter, 1991–97. Translated by John O'Kane as *Theology and Society in the Second and Third Centuries of the Hijra: A History of Religious Thought in Early Islam*. Leiden: Brill, 2017.

Zayn al-Dīn, Muḥammad Amīn. *Maʿa l-duktūr Aḥmad Amīn fī ḥadīth al-mahdī wa-l-mahdawiyya*. Najaf 1951; repr. Beirut 1413/1992.

al-Zuhaylī, Muḥammad ʿAlī. *al-Mahdī wa-Aḥmad Amīn*. Najaf 1950.

10

Public Piety and the Politics of Preaching among Female Preachers in Riyadh

Laila Makboul

Six months into my fieldwork studying the role of "intellectual female preachers" (*dāʿiyāt muthaqqafāt*) in Riyadh,[1] I was invited to the home of a *dāʿiya* whose views led me to reassess my conception of political quietism. Describing herself as one the first *dāʿiyāt* (sing. *dāʿiya*) in contemporary Saudi Arabia, I initially sought to understand how she perceived the role of a *dāʿiya* in society and as a religious authority.[2] As an example, I mentioned the preacher Nawāl al-ʿĪd, who is known for her engagement in the public sphere and her popularity on social media.[3] Recently, I attended al-ʿĪd's *lecture* titled "al-Ḥaḍāna al-fikriyya li-l-nashʾ" ("Intellectual upbringing for the youth") on how to protect adolescents from political extremism and religious deviance.[4] I assumed that al-ʿĪd, an exemplary public *dāʿiya* who combined religious teachings with public activism, was a case in point. However, the *dāʿiya*'s hesitant response about al-ʿĪd's engagement caught me by surprise. She found it problematic to engage in topics such as terrorism because, as she said, there are many issues to be considered. One challenge that she saw was the question of obedience to the ruler and whether it applied to non-Muslim rulers in Muslim lands. To illustrate this dilemma, she asked whether the Sunnīs of Iraq were obliged to obey former prime minister Nuri al-Maliki.[5] The question was left unanswered, but it opened a Pandora's box of challenging questions regarding the nature of political quietism. Her response revealed her wish to avoid certain political subjects, not because she found politics to be religiously objectionable—but because it could lead her to compromise her convictions, if her opinions went against what was considered politically correct. In fact, she explicitly stated that religion is politics and that part of religion is to criticize political decisions deemed objectionable.[6] Therefore, her unwillingness to engage in the subject of terrorism could be understood as a deliberate avoidance of certain political subjects, out of the conviction that it would lead to concessions she was not willing to make. In other words, eschewing certain political topics meant safeguarding her political independence when the political climate called for it.

In this framework, I explore the "politics" of political quietism among intellectual female preachers. I argue that political quietism constitutes a political behavior and thus departs from a binary understanding of politics in Islamic thought that defines it as either passivism or activism (i.e., an active involvement in political affairs to affect power or change policy).[7] Rather, political quietism is contingent on the context and the agents in question, which I seek to elucidate in my case study of intellectual female preachers in Riyadh. I therefore begin by characterizing the political landscape in the kingdom, before examining the *dāʿiyāt*'s relation to politics. I analyze this by examining the perceptions of Nāṣir al-Dīn al-Albānī's proclaimed policy of abandoning politics (*min al-siyāsa tark al-siyāsa*) and the politico-religious notions of obeying the ruler (*al-samʿ wa-l-ṭāʿa*). I look more closely into how *daʿwa* activities cultivate pious subjects. In line with anthropologist Saba Mahmood, I argue that these activities have the effect of transforming social and political fields[8] and are thus political, albeit quietist, in the sense that they do not involve disobeying the ruler. The chapter is based on data collected throughout my year-long ethnographic fieldwork exploration of *dāʿiyāt muthaqqafāt* in Riyadh in the period between 2015 and 2016. This data should not be read as the position held by all *dāʿiyāt* in this category, but simply as examples of my analysis of the specific topic. Like any other group, the views of these *dāʿiyāt* are as heterogeneous as they are. Notwithstanding their differences, those mentioned in this chapter do share some common perspectives and modes of engagement within the group of *dāʿiyāt muthaqqafāt* that I seek to highlight.

Saudi Salafism and the concept of political quietism

According to Koselleck, political quietism is inherently ambiguous, as concepts "possess a substantial claim to generality, and always have many meanings."[9] Consequently, its meanings are contingent upon the context of the phenomena referred to. In Saudi Arabia, quietism draws its specific denotation from, among other factors, the governing system of the country. Therefore, it is a challenge to recognize the various manifestations of political expressions in the context of Saudi Arabia, which is ruled by an absolute monarchy whose political legitimacy rests on a constitutional framework based on the Qur'ān and the prophetic *sunna*.[10] One common method used to identify political quietism in Saudi Arabia involves, as a point of departure, taking the existing contemporary Salafī groups[11] and delineating them according to their involvement and relationship with the government. In this classification, the quietists are identified as those who demonstrate absolute loyalty to the royal family; they are known as the *Jāmiyya* or the *Madkhaliyya* (named after its popular scholars, Muḥammad Amān al-Jāmī and Rabīʿ al-Madkhalī). On the opposite side, we find political activists influenced by different, often conflicting, political and social trends inspired by the *ṣaḥwa* movement.[12] In the middle are the traditional Wahhābī scholars, whose support for the social and political activism of the *ṣaḥwa* varies. Included in this last category are well-known scholars and former muftis such as ʿAbd al-ʿAzīz b. Bāz and Muḥammad b. ʿUthaymīn. I argue, the female preachers I discuss in this chapter belong to the category of the Wahhābī establishment but are influenced by the social activism of the nonviolent strand of the *ṣaḥwa* movement.

Placing the *Jāmī/Madkhalī* strand on the quietist end of the spectrum and the *ṣaḥwa* movement at the opposite end poses some challenges. The taxonomy of Salafism and the Wahhābī-*ṣaḥwa* synthesis that the *dāʿiyāt* present demonstrates that a continuum exists between the different strands; these preachers can be found at both ends and cannot easily be characterized as mere opposites. More importantly, the view that quietists are passive with regard to politics is erroneous. Clearly, a display of absolute loyalty to a ruler is as much an engagement in politics as opposing a ruler; loyalty, or the lack thereof, is not evidence of the "passivism" that generally characterizes quietism. In addition, the absolute obedience to the Muslim ruler that the *Madkhaliyya* advocate is contingent on a political context, that of a Muslim ruling over Muslim lands. The case of *Madkhalī*s joining military forces in Libya and some getting involved in the political uprising is a reminder of the importance of context in their decision to avoid or engage in politics.[13] By premising their obedience on the "Islamic" nature of the Saudi government, it follows that the *Madkhaliyya* and other Salafī groups are, in fact, arguing for a state that is, by definition, based on political Islam.

Instead of becoming caught up in the distinction between passivism and activism, I turn to an arguably more definable divergence based on methodology, that is, *how* do these Salafī groups approach political power. Here, we find a rich variety among the taxonomy of Salafīs, ranging from the de facto unconditional obedience of the *Madkhalī* trend to the *jihādī*s who deem the government illegitimate. Therefore, by focusing on a measurable variable, we can better examine the activities of the intellectual female preachers within the paradigm of political quietism in the context of contemporary Saudi Arabia. In the next section, I trace the women's conformist attitude toward political power back to their insistence on participating in the political process by engaging in *da'wa*, which is seen as part of state governance and thus lay politics.

"This state is a state of *daʿwa*": Appropriating the *dāʿiyāt*'s relation to the state

The title *dāʿiyāt muthaqqafāt*, a self-proclaimed denomination used by many of the preachers in this study, attests to the two main types of capital that these women lay claim to the religious and the cultural. The development of the intellectual field alongside the religious field facilitated the emergence of the *dāʿiya* in the Saudi public scene in the mid-1980s. This development was precipitated by the introduction of public education in the 1960s, which opened the field of religious studies to women beyond those who were descendants of well-known religious families.[14] These new female religious authorities graduated from institutions that were largely developed by members of the Syrian and Egyptian Muslim Brotherhood who had sought refuge from the repressive Nasserite and Baʿthist regimes. Prominent Syrian and Egyptian members of the brotherhood, such as Muḥammad al-Mubārak, Muḥammad Quṭb, and Mannāʿ al-Qaṭṭān, taught in various universities, where they redefined the curricula.[15] Those affiliated with the brotherhood introduced new religious sciences, such as Islamic culture, and "Islamized" other subjects.[16] By the mid-1980s, an emerging Islamic intelligentsia challenged the Saudi intelligentsia, which, until then, had been associated with liberal trends.[17] It was within this milieu that the *dāʿiyāt muthaqqafāt* emerged.

Like their male counterparts, intellectual female preachers began their careers in the educational system, first as students and later as academics in various universities. Many began preaching on university campuses. Among other activities, they set up gatherings to memorize the Qurʾān and disseminate religious lectures from cassette sermons by renowned scholar preachers, such as the late grand muftis Shaykh Ibn ʿUthaymīn and Shaykh Ibn Bāz.[18] Today, they all hold PhDs, teach in universities, lecture at religious gatherings, and supervise their own religious-intellectual centers. They are introduced by their educational qualifications, as "*duktūra*," and are thus distinguished from preachers who cannot draw on this intellectual authority and are instead simply referred to as *dāʿiya*, or *ustādha*.[19]

The *dāʿiyāt muthaqqafāt* regard themselves as guardians of the religious character of the kingdom, whereby they perform a form of "checks and balances" on the political leadership's upholding of *sharīʿa* and compose a sort of "executive branch" of religious affairs. I attended an event that demonstrated this—the inauguration ceremony of al-Ḥusnā, an organization that describes itself as the first scientific association for Islamic studies for women in the kingdom[20]; it consists of many intellectual female preachers, including Ruqayya al-Nayyāz and Najlāʾ al-Mubārak. A large part of the event's program was dedicated to exalting the kingdom's continuous efforts in *daʿwa* work. It was opened by Princess Hissa, the daughter of King Salman, and consisted of the recitation of poetry praising of Islam, the royal family, and the country. An introduction video of the organization was screened, showing a clip of King Salman stating that Saudi Arabia is "a state of *tawḥīd* and a state of *daʿwa*," whereupon the organizers vowed to uphold this cornerstone of the state with the organization's *daʿwa* efforts. The king's statement was taken from a speech made in a conference on *daʿwa* in 2007, in which he (then governor of Riyadh) reaffirmed the significance of *daʿwa* as an essential aspect of Saudi Arabia's existence, from the time of the first Saudi state and the political-religious alliance between the amir of Dirʿiyya, Muḥammad b. Saʿūd, and the religious reformer Muḥammad b. ʿAbd al-Wahhāb.[21]

The legitimization of the *dāʿiyāt*'s role as guardians of the religious character of the kingdom is drawn from their understanding of *iḥtisāb,* the doctrinal justification of *daʿwa. Iḥtisāb*, understood as the commanding of right and forbidding of wrongdoing (*al-amr bi-l-maʿrūf wa-l-nahy ʿan al-munkar*), is a term commonly used for the civil performance of this instruction.[22] In Nawāl al-ʿĪd's book on women's rights in Islam, it is the notion of enjoining right and forbidding wrong that she refers to when she argues for the right of women to give advice to those in power.[23] She holds that *iḥtisāb* is obligatory for both men and women, and concludes that women must "command to right and forbid wrong, and she may offer her plight to the rulers and perform her role in *al-amr bi-l-maʿrūf wa-l-nahy ʿan al-munkar* on behalf of the general public, her kinsmen, scholars and seekers of knowledge."[24] Consequently, *daʿwa* takes on a meaning beyond the religious endeavor of calling others to Islam—it can also involve an engagement with the political foundation of the kingdom itself. This is also in line with the analysis of social scientist Lacroix, who describes Saudi

Arabia's field of power[25] as made up of a political field, which consists of the royal family, and a religious field, composed of traditional religious scholars.[26] The very activist notion of *iḥtisāb* begs the question of how one might understand a *dāʿiya* (as noted at the beginning of this chapter) who refuses to engage in certain political topics. One explanation may be found in the proclaimed policy of abandoning politics (*min al-siyāsa tark al-siyāsa*), espoused by the renowned late Salafī scholar Muḥammad Nāṣir al-Dīn al-Albānī.

"From politics is to leave politics": Al-Albānī's policy of political disengagement

Few have been more controversial among Salafī groups than Muḥammad Nāṣir al-Dīn al-Albānī. Regarded as one the greatest figures of contemporary Salafī thought, his life and teachings have influenced a wide range of Salafī movements: from the Jamāʿa al-Salafiyya al-muḥtasiba (JSM) that became notorious for the messianic faction that led to the siege of Mecca in November 1979 to the loyalists of the *Madkhalī/Jāmī* strand within the wider *ahl al-ḥadīth* movement.[27] With regard to the subject of this chapter, it was al-Albānī's views on the political activism of the Muslim Brotherhood, and by extension, the *ṣaḥwa* movement, that provoked many to oppose him. In addition to finding faults with Ḥasan al-Bannā's lack of religious scholarship and accusing Sayyid Quṭb of incorporating Sufism, namely, Ibn ʿArabī's "unity of being" (*waḥdat al-wujūd*)[28] in his Qurʾānic commentary, al-Albānī criticized the movement for prioritizing politics over religious knowledge.[29] For al-Albānī, the prime concern for a Muslim should be purifying the Islamic creed (*ʿaqīda*) and inculcating the society with correct religious knowledge—endeavors he termed purification and education (*al-taṣfiya wa-l-tarbiya*).[30] Nevertheless, this did not mean that he disregarded the importance of an Islamic state; rather, he agreed with the aims of establishing an Islamic state but disagreed on the means by which to achieve it. He stated that religious purification and education were necessary conditions for its viability, claiming that "without these two fundamentals (correct knowledge) and (correct education based on this correct knowledge), it is impossible—I believe—to establish the foundations of Islam, the rule of Islam or the Islamic state."[31]

Al-Albānī's work has had a huge impact on the *daʿwa* movement. In effect, the call for purification and education was a call to *daʿwa*. According to al-Albānī, the only remedy for the social ills and the political deterioration in Muslim lands was a return to the religion as taught by the Qurʾān and the *sunna* (the prophetic tradition).[32] This necessitated the existence of qualified preachers who first worked on themselves and then taught the rest of the *umma*, the Muslim nation. He argued that any attempt to establish an Islamic state without sound religious knowledge would be, by default, futile and in vain.

How al-Albānī's ideas, such as the proclamation *min al-siyāsa tark al-siyāsa*, have been understood and practiced by some of the *dāʿiyāt* bring to the fore the underlying political effect of his work. When I asked a *dāʿiya* how she understood his policy of political disengagement, she started by clarifying that religion and politics are inseparable. Therefore, his statement had to be understood in its proper context.[33] To illustrate, she compared it with another statement, that "*min al-sunna tark al-sunna*" (lit., from the *sunna* is to leave the *sunna*), thus implying that part of *sunna* is to leave aspects of *sunna* in certain situations, such as not greeting a person who is sleeping, since that would disturb his or her rest and ultimately violate the *sunna* of the Prophet. In this regard, the *sunna* of greeting a Muslim with the expression *al-salām ʿalaykum* became secondary or even counterintuitive when it leads to the misdeed of disturbing someone. In similar ways, what was initially seen as a call to leave politics was in reality understood as a political act itself, according to the context. This idea is echoed in some books on women's *daʿwa*. For example, in a popular book by Muḥammad Mūsā l-Sharīf (a Saudi historian and a figure in the *daʿwa* movement) on the subject of female preachers, he writes that

> some topics political in nature are not possible to discuss in any event, and in some situations it is difficult to make an opinion about it. Therefore, it is better to leave [these subjects] than to touch upon them [*fa-tutrak wa-lā tuṭraq*], and if the *dāʿiya* is asked about them, she should reply with cleverness and intelligence.[34]

This further demonstrates the reasoning of the *dāʿiya* mentioned earlier in this chapter who did not feel comfortable talking about a controversial topic such as terrorism. A similar contextualization is important in understanding the notion of *al-samʿ wa-l-ṭāʿa*, a major trademark of traditional Salafism, and one that lies at the core of the conception of official political quietism in Saudi Arabia.

"Hearing and obeying"—Absolutism and its limitations

A three-day *ḥadīth* seminar[35] held by Ruqayya al-Muḥārib, a prominent preacher who is also known as a *muftiyya* (a female mufti)[36] among her students, revealed a detailed conception of the notion of hearing and obeying that deserves to be explored in length. The course covered over 900 *ḥadīth*s (from the collection of al-Bukhārī) that had been summarized by the sixth-/twelfth-century scholar Zakī l-Dīn al-Mundhirī and commented on by al-Albānī. Al-Muḥārib took time to explain some *ḥadīth*s more than others; one[37] of those she covered is listed under the section entitled "The best and worse of rulers"; it states,

> The best of your rulers are those whom you love and who love you, who invoke God's blessings upon you and you invoke His blessings upon them. And the worst of your rulers are those whom you hate and who hate you and whom you curse and who curse you. It was asked (by those present): Should we not overthrow them with the help of the sword? He said: No, as long as they establish prayer among you. If you then find anything detestable in them, you should hate their administration, but do not withdraw yourselves from their obedience.

In al-Muḥārib's exegesis of the *ḥadīth*, she made some important distinctions. The first pertains to the nature of the unjust leader's (*ḥākim ẓālim*) offense; she distinguishes between injustice in worldly matters and injustice in religious affairs. The second concerns the course of action incumbent on common people (*ʿawāmm al-nās*) versus that required by people of knowledge (*ahl al-ʿilm*).

In worldly matters, she gave examples of an unjust ruler as someone who allocates lands, properties, and benefits to himself, and appoints his own children, but who is nevertheless in control of Muslim lands (*qāʾim ʿalā bilād al-muslimīn*), where security is widespread, people are able to pray in the mosques, and the ruler protects the borders of the land. In this instance, and despite the ruler's mischief, it is better to remain under his authority than to withdraw one's obedience and engage in strife against him, because the latter would lead to sedition (*fitna*) and great harm. This, she posited, has been the classical understanding in the Sunnī tradition and is the obligation of common people. However, she also stated that if the ruler could be removed safely, without causing *fitna*, as has happened in some situations, then that would be beneficial.

In terms of religious matters and the unjust ruler, she had a much more detailed course of action, one that nevertheless applied to "people of knowledge"[38] and that she stated was also a part of the teachings of the Sunnī tradition. The first applied to a ruler who commits reprehensive actions (*munkar*) in religious matters but who might heed the advice of scholars. In this circumstance, the disavowal (*inkār*) should take place in private. In the second circumstance, when a ruler does not heed the private disavowal, his actions should be disavowed publicly, but then only by those with the necessary credentials to disavow them with knowledge (*ʿilm*) and evidence (*adilla*). It is not clear whether she also includes nonreligious figures, such as politicians and intellectuals. However, the following Qurʾānic verse was recited as proof for her claim: "Why do the rabbis and religious scholars not forbid them from saying what is sinful and devouring what is unlawful? How wretched is what they have been practicing."[39] This verse, and the following situation, specifies that the group that participates in the disavowal must be religious scholars. A third circumstance applies if the *inkār* results in their persecution and imprisonment, and as a result, people cannot benefit from their knowledge. In this case, the *ahl al-ʿilm* must instead disavow the ruler's atrocities in their hearts and focus their efforts on reforming the common people. The last and only circumstance that permits everyone to oppose the ruler is if he promotes blatant disbelief (*kufr bawāḥ*) and corrupts people's faith. This sequential understanding illustrates how obedience, although strict, also has its limitations. A demonstration of this can be discerned from a case in 2013, when al-Muḥārib tweeted that public *inkār* was necessary in response to the singing of a female artist, which took place during the yearly cultural festival of Janādriyya.[40]

It is equally important to understand the political implications of *daʿwa* work and its relation to political quietism. The *daʿwa* movement's work in cultivating piety in society is closely linked to their understanding of al-Albānī's injunction and their subsequent understanding of obedience, which includes the religious reform of the society.

The ruler and the common folk: A relation of congruence

In his work on the theory of congruence, social scientist Harry Eckstein argues that the relationship between authority patterns in "public government" and governance in "private units" consisting of collective individuals is one of congruence.[41] Using Norway as an example, he identified patterns of similarity between the governmental and other authority patterns in society, which, he argues, explain the democratic character of the country's governance. Expanding this idea to metaphysics, we can perceive the worldview of the *daʿwa* movement as a relationship of congruity, in which the well-being of the country and the competence of the government, along with its religious character, are contingent on the piety of the individuals in a society.

"Indeed, God will not change the condition of a people until they change what is in themselves."[42] This often-cited verse lies at the core of the work performed by the intellectual female preachers in *daʿwa*. In a commentary, or exegesis (*tafsīr*) lesson by Ruqayya al-Muḥārib,[43] she explained the Qurʾānic verses (68:17–33) about the story of the sons who inherited a garden from their pious father. Their father used to give a considerable amount of the produce to the poor. After he passed away, the sons thought that their father was foolish to help the poor and so decided that they would no longer share their produce. As a consequence of their decision, God sent a windstorm and ruined the whole garden. Drawing on the lessons from this story, al-Muḥārib emphasized the importance of sharing the blessings and wealth granted to the kingdom with those less fortunate. She reminded the audience that blessings are not limited to food and drinks, as the most important blessing to the country is Islam. She referred to the time prior to the call of Muḥammad b. ʿAbd al-Wahhāb as *jāhiliyya* ("ignorance"),[44] during which the people of the country used to rob caravans, lived in poverty, and worked as migrants in other countries. However, as a result of his *daʿwa*, security spread throughout the country and God gave them the blessings they share today. She ended the lesson by warning the audience of the increasing societal vices, the spreading of atheistic thoughts, and the growing failure to help the needy, all of which she feared would ultimately lead to the loss of the country's security and blessings.

Studying the female *daʿwa* movement in Egypt, anthropologist Saba Mahmood argues that the political efficiency of pious movements is a function of the work they perform in the ethical realm. Extending Mahmood's insight to female preachers, I argue that the political project of the *daʿwa* movement can only be understood through an exploration of their ethical practices.[45]

The lesson of al-Muḥārib demonstrates that the primary political capacity of the *daʿwa* movement lies in the work they perform in cultivating ethical practices among the subjects of the kingdom. For the *daʿwa* movement, the main concern is ethics and morals, which ultimately reflect on society as a whole. By affecting the way people live, the *dāʿiyāt* exert their influence on how subjects and politics are imagined and lived.

This view may explain al-Albānī's insistence that religious purification and education be the pivot of individual endeavors, and also the reason he criticized the state-centered social change of the Muslim Brotherhood. By the same token, there are political implications to avoiding political activity. Arguably, the divergence is more or less on a methodological level, in which those traditionally seen as political activists tend to emphasize the effects that the structure has on the agent, rather than the reverse. In other words, the ruling authorities are seen as a reflection of the character of the entire population. Therefore, the female preachers insist that the individual members of society must first be pious and live according to an ideal God-fearing society in order to affect the political governance of the state. Hence, the primary political activism is focused on cultivating pious subjects and countering everything that may conceivably undermine a life governed by piety.

Conclusions

The examples from the *dāʿiyāt muthaqqafāt* illustrate the challenge of limiting the understanding of political quietism to passivism in politics. Situated in the traditional strand of Salafism, although profoundly influenced by the social activities of the *ṣaḥwa* movement, these women provide rare insights into the ways in which political activism is closely related to context. Legitimating their work as an implementation of the religious characteristics of the political power, while at the same time belonging to the *daʿwa* movement that draws inspiration from al-Albānī's call for a rejection of lay politics, their diverse engagements can seem somewhat contradictory. However, through the lenses of the *dāʿiyāt*, I suggest that al-Albānī's political disengagement should be understood more as a methodological approach to politics in which the cultivation of pious subjects is a necessary and integral part. From dedication to Qurʾānic circles, the circulation of religious reminders (*adhkār*) on social media, to the minute discussions of proper face veiling, the goal of these engagements is to instill piety in the social realm, as this will reflect on the ruling power itself. This epistemological worldview based on a congruity between collective individual action and political power is crucial to understand the *dāʿiyāt*'s insistence on obeying the ruler. Since they regard the ruler as, ultimately, a reflection of the morals of his subjects, their engagement in politics lies foremost in creating a society of pious subjects.

Notes

1 This article is part of my PhD thesis, in which I examine the phenomenon of intellectual female preachers in Saudi Arabia and in Riyadh in particular. I explore the role of these female preachers in the public sphere, as both intellectuals and religious authorities.

2 All my interviewees have been anonymized, and only the names of lecturers in public seminars and conferences are mentioned.

3 As of March 2018, al-ʿĪd's Twitter account (@Nawal_Al3eed) had over five million followers and was thus by far the most followed account of any Saudi woman.

4 Nawāl al-ʿĪd, "Al-Ḥaḍāna al-fikriyya li-l-nashʾ" [The intellectual upbringing of the youth] (lecture, Riyadh, February 9, 2016).

5 *Dāʿiya* A, interview by author, February 23, 2016.

6 This reply came in response to my question regarding her opposition to the UN Convention on the Elimination of All Forms of Discrimination against Women (CEDAW).

7 Katrin Jomaa, "Quietism and Activism," in *Princeton Reference*, ed. Gerhard Böwering, Patricia Crone, and Mahan Mirza (Princeton, NJ: Princeton University Press, 2013), 446.

8 Saba Mahmood, *Politics of Piety: The Islamic Revival and the Feminist Subject* (Princeton, NJ: Princeton University Press, 2012).

9 Reinhart Koselleck, "Futures Past: On the Semantics of Historical Time," *Futures Past* (Cambridge, MA: MIT Press, 1985), 83.

10 The established custom and cumulative tradition based on the Prophet Muḥammad's example. "Sunnah," in *The Oxford Handbook of Islam and Politics*, ed. John L. Esposito (Oxford and New York: Oxford University Press, 2013).

11 The prime objectives of the reform movement known as Salafism were to purge the Islamic tradition of unconditional imitation (*taqlīd*) and reform the moral, cultural, and political conditions of Muslims. "Salafi," in *The Oxford Dictionary of Islam*, ed. John L. Esposito (Oxford: Oxford University Press, 2003). As a historically constructed concept, its meaning has been contested with different, often conflicting, interpretations ranging from those of the modernists who call for a greater use of reason in dealing with modern challenges to the purists, whose main efforts are to call people to orthodoxy and orthopraxy. Henri Lauzière, *The Making of Salafism: Islamic Reform in the Twentieth Century* (New York: Columbia University Press, 2016).

12 A local variation of the Egyptian version of the Muslim Brotherhood, the *ṣaḥwa* movement was characterized by a hybridization of Salafi creed and the social and political activism of the brotherhood. The movement, which began in the 1960s and culminated in the 1990s, consisted of tendencies inspired by both Ḥasan al-Bannā and Sayyid Quṭb. Today, the movement has arguably split into three competing factions consisting of the "new *ṣaḥwa*," which calls for moderation and is primarily occupied with social activism; the Islamo-liberals, who advocate nonviolent constitutional reforms; and the neo-*jihādī*s, who support al-Qāʿida and openly criticize the Saudi government. See Stéphane Lacroix, *Awakening Islam: The Politics of Religious Dissent in Contemporary Saudi Arabia*, trans. George Holoch (Cambridge, MA: Harvard University Press, 2011).

13 Ahmed Salah Ali, "Libya's Warring Parties Play a Dangerous Game Working with Madkhali Salafists," Atlantic Council, online: http://www.atlanticcouncil.org/blogs/menasource/libya-s-warring-parties-play-a-dangerous-game-working-with-madkhali-salafists.

14 Madawi al-Rasheed, *A Most Masculine State: Gender, Politics and Religion in Saudi Arabia* (New York: Cambridge University Press, 2013), 255.

15 Lacroix, *Awakening Islam*, 42–51.

16 Ibid., 45–48.

17 These former intelligentsia were known as technocrats (*tiknūqrāṭī*) or bureaucrats (*bīrūqrāṭī*); they emerged from the bureaucratization process that took place during the 1950s. ʿAbd al-Azīz al-Khiḍr, *al-Saʿūdiyya: Sīrat dawla wa-mujtamaʿ* (Beirut: Arab Network for Research and Publishing, 2010), 491–493.

18 Ruqayya al-Muḥārib, interview by author, September 28, 2016. Another common academic title is *ustādha*, which indicates some kind of higher education. Other labels that *dāʿiyāt* use for themselves are *kātibāt* (writers) or *akādīmiyyāt* (academics); these classifications often overlap, as a *dāʿiya* can also be an academic who publishes books and is therefore a writer as well. These qualifications give them greater flexibility in engaging in various topics outside religious-specific ones and enable them to become experts in a variety of disciplines.

19 al-Ḥusnā, "al-Nashra al-taʿrīfiyya" (Riyadh: al-Ḥusnā: Saudi Association for Islamic Studies, 2016).

20 Ibid.

21 ʿAlī l-Shithrī, "Al-Amīr Salmān: hādhihī l-dawla dawlat daʿwa mundhu taʾsīsihā wa-hiya l-ūlā li-annahā mahbiṭ al-waḥy wa-qiblat al-muslimīn," *al-Riyadh*, June 11, 2007.

22 Another term used is *ḥisba*, which usually applies to the institutionalization of this doctrine and often refers to the governmental agency Hayʾat al-Amr bi-l-Maʿrūf wa-l-Nahy ʿan al-Munkar (Committee for the Promotion of Virtue and the Prevention of Vice, CPVPV).

23 Nawāl al-ʿĪd, *Ḥuqūq al-marʾa fī ḍawʾ al-sunna al-nabawiyya* (Riyadh: N.p., 2006), 443–449, online: www.nawalaleid.com/cnt/lib/154.

24 Ibid., 449.

25 This is a concept taken from Pierre Bourdieu's social theory, in which the field of power is an amalgamation of all fields that have power over social fields. Since some fields are more dominant than others, a hierarchy exists in which some fields are often dependent on activity in another. Patricia Thomson, "Field," in *Pierre Bourdieu: Key Concepts*, ed. Michael James Grenfell (New York: Routledge, 2014). According to Bourdieu, the structure of a field is a *state* of the power relations among the agents or institutions engaged in the struggle. The struggle is for the monopoly of legitimate violence, or authority. Pierre Bourdieu, *Sociology in Question*, trans. Richard Nice (London: Sage, 1993).

26 Lacroix, *Awakening Islam*, 7.

27 The movement is similar to Wahhābism, in its literal reading of sacred texts, fierce opposition to Shīʿism and Sufism, and their close reading of Ibn Taymiyya. They differ from Wahhābism in methodology; while Wahhābīs are more concerned with

creed (ʿ*aqīda*) and tend to follow the Ḥanbalī school of jurisprudence, the *ahl al-ḥadīth* are mainly involved with law (*fiqh*) and call for a complete rejection of any imitation of the four canonical schools of Sunnī jurisprudence. Stéphane Lacroix, "Between Revolution and Apoliticism. Nasir al-Din al-Albani and His Impact on the Shaping of Contemporary Salafism," in *Global Salafism: Islam's New Religious Movement*, ed. Roel Meijer (London: Hurst and Co., 2009).

28 Ibid., 69.

29 Ibid.

30 Jacob Olidort, *The Politics of "Quietist" Salafism* (Washington, DC: Brookings, 2015).

31 Muḥammad Nāṣir al-Dīn al-Albānī, *al-Taṣfiya wa-l-tarbiya* (Amman: al-Maktaba al-Islāmiyya, 2000), 31, online: https://islamhouse.com/ar/books/344363/ (accessed March 7, 2018).

32 Ibid., 14–16.

33 *Dāʿiya* B, interview by author, September 28, 2016.

34 Muḥammad Mūsā l-Sharīf, *al-Marʾa al-dāʿiya: Maʿālim wa-ʿaqabāt wa-maḥādhīr* (Beirut: Dār al-Andalus al-Khaḍrāʾ, 2012), 36.

35 Ruqayya al-Muḥārib, "Zawāʾid Muslim ʿalā l-Bukhārī min *Mukhtaṣar Ṣaḥīḥ Muslim* li-l-imām Zakī l-Dīn al-Mundhirī" (seminar, Riyadh, November 12–14, 2015).

36 A title rarely given to female religious scholars in Saudi Arabia; it implies the authority to issue *fatwā*s, religious opinions. According to al-Muḥārib, she was granted the title by the late grand mufti of Saudi Arabia, Ibn Bāz, on the basis of her work in the field of *daʿwa*. Interviewed by author, September 28, 2016.

37 A *ḥadīth* from *Ṣaḥīḥ Muslim*, from a book compiled by al-Muḥārib's study circle, called *al-Najāḥ*.

38 Al-Muḥārib did not specify who she meant by *ahl al-ʿilm*. Based on the context, we can deduce that she was referring to experts in religious knowledge.

39 Qurʾān 5:63, Sahih International translation, online: https://quran.com/5/63.

40 Ruqayya al-Muḥārib, "#Iʿtidāʾ_ʿalā_ʿuḍū_hayʾa_bi-l-janādriyya," April 13, 2013. The hashtag came in response to the news that a member from the Hayʾat al-Amr bi-l-Maʿrūf wa-l-Nahy ʿan al-Munkar was attacked in his attempt to stop the show.

41 Harry Eckstein, "Congruence Theory Explained" (UC Irvine: Center for the Study of Democracy, 1997), online: https://escholarship.org/uc/item/2wb616g6 (accessed March 28, 2018).

42 Qurʾān 13:11, Sahih International translation, online: https://quran.com/13/11.

43 Ruqayya al-Muḥārib, "Tafsīr" (lecture, Riyadh, December 15, 2015).

44 *Jāhiliyya* is a notion that reoccurs in the narrative of the *dāʿiyāt*; it refers to a religious ignorance that they compare with the ignorance that was believed to exist in the pre-Islamic period.

45 Mahmood, *Politics of Piety*, 35.

Bibliography

al-Albānī, Muḥammad Nāṣir al-Dīn. *al-Taṣfiya wa-l-tarbiya* [Purification and education]. Amman: al-Maktaba al-Islāmiyya, 2000. Online: https://islamhouse.com/ar/books/344363/. Accessed March 7, 2018.

Ali, Ahmed Salah. "Libya's Warring Parties Play a Dangerous Game Working with Madkhali Salafists." Atlantic Council. November 3, 2017. Online: http://www.atlanticcouncil.org/blogs/menasource/libya-s-warring-parties-play-a-dangerous-game-working-with-madkhali-salafists. Accessed March 28, 2018.

Bourdieu, Pierre. *Sociology in Question*. Translated by Richard Nice. London: Sage, 1993.

Eckstein, Harry. "Congruence Theory Explained." UC Irvine: Center for the Study of Democracy, working paper. 1997. Online: https://escholarship.org/uc/item/2wb616g6. Accessed March 28, 2018.

al-Ḥusnā Saudi Association for Islamic Studies. "al-Nashra al-taʿrīfiyya" [Introductory pamphlet]. Riyadh: Saudi Association for Islamic Studies, 2015.

al-ʿĪd, Nawāl. *Ḥuqūq al-marʾa fī ḍawʾ al-sunna al-nabawiyya* [Women's rights in light of the prophetic *sunna*]. Online: http://nawalaleid.com/cnt/lib/154. Accessed March 28, 2018.

Jomaa, Katrin. "Quietism and Activism." In *The Princeton Encyclopedia of Islamic Political Thought*, edited by Gerhard Böwering et al. Princeton, 446–447. NJ: Princeton University Press, 2013.

al-Khiḍr, ʿAbd al-Azīz. *al-Saʿūdiyya: Sīrat dawla wa-mujtamaʿ* [Saudi Arabia: A biography of state and society]. Beirut: Arab Network for Research and Publishing, 2010.

Koselleck, Reinhart. *Futures Past: On the Semantics of Historical Time*. Translated by Keith Tribe. Cambridge, MA: MIT Press, 1985.

Lacroix, Stéphane. *Awakening Islam: The Politics of Religious Dissent in Contemporary Saudi Arabia*. Translated by George Holoch. Cambridge, MA: Harvard University Press, 2011.

Lacroix, Stéphane. "Between Revolution and Apoliticism: Nasir al-Din al-Albani and His Impact on the Shaping of Contemporary Salafism." In *Global Salafism: Islam's New Religious Movement*, edited by Roel Meijer, 58–80. London: Hurst and Co., 2009.

Lauzière, Henri. *The Making of Salafism: Islamic Reform in the Twentieth Century*. New York: Columbia University Press, 2016.

Mahmood, Saba. *Politics of Piety: The Islamic Revival and the Feminist Subject*. Princeton, NJ: Princeton University Press, 2012.

al-Muḥārib, Ruqayya. "#Iʿtidāʾ ʿalā_ʿuḍū_hayʾa_bi-l-janādriyya" [Attack against Hayʾa member in Janadriyya]. Twitter post, April 13, 2013. https://twitter.com/rokaya_mohareb_/status/322538495992283137.

al-Muḥārib, Ruqayya. "Zawāʾid Muslim ʿalā l-Bukhārī min *Mukhtaṣar Ṣaḥīḥ Muslim* li-l-imām Zakī l-Dīn al-Mundharī" [Additional appendix of Muslim to al-Bukhārī

from *Mukhtaṣar Ṣaḥīḥ Muslim* by Imam Zakī l-Dīn al-Mundharī]. Seminar, Riyadh, November 12–14, 2015.
Olidort, Jacob. *The Politics of "Quietist" Salafism*. Washington, DC: Brookings, 2015.
al-Rasheed, Madawi. *A Most Masculine State: Gender, Politics and Religion in Saudi Arabia*. New York: Cambridge University Press, 2013.
"Salafi." *The Oxford Dictionary of Islam*. Edited by John L. Esposito. Oxford, UK: Oxford University Press, 2003.
"Sunnah." *The Oxford Handbook of Islam and Politics*. Edited by John L. Esposito. Oxford, UK and New York: Oxford University Press, 2013.
al-Sharīf, Muḥammad Mūsā. *al-Marʾa al-dāʿiya: Maʿālim wa-ʿaqabāt wa-maḥādhīr* [The female preacher: Outlines, obstacles and precautions]. Beirut: Dār al-Andalus al-Khaḍrāʾ, 2012.
al-Shithrī, ʿAlī. "al-Amīr Salmān: hādhihī l-dawla dawlat daʿwa mundhu taʾsīsihā wa-hiya l-ūlā li-annahā mahbiṭ al-waḥy wa-qiblat al-muslimīn" [Prince Salman: This country has been a country of *daʿwa* since its establishment, because, first and foremost, it is the cradle of revelation and the prayer direction of Muslims]. *Al-Riyadh*, June 11, 2007. Online: http://www.alriyadh.com/256427. Accessed March 28, 2018.
Thomson, Patricia. "Field." In *Pierre Bourdieu: Key Concepts*, edited by Michael James Grenfell, 65–80. New York: Routledge, 2014.

11

The Gülen Movement in Azerbaijan: Political Quietism or *Taqiyya*?

Fuad Aliyev

Introduction

The post-Soviet Republic of Azerbaijan has been experiencing an Islamic revival since its independence in 1991. This process has involved domestic as well as transnational Islamic activism. Given the sectarian differences among the population, the revival process also encompasses an element of conflict between Shīʿī and Sunnī activists and groups.

The Gülen movement (or Hizmet movement), a Turkish network of Fethullah Gülen's followers, is one of the most active faith-based networks in Azerbaijan. It targets a diverse stratum of the population—the rich urban elite, provincial people, the poor, businessmen, and youth. However, the movement differs from others in the way it operates—generally, religious ideology is hidden behind a façade of secular media, educational, social, and business institutions. The Gülen movement ignored the issues that are important to marginalized religious activists and devout Muslims in Azerbaijan, like the ban on *ḥijāb* in schools and for passport photos, the closure of mosques, social discrimination against veiled women and bearded men, and other related social problems.

The Gülen movement's passive approach to the fate of Islam in Azerbaijan led other Islamic activists to criticize them for un-Islamic behavior, introducing innovations (*bidʿa*), ignoring the problems of religious Muslims, and for having a hidden political agenda. The question is, what makes the Gülen movement in Azerbaijan so different from the other locally operating Islamic movements and how does it differ from its operations in Turkey and other countries? Does it naturally emanate from the ideology of declared political quietism? Or is this "quietism" really the chameleon-like pragmatism of a movement trying to work in a country with limited opportunities by integrating itself into the local circumstances and waiting for momentum? That is, are they practicing a form of *taqiyya* (religious dissimulation in Islam, sometimes observed when Muslims are threatened, persecuted, or oppressed)? In this chapter, I address these questions by exploring the history, organizational structure, and current developments of the Gülen movement in Azerbaijan.

Turkish religious influence and the Gülen movement in Azerbaijan

Turkish religious influence represented by state and non-state religious organizations headquartered in Turkey is widespread in post-Soviet Azerbaijan. These organizations have played a crucial role in the revival of Sunnī Islam in Azerbaijan, which is predominantly Shīʿī.[1] Moreover, Turkish religious influence in Azerbaijan was probably more powerful than Turkish influence in other post-Soviet countries, given the historic, geographic, linguistic, and cultural closeness.

Turkish religious actors in Azerbaijan can be divided into three groups: the official public entity—the state board for religious affairs of the republic of Turkey (Diyanet), followers of Sufi orders, and Nurcular.

The Diyanet has been extremely active in Central Asia, Georgia, and particularly in Azerbaijan. It is a huge organization mandated to organize matters related to the beliefs, worship, and moral principles of Islam. Turkey uses the Diyanet as an instrument to increase its Islamic presence in the region.[2] It has constructed numerous mosques, publishes and disseminates large amounts of religious literature, funds the theology department at Baku State University, and contributes to various educational projects.

The followers of Sufi orders in Azerbaijan are restricted and mainly operate in the regions Sheki, Qazakh, Gabala, Goycay, and Aghdash, where there is a significant Sunnī population. There are also orders in Baku. The Sufis are mainly followers of the Naqshbandiyya order. Among the most well-known official Sufi institutions are the Mahmut Ziya Hudayi Foundation, the Süleymancılar, and the community of Osman Nuri Topbaş.

Among the Turkish religious organizations in Azerbaijan, the most effective and successful is the Gülen movement of Nurcu origin; for decades it has advanced Turkey's soft power globally.[3]

The so-called Nurcular—disciples of Said Nursi (1876–1960)—were among the first to engage in religious activities in post-Soviet Azerbaijan. The group is named after Said Nursi, an influential figure in the religious affairs of Kemalist Turkey; his philosophy and teachings were collected in a book called *Risale-yi nur*. He opposed secularism and Mustafa Kemal Ataturk's policies and was arrested and imprisoned in 1935 for eleven years.[4] Nursi's movement was a semi-secret, highly motivated network of obedient followers, and thus, has often been considered a threat by the Turkish government. Today, the Nurcular are divided into groups, most of whom are involved in business, education, and faith-based activism.

The movement of Fethullah Gülen is the most powerful, elaborate, and widespread group among the Nurcular. Gülen managed to create a strong, vertically structured organization of devoted followers.[5] A number of characteristics distinguish it from the other followers of Said Nursi: it has a clear hierarchy, stricter discipline, secret statutes, and a focus on the media and business institutions rather than religion.[6] For instance, the typical city-level Turkish cell is usually organized into the following levels: *şagirdler* (students), *uy imam*s (leaders of groups of five people), *semt imam*s (associations of five people based on the urban district or educational institution), and *bolge imam*s (head of district/region level). Students are recruited and controlled at the local level by *abi*s (brothers) or *abla*s (sisters). According to the experts I have interviewed, the confidentiality of the network is crucial and strictly maintained.[7] The movement has substantial financial resources to fund its social activities and political power, in both Turkey and abroad.[8] According to some experts, it is the largest religious movement in Turkey.[9]

The presence of the Gülen movement in Azerbaijan dates to the early 1990s, when the movement opened schools and took on a significant role in the social and educational life of Azerbaijan. The Gülen movement established itself in Azerbaijan just after its independence from the Soviet Union. Moreover, Azerbaijan was the first country outside Turkey where schools were opened—this began in 1992.[10] The history of the movement's first steps in the country started with the visit of İlhan İşbilen, the general manager of the newspaper *Zaman*; he began by establishing contacts with the government for the movement's activities. As a result, the movement opened *Zaman* newspaper, the first school, Samanyolu TV, and a number of business entities and companies. In the meantime, Ali Bayram, the head representative of the movement's Güney-Doğu region, visited the head of the Nakhchivan Autonomous Republic, at that time Heydar Aliyev, who later became the president of Azerbaijan, and the Gülen movement continued to support the region during the Armenian blockade.[11]

The Gülen movement was never directly and openly involved in religious activities; rather, the dissemination of Gülen-Nursi ideas occurred through informal personal contacts among students and instructors, and businesses.[12] Influencing the local elites helped the movement promote its values, but more importantly, enabled it to obtain business and political support.

Moreover, the schools established by the Gülen movement did not have any serious problems with the government of Azerbaijan until 2014, when they were shut down, presumably at the request of the AKP government in Ankara, who tried to thwart Gülen followers by all means and wherever possible.[13] However, the AKP government was not successful in its efforts to suppress Gülen's influence in Azerbaijan. According to Azerbaijani journalist Aqil Alesger, Gülen-affiliated schools continue to operate, but under new names and with "new" founders: university preparation courses called *araz* have been replaced by other courses with different names, usually related to the newly established Guven Printing House (the sole provider of training material and the testing center for all the schools), while the staff of the lyceums owned by Çağ Oyretim (a company affiliated with the Gülen movement) that were shut down are now involved in managing and teaching at the newly established "Istek Lyceums" network.[14]

As noted, the Gülen movement avoided direct missionary activity and promoted its brand of Islam indirectly and informally through personal communications and networking. As seen from the diagram below, the Gülen movement is the only "faith-based" movement that created its own education system, business empire, and ran TV, radio, and press institutions in Azerbaijan; no other Turkish group has gained so much influence. Hundreds of various Turkish and local business enterprises are part of the network, either as active members and donors or as sympathizers. Gülen supporters were a part of Azerbaijan International Turkish Industrialists' and Businessmen's Association (TUSIAB), which coordinated the businesses affiliated with the movement, those owned by local members or those that indirectly supported the Gülen movement. However, after 2013, under pressure from the Turkish government, the state of Azerbaijan began a gradual purge of this organization.

The network institutions were mutually supportive and cooperative. Members of the Gülen network are required by their "elder" brothers/sisters in the network to buy from Gülen-affiliated shops, eat in places that are part of the

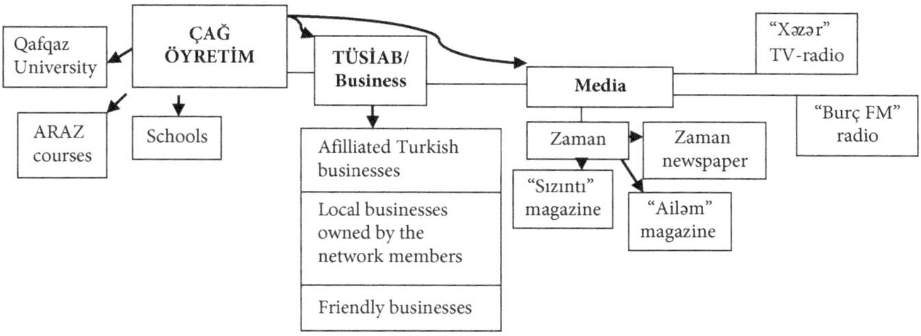

Figure 11.1 The Gülen network scheme in Azerbaijan before 2014.

network, and watch only STV or Xazar TV, Xazar radio, or Burc FM radio, and read periodicals and publications owned by *Zaman*.[15]

The Gülen movement is structured in circles that correspond to the degrees to which someone adheres to the values of Fethullah Gülen and then makes an institutional commitment.[16] The central circle is the *cemaat* (Turkish for "community"), which is the core in the hierarchy, where Gülen's closest and most trusted followers can be found. The second circle is the *arkadaşlar* (Turkish for "friends"), an expansive network of followers who live according to Gülen's teachings—these people work to help achieve the movement's objectives. The third circle is made up of sympathizers—supporters of the movement and those who occasionally participate in its activities, but are not necessarily aware of Gülen's teachings (e.g., journalists, business people, public officials, former alumni of the movement's schools, and friends). Finally, there are consumers—the recipients of the movement's products (e.g., education, businesses); their value is mainly as consumers.[17] The third and fourth circles are not necessarily formal parts of the network but are utilized to serve the needs and objectives of the movement. This makes the Gülen movement a Muslim faith-based organization that has been able to achieve a sophisticated and not fully identifiable network of support.

Political quietism or *taqiyya*?

In the social sciences, there are various approaches to political quietism. For instance, Bernard Lewis defines "quietism" as something opposite to "activism" and highlights the conditional nature of political quietism in Islam, in which quietism is only practiced when Muslims are compelled, "because the alternatives are worse, and because only in this way can the basic religious and legal prescriptions of Islam be maintained."[18] In this chapter, I define political quietism as the acceptance, by a faith-based movement, of existing circumstances, their withdrawal from political affairs, and skepticism about the feasibility of establishing an "Islamic state" or even "Islamic government."[19] We define *taqiyya* as the practice of religious dissimulation in Islam when under threat, persecution, or compulsion. The question is whether withdrawing from political affairs in the case of Azerbaijan was the Gülen movement's strategy or a tactical move allowed by Islam to enable its adherents to survive and expand under the circumstances, with the objective of changing in the future, when they are stronger, more powerful, and more influential.

The Gülen movement is believed to have long-term goals; for this reason, they work with the younger generation and thus invest in its future.[20] They try to solve all the problems their followers may face, from education to employment and accommodation. Upon the completion of their studies, Gülen's followers can work in the companies that are linked to the overall structure and are also encouraged to work in the public sector. In exchange for obedience, students and other members are taken care of by the network, which addresses their educational, employment, and accommodation needs. This strategy ensures their access to the future elite and strengthens the positions of their followers, supporters, and sympathizers in all spheres—politics, business, education, media, and civil society.

One of the graduates of Gülen's schools that I interviewed described the way students were approached, depending on their potential:

> As a student of Gülen's school, I can say that the environment in these schools was very friendly and heartwarming. The language of education was English. It was a very good way of promotion, especially at those times [in the 2000s]. In the first years of education, pupils were taught only the basics of the religion and a lot about patriotism. Moreover, the first years were also memorable, with teachings to love Islam and one's parents, but there were no religious studies courses. There were some students, who conducted the daily Muslim prayers, but teachers and *abi*s were actually against it. Intensive religious instruction mainly starts in the ninth year, for the students who are either successful in classes or took leading places in the various science Olympics. The rest of the students were taught in the tenth or eleventh years. In any case, everything was done secretly. Pupils were warned not to tell anyone about the literature distributed and so on.

> When students graduate, they keep in touch with them and show their assistance in Azerbaijan as well as in foreign countries.[21]

The movement's operational environment in Azerbaijan does not provide much opportunity for political activism; any political opposition by Islamic movements is immediately and harshly responded to and ended (the Azərbaycan İslam Partiyası, Cümə Məscidi icması, Müsəlman Birliyi, etc.).[22] The Gülen movement understood this and adjusted its language and actions accordingly. This is a perspective and position that other faith-based actors have not taken. As a result, the Gülen movement has been the most successful in terms of its capacity to deliver attractive messages to target audiences and to adapt to local conditions—two factors that are critical for transnational religious actors to achieve their objectives.

Given the secular nature and cautious attitude toward independent and foreign religious activism, the Gülen movements' secular form and humanitarian and educational messages worked well among the general public and the government in Azerbaijan. The capitalist pragmatism and business activities of all levels of the movement helped position it as a friend not only of Azerbaijan but also of the ruling elite in particular. Gülen's followers in Azerbaijan adapted to the local conditions for faith-based activism by avoiding open religious propaganda, to say nothing of open criticism of the government; rather, they operated purely as an educational, humanitarian, and business network.[23] According to Turkish researcher Bayram Balci:

> The movement adopted a unique action plan that largely surpassed the religious sphere to which previous organizations had limited themselves. It opted to tailor its strategy to the customs, needs, and expectations of its host countries, determining references to religion and Turkishness on a case-by-case basis according to local sensibilities, the social and ideological environment, and the degree of openness and acceptance encountered on the ground, which may vary within the same country.[24]

In general, in 2009 and 2010 the Nurcu network in Azerbaijan (not Gülen followers, specifically) was subject to significant criticism by the local media, which accused it of brainwashing the youth and turning them into obedient novices. Also in 2009 and 2010, several waves of anti-Nurcu reports and negative media coverage were accompanied by the occasional arrests of Turkish nationals for distributing religious propaganda and encouraging extremism. The reasons for these developments are not clear, and such campaigns may have been initiated by the political or business opponents of the movements. For example, numerous media reports featured "confessions" of former network members, who wrote about their recruitment and revealed brainwashing methods and information about the movement's strict hierarchical organizational structures. According to the media reports, the movement tried to bring the youngsters studying in their schools into the *ishik evi* or *yurd* houses—these are apartments large enough to accommodate more than fifteen students and three or four *abis* or *ablas*. In these houses, they were given lessons on the teachings of Said Nursi.[25] The head of Azerbaijan's spiritual board of the Caucasus Muslims—the de facto ministry of Islamic affairs—Shaykh al-Islam Hajji Allahshukur Pashazade, was also, on several occasions, critical of Nurcu ideology and their activities in Azerbaijan and may have been behind these anti-Nurcu campaigns.[26]

Although Fethullah Gülen's name was not always mentioned in this anti-Nurcu rhetoric, in the public view, his followers were also a part of this network. In fact, the Nurcu activists in Azerbaijan who were arrested were usually the youth (either Azerbaijani or Turkish) who spread Said Nursi's works; no direct affiliates of Gülen have been ever prosecuted. Other less "quietist" non-Gülen Nurcu activists have been involved in direct religious activities, *madrasas*, etc., especially in the regions of Azerbaijan. And often the negative coverage was about other Nurcular (e.g., Mustafa Sungur followers) rather than Gülen's network.[27]

It should be mentioned that Azerbaijan's political opposition did not appreciate the pro-governmental orientation of the Gülen movement. Thus, opposition and independent political and social activists also strongly criticized Gülen's followers, who stressed their "hypocrisy" and "opportunism" for turning a blind eye to the "continuous restrictions on the freedom of expression and assembly" in the country and for regularly praising Azerbaijan's leadership.[28] According to those I interviewed for this chapter, the graduates of Gülen schools, teachers, and *abis* in general tried to avoid political discussions; in fact, any oppositional views of students were not welcome and were counteracted. Only pro-government political attitudes were allowed and supported.

Besides negative attitudes toward the Gülen movement from some secular media outlets and political opposition, the movement's relations with other major religious activists in Azerbaijan were also tense. As noted, Azerbaijan's Shaykh al-Islam was critical of all Turkish movements and publicly criticized Nurcular, of which Gülen is a part. Many independent Shīʿī and Sunnī activists see the movement as conformist and hypocritical because the Gülenists were silent about the *hijāb* ban in schools, the closing of some mosques (including Turkish mosques), the attempts to ban the *adhān*, the Baku city administration, the persecution of bearded men, and other similar problems that directly affected the everyday lives of many practicing Muslims regardless of their sectarian affiliation.[29] For instance, according to informal interviews with Shīʿī religious leaders in Azerbaijan, the movement was labeled as non-Islamist and applied *taqiyya* as a political maneuvering tool to avoid prosecution, strengthen over time, come to power, and advance its interests as well as the interests of Turkey against the Azerbaijan's Shīʿī majority. On the other hand, Azerbaijani Salafis have been critical of the movement's methodological and especially theological innovations and viewed them as "people of *bidʿa*" who were "misled."[30]

However, this partial public opposition to Nurcu activism did not undermine the overall success, and ultimately the Gülen movement in Azerbaijan and elsewhere did well practicing this strategy (or tactic) of political quietism. This was the case until the 2013 conflict with the AKP government in Turkey.

The AKP-led government recognized the global influence of the Gülen movement, and its benefits to Turkey, particularly the way it enhanced Turkey's soft power.[31] Initially, Gülen's followers cooperated closely with the AKP, and some of the Gülen-affiliated public figures even joined the AKP party. This coalition was based on common Islamic roots and similar interests. This was also true with regard to Turkey's interests in Azerbaijan. For instance, the visit by Prime Minister Recep Tayyip Erdogan to Baku in January 2003 was organized by business circles related to the Gülen movement.[32] Erdogan and Fethullah Gülen shared the same social base and for years held similar ideas and objectives.

Gülen's followers in the Turkish security forces are believed to have played a crucial role in the so-called Ergenekon and Sledgehammer cases in 2008, which led to the arrest of Turkish army officers and purged the army of Kemalists.[33] United against the same enemy, they forgot their differences, until their common threats were defeated.[34]

After Erdogan's campaign against Gülen's school network in Turkey in late 2013, Fethullah Gülen's followers in the security forces and judiciary effectively sought to undermine Erdogan's authority and accused members of his family and inner circle with corruption.[35] Erdogan pushed back by firing thousands of judiciary personnel and police officers or moving them to other jobs, shutting down the investigation, and increasing pressure on Gülen's religious, educational, and commercial network.[36] In July 2016, the government immediately associated the unsuccessful coup by some army officers with Gülen; this was the most critical conflict and led to the movement's decline in Turkey and many other places, including Azerbaijan. Erdogan used this opportunity to eliminate the supposed followers and sympathizers of Fethullah Gülen from all branches of power.

Although the Gülen movement has long positioned itself as a social movement (i.e., one that is society-centric) that integrates itself into the society, there are some signs that it is "reformist" in the sense that it hopes to control the state or shape policies by forming an interest group within the government or in alliance with other interest groups.[37] From the beginning of the movement's operations in Azerbaijan, it targeted either the children of the current elite, through their involvement in education institutions, or talented young people, who could become future technocrats, business, and political elites. According to informal sources and experts, there were and still may be several members of the parliament (both pro-government and opposition) and high-ranking officials in the president's office and other governmental bodies who are either affiliated to or supportive of the movement.

Given that the Gülen movement is elite-based and strongly hierarchical, there have long been speculations about its hidden agenda. I would conclude that these speculations, now fueled by recent developments in Turkey, indicate that the goal of the movement is not actually to "integrate" into the present government, but "accommodate" it in the long term, and/or the Gülen movement could be practicing *taqiyya* in its operations.[38] Thus, the post-Islamist integrative society-centered activism exercised by the Gülen movement is not political quietism but a post-modernist practice of classic *taqiyya*.

The secretive nature of the Gülen movement, its Christian missionary-style tactics, and its external disassociation from religious and political activism, in which it focuses on education and business, are reminiscent of its activities in Turkey twenty years ago when opportunities were much narrower, and the movement's behavior was much different and extremely cautious. This might be the case again for the Gülenists in Turkey for years to come given the current unprecedented level of pressure by the AKP government.

Whatever the real motivation behind and the extent to which the accusations against the Gülen movement can be substantiated, one thing is clear: for years, Gülen's followers and sympathizers, under the banner of political quietism, were infiltrating the government, political parties, law enforcement agencies, the army, the judiciary, and the business elite in Turkey to the extent that they managed to establish a parallel to the formal authorities and thus challenge a strong government with ambitious and charismatic leaders. Indeed, the movement could have been attempting to build a kind of "parallel state" as defined by President Erdogan in Turkey and as recent developments have demonstrated, even if one dismisses all the hysteria, exaggerations, and conspiracy theories surrounding these claims. It is now more evident that this apolitical stance and outer integration was a matter of tactics rather than a strategy for Turkey and could be the case for other areas.

The case of Azerbaijan also demonstrates that continuous pressure from the AKP government has led to certain policy measures against the Gülen movement and limited its presence in the social and economic affairs of Azerbaijan. The reason behind the Azerbaijani government's unwillingness to preclude the movement's presence and influence can be explained by two decades of its active "elite penetration" and growing political influence under the label of political quietism. There might be extreme resistance to such attempts to preclude the movement in Azerbaijan, given that the network has been functioning in the country since 1993 and was supported by the government all the time it was deeply rooted in all spheres, from the economy to the education system. It is natural that there will be reluctance to resist this movement, given the benefits it has brought. Moreover, there are direct or indirect links between Gülen-related institutions and companies and decision-makers in Azerbaijan. However, now no one is likely to want to be affiliated with Fethullah Gülen, and many members of the Gülen movement and friends of Gülen have outwardly turned their backs on him and even criticized the movement and its actions in Turkey.[39] This worsening operational environment and the new challenges it now faces could lead the Gülen movement to enter a new level of *taqiyya*.

Conclusion

The Gülen movement has been the most successful faith-based social movement in post-Soviet Azerbaijan. It effectively utilized available opportunities and positioned itself as a nonreligious, apolitical movement that accepts the existing status quo and rules of the game. Its international business networks, charities, foreign lobbying capacities, and successful educational institutions have made it a close and valuable ally of the official government in Baku.

Given the current relations between the state and religious organizations, the perceived threat of Iranian religious influence, and the spread of al-Qāʾida Daesh (ISIS) terrorism in Azerbaijan, the Gülen movement positioned itself as an alternative version of moderate, "politically acceptable" Islam. Without making direct references to religion, it played by the established rules and supported the ruling elite. Thus, the Gülen movement demonstrated a lack of political ambition and its full support for the ruling party in Azerbaijan, in what would seem to be a brilliant example of political quietism.

However, after the recent developments in Turkey and with new information on the network's expansionist operations and attempts to penetrate the elite in Azerbaijan, it is increasingly difficult for the Gülen movement to maintain the same claims regarding its apolitical intentions and quietism. Now the arguments of those who considered the movement's integrative approach quasi-quietist and just an example of a postmodernist version of *taqiyya* have much greater weight.

The movement's transformation and changing operational forms, as well as the fact that most of the businesses and some public figures considered to be affiliated with the movement have maintained their positions, can be explained by a certain level of resistance and unwillingness to fully eliminate the presence of the Gülen movement in Azerbaijan. Moreover, many members and friends now outwardly "forget" about their previous connections and love for Fethullah Gülen, and sometimes even criticize him and his supporters in Turkey; this is an example of either mass betrayal or higher levels of *taqiyya* in response to the changing environment.

Notes

1 B. Balci and A. Goyushev, "Changing Islam in Post-Soviet Azerbaijan and Its Weighting on the Sunni/Shiite Cleavage," in *The Dynamics of Sunni-Shia Relationships: Doctrine, Transnationalism, Intellectuals and the Media*, ed. B. Maréchal and S. Zemni (London: Hurst, 2012).

2 A. Raufoglu, "Turkey's Diyanet Sparks Concerns in Central Asia and Caucasus," *Southeast European Times*, March 13, 2012, online: http://turkey.setimes.com/en_GB/articles/ses/articles/reportage/2012/03/13/reportage-01 (accessed May 2013).

3 F. Aliyev, "Islam and Turkey's Soft Power in Azerbaijan: The Gülen Movement," in *Religion and Soft Power in the South Caucasus*, ed. A. Jödicke (New York: Routledge, 2018).

4 B. Balci, "Fethullah Gülen's Missionary Schools in Central Asia and Their Role in the Spreading of Turkism and Islam," *Religion, State & Society* 31, no. 2 (2003): 151–177; A. Şık, "İmamın Ordusu," online: http://xeberler.files.wordpress.com/2011/04/51984426-dokunan-yanar.pdf (accessed January 11, 2018).

5 F. Aliyev, "Islamic Activism as a Social Movement: Recent Issues of Religion and Politics in Azerbaijan," *Caucasus Analytical Digest* 72 (April 29, 2015): 3–5.

6 Şık, "İmamın Ordusu"; T. Keskin, "Market-Oriented Post-Islamism in Turkey," in *Secular State and Religious Society: Two Forces in Play in Turkey*, ed. B. Turam (New York: Palgrave Macmillan, 2012), 121–142; Balci, "Fethullah Gülen's Missionary Schools"; Aliyev, "The Gülen Movement in Azerbaijan," *Current Trends in Islamist

Ideologies 14 (December 2012), 90–103, online: https://www.hudson.org/content/researchattachments/attachment/1160/20130124_ct14aliev.pdf (accessed July 29, 2018); Aliyev, "Islamic Activism as a Social Movement."

7 Aliyev, "Islam and Turkey's Soft Power."

8 Aliyev, "Islamic Activism as a Social Movement."

9 J. Alekperov, "«Турецкий гамбит» и взгляд из-за океана," online: http://1news.az/authors/130/20120620030903621.html#page999 (accessed July 2012).

10 N. Goksel, "Religiously-Inspired Bonding: Changing Soft Power Elements in Turkey's Relations with Azerbaijan," *Center for Conflict Prevention and Early Warning* 4, no. 8 (2011), online: http://www.cpc-ew.ro/occasional_papers/008.pdf.

11 Aliyev, "Islamic Activism as a Social Movement."

12 Aliyev, "Islamic Activism as a Social Movement."

13 B. Balci, "The Gülen Movement and Turkish Soft Power," *Carnegie Endowment for International Peace*, February 4, 2014, online: http://carnegieendowment.org/2014/02/04/g%C3%BClen-movement-and-turkish-soft-power (accessed January 11, 2018).

14 A. Alesger, "Azərbaycanda fətullahçılar 'vuruldu' yalanının pərdəarxası və ya yerli 'imamlar' kimlərdir?" *Yeni Cag*, July 27, 2016, online: http://yenicag.az/azerbaycanda-fetullahcilar-vuruldu-yalaninin-perdearxasi-ve-ya-yerli-imamlar-kimlerdir-arasdirma/ (accessed August 2016).

15 T. Turan, "Keçmiş Nurçu Tələbənin Etiraflari," *Yeni Müsavat*, May 28, 2009, online: http://www.musavat.com/new/%C3%96lk%C9%99/53858-KE%C3%87M%C4%B0%C5%9E_NUR%C3%87U_T%C6%8FL%C6%8FB%C6%8FN%C4%B0N_ET%C4%B0RAFLARI (accessed August 2012).

16 J. Hendrick, *Gülen: The Ambiguous Politics of Market Islam* (New York: New York University Press, 2013).

17 Ibid.

18 Bernard Lewis, "On the Quietist and Activist Traditions in Islamic Political Writing," *BSOAS* 49 (1986), 142.

19 A. Sachedina, "Forms of Political Participation in Muslim Political Heritage," in *Comparative Political Thought: Theorizing Practices*, ed. M. Freeden and A. Vincent (New York: Routledge, 2013).

20 Aliyev, "Islam and Turkey's Soft Power."

21 Personal interview, Baku, May 2013.

22 Aliyev, "Islamic Activism as a Social Movement."

23 Aliyev, "Islam and Turkey's Soft Power."

24 B. Balci, "What Future for the Fethullah Gülen Movement in Central Asia and the Caucasus?" *Central Asia Caucasus Analyst*, July 2, 2014, online: https://www.cacianalyst.org/publications/analytical-articles/item/13006-what-future-for-the-fethullah-g%C3%BClen-movement-in-central-asia-and-the-caucasus (accessed January 11, 2018).

25 A. Yunusov, *Islamic Palette in Azerbaijan* (Baku: Adiloglu, 2012).
26 Aliyev, "Islamic Activism as a Social Movement."
27 Yunusov, *Islamic Palette.*
28 E. Mamedov, "Azerbaijan: Evaluating Baku's Attitude Toward the Gülen Movement," online: Eurasia.net, February 16, 2012: http://www.eurasianet.org/node/65013 (accessed January 11, 2018).
29 Aliyev, "Islamic Activism as a Social Movement."
30 Balci and Goyushev, "Changing Islam in Post-Soviet Azerbaijan."
31 Balci, "The Gülen Movement and Turkish Soft Power."
32 J. Rohozifski, "Azerbaijan and Turkey: The Light and Shade of 'Turkish' Brotherhood," online Oval.az, February 22, 2016, http://oval.az/azerbaijan-and-turkey-the-light-and-shade-of-turkish-brotherhood/ (accessed January 11, 2018).
33 D. Rodrik, "Is Fethullah Gülen behind Turkey's Coup?" Dani Rodrik's weblog, July 23, 2016, online: http://rodrik.typepad.com/dani_rodriks_weblog/2016/07/is-fethullah-g%C3%BClen-behind-turkeys-coup.html (accessed January 11, 2018).
34 Balci, "The Gülen Movement and Turkish Soft Power."
35 J. Dorsey, "Who Is Fethullah Gülen? A Modernizer or a Wolf in Sheep's Clothing?" *Huffington Post*, July 17, 2016, online: http://www.huffingtonpost.com/james-dorsey/who-is-fethullalh-gulen-a_b_11043092.html (accessed January 11, 2018).
36 Ibid.
37 Aliyev, "Islamic Activism as a Social Movement."
38 Aliyev, "Islam and Turkey's Soft Power."
39 Alesger, "Azərbaycanda fətullahçılar."

Bibliography

Alekperov, J. "«Турецкий гамбит» и взгляд из-за океана" [The "Turkish gambit" and the view from over the ocean]. Online: http://1news.az/authors/130/20120620030903621.html#page999. Accessed July 2012.

Alesger, A. "Azərbaycanda fətullahçılar 'vuruldu' yalanının pərdəarxası və ya yerli 'imamlar' kimlərdir?" [Who are the hidden or local "imams" of the "Fethullah-followers are under attack in Azerbaijan"]. *Yeni Cag*, July 27, 2016. Online: http://yenicag.az/azerbaycanda-fetullahcilar-vuruldu-yalaninin-perdearxasi-ve-ya-yerli-imamlar-kimlerdir-arasdirma/. Accessed August 2016.

Aliyev, F. "The Gulen Movement in Azerbaijan." *Current Trends in Islamist Ideologies* 14 (December 2012): 90–103. Online: https://www.hudson.org/content/researchattachments/attachment/1160/20130124_ct14aliev.pdf. Accessed July 29, 2018.

Aliyev, F. "Islam and Turkey's Soft Power in Azerbaijan: The Gülen Movement." In *Religion and Soft Power in the South Caucasus*, edited by A. Jödicke. New York: Routledge, 2018.

Aliyev, F. "Islamic Activism as a Social Movement: Recent Issues of Religion and Politics in Azerbaijan." *Caucasus Analytical Digest* 72 (April 29, 2015): 3–5.

Balci, B. "Fethullah Gülen's Missionary Schools in Central Asia and Their Role in the Spreading of Turkism and Islam." *Religion, State & Society* 31, no. 2 (2003): 151–177.

Balci, B. "The Gülen Movement and Turkish Soft Power." *Carnegie Endowment for International Peace*. February 4, 2014. Online: https://carnegieendowment.org/2014/02/04/g-len-movement-and-turkish-soft-power-pub-54430. Accessed July 29, 2018.

Balci, B. "What Future for the Fethullah Gülen Movement in Central Asia and the Caucasus?" *Central Asia Caucasus Analyst*. July 2, 2014. Online: https://www.cacianalyst.org/publications/analytical-articles/item/13006-what-future-for-the-fethullah-g%C3%BClen-movement-in-central-asia-and-the-caucasus. Accessed January 11, 2018.

Balci, B., and A. Goyushev. "Changing Islam in Post-Soviet Azerbaijan and Its Weighting on the Sunni/Shiite Cleavage." In *The Dynamics of Sunni-Shia Relationships: Doctrine, Transnationalism, Intellectuals and the Media*, edited by B. Maréchal and S. Zemni, 195–215. London: Hurst, 2012.

Dorsey, J. "Who Is Fethullah Gülen? A Modernizer or a Wolf in Sheep's Clothing?" *Huffington Post*. July 17, 2016. Online: http://www.huffingtonpost.com/james-dorsey/who-is-fethullalh-gulen-a_b_11043092.html. Accessed January 11, 2018.

Goksel, N. "Religiously-Inspired Bonding: Changing Soft Power Elements in Turkey's Relations with Azerbaijan." *Center for Conflict Prevention and Early Warning* 4, no. 8 (2011). Online: http://www.cpc-ew.ro/occasional_papers/008.pdf.

Hendrick, J. *Gülen: The Ambiguous Politics of Market Islam*. New York: New York University Press, 2013.

Keskin, T. "Market-Oriented Post-Islamism in Turkey." In *Secular State and Religious Society: Two Forces in Play in Turkey*, edited by B. Turam, 121–142. New York: Palgrave Macmillan, 2012.

Lewis, Bernard. "On the Quietist and Activist Traditions in Islamic Political Writing." *BSOAS* 49, no. 1 (1986): 141–147.

Mamedov, E. "Azerbaijan: Evaluating Baku's Attitude Toward the Gülen Movement." Online: Eurasia.net, February 16, 2012: http://www.eurasianet.org/node/65013. Accessed January 11, 2018.

Raufoglu, A. "Turkey's Diyanet Sparks Concerns in Central Asia and Caucasus." *Southeast European Times*. March 13, 2012. Online: http://turkey.setimes.com/en_GB/articles/ses/articles/reportage/2012/03/13/reportage-01. Accessed May 2013.

Rodrik, D. "Is Fethullah Gülen behind Turkey's Coup?" Dani Rodrik's weblog, July 23, 2016. Online: http://rodrik.typepad.com/dani_rodriks_weblog/2016/07/is-fethullah-g%C3%BClen-behind-turkeys-coup.html. Accessed January 11, 2018.

Rohozifski, J. "Azerbaijan and Turkey: The Light and Shade of 'Turkish' Brotherhood." Online: Oval.az, February 22, 2016. Online: http://oval.az/azerbaijan-and-turkey-the-light-and-shade-of-turkish-brotherhood/. Accessed January 11, 2018.

Sachedina, A. "Forms of Political Participation in Muslim Political Heritage." In *Comparative Political Thought: Theorizing Practices*, edited by M. Freeden and A. Vincent, 126–140. New York: Routledge, 2013.

Şık, A. "İmamın Ordusu" [The army of imam]. Online: http://xeberler.files.wordpress.com/2011/04/51984426-dokunan-yanar.pdf. Accessed January 11, 2018.

Turan, T. "Keçmiş Nurçu Tələbənin Etiraflari" [Confessions of a former Nurcu student]. *Yeni Müsavat*, May 28, 2009. Online: http://www.musavat.com/new/%C3%96lk%C9%99/53858-KE%C3%87M%C4%B0%C5%9E_NUR%C3%87U_T%C6%8FL%C6%8FB%C6%8FN%C4%B0N_ET%C4%B0RAFLARI. Accessed August 2012.

Yunusov, A. *Islamic Palette in Azerbaijan*. Baku: Adiloglu, 2012.

12

The Neo-Traditionalist Critique of Modernity and the Production of Political Quietism

Walaa Quisay

Introduction

The production of a form of political quietism in the religious landscape of Western Islam commends itself to multiple scopes of interpretation. Indeed, the politically charged climate after 9/11, the wars in Iraq and Afghanistan, the turmoil after the Arab Spring, and the increased rise of Islamophobia led Muslims to simultaneously engage and disengage with politics. Against this political backdrop, a group of Sufi-inclined neo-traditionalist *shuyūkh* (sing. *shaykh*) gained popularity. They stressed the Muslim community's need for introspection as opposed to political action. Their discourse affirmed the importance of connecting to the religious tradition, which had been obscured by modernity. In this chapter, I focus primarily on the philosophical production of political quietism of three popular neo-traditionalist *shuyūkh* in the West—Hamza Yusuf, Abdal Hakim Murad, and Umar Faruq Abd-Allah. In their critique of modernity, the positioning of notions of authority is essential to the production of political quietism. These *shuyūkh* juxtapose the Islamic "tradition"—as layered, structured, and essentially "enchanted," and they also recognize authority and hierarchy—with modernity. Modernity, in turn, represents paradigmatic ruptures in systems of meaning and established hierarchies of the past. Political quietism becomes a means by which some semblance of authority is maintained. Therefore, they formulate their religious contentions with reference to social science literature on religion, tradition, and modernity. Here, I highlight how the process of meaning-making is interlinked and how it reaffirms authority in the political philosophy of these three neo-traditionalist *shuyūkh*.

Hamza Yusuf, Abdal Hakim Murad, and to a lesser degree Umar Faruq Abd-Allah are all leading religious authorities in the West. Their popularity extends beyond young members of the community. They have been involved in several international campaigns spearheaded by governments in the Middle East and in the West to combat religious extremism and promote intra-religious tolerance.[1] Among their religious following, the *shuyūkh* represent a wealth of intellectual depth absent in other religious groups in the West. They act as both spiritual philosophers and sociologists of the modern world. Additionally, they were considered among the top 500 most influential Muslims.[2] At the outset, "neo-traditionalism" as a religious concept needs to be defined. Abdullah Bin Hamid Ali—a faculty member at Zaytuna College and one of Hamza Yusuf's colleagues—explains,

> When I say that I am a "neo-traditionalist," what I mean by it is that I incline towards and participate in the movement to return to the classical adherence to the schools of Islamic law (4 Sunni Schools), the study and contextualization of mainstream Sunni doctrine (viz., Ash'ari, Maturidi), and the study and practice of traditional text-based Islamic spirituality (historically referred to as Sufism).[3]

This is based on the understanding that *ahl al-sunna wa-l-jamāʿa*, in the past, belonged to one of the four recognized *maddhabs*—Ḥanafī, Shāfiʿī, Mālikī, and Ḥanbalī. They followed one of the two schools of *ʿaqīda*—the Ashʿarī or the Māturīdī[4]—and belonged to a Sufi order (*ṭarīqa*). They have received traditional knowledge—both exoteric and esoteric—through an unbroken chain of transmission. Their religious authority is derived through this process of transmission. The neo-traditionalists thus consider themselves custodians of the tradition that has been marginalized and obscured by modernity.

Locating the quietism in the *shuyūkh*'s discourse on tradition is an arduous task. This is due to the elusiveness of the concept in and of itself. According to Robert Gleave, when one refers to political quietism in the Islamic context, this could indicate one of five positions held and encouraged by religious scholars.[5] It could be a categorical rejection of forms of rebellion against the governing authorities. "Rebellion" could refer to armed action or nonviolent rebellion that leads to the overthrow of these governing authorities. Second, it could refer to a refusal to engage in forms of political activism. This stance often entails a theological critique of the religious premises on which "Islamism" is based. Third, political quietism could be understood as a complete rejection of working with any form of political power based on the idea that it is entirely corrupting. On the other hand, quietism could represent an unconditional loyalty to the ruling power. Last, Gleave explains that political quietism could refer to the acceptance of the legitimacy of the ruling power—regardless of who they may be. These are not apolitical stances; each makes very clear political statements. They are also not mutually exclusive. In the case of the *shuyūkh*, they make an argument for each one of these five positions, albeit they apply them selectively. In this chapter, I focus on two dimensions of political quietism—rejecting rebellion and Islamist activism, and affirming the legitimacy and the necessity of ruling authorities. In this case, Islamist activism represents the fragmentation inherent in modernity, while the state represents the stability that ensures a continuity in the tradition.

Islamism as a result of the Protestantization of Islam

The fragmentary force of Islamism was developed through the epistemic structures of modernity. Its main features are said to include rupture or break with tradition, the deconstruction of authority, rationalization, objectification of meaning, and the eventual loss of the comprehension of transcendental meaning altogether. Therefore, the neo-traditionalists' critiques of modernity and of Islamism are deeply interlinked.[6] The so-called Islamic modernists of the nineteenth century paved the road,[7] in epistemological terms, to the rise of Islamist movements. Muslims, with the advent of modernity, have "sunk into theological shallowness that allows violent fundamentalists to fill the vacuum."[8] Abdal Hakim Murad explains this epistemological structure by defining Islamic modernism as "a *danse macabre* flirting with the spiritual death of the Enlightenment."[9] That is to say, Islamic modernism will inevitably lead to nihilism. Its objectification and secular rationalization of the transcendent through the epistemological paradigms of the Enlightenment voids the faith of all structures of meaning; its revolutionary tendencies depend on this intellectual mayhem. Hamza Yusuf expands on this genealogy of ideas by locating the origins of modern revolutionary violence and fragmentation in the French Revolution.[10] Muslims have lost something of the past; the spiritual and political order of the tradition maintained a form of hierarchy and spiritual harmony. Modernity has alienated Muslims from their religious tradition. Now as modern "autonomous subjects," Muslims feel a need to dictate or inform their own realities without faith in the grander designs of God, thereby externalizing *jihād* and disregarding its internal truth. In doing so, Muslims have lost the concept of a meaningful cosmos.

Thus far, the "tradition" has involved the notion of a harmonious cosmos, enchantment, esoteric and exoteric authority, and meaning. The agency of the believer is mediated by these layers of authority. This of course changed in the neo-traditionalist narrative with the Muslim "secular age." The story begins with the Wahhābī "Protestantization" of Islam in the eighteenth century. The Wahhābī movement sparked a transformation in the way Muslims approached their faith. It first began by deconstructing methodological and scholarly authorities in the religion. It sparked a change in notions of agency, most importantly, by attacking Sufi practices such as visiting shrines and asking for the intercession of saints. The *shuyūkh* contend that the Wahhābī movement instigated the process of disenchantment. The nineteenth century proved to be a paradigmatic moment of modernist fragmentation. So-called Islamic modernists, such as Muḥammad ʿAbduh, Jamāl al-Dīn al-Afghānī, and Rashīd Riḍā in the Arab East and Ben Bādīs and al-Fāsī in the Arab West and their South Asian reformist counterparts like Sayyid Aḥmad Khān and Muḥammad Iqbāl, in awe of Western colonial advancement and convinced of their own technological inferiority, attacked institutions of Islamic spirituality or scholastic authority. As Hamza Yusuf puts it, "They believed that the Muslims were far too 'otherworldly'—that the Sufis had taken hold of their understanding to such a degree that they really forgot about the world itself."[11] They borrowed notions of rationality and anti-institutional theological stances entrenched in post-Enlightenment modernist thought. Colonialism, Yusuf contends, "undermined the spiritual authority of the scholars of Islam, making them appear backward and foolish by promoting the idea that the scholars' religious cosmologies paled before the impressive pillars of modern science."[12] ʿAbduh, who was no more than a "stooge" for the British Empire,[13] essentially secularized the study of Islam. In so doing, he and his reformist counterparts innovated an epistemic shift in the way Muslims understand their religious tradition that was totally divorced from the Islamic tradition.

The "Islamic modernists" of the nineteenth century then paved the epistemological road to the rise of Islamist movement, just as the Wahhābī movement did in the eighteenth century. The forefathers of the Salafiyya movement and the student of Muḥammad ʿAbduh—Rashīd Riḍā—were instrumental to the ideological formation of the first and most prominent Islamist group—the Muslim Brotherhood.[14] Yusuf explains that the founder of the Muslim Brotherhood—Ḥasan al-Bannā—was the ideological product of Riḍā's religious school of thought.[15] These activist tendencies gave rise to new notions of selfhood, what Charles Taylor calls the "buffered" self. Not only has it separated the self from its rightful position in the order of the cosmos, but it also positioned the self, rather than God, as the center of the cosmos.

According to Abdal Hakim Murad, in an attempt to govern the meanings of the faith, Islamism reified them. This process of reification voided religious practice of all transcendental meanings.[16] Religious tenets with a metaphysical reality became symbols used for political instrumentalization. Islamism made "the religion a refuge for angry youth who use it as a political platform to rage against the injustice of the West."[17] The harmonious cosmological order has been disrupted, authorities have fragmented, religious practice has been externalized, and meanings have been voided.

In the neo-traditionalist narrative on the Muslim "secular age," the sense of loss of meaning has been amplified. In this "secular age," Muslims have become disenchanted and are heading down a road to nihilism. Abdal Hakim Murad argues that "we are no longer in a story. We don't have a narrative. Even when old stories intrude they void its meaning; take out the eschatology."[18] He is essentially explaining what Charles Taylor held to be the features of our secular age. Our age is haunted by a distant memory of a cosmos that had once been enchanted.[19] However, meanings are now stripped of their claim to truth or relation with transcendence. He explains that "we are enjoying the enormous free void that is freed by the departure of ontology, metaphysics, ethics and everything that used to restrict and restrain us."[20] This void is the nihilism inherent in disenchantment. Is the Western Muslims' disenchantment and quest for meaning the same as that which Taylor outlined as describing a secular age? Are Muslims in the West facing the anxieties of a distinctly post-Christian secular age? Additionally, does political stability always maintain transcendental meaning? Is authority inherently meaningful? Lastly, how can the attempt to insert meaning into modern political authority be read in the light of Taylor's notion of re-enchantment?

Order and authority in the cosmos

The standing of political leadership in the tradition represents order in a fragmenting world. Political leadership, even when it is corrupt, is seen as absolutely essential. Hamza Yusuf explains in an interview,

> By glorifying our leaders and our *ʿulamāʾ* God will rectify our world and the hereafter. When we denounce our leaders and *ʿulamāʾ*, we lose our *dunyā* and our hereafter. Exalting the leaders is the basis for society. If the government is not respected and [instead is] abused, how will the people feel secure? The greatest blessing of Allah onto people is security.[21]

In another interview he says, "most rulers are oppressors in one way or another."[22] At the outset these may seem to be contradictory views. If most leaders are oppressive in one way or another, how is it possible that God will be pleased when people glorify them? The function of political leadership, even when oppressive or corrupt, is to create a semblance of order. Disorder, political strife, and anarchy are disruptive forces in an otherwise harmonious cosmos. Political oppression is a way for God to test the faith of his servants; will they direct their *jihād* internally or externalize it? For this reason, righteous people and scholars refused to engage with politics. According to Hamza Yusuf, the four imams—Abū Ḥanīfa, al-Shāfiʿī, Ibn Ḥanbal, and Mālik—never engaged in politics.[23] Despite this being a highly disputed claim, it is indicative of the way in which the neo-traditionalists depict the tradition.[24] The question of agency, as understood in what the neo-traditionalists call Islamic cosmology, resurfaces once again. The political authority, despite the overwhelming probability that it will be oppressive, represents a fixed reality that ensures order. *Fitna,* which Hamza Yusuf translates as "political strife,"[25] represents fragmentation and dissolution. If an individual believer were to participate in *fitna* or increase this fragmentation, this would threaten the harmony of the cosmos. Human agency is relegated to the place of devotion, prayer, and acquiring knowledge; by contrast, it is up to the divine to change political authority. This was how traditional Muslims understood the order of the cosmos.

Traditional Muslims in the past recognized their position in the cosmos. They accepted and internalized the notion of anthropic realism—the belief that human beings and the cosmos fit together or belong together.[26] Implicit in this cosmos-centric vision is the acceptance of a deeper metaphysical reality. This inward knowledge of metaphysics was manifested in *taṣawwuf* and assembled in the structures of *ʿaqīda*.[27] Both the natural and what is man-made exist within this cosmic system that accepted the metaphysical reality of the necessary existence and power of God.[28] In the tradition, Muslims recognized that the cosmos was organized, layered, and meaningful; they had an understanding of recognized authorities. The notion of authority and hierarchy becomes especially important because they provide a sense of stability—be it the epistemic stability of "orthodoxy" or a political stability. Authority also assumes inherent esoteric and exoteric truths that imbue the cosmos with meaning and, in doing so, relegates meaning beyond the human agent. Therefore, belief is not a matter of volition, but the recognition of an objective reality that exists outside the human agent.[29] Religious authorities, be they the methodological authority of a specific *madhhab* or that of a religious scholar who personifies it, do not derive their authority merely from outward knowledge; they also carry a form of gnosis absent but recognized by individual Muslims. Umar Faruq Abd-Allah therefore defines tradition as the "reception of a rich past, a profound past with metaphysics, theology and law and a deep understanding of civilisation that we receive not just in word but in spirit."[30] The scholars, their religious methods, and saintly authority are signifiers of a porous cosmos.[31] Their charismata or *karamāt* show that the world is open and vulnerable to the enchanted "outside" world.

The greatest transformation emblematic of our time, according to Taylor, is the shift from a cosmos-centric view to a universe-centric one. "Taylor encapsulates this imaginary shift as … the move of spontaneously imagining our cosmic environment as an ordered, layered, hierarchical, shepherded *place* to spontaneously imagining our cosmic environment as an infinite, cavernous, anonymous *space*."[32] The cosmic environment essentially becomes devalued, voided of "charged" meanings and decentered from any notion of objective truth. Unlike the "porous self" of pre-modernity, the human agent becomes what he calls the "buffered self." Smith defines the "buffered self" as one "no longer vulnerable to the transcendent or the demonic."[33] Unlike the porous self, there is a clear boundary and a defined agency separate and even superior to the cosmic order. Human beings are then free to reorder the universe and assign symbolic meanings to it.[34] Taylor argues that even this disenchanted age is haunted by the idea of transcendence. Smith says, "We live in the twilight of both gods and idols that have refused to depart. We become tempted by belief by intimations of transcendence."[35] According to Taylor, humans therefore seek meanings, paradoxically, by assigning meanings and arranging them. The notion of meaning here is used in the sense of the "meaning of life" or of a relationship as having great "meaning" for us.[36] The shift in the location of meaning from objects and the cosmos to the mind of the individual, buffered self is the key signifier of the secular age rather than belief in God or lack thereof; therefore, in reality, the instinct for re-enchantment does not enchant the cosmos. Still, it is the hope of regaining a system of meaning that can anchor humans to the transcendent.

Assigning meaning, re-enchantment, and the production of political quietism

The way Abdal Hakim Murad explains the economic problems of modernity is a prime example of the link between the metaphysical and the political. In a lecture he presented titled "Britain's void of meaning," he locates the roots of our economic woes to 1914, when the gold standard began to crumble because Germany no longer used it.

> In many ways that is a more fundamental transformation than the beginning of the genocidal mega-conflicts of the 20th century because wars come and they go but we are still off the gold standard. What does that mean? It means from a shariʿah perspective that we are de-centred, that meaning is gone that there is no refereniality. [Gold] is the material because it's to do with the sun. It is to do with cosmos itself. Its inherently valuable.[37]

In the hierarchy of material, gold reaffirms the centrality of a cosmos-centric vision and therefore maintained the structures of meaning. By contrast, now money has no point of reference and refers only to its symbolic imagined worth. This fragmentation of solid referential truths makes sense to a postmodern state, which does not accept objective truths.

The juxtaposition of gold, as essential to the order and meaning of the cosmos, and "genocidal mega-conflicts," as relatively inconsequential, is an interesting point of analysis. Murad's point is not to belittle the scale of suffering caused by genocides of the twentieth century. Rather, he explains that the material loss of life could be overcome and not disorient one from the coordinates of the cosmos, while when the gold standard was dropped, the coordinates were lost. It is easy to see how a statement such as this can lead to the production of political quietism. The primary concern is not material existence, but the esoteric symbols that anchor this existence to the transcendent. This, however, highlights a tension since these genocides were a result of the formation of the modern nation-state, as Wael Hallaq points out. He says, "It is impossible not to conclude that the genocides and atrocities of the twentieth century (and the present one) are the direct product of the phenomenon of the nation-state."[38] He then quotes Finlayson that "as a dialectic of modernity, nationalism is the pay-off for a disenchanted world, the mythic, naturalised, non-rational fantasy produced by the demythologising, 'rational' development of the state."[39] The question, therefore, that presents itself is, what are the limits of meaning-making?

The concept of a nation in of itself becomes enchanted in the sense that the nation forms a hierarchy by which to counter fragmentation. In this sense, we can assign metaphysical meanings to the idea of citizenship and country.[40] The structures and internal mechanisms of the state ought to be respected and engaged with. For example, in the context of a country that would normally not allow protests, Muslims should not engage in them.[41] However, as Hamza Yusuf has argued, because protesting is a part of the structure on which the state is built, it is morally incumbent on American Muslims to engage in such protests as a great American tradition.[42] This shifts again depending on whether or not protests institutionally challenge the authority of the state. However, the modern nation-state propagates the supremacy of the epistemological ideals of secular modernity;[43] thus, there is an inherent tension. The nation-state itself does not make that metaphysical claim. As Finlayson argues,

> [the nation] comes to stand in for a guiding force of social and individual life. This in turn leads to identification with the nation and its figureheads as the grounding for subjectivity. Nationalism offers autonomy (self-determination) and particularity in the form of subjugation to a universal. It is an instituting moment for the self, society and the state .... Humanity no longer worships gods but rather itself as the transcendental nation.[44]

In the Anglo-American context, the position of the state in the discourse of the *shuyūkh* becomes even more precarious. Affirming it as an authority in the face of political and social fragmentation thereby reproduces forms of political quietism. Many Muslim activists have been especially critical of the *shuyūkh* on that front and vice versa. This political quietism exists in two domains reflecting four of the politically quietist positions that Gleave outlines.[45] The first domain rejects all forms of "rebellion" and is very critical of the role of activism. In recent years, this position has been illustrated by a deep mistrust of the "Left–Muslim" alliance and Islamist activism. The second domain calls for the acceptance and affirmation of the legitimacy of the state and calls for loyalty to it. These positions are complicated by the heightened rise of Islamophobia, racism, and Anglo-American military interventions in Muslim countries. Therefore, they are often coated in apologetics rather than in clear political and religious statements.

Hamza Yusuf's criticism of the "Left–Muslim" alliance generated much debate and controversy after his appearance in the Reviving Islamic Spirit (RIS) conference in 2016.[46] On stage, Yusuf was asked by a presenter, Mehdi Hassan, how Muslims could better show solidarity with other anti-racist struggles such as the "Black Lives Matter" (BLM) movement. He responded by first stating that the United States, in terms of its laws, is one of the least racist societies. He then went on to say that there is not a word for "racism" in Arabic; there are modern words, but not "classical" ones. He then said that out of the 15,000–18,000 homicides in the United States, 50 percent of them are black on black crimes. There are twice as many whites shot by the police, but no one shows these videos.[47] Yusuf was severely criticized by imams and activists, prompting him to release an apology and a clarification of his position. He said,

> My point is that the biggest crisis facing the African American community in the United States is not racism but the breakdown of the Black family ... We have to be very careful, especially as minority communities, in falling in the agendas of other people. There are people in the United States who would like to see a race war; who would like to see violence in our communities. We have anarchists who want to see a complete breakdown of society.[48]

The anarchists he is referring to here are the activists on the Left and especially those active in the BLM movement.

There is much that could and has been said about the controversy from the vantage point of race politics and white privilege[49]; however, here my scope is limited to a discussion of the production of political quietism and order. In these statements, Yusuf makes four points. He invokes the authority of the "sacred tradition" as something that epitomizes truth. Racism being a modern construct, its mechanisms are therefore a result of the breakdown of reality and are not an essential point of analysis in of itself. Second, he points out that the state's antidiscrimination laws are some of the best. This, in turn, affirms the legitimacy of the state and shields it from criticism. On the other hand, the burden of stabilizing the community and ending the violence falls on the black community. Lastly, Yusuf locates and warns of the problem of fragmentation. The main problem is not racism, but the breakdown of the black family, and if Muslims are not perceptive, they will follow the whims of those who wish to deepen the fragmentation of society. The United States—as a nation with its legal apparatuses—demands a form of loyalty. Activism in turn becomes synonymous with anarchism. This engenders fragmentation, which further exacerbates problems faced by the African American community. Yusuf's political quietism in this instance becomes a call for loyalty to the state, introspection on the level of the people, and a warning against fragmentation.

The *shuyūkh* found the religious Right to be a natural ally in their anti-activist, statist, and quietist approaches. Abdal Hakim Murad called for a "sacred alliance of conservative believers." Traditionalists of all faiths seem to have similar concerns regarding the breakdown of traditional social order and systems of meaning inherent in it.[50] To add to this point, Hamza Yusuf argued,

> One of our major problems right now is our inability to speak to the Right. I think before 2001, we had a lot of Muslims who were registered Republicans. ... That's no longer the case. Millennials have shifted incredibly towards the Left, so we don't have an ability to talk to them, and I think Republicans, when they hear a certain type of speech they immediately shut down, and for me, looking at people, I think the biggest opportunity that we have is to recognize that there are a lot of decent people out there.[51]

Indeed, the moral alliance with the Right extends beyond an agreement on a set of socially conservative issues such as their stances on LGBTQ rights, family values, and anti-secular initiatives.[52] It permeates issues of concern to the Muslim community itself.

Upon the election of Donald Trump, the Muslim community mobilized to protest his policies, especially the so-called Muslim ban.[53] Hamza Yusuf rejected the efficacy of such initiatives. He said,

> We have too much work to do, not protesting, not lighting fires, not saying, "Trump is not my president." He is, and that is how our system works: by accepting the results and moving on. Now we have to work to make sure our educational, political, and scientific institutions, which are some of the finest in the world, are protected and perfected.[54]

Indeed, this has been, arguably, the philosophy of Hamza Yusuf since the 9/11 attacks. He has worked with many of these governments, in the belief that advising them could bring greater benefit to the Muslim community.[55] Islamophobia is a marginal issue, since all minority communities in the past had to face racism as a rite of passage.[56] Hamza Yusuf was appointed one of George Bush's religious advisers. Yusuf was successful in dissuading Bush from naming his "military's impending operation in Afghanistan, "Infinite Justice," because it would offend Muslims, who believe the only source of infinite justice is God. Mr. Bush responded by changing the operation's name to "Operation Enduring Freedom.""[57]

Working with governments does not necessarily absolve them when they err; in fact, that is not even the point. Political quietism is based on the understanding that order is needed for metaphysical meanings to be realized and working within the framework of the state could ensure that. Yusuf makes this point in the RIS conference by saying,

> One, keeping recognition that we have a metaphysical lens that we look at the world with, and always seeing God behind these things. God is in charge: Trump is a servant of God (ʿabd Allāh), just like everyone else. He'll either serve with good or with evil, but he will serve God. And so it's important for us, as people who want and aspire to be servants of good to be that good in the world so that other people can see that. I am a deep believer in *fitra*, in that principal nature of human beings. The *fitra* is good, and we should allow people, even the worst people, to change.[58]

Quietism, therefore, becomes a means by which believers allow the cosmic will of God to be manifest. This is indeed tied to the "traditional" outlook the *shuyūkh* urge Muslims to maintain. The ruptures caused by modernity, along with the fragmentation inherent in activist political philosophy, alienated mankind from a cosmos-centric vision.

In conclusion, neo-traditionalist *shuyūkh* construct state authority as something essential to an Islamic cosmology. The decline of this state authority is another symptom of the fragmentation of modernity. To the neo-traditionalists, the authentic, traditional cosmos-centric view is differentiated from the modern universe-centric one in terms of authority and the order of the cosmos, centrality of God, meaning, and through the changing notions of agency and selfhood. In this chapter, I follow the neo-traditionalists' story of the Muslim "secular age." The enchanted cosmos, before the advent of modernity, was inherently meaningful. It recognized the metaphysical realities of objects. The spiritual and political orders maintained a sense of harmony. When the political order was in disarray, the spiritual orders dissuaded the people from following the *fitna*. The Protestantization of Islam, via the Wahhābī movement, and the later Islamic modernists—who forged their epistemology on colonial modernity—divorced the cosmos from its metaphysical realities. These modern religious movements constructed new notions of Islamic selfhood that decried any form of authority and thereby caused fragmentation and a loss of meaning. Therefore, in reasserting the need for authority, the neo-traditionalists infuse meaning into an otherwise modern political authority. This is precisely Taylor's critique of attempts at re-enchantment. Meanings are assigned and not inherent to the object of meaning; thus, they become contestable. This is perhaps the dilemma that the neo-traditionalists must attempt to resolve; the modern nation-state does not recognize transcendence or metaphysics. Still, it maintains a semblance of order that engenders meaning in an otherwise fragmented reality.

Notes

1 "2014 Forum for Promoting Peace in Muslim Societies," Abu Dhabi, March 9–10, 2014, online: http://peacems.com/wp-content/uploads/2014/09/Pursuite-of-Peace-Morocco-Red-Cover.pdf (accessed October 18, 2017). *A Common Word between Us and You* (Amman: Royal Aal Al-Bayt Institute for Islamic Thought, 2012), ebook, online: http://www.acommonword.com/signatories/ (accessed March 28, 2018).

2 "Hanson, Sheikh Hamza Yusuf: The Muslim 500," Themuslim500.com, 2017, online: http://themuslim500.com/profile/sheikh-hamza-yusuf-hanson (accessed March 28, 2018); "Winter, Timothy (Sheikh Abdal-Hakim Murad): The Muslim 500," Themuslim500.com, 2017, online: http://themuslim500.com/profile/timothy-sheikh-abdal-hakim-murad-winter (accessed March 28, 2018); "Abdullah, Dr Umar Faruq: The Muslim 500," Themuslim500.com, 2017, online: http://themuslim500.com/profile/dr-umar-faruq-abdullah (accessed March 28, 2018).

3 Abdullah Ali, "'Neo-Traditionalism' vs 'Traditionalism,'" *Lampost Education Initiative*, January 22, 2012, online: www.lamppostproductions.com/neo-traditionalism-vs-traditionalism-shaykh-abdullah-bin-hamid-ali/ (accessed February 15, 2017).
4 This does not apply to followers of the Ḥanbalī *madhhab*.
5 Robert Gleave, see Chapter 5 of this book.
6 Scott Alan Kugle, *Rebel between Spirit and Law: Ahmad Zarruq, Sainthood, and Authority in Islam* (Bloomington and Indianapolis: Indiana University Press, 2006), 9.
7 The main figures identified by Hamza Yusuf are, in the Arab East, Muḥammad ʿAbduh, Jamāl al-Dīn al-Afghānī, and Rashīd Riḍā and, in the Arab West, Ben Badīs and al-Fāsī. See Merciful Servant, "Transcript of Lectures by Shaykh Hamza Yusuf," December 28, 2014, online: https://rully02.files.wordpress.com/2014/12/lectures-by-syaikh-hamza-yusuf.pdf (accessed April 3, 2018), 307–308.
8 Kugle, *Rebel between Spirit and Law,* 9.
9 Abdal Hakim Murad, "Contentions," online: www.masud.co.uk/ISLAM/ahm/contentions.htm (accessed February 15, 2017).
10 MBC, "Rihla maʿa Hamza Yusuf," TV program, 2016.
11 Hamza Yusuf and Tariq Ramadan, "Rethinking Reform," debate, University of Oxford Union, Oxford, May 26, 2010.
12 Islam on Demand, "The Concept of Ihsan—by Hamza Yusuf (Foundations of Islam Series: Session 4)," YouTube video, posted March 16, 2011, https://www.youtube.com/watch?v=SLhogmk-Wug (accessed February 15, 2017).
13 Yusuf and Ramadan, "Rethinking Reform."
14 Ana Belén Soage, "Rashid Rida's Legacy," *Muslim World* 98, no. 1 (January 2008), 1–23.
15 Yusuf and Ramadan, "Rethinking Reform."
16 Abdal Hakim Murad, *Commentary on the Eleventh Contention* (Istanbul: Quilliam Press Ltd., 2012), 124.
17 Hamza Yusuf and Zaid Shakir, *Agenda to Change Our Condition* (California: Sandala, 2013), 5.
18 The Ink of Scholars channel, "Britain's Void of Meaning—Timothy Winter," YouTube video, posted October 26, 2014, https://www.youtube.com/watch?v=D5UTDzfS0Wc (accessed February 15, 2017).
19 James K. A. Smith, *How (Not) to Be Secular: Reading Charles Taylor* (Grand Rapids, MI: Wm. B. Eerdmans Publishing, 2014), 26.
20 The Ink of Scholars channel, "Britain's Void of Meaning—Timothy Winter."
21 Turkī l-Dakhīl, "Iḍāʾāt: Hamza Yusuf," filmed October 2011, Al-Arabiya Channel, posted October 2011, https://www.youtube.com/watch?v=WhV791UyT0o (accessed January 13, 2016).
22 Merciful Servant, "Transcript of Lectures by Shaykh Hamza Yusuf," 76.

23 Inkofknowledge, "Is Islam a Political Ideology?—Shaykh Hamza Yusuf: Powerful," YouTube video, posted November 26, 2016, https://www.youtube.com/watch?v=872N34Jxiw8&t=1s (accessed February 15, 2017).

24 Interestingly, in Umar Faruq Abd-Allah's academic book, he mentions claims that Imam Mālik supported the rebellion of Muḥammad al-Nafs al-Zakiyya. This history is absent or marginal in the public discussions on political engagement and the tradition. Umar F. Abd-Allah, *Mālik and Medina: Islamic Legal Reasoning in the Formative Period* (Leiden: Brill, 2013), 44.

25 Hamza Yusuf, "The Crisis of ISIS: A Prophetic Prediction," YouTube video, posted September 19, 2014, https://www.youtube.com/watch?v=hJo4B-yaxfk (accessed February 15, 2017).

26 Umar Faruq Abdullah, "Modernist and Post-Modernist Belief," part 4, Rihla, 2016.

27 Abdullah, "Modernist and Post-Modernist Belief," part 1.

28 Ibid., part 3/a.

29 Ibid., part 2.

30 Ibid., part 1.

31 Hamza Yusuf, "The Miracles of the Awliya," YouTube video, posted July 28, 2012, https://www.youtube.com/watch?v=7gwqus452ns (accessed February 15, 2017).

32 Smith, *How (Not) to Be Secular*, 70–71.

33 Ibid., 140.

34 Ibid., 39.

35 Ibid., 3–4.

36 Charles Taylor, *A Secular Age* (Cambridge, MA: Harvard University Press, 2007), 31.

37 The Ink of Scholars channel, "Britain's Void of Meaning—Timothy Winter."

38 Wael B. Hallaq, *The Impossible State: Islam, Politics, and Modernity's Moral Predicament* (New York: Columbia University Press, 2014), 80.

39 Alan Finlayson, "Psychology, Psychoanalysis and Theories of Nationalism," *Nations and Nationalism* 4, no. 2 (1998), 153.

40 Marie Juul Petersen and Osama Arhb Moftah, "The Marrakesh Declaration: A Muslim Call for Protection of Religious Minorities or Freedom of Religion?" *Religion and the Public Sphere* (London School of Economics, 2017), online: http://blogs.lse.ac.uk/religionglobalsociety/2017/05/the-marrakesh-declaration-a-muslim-call-for-protection-of-religious-minorities-or-freedom-of-religion/ (accessed July 30, 2018).

41 Tobygeral, "Interview of Sh. Hamza Yusuf w/Tim Winter (3/3)," YouTube video, posted May 2013, https://www.youtube.com/watch?v=v_URekMEVdU (accessed January 13, 2016).

42 Scott Korb, *Light without Fire: The Making of America's First Muslim College* (Boston: Beacon Press, 2013), 56.

43 Talal Asad, "Religion, Nation-State, Secularism," in *Nation and Religion: Perspectives on Europe and Asia* (Princeton, NJ: Princeton University Press, 1999), 178–196.
44 Finlayson, "Psychology, Psychoanalysis and Theories of Nationalism," 153.
45 Gleave, see Chapter 5 of this book.
46 "Reviving the Islamic Spirit: 2016," Risconvention.com, 2017, http://risconvention.com/2016/.
47 *Rabwah Times*, "U.S. Muslim Cleric Hamza Yusuf Calls Trump 'A Servant of God' During Racist Rant against Black Lives Matter," *Rabwah Times*, December 25, 2016, https://www.rabwah.net/muslim-hamza-yusuf-racist-rant/ (accessed February 15, 2017).
48 Amro Abu Alhasan, "Hamza Yusuf Responding to Yesterday's Issues," Facebook, December 25, 2016, https://m.facebook.com/story.php?story_fbid=598246803714989&id=100005890233017.
49 Black Muslim Psychology.org, "#RIS2016 Shaykh Hamza Yusuf Controversy," January 5, 2017, online: http://www.blackmuslimpsychology.org/ris2016controversy (accessed March 28, 2018).
50 Abdal Hakim Murad, "A Sacred Alliance of Conservative Believers," YouTube video, posted July 13, 2017, https://www.youtube.com/embed/QbIo65dKk0o (accessed March 28, 2018).
51 Black Muslim Psychology.org, "#RIS2016 Shaykh Hamza Yusuf Controversy."
52 Yahya Birt, "Blowin' in the Wind: Trumpism and Traditional Islam in America," *Medium* 2017, online: https://medium.com/@yahyabirt/https-medium-com-yahyabirt-blowin-in-the-wind-trumpism-and-traditional-islam-in-america–40ba056486d8 (accessed March 28, 2018).
53 Rachael Revesz, "Muslim Leaders Hold Emergency Rally on Eve of Donald Trump's Muslim Ban," *Independent*, January 25, 2017, online: http://www.independent.co.uk/news/world/americas/muslim-leaders-cair-donald-trump-president-ban-rally-emergency-new-york-a7546581.html (accessed March 28, 2018).
54 H. Yusuf, "We Shall Overcome," *Sandala*, November 15, 2016, online: https://sandala.org/we-shall-overcome/ (accessed April 3, 2018). Also see Yahya Birt, online: https://medium.com/@yahyabirt/https-medium-com-yahyabirt-blowin-in-the-wind-trumpism-and-traditional-islam-in-america–40ba056486d8.
55 Finlayson, "Psychology, Psychoanalysis and Theories of Nationalism," 153. Zareena Grewal, *Islam Is a Foreign Country: American Muslims and the Global Crisis of Authority* (New York: New York University Press, 2013), 307.
56 Al Jazeera English, "Riz Khan—Hamza Yusuf," YouTube video, posted June 13, 2007, https://www.youtube.com/watch?v=ve0Sgm0PFyk (accessed February 15, 2017).
57 Laurie Goodstein, "U.S. Muslim Clerics Seek a Modern Middle Ground," *New York Times*, June 18, 2006, online: http://www.nytimes.com/2006/06/18/us/18imams.html (accessed March 28, 2018).
58 *Rabwah Times*, "U.S. Muslim Cleric Hamza Yusuf."

Bibliography

"2014 Forum for Promoting Peace in Muslim Societies." Abu Dhabi, March, 9–10, 2014. Online: http://peacems.com/wp-content/uploads/2014/09/Pursuite-of-Peace-Morocco-Red-Cover.pdf. Accessed October 18, 2017.

Abd-Allah, Umar F. *Mālik and Medina: Islamic Legal Reasoning in the Formative Period.* Leiden: Brill, 2013.

"Abdullah, Dr Umar Faruq: The Muslim 500." Themuslim500.com, 2017. http://themuslim500.com/profile/dr-umar-faruq-abdullah. Accessed April 3, 2018.

Abdullah, Umar Faruq. "Modernist and Post-Modernist Belief." 4 parts. *Rihla*, 2016.

Abu Alhasan Amro. "Hamza Yusuf Responding to Yesterday's Issues." Facebook December 25, 2016. Online: https://m.facebook.com/story.php?story_fbid=598246803714989&id=100005890233017.

Al Jazeera English. "Riz Khan—Hamza Yusuf." YouTube video, posted June 13, 2007. Online: https://www.youtube.com/watch?v=ve0Sgm0PFyk. Accessed February 15, 2017.

Ali, Abdullah. "`Neo-Traditionalism' vs `Traditionalism.'" *Lamppost Education Initiative*. January 22, 2012. Online: www.lamppostproductions.com/neo-traditionalism-vstraditionalism- shaykh-abdullah-bin-hamid-ali/. Accessed March 28, 2018.

Asad, Talal. "Religion, Nation-State, Secularism." In *Nation and Religion: Perspectives on Europe and Asia*, edited by Peter van der Veer and Hartmut Lehmann, 178–196. Princeton, NJ: Princeton University Press, 1999.

Bilgrami, Akeel. *Secularism, Identity, and Enchantment.* Cambridge, MA: Harvard University Press, 2014.

Birt, Yahya. "Blowin' in the Wind: Trumpism and Traditional Islam in America." *Medium*, 2017. Online: https://medium.com/@yahyabirt/https-medium-com-yahyabirt-blowin-in-the-wind-trumpism-and-traditional-islam-in-america-40ba056486d8. Accessed March 28, 2018.

Black Muslim Psychology.org. "#RIS2016 Shaykh Hamza Yusuf Controversy." *Black Muslim Psychology*, 2016. Online: https://www.blackmuslimpsychology.org/ris2016controversy. Accessed March 28, 2018.

A Common Word between Us and You. 5th ed. Amman: Royal Aal Al-Bayt Institute for Islamic Thought, 2012. Ebook: http://www.acommonword.com/signatories/. Accessed March 28, 2018.

al-Dakhīl, Turkī. "Iḍā'āt: Hamza Yusuf." Al-Arabiya Channel, posted October 2011. Online: https://www.youtube.com/watch?v=WhV791UyT00. Accessed January 13, 2016.

Finlayson, Alan. "Psychology, Psychoanalysis and Theories of Nationalism." *Nations and Nationalism* 4, no. 2 (1998): 145–162.

Gane, Nicholas. *Max Weber and Postmodern Theory: Rationalization versus Re-Enchantment.* New York: Springer, 2002.

Goodstein, Laurie. "U.S. Muslim Clerics Seek a Modern Middle Ground." *New York Times*. June 18, 2006. Online: http://www.nytimes.com/2006/06/18/us/18imams.html. Accessed March 28, 2018.

Grewal, Zareena. *Islam Is a Foreign Country: American Muslims and the Global Crisis of Authority*. New York: New York University Press, 2013.

Hallaq, Wael B. *The Impossible State: Islam, Politics, and Modernity's Moral Predicament*. New York: Columbia University Press, 2014

"Hanson, Sheikh Hamza Yusuf." Themuslim500.com. Online: http://themuslim500.com/profile/sheikh-hamza-yusuf-hanson. Accessed March 28, 2018.

Ink of Scholars Channel. "Britain's Void of Meaning—Timothy Winter." YouTube video, posted October 26, 2014. Online: https://www.youtube.com/watch?v=D5UTDzfS0Wc. Accessed February 15, 2017.

Inkofknowledge. "Is Islam a Political Ideology?—Shaykh Hamza Yusuf—Powerful." YouTube video, posted November 26, 2016. Online: https://www.youtube.com/watch?v=872N34Jxiw8&t=1s. Accessed March 28, 2018.

Islam on Demand. "The Concept of Ihsan—by Hamza Yusuf (Foundations of Islam Series: Session 4)." YouTube video. Posted March 16, 2011. https://www.youtube.com/watch?v=SLhogmk-Wug. Accessed March 28, 2018.

Korb, Scott. *Light without Fire: The Making of America's First Muslim College*. Boston: Beacon Press, 2013.

Kugle, Scott Alan. *Rebel between Spirit and Law: Ahmad Zarruq, Sainthood, and Authority in Islam*. Bloomington and Indianapolis: Indiana University Press, 2006.

MBC. "Rihla maʿa Hamza Yusuf." TV Program, 2016.

Merciful Servant. "Transcript of Lectures by Shaykh Hamza Yusuf." December 28, 2014. https://rully02.files.wordpress.com/2014/12/lectures-by-syaikh-hamza-yusuf.pdf. Accessed March 28, 2018.

Murad, Abdal Hakim. *Commentary on the Eleventh Contention*. Istanbul: Quilliam Press, 2012.

Murad, Abdal Hakim. "Contentions." Online: www.masud.co.uk/ISLAM/ahm/contentions.htm. Accessed February 15, 2017.

Murad, Abdal Hakim. "A Sacred Alliance of Conservative Believers." YouTube video. Posted July 13, 2017. Online: https://www.youtube.com/embed/QbIo65dKk0o. Accessed March 28, 2018.

Onlyagame. "A Secular Age (8): Subtraction Stories." October 16, 2008. Online: http://onlyagame.typepad.com/only_a_game/2008/10/a-secular-age-8-subtraction-stories.html. Accessed February 15, 2017.

Petersen, Marie Juul, and Osama Arhb Moftah. "The Marrakesh Declaration: A Muslim Call for Protection of Religious Minorities or Freedom of Religion?" *Religion and the Public Sphere*. London: London School of Economics. Online: http://blogs.lse.ac.uk/religionglobalsociety/2017/05/the-marrakesh-declaration-a-muslim-call-for-protection-of-religious-minorities-or-freedom-of-religion/. Accessed July 30, 2018.

Rabwah Times. "U.S. Muslim Cleric Hamza Yusuf Calls Trump 'A Servant of God' during Racist Rant against Black Lives Matter." December 25, 2016. Online: https://www.rabwah.net/muslim-hamza-yusuf-racist-rant/accessed. Accessed February 15, 2017.

Revesz, Rachael. "Muslim Leaders Hold Emergency Rally on Eve of Donald Trump's Muslim Ban." *Independent*. January 25, 2017. http://www.independent.co.uk/news/world/americas/muslim-leaders-cair-donald-trump-president-ban-rally-emergency-new-york-a7546581.html. Accessed March 28, 2018.

"Reviving the Islamic Spirit–2016." Risconvention.com, 2017. Online: http://risconvention.com/2016/.

RT America. "On Contact: The Perversion of Islam with Hamza Yusuf." YouTube video, posted October 22, 2016. https://www.youtube.com/watch?v=W_-V0-6XOXM&t=741s. Accessed February 15, 2017.

Smith, James K. A. *How (Not) to Be Secular: Reading Charles Taylor*. Grand Rapids, MI: Wm. B. Eerdmans Publishing, 2014.

Soage, Ana Belén. "Rashid Rida's Legacy." *Muslim World* 98, no. 1 (January 2008): 1–23.

Taylor, Charles. *A Secular Age*. Cambridge, MA: Harvard University Press, 2007.

Tobygeral. "Interview of Sh. Hamza Yusuf w/Tim Winter (3/3)." YouTube video, posted May 2013. https://www.youtube.com/watch?v=v_URekMEVdU. Accessed March 28, 2018.

Weber, Max. "Science as a Vocation." In *Science and the Quest for Reality*, edited by Alfred I. Tauber, 382–394. Basingstoke: Palgrave Macmillan UK, 1946.

"Winter, Timothy (Sheikh Abdal-Hakim Murad)." The Muslim 500, 2017. Online: http://themuslim500.com/profile/timothy-sheikh-abdal-hakim-murad-winter. Accessed March 28, 2018.

Yusuf, Hamza. "The Crisis of ISIS: A Prophetic Prediction—Sermon by Hamza Yusuf." YouTube video, posted September 19, 2014. Online: https://www.youtube.com/watch?v=hJo4B-yaxfk. Accessed February 15, 2017.

Yusuf, Hamza. "The Miracles of the Awliya." YouTube video, posted July 28, 2012. Online: https://www.youtube.com/watch?v=7gwqus452ns. Accessed February 15, 2017.

Yusuf, Hamza. "We Shall Overcome." *Sandala*, November 15, 2016. Online https://sandala.org/we-shall-overcome/. Accessed April 3, 2018.

Yusuf, Hamza, and Zaid Shakir. *Agenda to Change Our Condition*. California: Sandala, 2013.

Index

ʿAbbās II, Shah 41
ʿAbbāsids caliphate 19, 27 n.19, 40, 65, 86
Abd-Allah, Umar Faruq 241–2, 247, 254 n.24
ʿAbd al-Rāziq, ʿAlī 46–7
ʿAbd al-Razzāq 67, 74 n.26
ʿAbduh, Muḥammad 45, 244
Abou El Fadl, Khaled 115, 125 n.49
absolutism 36, 40
    and limitations 215–17
Abū Bakr 63–72
Abū l-Ḥasan ʿAlī l-Nadwī 22
Abū Ḥanīfa, Nuʿmān b. Thābit 37–8, 52 n.20, 68, 82, 152, 246
action-neutral position, *kufr* 7, 23–4
activism 15, 19, 189, 210–11, 230, 250
    al-Khūʾī's 48
    political 1, 10, 22, 35–6, 39, 42, 44, 46, 131–2, 176, 210–11, 219
    religious 20, 231
    social 22–3, 131, 211, 220 n.12
    vs. quietism 8, 19, 34
African Constitutionalism and the Role of Islam (An-Na'im) 182
Ahkām al-sulṭāniyya wa-l-dīniyya (*al-Māwardī*) 42
ahl al-bayt 19, 136
ahl al-dhimma 152–3, 157
ahl al-ḥadīth movement 91 n.2, 214, 222 n.27
ahl al-sunna 68, 242
Akhbār al-shuyūkh (al-Marrūdhī) 87
AKP government in Turkey 228, 233–5
al-Afghānī, Jamāl al-Dīn 45, 244
al-Albānī, Muḥammad Nāṣir al-Dīn 9–10, 20, 49, 56 n.78, 101, 210, 214–15, 217–19
Āl al-Shaykh, Muḥammad Ibn Ibrāhīm 49
al-Anṭākī, Muḥammad Marʿī l-Amīn 201 n.52
al-ʿAskarī, al-Hasan 187
al-Awdī, al-Afwah 42
al-ʿAymakī, Abū Bakr 151
al-Baladhūrī, Aḥmad b. Yaḥyā 27 n.19
al-Balkhī, Abū Muṭīʿ 68
al-Bannā, Hasan 136, 202 n.54, 214, 220 n.12, 244
al-Bāqir, Muḥammad 39, 100, 186
al-Bukhārī, Muḥammad b. Ismāʿīl 53 n.31
al-Buralī, Mulla Murtaḍā b. Ḥusayn 161
al-Chukhī, Muḥammad ʿAlī 159–60, 165 n.55
al-Dārimī, Aḥmad b. Saʿīd 63–5, 67–9
al-Durra al-nafīsa treatise (al-ʿUradī) 160–1
Alesger, Aqil 228
al-Fiqh al-akbar (Abu Hanifa) 37, 52 n.20, 52 n.24
al-Fitan (al-Marwazī) 84
al-Fārābī, Abū Naṣr 21, 28 n.32
al-Fukaykī, Tawfīq 192
al-Gharnāṭī, Abū Ḥāmid 151
al-Ghazālī, Abū Ḥāmid 21, 41
al-Ghāzī Qumūqī, ʿAlī l-Kabīr 152
al-Ghimrāwī, Shāmil 148, 150–1, 156, 159
al-Ghimrī, Ghāzī Muḥammad 148
al-Ḥawālī, Safar b. ʿAbd al-Raḥmān 20
al-Ḥusayn, ʿAlī b. 65–6, 81, 132, 187, 189–90, 198 n.24
al-Ḥusaynī, Aḥmad 109
al-Ḥusnā organization 213
ʿAlī 63–5, 68–72, 72 n.4, 99
al-ʿĪd, Nawāl 209, 213, 219 n.3
ʿAlids 19, 27 n.19, 186
ʿAlī l-Karakī, Shaykh 42
ʿAlī l-Riḍāʾ 139 n.1
ʿAlī Shāh, Muḥammad 134
Ali Shariʿati 54 n.51
Aliyev, Fuad 7, 10
Aliyev, Heydar 228
al-Karābīsī, al-Ḥusayn 83
Āl Kāshif al-Ghiṭāʾ, Muḥammad al-Ḥusayn 190
al-Khallāl, Aḥmad b. Muḥammad 82
al-Khūʾī, Abū l-Qāsim 192–4

al-Khūʾī, Sayyid Abū l-Qāsim 47–8
al-khulafāʾ al-rāshidūn (rightly-guided caliphs) 4, 9, 63–4, 67, 70, 72 n.1, 146, 178
al-Kulaynī, Muḥammad b. Yaʿqūb 133, 187, 192, 196 nn.10–11
Allahshukur Pashazade, Shaykh al-Islam Hajji 232
al-Maghribī, Abū l-Qāsim 109–10
al-Mahdī wa-l-mahdawiyya (Amīn) 199 n.33
al-Maliki, Nuri 209
al-Maʾmūn 87
al-Maqdisī, Abū Muḥammad ʿĀṣim 20, 22–4, 28 n.37, 29 n.39, 48–9, 101
al-Marāghī, Muḥammad Muṣṭafā 192
al-Marrūdhī, Aḥmad b. Muḥammad 82–3, 87–8
al-Marwazī, Nuʿaym b. Ḥammād 84
al-Māwardī, Abū l-Ḥasan 21, 42, 159
alms tax (*zakāt*) 103
al-Mudallisūn (al-Karābīsī) 83
al-Mufīd, Shaykh 39–40, 42
al-Muḥārib, Ruqayya 215–18, 221 n.18, 222 n.36, 222 n.38, 222 n.40
al-Mukhtaṣar (al-Ghāzī-Qumūq) 152
al-Mulk, Niẓām 41
al-Mundhirī, Zakī l-Dīn 216
al-Murghim treatise 151
al-Murtaḍā, al-Sharīf 42, 100, 102–4, 108, 119, 123 n.37, 123 n.41
  academic scholarship on treatise of 112–18
  treatise on working for government 108–12
al-Muʿtaṣim 88
al-Mutawakkil 85–6, 89
al-Nadīm, Muḥammad b. Isḥāq 67
al-Narāqī, Aḥmad 188, 197 n.17
al-Nawawī, Muḥyī l-Dīn 158
al-Qāʿida 23
al-Qaṭṭān, Yaḥyā b. Saʿīd 68
al-Qazwīnī, Zakariyyā 151
al-Rashīd, Hārūn 89
al-Risāla al-sharīfa (al-Thughūrī) 145, 154, 161
  concept of *hijra* in 154–8
al-Sabzawārī, Muḥammad Bāqir 116
al-Ṣādiq, Jaʿfar 39, 108–9, 139 n.5, 186–7
al-Ṣadr, Muḥammad Bāqir 48
al-Ṣadr, Muḥammad Ṣādiq 190
al-Sarhan, Saud 4–5, 8–9, 11 n.2, 29 n.38, 38–9
al-Shaʿbī 64–5
al-Sharīf, Muḥammad Mūsā 215
al-Sharqawī, ʿAbdallāh b. Ḥijāzī b. Ibrāhīm 152
al-Shīrāzī, Mīrzā Ḥasan 188, 197 n.16
al-Sijistānī, Abū Dāwūd 71–2
al-Siyāsa al-sharʿiyya (Ibn Taymiyya) 41
al-Ṭabarī, Abū Jaʿfar Muḥammad 27 n.19
al-Ṭahṭāwī, Rifāʿa Rāfiʿ 44–5
al-Ṭayālisī, Abū Dāwūd 70–1
al-Taymī, Sulaymān 68
al-Thawrī, Sufyān 67, 70, 72, 81, 105
al-Thughūrī, ʿAbd al-Raḥmān 145, 149, 154–8, 161–2
al-Thughūrī, Ḥājjī Muḥammad 148–9
al-Tunīsī, Khayr al-Dīn 6, 9, 171–2, 174–9, 181–2
  constitutional theory of (*see* constitutionalism)
al-Ṭūsī, Muḥammad b. Ḥasan 113, 116, 123 n.41, 124 n.43
al-Ṭūsī, Nāṣir al-Dīn 43
al-ʿUradī, Murtaḍā ʿAlī 151, 159–61
al-ʿUthaymīn, Muḥammad b. Ṣāliḥ 23, 211
al-Wansharīsī, Aḥmad b. Yaḥyā 157
al-Yamānī, Aḥmad 152
al-Yāmī, Zubayd 64
al-Zanjānī, ʿAbd al-Karīm 192
al-Zarqāwī, Abū Muṣʿab 24, 49
Amīn, Aḥmad 191, 199 nn.33–4
Amir-Moezzi, Mohammad Ali 132
An-Na'im, Abdullahi Ahmed 182
Ansari, Hassan 186
Arab Spring movement 181
Arjomand, Said Amir 39, 41–2, 115, 125 n.56, 197 n.19
Asín Palacios, Miguel 3
Asrār-i hizārsāla (Hakimzāda) 135
Assmann, Aleida 200 n.37
Azerbaijan. *See* Gülen movement in Azerbaijan

Baghdadi *isnād* 65
Balci, Bayram 231
Basran *isnād* 65–6, 68–9

Bell'uomo, Gottardo 16–17, 25 n.4
Bengel, Johann Albrecht 33
Black Lives Matter (BLM) movement 249–50
Bourdieu, Pierre 221 n.25
Böwering, Gerhard 25 n.1
Brunner, Rainer 6–7, 202 n.55
Budshīshiyya 101
bureaucrats (*bīrūqrāṭī*) 221 n.17
Burūjirdī, Sayyid Ḥusayn 47, 134, 190
Bush, George 251
Būyid dynasty 187

Calder, Norman 116–17, 124 n.44, 125 n.56
Cancian, Alessandro 5, 8–9
Catherine II 151
Caucasus 145, 151–6, 159–62
  burned Sogratl (1877) 146
  Caucasus Muslims 147–8, 151, 158–9, 232
  history of Islamic culture in 146–50
Chechnya 145, 149, 151, 162
Ché Guevara 185
Chishtiyya 43–4, 54 n.56
civilizational cycle, *dawla* as 19–20
colonialism 6, 45, 47, 50, 172, 244
confrontational position, *kufr* 4, 7, 23–4
constitutionalism 9, 171–2
  Islamic 173–4, 181–2
  representation 177–80
  restricting/defining power 180–1
  rule of law 175–7
The constitutional revolution (1906) 134
"constitution of Medina," Muḥammad's 173–4
Cook, Michael 1, 8, 11 n.1, 19, 27 n.18, 27 n.20, 36, 39, 52 n.25, 75 n.29, 102, 120 n.9
Corbin, Henry 132, 136
Crone, Patricia 39, 73 n.5, 100
customary law (*ʿādāt*) in Dagestan 148

Dabashi, Hamid 53
Dagestan 146, 149, 159, 162
  annexation of Chechnya and 145
  customary law (*ʿādāt*) in 148
  historical literature of 147
  irregular cavalry 156
  legal works 145, 151–2
  martyrs of 149
  migration 149–50
  Muslim scholars in 160–1
dāʿiya 209, 212–15, 221 n.18
dāʿiyāt muthaqqafāt in Riyadh 209–10, 217–19, 219 n.1
  relation to state 212–14
dār al-ḥarb 151–3, 155, 161
dār al-islām 146, 149, 151–4, 159, 161
dār al-kufr 146, 154
daʿwa movement 48–9, 210, 212–14, 217–19
dawla (state) 8, 27 n.19
  as civilizational cycle 19–20
Dawla Islamiyya fī l-ʿIrāq wa-l-Shām (ISIS) 23
De Molinos, Miguel 2–3, 16–17, 20, 25 n.5, 26 n.11, 33
Denny, Frederick 173–4
De oratione et meditatione (On oration and meditation) (Peter of Alcántara) 2
d'Herbelot, Barthélemy 3
dhimmī 173, 175
dīn wa-dawla (religion and state) 20
Dithār, Muḥārib b. 68
Diyanet, Turkey 226

Eckstein, Harry 217
ecumenicalism 6
El Omari, Racha 42
Enayat, Hamid 40
Encyclopedia of Religion 33–4
Epictetus 194
epistemology, European 44
Erdogan, Receb Tayyip 233
The Eternal Martyr (Najafābādī) 189

faith-based social movement. *See* Gülen movement in Azerbaijan
The Fall and Rise of the Islamic State (Feldman) 182
Falsafī, Abū l-Qāsim 47
fatwās/fatāwā 148, 152–3, 160, 188, 193, 197 n.16, 222 n.36
Feldman, Noah 182
Finlayson, Alan 248–9
fiqh (Islamic jurisprudence) 103, 105–6, 110, 114, 117, 122 n.21, 123 n.41, 154
first civil war 36, 38, 189

fitna 9, 82, 84–5, 189, 216, 246
five-caliph hypothesis 70–1
Formen des Vergessens (Assmann) 200 n.37
Foucault, Michel 35
four-caliph hypothesis 68, 70–1

"genocidal mega-conflicts" 248
Ghalib, Mirza 44
ghayba (occultation), imam's 99–100, 103–4, 112–13, 115, 117, 187
Gizbulaev, Mogamed 5
Gleave, Robert 5, 8, 242–3, 249
Glei, Reinhold 27 n.24
Goldziher, Ignác 86
Gorski, Philip 43
governance-orientation 3–4, 22–4
government,181, 188–9, 217, 227–8, 251
  al-Murtaḍā's treatise on working for 108–12, 118
  Islamic 131, 133, 230
  types of (al-Murtaḍā) 112–13
  working in legal context 104–8
guidance-orientation 3–4, 22
Gülen, Fethullah 225, 227–9, 232–3, 235
Gülen movement in Azerbaijan 7, 10, 225, 230, 233–6
  operational environment 231
  Turkish religious influence and 226–9
Gunābādī, Sulṭān ʿAlī Shāh 137–8

Haarmann, Ulrich 198 n.21
ḥadīth 9, 49, 63, 65, 67, 69, 71, 72 n.1, 104–5, 108, 110, 118, 121 n.19, 122 n.20, 154–5, 187, 192, 216
Haider, Najam 42
Hakimzāda, ʿAlī Akbar 135
Hallaq, Wael 248
Hamid Ali, Abdullah Bin 242
Ḥanbalī school of jurisprudence 4–5, 8, 38, 102, 222 n.27
Hartung, Jan-Peter 3–4, 8, 25 n.2, 27 n.28, 28 n.34
Hāshimīs 186
Hassan, Mehdi 249
Hayʾat Kibār al-ʿUlamāʾ (council of scholars) 23, 28 n.36
hegemony 44, 135
Hendrickson, Jocelyn 153
hijra (migration) 145, 149, 151–3, 159–61
  in *al-Risāla al-sharīfa* 154–8
Hinds, Martin 73 n.5
ḥisba 36–7, 50, 52 n.14, 221 n.22
historical study of political quietism 51 n.9
  early caliphate 35–44
  era of empire 40–4
  modern era 44–50
Hizmet movement. *See* Gülen movement in Azerbaijan
Ho Chi Minh 185
Hodgson, Marshall 35–7
ḥudūd (punishments for crimes) 106, 119
Hurvitz, Nimrod 89

Ibn ʿAbd al-ʿAzīz, ʿUmar 63–72, 81, 175
Ibn Abī ʿĀṣim 65, 74 n.13
Ibn Abī Shayba, ʿAbdallāh b. Muḥammad 70
Ibn al-Farrāʾ, Abū Yaʿlā 67
Ibn al- Ḥārith, Khālid 68
Ibn al-Jawzī, ʿAbd al-Raḥmān b. ʿAlī 53 n.27
Ibn al-Musayyab, Saʿīd 66, 70
Ibn al-Qāsim 105–6
Ibn al-Shikhkhīr, Muṭarrif 82
Ibn al-ʿUthaymīn, Muḥammad 49
Ibn al-Zubayr, ʿAbdallāh 70, 81–2, 84
Ibn Bāz, ʿAbd al-ʿAzīz 23, 49, 211
Ibn Ḥajar al-ʿAsqalānī 67, 72, 160
Ibn Ḥanbal, Aḥmad 4–5, 10, 38–9, 53 n.27, 64, 67, 69–70, 72 n.1, 72 n.4, 76 n.40, 81, 85–6, 93 n.31
  quietist doctrine of 82–5
  relationship to authority 86–90
Ibn Ḥanbal, Ḥanbal b. Isḥāq 86, 88, 93 n.28, 94 n.50
Ibn Ḥanbal, Ṣāliḥ b. Aḥmad 88–9, 94 n.44, 94 n.50
Ibn Ḥayy, al-Ḥasan 83
Ibn Isḥāq, Muḥammad 173
Ibn Jamāʿa 40–1
Ibn Khaldūn 180
Ibn Manẓūr, Abū l-Faḍl 26 n.16
Ibn Masʿūd, ʿAbdallāh 67
Ibn Mūsā, Sulaymān 38
Ibn Rāhawayh, Isḥāq 86, 89
Ibn Rajab, ʿAbd al-Raḥmān b. Aḥmad 71
Ibn Saʿd 52 n.19, 65, 68, 72 n.4
Ibn Shabbawayh, Aḥmad 85, 93 n.31

Ibn Sulaymān, Muʿtamir 68
Ibn Ṣurad, Sulaymān 84
Ibn Taymiyya, Taqī l-Dīn Aḥmad 21, 28 n.31, 40–1, 53 n.40
Ibn ʿUmar 65, 72, 74 n.13, 76 n.40, 81–2
Ignacius of Loyola 17
iḥtisāb (doctrinal justification of *daʿwa*) 213–14
imāma/imamate (leadership) 1, 42, 99, 186–7, 192, 246
  Caucasus 145, 147, 149, 151, 156, 160–1
Imam al-Khoei Foundation 48
Imāmī/Imāmism 42, 53 n.35, 100–4, 115, 117–19, 186
  political legitimacy in jurisprudence of 103–4
  and quietism 99–103, 119, 120 n.9
intellectual female preachers (*dāʿiyāt muthaqqafāt*). *See dāʿiyāt muthaqqafāt* in Riyadh
Iqāmat al-burhān ʿalā irtidādʿurafāʾ Dāgistān (al-Ghimrī) 148
Iran 7, 9, 115, 133–7, 185, 188–9
ʿIrfān 136
irjāʾ (postponing/deferring judgment to God) 37
İşbilen, İlhan 227
Islam and the Foundations of Political Power (ʿAbd al-Rāziq) 46
Islamic Ecumenism (Brunner) 202 n.55
Islamism
  Islamic constitutionalism 173–4, 181–2
  Islamic cosmology 244–8, 252
  Islamic jurisprudence (*fiqh*) 103, 105–6, 110, 114
  Islamic modernists 243–4, 252
  Islamic state 121 n.14, 135, 173, 214–15, 230
  Islamization in Dagestan 146
  Protestantization of Islam 243–5
  terms in study of Islam 17–20
Islamophobia 241, 249, 251
isnāds 64–6, 69

jāhiliyya (ignorance) 218, 222 n.44
Jamāʿa al-Salafiyya al-Muḥtasiba (JSM) 214
Jamāʿat al-Taqrīb Bayn al-Madhāhib al-Islāmiyya association 190, 193–4, 200 n.37
Jāmiyya/Madkhaliyya 211–12, 214
jihād 2, 20, 47–9, 101, 149, 151, 153, 155, 158–9, 188, 243, 246
Jomaa, Katrin 15, 25 n.1, 26 n.14, 120 n.9
Jubayr, Saʿīd b. 83
just ruler (*al-sulṭān al-ʿādil*) 113, 115, 123 n.41, 124 n.43, 125 n.49. *See also* unjust ruler (*al-sulṭān al-jāʾir*)
The Just Ruler in Shiʿite Islam (Sachedina) 115
Juynboll, G. H. A. 198 n.22

Kamali, Mohammad Hashim 52 n.14
Karbalāʾ 132, 186, 189–90, 198 nn.24–5
Kāshānī, Mullā Muḥsin Fayḍ 41
Kashf al-asrār (Khomeini) 135
Kasravī, Aḥmad 135
Keddie, Nikki 120 n.9
Kemper, Michael 160
Khan, Sayyid Ahmed 45
Khārijī political theology 37
Khawārij 35–6, 38
Khomeini, Ayatollah Ruhollah 7, 48, 131–6, 185, 188–9, 194, 197 n.19, 197 n.20, 202 n.53
Khumm, Ghadīr 70
khurūj (rebellion) 1, 39, 44, 48, 82, 85–6, 91 n.9, 100–2, 242–3, 249
Kīlānī, Muḥammad Sayyid 46
Kitāb al-īmān wa-l-kufr (al-Kulaynī) 133
Kitāb al-ṭabaqāt al-kubrā (Ibn Saʿd) 52 n.19
Kleidosty, Jeremy 6, 9
Koselleck, Reinhart 210
Krachkovskii, I. 147
Kufa 64–5, 67, 71–2, 75 n.29, 195 n.4
  Kufan *isnād* 64–5, 67
kufr (unbelief) 4, 23, 49, 161, 217

Lacroix, Stéphane 213–14, 222 n.27
land reform programs, Shah's 47
Lav, Daniel 20, 27 n.27
"Left–Muslim" alliance 249–50
Levi Della Vida, Giorgio 50–1
Lewis, Bernard 8, 18–19, 26 nn.13–14, 28 n.29, 40, 53 n.37, 194 n.1, 229–30

Madelung, Wilferd 72 n.2, 104, 109–10, 112–17, 121 n.18, 123 n.34, 123 n.41, 124 nn.43–4, 125 n.49, 125 n.52
madhhab 193, 242, 246

Ḥanbalī 38
Shāfiʿī 151
Mahmood, Saba 210, 218
Makboul, Laila 6, 9–10
marjaʿ al-taqlīd 188, 190
Marxism 135
Masʾala fī ʿamal maʿa l-sulṭān (Murtaḍā) 108
Medinan *isnād* 65
Melchert, Christopher 4, 9
Mervin, Sabrina 199 n.28, 200 n.39
Michot, Yahya 41
Millat Ibrāhīm (Al-Maqdisī) 24, 29 n.39
Miller, William M. 141 n.21
millet system, Ottoman 175
Mirza, Kazem-bek 151
Modarressi, Hossein 116, 118, 124 n.44, 125 n.52
modernity, Islamic 241, 243, 248, 251–2
Moosa, Ebrahim 4, 8–9
Mosaddegh, Mohammad 47, 134
Motahhari, Morteza 135
Muʿāwiya b. Ḥudayj 63, 66, 68
muftiyya (female mufti) 215
Mughniyya, Muḥammad Jawād 190–2, 194, 200 n.40, 202 n.53
muḥaddith 91 n.2
Mukarram, Ahmed 3, 22, 28 n.33
Murad, Abdal Hakim 241–2, 245, 247–8, 250
Murjiʾa 19–20, 36–8, 46, 49, 52 n.19, 68
Muslim Brotherhood 212, 214, 218, 220 n.12, 244
Muslim community 35–41, 44–6, 81, 85–6, 100, 135, 147, 179, 241, 251. *See also* *umma* community
Muslim World League, Mecca-based 28 n.37
Musnad Aḥmad ibn Ḥanbal (Ibn Ḥanbal) 66, 83
muwādaʿa (quietism) 1, 18
mysticism, religious 136–8

nāʾib group, Shāmil's 149
Najafābādī, Niʿmatullāh Ṣāliḥī 189
Naṣīḥat al-mulūk (al-Ghazālī) 41, 106–7, 112
nation-state 46, 49, 248–9, 252
Neoplatonism of Islam 136
neo-traditionalism 242
Niʿmatullāhī (religious order) 131, 137
Nizami, K. A. 43, 54 n.55
non-Muslim rule 5–6, 149, 153, 158–9, 209
Nūr ʿAlī Shāh II 137, 141 n.21
Nurcular 226–7, 231–3
Nūr ʿhav Shāh II 141 n.21
Nūrī, Shaykh Faḍlallāh 188
Nursi, Said 227–8, 232

Olidort, Jacob 56 n.78
Ottoman Empire 6, 8, 146, 149, 159, 162, 172, 177

Pahlavi, Mohammad Reza 134
Pahlavi, Reza Shah 134
passivism in politics 210–11, 219
Paul, Jürgen 54 n.56
Peter of Alcántara 2
Petrucci, Pier Matteo 26 n.6
pietism 17
political activism 1, 10, 22, 35–6, 39, 42, 44, 46, 131–2, 176, 210–11, 219
political contestation 35, 38
political leadership 245–6
political quietism 2–4, 6, 8–10, 18–23, 25, 33–5, 39, 44–6, 50, 102, 172, 209, 229–35, 241–3, 247–52, 248–51
  historical study of (*see* historical study of political quietism)
  intellectual female preachers 210
  Saudi Salafism and 210–12
  in Shīʿism 132–3
  Yusuf's 250
"political responsibility," Hodgson's 35–7
political theology 33, 36, 40–1
  activist 42
  Khārijī 37
  Muslim 35, 45–6
  quietist 35, 50, 54 n.51
post-Soviet Azerbaijan 226–7
pragmatic political quietism 102, 104, 119
prayer of quiet (*orazione di quiete*) 16
The Princeton Encyclopedia of Islamic Political Thought (Böwering), Jomaa's entry in 15, 25, 25 n.1, 26 n.14, 120 n.9
Prophet Muḥammad 3, 19, 38, 49, 99, 146, 153, 174, 178, 186, 192
Protestantization of Islam 243–5, 252

proto-Shīʿa 36–7
purity *vs.* pragmatism 8–10
Pushkin, Alexander 156

qaʿadat al-Khawārij (the quietist Khārijīs) 2
Qajar monarchy 133, 137–8
Qavāʿid al-salāṭīn 41–2
quietism 1–2, 8, 15–17, 19–20, 24–5, 26 n.14, 34–6, 38–40, 174, 176–7, 180, 185–7, 189, 193, 210, 251
  Christian 2, 33
  for Ibn Ḥanbal 39, 82–5
  and Imāmism 99–103
  Lewis's 18–19, 229–30
  political (*see* political quietism)
  with political activism 42
  in practice 86–90
  semantics of 7–8, 16–17, 26 n.10
  in *shuyūkh* 242
  in Sunnī jurisprudence 81–2
  vs. collaboration 85
"Quietism and Activism," Jomaa's entry in 15, 120 n.9
quietist *jihādī*/activist 20, 24
quietist political theology 35
Quietist Salafism/Salafis 48–9
Quisay, Walaa 7, 10
Qulzum: Uqiyānūs-i bī-karān-i maʿārif-i Ahl-i Bayt (Nūr ʿhav Shāh II) 141 n.21
Qummī, Muḥammad Taqī 190–1, 199 n.34
Qurʾān 34, 36–7, 52 n.14, 153–4, 157, 192–3, 212, 214, 217–18
Quṭb, Sayyid 136, 214, 220 n.12

Rābiṭat al-ʿĀlam al-Islāmī (Muslim World League) 28 n.37
racism 249–51
Rebellion and Violence in Islamic Law (Abou El Fadl) 115
Reichmuth, Stefan 27 n.24
religiosity, De Molinos's 2
religious activism 20, 231
religious law, types 192
Reviving Islamic Spirit (RIS) conference 249, 251
Riḍā, Rashīd 244
rightly-guided caliphs (*al-khulafāʾ al-rāshidūn*) 4, 9, 63–4, 67, 70, 72 n.1, 146, 178
rāʿin–raʿiyya binary 21, 28 n.30
Risāla fī dār al-ḥarb treatise (al-Buralī) 161
Risale-yi nur (Nursi) 227
Riyadh 209–10, 219 n.1
Rizek, Ali-Rida 122 n.29
Roberts, Nicholas 4, 8–9
Russian Empire 145, 149, 156
  Caucasian Muslims 148, 151–2, 158–9
  colonial encroachment in Caucasus 151, 153, 155
  execution of al-Thughūrī 149
  imperial Russian army 156–7
  Islamic arguments and polemics against 159–62

Sachedina, Abdulaziz 115
Saddam Hussein 48
Saʿdī of Shiraz 44
Safavid dynasty 119, 136, 188
Safīna, Abū Abd al-Raḥmān 69, 71, 76 n.39
ṣaḥwa movement 211, 214, 219, 220 n.12
Salafis/Salafism 35, 48–9, 56 n.78, 101, 210–12, 214–15, 219, 220 n.11
Sangalajī, Ḥasan Sharīʿat 135
Saudi Arabia 49, 210–13, 215, 219 n.1, 222 n.36
  egalitarian ethos of 8, 35–6
Schacht, Joseph 52 n.20
secular age, Muslim 244–5, 252
Segneri, Paolo 26 n.6
The Shadow of God and the Hidden Imam (Arjomand) 115
Shah, Nādir 148, 193
Shaltūt, Maḥmūd 193
Sharaf al-Dīn, ʿAbd al-Ḥusayn 190
Sharḥ ʿalā l-Mukhtaṣar al-Dāgistanī (al-Sharqawī) 152
sharīʿa (*al-siyāsa al-sharʿiyya*) 21–3, 42, 47, 100, 102, 111, 115, 118, 135, 145, 148, 152, 160, 175, 178–81, 183 n.8, 213
Shīʿism/Shīʿī tradition 1, 5–6, 9, 39, 41–2, 47–8, 54 n.51, 65, 67, 99–101, 115–16, 121 n.19, 131–2, 135, 137, 185–9, 190–4, 195 n.4, 195 n.7, 198 n.24
  ʿAbd al-Razzāq's 74 n.26
  clerics 35, 47

ḥadīth 187
political quietism in 132–3
to Sunnism 193
theology 34
shūrā (consultation) 50, 178–9, 182
shuyūkh, neo-traditionalist 241–4, 249–52
Siyāsat nāma (al-Mulk) 41
Smith, James K. A. 247
social activism 22–3, 131, 211, 220 n.12
social quietism 102
Spiritual Exercises of Ignacius of Loyola 17
Spiritual Guide, de Molinos's 17
spirituality 3, 16, 43, 102, 244
state-sustaining position, *kufr* 4, 23
Stewart, Devin 200 n.39
St. Paul 34
Sufi Khālidiyya 155
Sufi Shīʿism 5, 8–9, 137
Sufism (*taṣawwuf*) 18, 43, 54 n.55, 214
in Azerbaijan 226
and politics 136–8
sulṭān 88, 105–6, 110–11, 113–14, 117, 119, 121 n.18, 124 n.41
Sunna (prophetic) 46, 71, 106, 153, 211, 214–15
Sunnī Islam 1, 5–6, 9, 34, 39, 41–2, 48, 63, 68–71, 90, 100–1, 118, 190, 193–4, 216
ḥadīths 4, 63, 67
jurists 155
quietism in 81–2
to Shīʿism 193
theology 34
The Surest Path to Knowledge Concerning the Conditions of Countries (al-Tunīsī) 171–2, 174, 177

ṭāʿa shāmiyya (Syrian obedience) 38
tafḍīl (preference) 38, 63, 66
Tanzimat-era 44, 176, 181, 183 n.12
taqiyya (dissimulation) 9, 35, 39, 43, 111, 115, 117, 191, 226, 229–36
taqrīb movement 190, 192, 194
Taylor, Charles 244–5, 247, 252
technocrats (*tiknūqrātī*) 221 n.17
Teresa of Ávila 2
Thomson, Patricia 221 n.25
three-caliph hypothesis 65–7
Trump, Donald 251
Tughluq, Muḥammad bin 43
Tunisia 6, 9, 171–2, 176, 181
Twelver Shīʿism (*al-shīʿa al-ithnā ʿashariyya*) 5–6, 8, 99–100, 114–15, 132, 134, 185–7, 195 n.4
two-caliph hypothesis 65, 71

ʿUdhāfir, Muḥammad b. 109, 123 n.31
ulamā (religious scholars) 3, 8–9, 28 n.37, 49–50, 133, 135–6, 172, 180–2, 187–8
Umayyad caliphate 36, 38, 64–6, 86, 90, 108, 186, 189
umma community 1, 45, 173, 178–9, 181, 192, 215. *See also* Muslim community
United States 249–50
Universal Declaration of Human Rights 138
unjust ruler (*al-sulṭān al-jāʾir*) 34, 41–2, 84–5, 100, 105–8, 110–12, 116–19, 121 n.19, 123 n.34, 124 n.44, 216. *See also* just ruler (*al-sulṭān al-ʿādil*)
ustādha 213, 221 n.18
Uṣūl al-kāfī (al-Kulaynī) 195 n.7, 196 n.11, 201 n.45
Uṣūl min al-Kāfī (al-Kulaynī) 133
ʿUthmān 63–72, 189
ʿUthmānī, Ibn Saʿd's 68
ʿUthmāniyya 65, 70
developmental stages of 68

van Ess, Josef 72 n.2
Verskin, Alan 153
voenno-narodnoe upravlenie (military people's administration) 145

Wagemakers, Joas 20, 23, 27 n.25, 56 n.83, 101
Wahhabi movement 211, 221–2 n.27, 244, 252
Wallerstein, Immanuel 44
Waqfāt maʿa thamarāt al-jihād (al-Maqdisī) 24
Waṣiyya 68
Watt, Montgomery 37
Weber, Max 16–17, 22, 28 n.35
Wiktorowicz, Quintan 48

wilāyat al-faqīh (sovereignty of jurist) 7, 48, 131, 188–9, 202 n.53

Yavari, Neguin 47
Yazīd I 81, 132
Yusuf, Hamza 241–6, 248–51, 253 n.7

Zakat tax, religious 103
ẓālim 110, 116, 119, 121 n.19, 124 n.44
Zaman, Muhammad Qasim 19–20, 27 n.22
Zaydī 42, 67, 187
Zelkina, Anna 151

CPSIA information can be obtained
at www.ICGtesting.com
Printed in the USA
LVHW111912031221
705203LV00004B/97

9 780755 64504